CW00497595

Office Skills for
New CLAiT and
CLAiT Plus 2006

for Office XP

Office Skills for

New CLAiT and CLAiT Plus 2006

for Office XP

ALAN CLARKE

Hodder Arnold

A MEMBER OF THE HODDER HEADLINE GROUP

Orders: please contact Bookpoint Ltd, 130 Milton Park, Abingdon, Oxon OX14 4SB. Telephone: (44) 01235 827720, Fax; (44) 01235 400454. Lines are open from 9.00–5.00, Monday to Saturday, with a 24 hour message answering service. You can also order through our website: www.hoddereducation.co.uk

British Library Cataloguing in Publication Data
A catalogue record for this title is available from The British Library

ISBN 0 340 91535 8
ISBN-13 978 0 340 91535 6

First published 2006
Impression number   10 9 8 7 6 5 4 3 2 1
Year   2011 2010 2009 2008 2007 2006
Copyright © 2006 Alan Clarke

All rights reserved. No part of this publication may be reproduced or transmitted in any form or by any means, electronic or mechanical, including photocopy, recording, or any information storage and retrieval system, without permission in writing from the publisher or under licence from the Copyright Licensing Agency limited. Further details of such licences (for reprographic reproduction) may be obtained from the Copyright Licensing Agency Limited, of Saffron House, 6–10 Kirby Street, London EC1N 8TS.

Every effort has been made to trace and acknowledge ownership of copyright.
The publishers will be glad to make suitable arrangements with any copyright holders whom it has not been possible to contact.

Typeset by Fakenham Photosetting Limited, Fakenham, Norfolk
Printed and bound in Dubai for Hodder Arnold, an imprint of Hodder Education, a member of the Hodder Headline Group, 338 Euston Road, London NW1 3BH.

Contents

New CLAiT   LEVEL 1

CLAiT Plus   LEVEL 2

This book contains chapters from *New CLAiT 2006 for Office XP* (ISBN 0340915374) and *CLAiT Plus 2006 for Office XP* (ISBN 0340915331), both by Alan Clarke.

Acknowledgements

To my wife and sons for their support, and particularly to Peter for his practical assistance and suggestions.

The author and publisher wish to acknowledge the Microsoft® Corporation for the use of captured screen images.

Screen shots reprinted by Microsoft Corporation.

OCR does not endorse the use of one software package over another, and all CLAiT qualifications are written in generic form. This book is written using the Microsoft® Office suite as examples, simply to provide clear support to the majority of candidates who will be using that package. The use of any other form of software is equally appropriate and acceptable to OCR.

Introduction

In a modern society it is essential to have Information and Communication Technology (ICT) skills and knowledge. OCR has developed a suite of ICT user qualifications at levels 1, 2 and 3. This book covers the content required for the level 1 and 2 qualifications, New CLAiT 2006 and CLAiT Plus 2006 respectively.

New CLAiT is an initial information and communication technology qualification that does not assume that you have any prior experience of using computers, applications (e.g. word processing) or accessing the Internet. It is offered by OCR, a major qualification awarding body. The qualification conforms to the National Qualifications Framework.

CLAiT Plus is a level 2 qualification for Information and Communication Technology (ICT) users.

In August, 2005 New CLAiT and CLAiT Plus were revised to produce a straightforward structure of eight units for each qualification. You can achieve a Certificate by completing three units or a Diploma by completing five. Ten units are covered within this book. For both the Certificate and Diploma you must complete the core unit (unit 1) amongst your chosen units.

There are no formal entry requirements for either qualification. However, CLAiT Plus assumes that you have the skills and knowledge of ICT provided by New CLAiT. This book is based on Microsoft Office XP® although a large part of the material should be suitable for other versions of Office.

The assessment of each unit is based on a practical test which places an emphasis on undertaking a task by accurately following instructions. For most units there is a choice of assessment methods such as local or computer-based assessment. Your local tutor will be able to provide you with detailed guidance about the nature of the assessment.

Unit 1

File management and e-document production

This chapter will help you to use a computer, manage your data and produce documents. You will be able to:

- identify and use a personal computer, monitor, keyboard and mouse
- identify and use operating system software
- use an operating system to create and manage files and folders
- identify and use a word processor to enter text, numbers and symbols
- format basic paragraphs and document properties

The chapter covers the contents of the New CLAiT mandatory unit. It contains information and helps you practise the skills which are essential to the successful completion of the unit.

Assessment

This unit does not assume any previous experience of using a computer. You will be assessed through a practical realistic assignment which is designed to allow you to demonstrate your knowledge and skills against each objective. Your tutor can provide you with more guidance.

What is a computer?

A computer consists of two main components: hardware and software. The hardware is the physical element of the equipment that you can see when you look

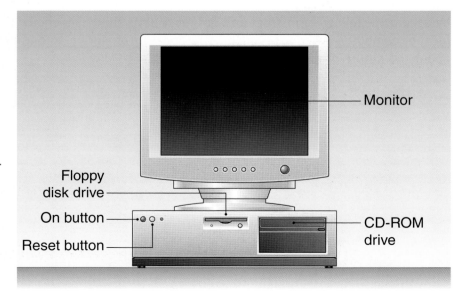

Figure 1.1 Desktop computer

at a computer. Figure 1.1 illustrates a desktop computer, Figure 1.2 shows a tower computer and Figure 1.7 a laptop computer. These are some of the variations of personal computers. In the first two examples you will see a monitor which resembles a television, a box that contains the electronic heart of the computer (Central Processing Unit), a keyboard (Figure 1.6) and a mouse (Figure 1.8). The laptop computer integrates these features into a single structure. The views of the computer may seem complicated and you may wonder what the purposes of all the parts and connections are. For OCR New CLAiT you do not need to know but if you are interested you will find an explanation in the summary section at the end of the chapter.

All computers are different so when you look at your own computer it will be similar but not identical. The on-switch is often positioned on the front of the computer but in many models there is a second switch on the back of the computer. The second switch is usually the power supply control so it needs to be on in order for the front switch to operate. When the computer is switched on a small light near to the on-switch is sometimes illuminated.

Software is the set of instructions that controls the hardware. It controls the operations of the hardware such as saving information, electronic communications, word processing and many other applications. Software is divided into two main types.

The operating system – this is the program that controls and connects the application software and hardware. It provides all the standard features of the computer (e.g. saving information, printing and display of information on the monitor screen). This book is based on the Microsoft® Windows® XP operating system. However, there are other Microsoft® operating systems and also other completely different systems (e.g. Linux).

Figure 1.2 Tower computer

Applications – these are programs that help you carry out specialist tasks (e.g. word-processing, drawing pictures, communicating and designing presentations). The later chapters consider applications in considerable detail.

Exercise 1

Investigate the hardware

1 Before you switch on your computer, and with all the hardware disconnected from the power supply, carry out a visual inspection of the equipment. Observe the different connections and pieces of hardware.

2 Identify whether the computer is a desktop, tower or laptop, then locate the printer, keyboard (Figure 1.6) and mouse (Figure 1.8). These are the main components of a computer system's hardware. If you are considering a laptop then identify how these features are incorporated into the structure.

3 Inspect the back of the computer and you will observe a number of connections and cables. These link the different parts together and allow information to pass between the different elements (e.g. the computer sends information to the printer so it can produce a document).

4 Locate the on-switch or switches.

Switching on

When you switch on a computer you are instructing the operating system, which is software stored on the computer's hard disk, to start the computer following a set procedure. If the computer is connected to the power supply then you will hear the hard disk making noises while searching for instructions. The monitor will display some of the instructions but these are probably meaningless to all but those users at an expert level.

You may notice that the light on the floppy disk drive or other parts of the computer are illuminated. The standard start up (or 'boot up') procedure involves checking the floppy drive for a disk. If you have left one in the drive then the start-up sequence will be interrupted. This seems unusual but is actually a safety feature – if you have a hard disk failure it allows you to investigate the problem.

After a few moments the Microsoft® Windows® logo will apear on the screen. The system will continue to make noises until eventually the logo disappears and is replaced by what is known as a dialog box in the middle of the screen. This will ask you for your user name and password . You can change both once you have access to the computer. Once you have entered the correct name and password you click on to the OK button using the mouse pointer. This will present you with the Microsoft® Windows® desktop (Figure 1.3). This illustration has been kept very simple but on many desktops there will be many small pictures (known as icons) representing different software applications.

Figure 1.3 shows some icons on the main desktop area. Three important ones are:

- My Computer – this links you to the areas of the computer where information is stored (known as drives). Drives include the hard disk which stores the bulk of the information as well as CD-ROM and floppy disk drives which allow information to be placed in portable form. My Computer also links you to resources connected to the computer, such as printers

Figure 1.3 Microsoft® Windows® desktop

- Recycle Bin – this is a place where deleted files are kept so that if you make a mistake you can reclaim them

- Application icons – these allow you to load the application (e.g. Microsoft® Word)

At the bottom of the desktop there is a grey bar – the taskbar. At the right end of the taskbar is an area called the status area in which a range of small icons are shown. These represent programmes that are currently working. Other icons on the toolbar allow you to access the applications they represent while on the left end is the button called Start. Clicking on this provides access to a range of applications and other services and is also the way to switch off the computer.

Exercise 2

Switching on (booting up) your computer

1 With the computer, monitor and other hardware connected to the power supply, press the on-switch on the front of the computer and on the monitor. In both cases a small light will be illuminated and you will hear the whirring and clicking sounds of the computer starting.

2 If nothing happens then check that the power switch at the rear of the computer is in the on position.

3 Observe what happens – the time to start (boot) the computer can vary considerably depending on what is connected to the machine and how it is configured, so do not be concerned if it takes a few minutes.

4 Eventually you will see the dialog box requesting your user name and password. Once these have been entered you will see something similar to Figure 1.3 appear.

Opening applications

There are several ways of loading an application such as a word processor (Microsoft® Word) or a spreadsheet (Microsoft® Excel®). The two most used are:

- the Start button
- the application icon displayed on the Windows® desktop

In the bottom left-hand corner of the Windows® desktop (Figure 1.3) is a button called Start. This allows you to access many applications and standard features of the operating system. If you single click on Start, a menu will pop-up, which is shown in Figure 1.4. If you place the mouse pointer over the All Programs item it will become highlighted (i.e. the background will change colour) and a new menu, the programs menu, will appear alongside. This is shown in Figure 1.5.

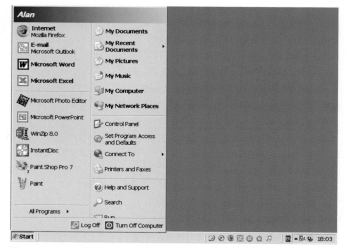

Figure 1.4 Start menu

The programs menu will vary in length and number of items depending on what applications you have installed on your computer. In this case all the Microsoft® Office XP applications are available to you. You should notice that All Programs and other items sometimes have a small black triangle next to them. This indicates that if you highlight this item by placing your mouse pointer over it, then another menu will open.

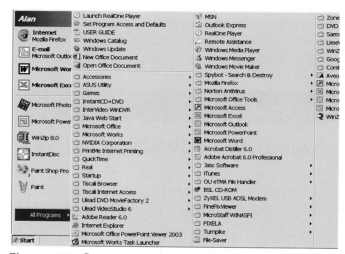

Figure 1.5 Programs menu

To load Microsoft® Word single click on the Microsoft® Word option on the All Programs menu (Figure 1.5). The Microsoft® Word application will open. An alternative way of loading Microsoft® Word is to double click on the Microsoft® Word icon on the Windows® desktop.

Switch off

Switching off a computer must be done in the correct way or you run the risk of damaging your system. To switch off a computer using the Microsoft® Windows® XP operating system requires you to click on the Start button. A menu (list of options) will appear (Figure 1.4) and if you select the Turn Off Computer option then a small box entitled Turn off computer will appear.

The Turn off computer box provides several options and in most cases you will want to select Turn Off. You select an option by clicking on its icon. If you click on the Cancel button you will return to the desktop. If you position your pointer over an option then a short statement will appear explaining its purpose.

The process of shutting down involves the computer making noises and the screen showing a variety of images. The time required to complete the process varies but does not take very long. When the shut down is complete, the light on the computer will be switched off. However, the light on the monitor will still remain on until you press its switch.

Input

Users communicate with computers using input devices such as:

- a keyboard (Figure 1.6)
- a mouse (Figure 1.8)

There are a variety of input devices depending on how you need to interact with the computer system. When you input information into the computer it usually responds by displaying the information on the monitor screen.

A keyboard is similar to a typewriter and is designed to allow you to enter text into the computer. A keyboard and a typewriter have alphabetical keys and are laid out identically. There are also other keys which are common to them both, for example:

Figure 1.6 **Keyboard**

- space bar
- capital lock
- shift
- punctuation keys

The major difference, however, is that the keyboard has a number of additional keys. These are:

- a row of number keys towards the top of the keyboard and a separate number pad on the right
- enter keys which are used to confirm that you want to enter information into the computer
- a top row of keys labelled F1 to F12 which carry out particular functions
- a number of other special purpose keys whose role will gradually emerge as you work through the book

Exercise 3

Exploring the keyboard

1 Take a look at the keyboard. You will notice that it is divided into four main areas:

- function keys across the top of the keyboard
- number pad on the right of the keyboard
- main alphabetical keys – notice the QWERTY layout (this is the sequence of alphabetical keys along the top left of the lettered keys)

- various other keys some sandwiched between the QWERTY keys and number pad areas (e.g. Delete)

2 Identify the following keys: Ctrl, Alt, Home, Pg Up and Num Lock. These are special purpose keys, and eventually you will learn their purposes. For the moment you simply need to know where they are. This will help you once you start to use applications.

3 To enter uppercase letters requires that the shift and character keys are pressed together. This is also the way symbols on the top half of some of the keys are entered.

4 Some keyboards have a small Microsoft® Windows® symbol on a key. This is a shortcut equivalent to pressing the Start button on the taskbar. This might not seem useful at the moment but its importance will become apparent later.

There are other types of keyboard and various specialist ones have been devised for particular tasks.

Figure 1.7 illustrates a laptop computer keyboard. This is smaller and so is suitable for a laptop computer which is designed to be portable. The main difference from a desktop keyboard is the lack of a number pad.

A mouse is a small palm-sized device which is usually connected to your computer by a cable, although wireless mice are now becoming very popular. Many new computers are now supplied with a wireless mouse. The mouse is linked to an on-screen pointer which normally appears as an arrow and mirrors the movements made by the mouse.

Figure 1.7 Laptop Computer

Figure 1.8 shows a two-button mouse which is the type most widely used, but single and three-button mice are also available. This book will only discuss a two-button mouse.

Figure 1.8 Mouse

If you move the mouse, the on-screen pointer moves in the same way. If you move right, the pointer goes right, if you move left then the pointer goes left, and so on. The buttons on the mouse allow you to communicate with the computer.

Other input devices exist which will also control a screen pointer. A trackball works by manipulating a ball and clicking buttons to control the pointer and make selections. Laptop computers have a variety of devices using touch buttons, pads and thumb balls to control on-screen pointers.

Note: The mouse often sits on a small mat which is called, not surprisingly, a mouse mat. This helps the mouse move smoothly across the surface.

Exercise 4

Using a mouse – right-handed users

1 Place your right hand with your index finger on the left-hand button and your middle finger on the right button.

2 Move the mouse and watch how the pointer responds on the screen.

3 Practise using the mouse until you are comfortable – move the pointer up, down, left, right and diagonally until you can accurately control the pointer. Notice where you move the mouse to achieve the desired result.

Alternative Exercise 4

Using a mouse – left-handed users

1 You can adjust a mouse to make it suitable for left-handed people. This involves clicking on the Start button and Control Panel to reveal the Control Panel window. Double click on the Mouse icon. This will reveal the Mouse Properties window and you can select the left-handed option by clicking on the radio button labelled Switch primary and secondary buttons and then the OK button.

2 Place your left hand with your index finger on the right-hand button and your middle finger on the left button.

3 Move the mouse and watch how the pointer responds on the screen.

4 Practise using the mouse until you are comfortable – move the pointer up, down, left, right and diagonally until you can accurately control the pointer. Notice where you move the mouse to achieve the desired result.

Note: remember that if you select the left-hand mouse options then you will need to take this into account when reading the instructions in this book.

It is very important that you learn to use a mouse accurately and effectively. This will take practice. The main skills are:

- accurately moving the on-screen pointer until it touches objects on the screen. Often they will be animated or a text box will appear to explain their purpose.
- single clicking the left mouse button to communicate a command to the computer to select something
- single clicking the right mouse button to communicate a command to the computer to show some extra features such as revealing an extra menu of choices
- double clicking the left mouse button which communicates a command to the computer to start a process

■ clicking and dragging (if you press the left-hand mouse button but do not release it while the pointer is resting on an object on the screen and then you move the mouse, the object will be dragged across the screen until you release the button)

Exercise 5

Practising your mouse skills

1 You can practise your mouse skills in many ways but it can be fun to play a game which is supplied as part of the Windows® operating system. This is a card game called Solitaire played using the mouse pointer to move the cards.

2 To load the games program requires using the mouse and can be quite a challenge if this is the first time you have used a mouse – but do keep trying.

3 The first step is to single click with the left mouse button on the Start button. A list of options will appear above the button. This is called a menu and is a standard way of presenting an option in Microsoft® Windows® and in applications.

Step 1: Slide the mouse up the menu until you highlight the All Programs option (the background changes to a new colour).

Step 2: At the end of the word Programs you will see a small pointer (triangle) which tells you that there are more options available. If you leave the mouse pointer over All Programs a new menu will appear to the right.

Step 3: Slide your mouse pointer in a straight line to the right until you highlight an option in the new menu, then move the pointer up the menu until you reach the option Games.

Step 4: If you leave your pointer over Games another menu to the right will appear. Again, in a straight line slide your pointer to the right until a new option is highlighted. Move the pointer until it is now over the option Solitaire.

Step 5: With the option highlighted, single click the left mouse button and you will see the Solitaire game appear. It will provide you with an opportunity to practise moving and controlling the precise direction of the mouse pointer.

4 Figure 1.9 illustrates the Solitaire game after a few cards have been played. The game has the same rules as the card game. You turn cards over by single clicking on the pile. Move cards by clicking the left mouse button on the one of your choice and holding the button down and dragging the card to its new location.

5 Try to play a game. If you find that every time you drag a card to a new location it returns to its original position, it is because you are making an illegal move.

6 Keep playing until you are confident about dragging and dropping and clicking with the left button. These are key elements in using a mouse but there are two further important actions. These are double clicking and single clicking with the right mouse button and there will be opportunities to improve these skills in other parts of the book. However, double clicking (which is clicking the left mouse button twice rapidly) needs practise. People often find it difficult initially to click twice quickly enough. If you find that after

double clicking no action results, it is probably because you are leaving too long an interval between the clicks. Keep trying to click twice as quickly as you can. You will eventually get it right.

7   To close the Solitaire window you need to single click with the left mouse button on the button marked with an X in the top right-hand corner of the Solitaire window. Figure 1.9 shows the three buttons that allow the window to be minimised to a button on the Desktop taskbar, maximised to fill the entire display, or closed (i.e. buttons left to right). Experiment with expanding the window to fill the whole display and minimising it to a button. When the window is maximised you can reduce it in size by using the same buttons.

8   These controls appear on all windows. It is a standard part of the operating system. Applications can be displayed as a window (a rectangular area), the whole display or a single button on the taskbar.

9   When you have finished playing Solitaire, close the window.

Graphic User Interface

Microsoft® Windows® and the vast majority of modern software uses a Graphical User Interface (GUI). A GUI is a highly visual interface combining the use of a pointing device (e.g. a mouse) with visual links to applications, commands and options. The visual links take the form of small pictures called icons, buttons (small rectangles) or menus (i.e. lists of options). GUIs are easy to learn and to use since you do not need to remember a large number of commands, but only to recognise them when they appear on the screen. Most GUIs are consistent meaning that you can work out what to do even when you are using a new part of the system.

A key feature of a GUI, Microsoft® Windows® and Office is the window. This is a rectangular enclosed area in which applications, files and messages are displayed. Windows can be moved and resized (i.e. a window can fill a whole screen or be reduced to small picture on the edge of the display). Windows can be stacked on top of each other so that at first you can sometimes lose a window because it is hidden under another one.

While you are still learning about Windows®, using a mouse and GUIs, you probably feel confused and uncertain but this will change with practice. GUIs have made learning about using information and communication technology far easier than earlier computers based on command interfaces.

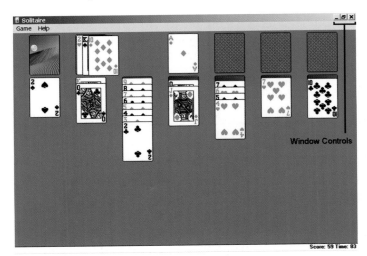

Figure 1.9 Solitaire

Storing and locating information

Computers have a permanent store for information, programs (applications) and data. This is called the hard disk or hard drive and it can hold an enormous amount of information. It is often designated by the letter C with a colon, so drive C: is the hard drive. The hard disk is normally a permanent part of the computer, although there are computers that allow you to remove a hard drive, but these are relatively rare. Information can be stored in smaller amounts on a floppy disks which is a portable storage device that you can carry from one computer to another. The floppy drive is often designated as the A: drive.

Figure 1.10 illustrates a floppy disk. The disk is inserted into the drive with its label on the top, the metal slider entering first. The disk is firmly pushed into the drive until it clicks. It is not possible to insert a disk the wrong way round so if it does not go in, you are holding it the wrong way up.

There are other portable storage devices that can hold far more data than a floppy disk. The memory stick is a small device which you can plug into a computer's USB port. It then becomes a new drive on to which you can store information. Memory sticks are sometimes called flash or pen drives and even dongles. Some computers have CD-RW (i.e. compact disc read write) or DVD-RW (i.e. DVD read write) drives which enable you to save information on to disks.

Figure 1.10 Floppy disk

Exercise 6

Inserting a floppy disk

1 Try to insert a floppy disk into the drive (Figure 1.1 and 1.2). Remember to push the disk firmly into the drive, but if it will not enter then check you are inserting it the right way (i.e. label on top and metal slider first).

2 The floppy will make a noise when it is in place and it will be inside the computer so that you cannot reach it. To remove the disk you need to press the button which is located near to the drive. This button will pop out as the floppy disk is pushed in.

3 Press the button and see the disk emerge.

4 Repeat the action of inserting and removing the disk until you are confident.

The Windows® operating system provides you with the means to search the hard disk and floppy disks when they are inserted into the drive. Windows® Explorer lets you view the contents of the computer drives. Figure 1.11 illustrates Windows® Explorer showing the contents of the C: drive (hard drive).

Windows® Explorer is a file management application provided within Microsoft® Windows®. The Explorer's application window is divided into a number of areas. These are:

- Title bar (e.g. Local Disk (C:))
- Menu bar
- Toolbar
- Address (i.e. shows the location or path of the highlighted folder)
- Folders (left-hand side of the display) – showing the structure of folders stored on the hard disk, floppy disks, CD-ROMs or other storage media. A plus sign indicates that the folder has more folders stored within it. If you click on the plus sign, the structure will be opened up to show these folders. The revealed folders can also be marked with a plus sign, indicating further folders stored within the revealed one.
- Contents of the folder (right-hand side of the display). This shows the files and folders stored within the highlighted folder.

Information is stored in a computer in what are known as files. All files have a unique name and they are normally grouped with related files and stored within folders. This is rather similar to the storage of paper records in cardboard files and it is intended to help you locate them again when you have a large number of files. In the computer it is also possible to store folders within other folders. In Figure 1.11 you will notice many small plus signs in the left-hand area of the display.

This indicates that these folders contain other folders. Clicking on the plus sign will open up the folder to reveal what it contains. These are shown in the right-hand window. Figure 1.12 shows a group of folders within the Documents and Settings folder each with a unique name.

Figure 1.13 shows the folders stored within the Alanc folder. Two folders are revealed and if the My Documents folder is highlighted then the files stored in the folder are shown. The different types of files take on different forms or formats depending on the information they contain. Here we see examples of Microsoft Word, Text Document, PUB file (i.e. desktop publishing) and Bitmap Image.

Windows® Explorer provides functions in the File menu to delete or rename your files. You highlight the file you need to work on by single clicking on it, then select the File menu and the options Delete or Rename. In the Edit menu you are also provided with options to copy (Copy and Paste) or move (Cut and Paste) the file to another folder.

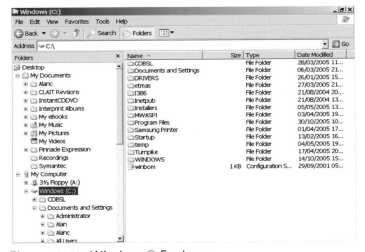

Figure 1.11 Windows® Explorer

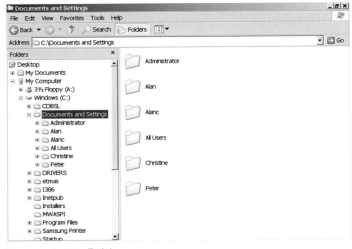

Figure 1.12 Folders

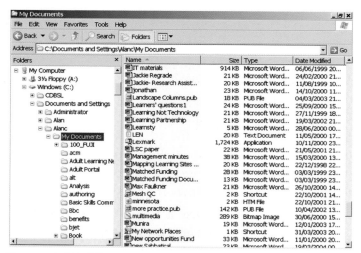

Figure 1.13 Files

It is not always easy when you first start to use a computer to distinguish between different types of files. Applications (e.g. word processors) are stored as files, documents produced by the applications are also stored as files and so on. In a way everything is a file. You distinguish between them by considering the small picture (icon) in front of the file name and the extension at the end of the name (i.e. the letters following the full stop – .bmp, .gif, .doc and .txt). There are many different types of files.

You can change the appearance of folders and files in Windows® Explorer and in other Microsoft® applications. They can appear as:

■ Icons

■ Tiles (e.g. Figure 1.12)

■ Details (e.g. Figures 1.11 and 1.13)

■ List (i.e. similar to details but without the information about size, type and date of modification)

■ Thumbnails (i.e. useful if you are viewing pictures since each appears as a small image making it easy for you to select the one you want)

In order to change the appearance within Windows® Explorer select the View menu and choose the appropriate option (i.e. icons, tiles, list, details and thumbnails). Alternatively choose the View icon on the toolbar and the options will be displayed allowing you to select one. The selected option is shown by a black dot placed alongside the item.

Exercise 7

Windows® Explorer

1 Open Windows® Explorer by clicking on the Start button, then highlighting All Programs and then Accessories to reveal a menu of options. Click on the Windows® Explorer item. This will open Explorer (Figure 1.11).

2 Explore the application by clicking on the plus signs to open up the folder structure. Keep clicking on new plus signs that are revealed and observe what changes.

3 Highlight a folder in the left-hand list and observe the changes in the right-hand area of the window. This area shows what a highlighted folder contains. You can also click on folders in the right-hand area to open them. Again notice any changes this causes.

4 When you click on a folder in the left-hand list you will notice the picture of the folder itself changes to look like an open folder.

continued

5 Use Explorer to investigate what is stored on the computer's hard disk. However, do not select Delete or Rename or any option within the menus since you may cause changes that harm your computer.

6 When you have investigated the structure, close Explorer by clicking on the Close button in the top right-hand corner of the window or select the File menu and the Close option.

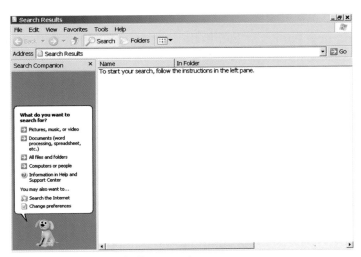

Figure 1.14 Search Companion

If you use a computer regularly, you will find that you have many hundreds of folders and files. Although they all have individual names, in order to find them you will need to remember the name of the file and in which folder you stored it. This is further complicated by storing folders inside other folders. The Windows® operating system provides you with a way of finding files and folders, if you cannot remember a particular file location.

If you click on the Start button, a menu will pop up containing an option called Search (in other versions of Windows® this is sometimes called Find). If you click on Search, the Search Companion window appears (Figure 1.14).

Exercise 8

Finding a file

1 Load the Search Companion window (Figure 1.14). On the left-hand side of the window are a series of options to help you search for different types of files and folders (e.g. Documents). Select the Documents option by clicking on it and observe what happens (Figure 1.15). The display changes to ask you to specify the nature of the file you are seeking (e.g. name or

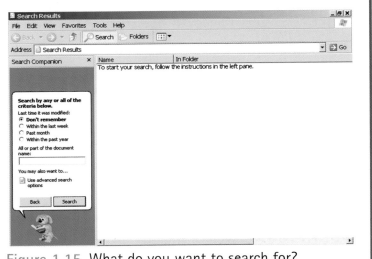

Figure 1.15 What do you want to search for?

part of the name of the file and the last time you changed it). Enter the name of a file (e.g. clait) and select the Don't remember option and click on the Search button. If you make a mistake you can go back a step by selecting the Back button.

2 Observe what happens and you should see the search results on the right-hand side of the display fill with a list of files and folders. These all have your search term in their titles.

3 When the search is completed you will need to review the list to identify the particular file you are searching for. If you want to open the file, double click on the chosen item. The file will open inside the application which created it (e.g. text files in a text editor).

4 Explore the search function by entering new names, selecting different modification dates and try the advanced search functions (i.e. click on Use advanced search options). Try the different options and see what happens.

5 The advanced search options let you search specific drives and offers two additional features:

 – What size is it? (i.e. lets you specify the size of the file you are seeking)

 – More advanced options

The more advanced options include allowing you to specify case sensitivity (i.e. match file name with lowercase or capital letters).

6 Continue until you are confident in locating files. Try locating files on a floppy disk (A:) as well as on the hard disk (C:).

7 Close the function by using the Close button in the right-hand corner of the window.

Create and manage files and folders

In addition to being able to find files and folders it is important that you are able to manage them. The Microsoft® Windows® operating system provides a range of functions to allow you to:

- Create and name folders (directories)
- Open, close and save files
- Delete files and folders
- Rename files and folders
- Print the file structure
- Cut, copy and paste
- Move files and folders
- Copy files and folders

Windows® Explorer is designed to manage your files and folders. It allows you to create, delete and rename files and folders. The File menu (Figure 1.16) offers you functions to Create, Delete, Open, Close and Rename files and folders. The Edit menu has the options of Cut, Copy, Paste, Move and Copy files and folders.

Figure 1.16 shows the following functions:

- **New** – create a new folder in the folder currently being viewed in Windows® Explorer
- **Delete** – deletes the file or folder highlighted
- **Rename** – allows you to change the name of the file or folder highlighted

Other options are available within the Edit menu:

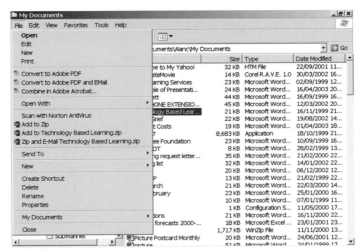

Figure 1.16 Manipulating files and folders

- **Move To Folder ...** – moves the highlighted file or folder to a new folder (this is the same process as Cut and Paste)
- **Copy To Folder ...** – copies the highlighted file or folder to a new folder (this is the same process as Copy and Paste)
- **Undo** – this lets you change your mind, since it undoes the last action you have undertaken
- **Cut** – enables you to cut out a file or folder with the intention of moving it to a new location using the Paste option
- **Copy** – allows you to copy a file or folder to a new location using the Paste option but leaving the original file or folder unaffected.
- **Paste** – lets you place a copied or cut file or folder in a new location

Exercise 9

Manipulating folders

1 Insert a floppy disk into the drive.

2 Open Windows® Explorer by clicking on the **Start** button, highlighting **All Programs** and then **Accessories** and selecting **Windows® Explorer**. The application will appear (Figure 1.11) either in a window or filling the whole screen.

3 Click on the 3½ Floppy (A:) option (Figure 1.17). If the floppy is empty then no files or folders will be shown on the right-hand side of the

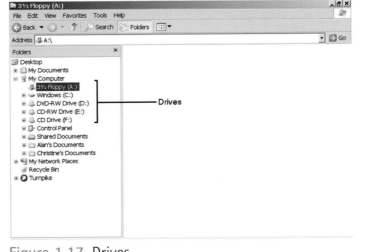

Figure 1.17 Drives

display. If you cannot see the 3½ Floppy (A:) option, scroll up and down the window or click on My Computer folder to display the drives. 3½ Floppy (A:) is at the top of the list.

4 You are going to create a new folder so select the File menu, highlight New and click on the Folder option. A new folder will appear on the right-hand side of the display with the name New Folder. The cursor (a cursor is a small flashing bar that shows you where your text will appear when you enter it from the keyboard) will be flashing in the name box and you should type a name for the folder using the keyboard. In this case call it Master.

5 The Master Folder is stored on the floppy disk because this was the drive selected when the folder was created.

6 Double click on Master in the left-hand side and you will see the right-hand side is empty because this folder is empty. However, on the left hand side the Master Folder will appear (Figure 1.18) and because it has been selected, the folder icon is shown open.

7 Create a new folder and name it Master1. Open Master1 and create another new folder called Master2. You now have three folders stored one within another. Figure 1.19 shows the structure.

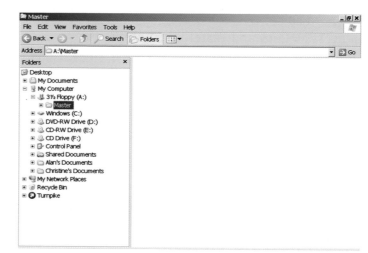

Figure 1.18 Master folder open

8 Highlight the Master1 folder by clicking on it, then select File menu and the Rename option. You can change the name to New Master. Repeat the process for Master2 and rename it Modern Master.

9 Highlight Modern Master (single click) and then select the Copy tool (alternatively select the Edit menu and the Copy option). Highlight the Master folder and select the Paste tool (alternatively select the Edit menu and Paste option). You will see the Modern Master folder copied into the Master Folder. The original Modern Master folder is still in place. Figure 1.20 shows the new structure.

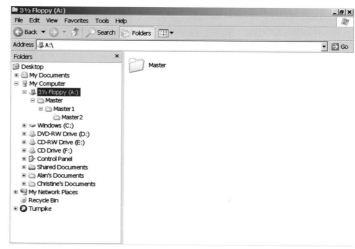

Figure 1.19 Structure

10 The process of using a function has now been illustrated. You must highlight the folder you wish to operate on and then select the function. Now practise using the other functions. The undo function lets you remove your last action so none of your changes need to be permanent:

- Delete a folder

- Cut and paste a folder

- Copy To

- Move To

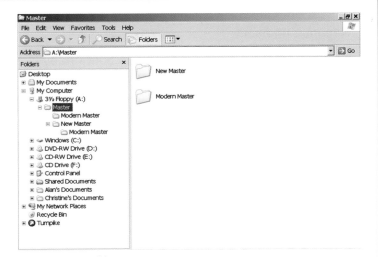

Figure 1.20 **New structure**

11 When you select either Copy To or Move To a new window appears called Move Items or Copy Items (Figure 1.21). This allows you to find the folder you want to copy or move the file or folder to. Notice that in the Copy Items or Move Items window, you can create a new folder using the Make New Folder button in the bottom left-hand corner of the window.

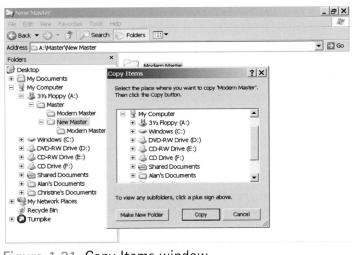

Figure 1.21 **Copy Items window**

12 Continue trying the different functions until you are confident.

13 Close Windows® Explorer by clicking on File menu and the Close option.

Creating and printing documents

The Windows® operating system includes other applications in addition to Windows® Explorer. These include:

- Microsoft® Paint – a straightforward drawing application
- Microsoft® WordPad – a basic word processor

- Microsoft® Notepad – a text editor which is a limited word processor
- Microsoft® Calculator – an on-screen calculator
- Address Book – this allows you to keep details of peoples names, email addresses and telephone numbers

These can be accessed in a similar way to Solitaire by clicking the Start button, highlighting the All Programs and Accessories options in the menu and then single clicking on the application of your choice. In addition to these applications you can install other ones. This book is largely based on Microsoft® Office XP which is an integrated suite of products.

Word processors are one of the most widely used computer applications. In the next exercises, you are going to use Microsoft® Word (Figure 1.22) to create a short document, save it to floppy disk and print it. Microsoft® Word is a powerful word processor though there are many other word processors available and other applications such as text editors. The difference between a word processor and a text editor is mainly the degree of sophistication. Text editors are used principally for producing simple messages while a word processor provides the tools for writing a wide range of documents (e.g. from a letter to a book). Word processors provide tools for presenting and formatting information and are often WYSIWYG, which stands for What You See Is What You Get. This means that the way the words are presented on the screen is how they will be printed. They help you write by providing a wide range of features and functions such as spelling and grammar checkers and offer you considerable freedom to change the words, presentation, layout and appearance of your documents.

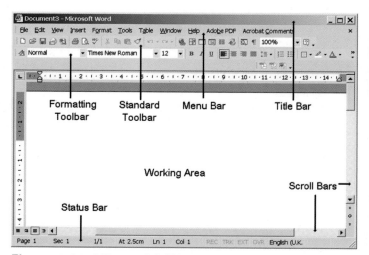

Figure 1.22 Microsoft® Word

If you have never used a keyboard to enter text it may feel strange at first, but you will rapidly realise how useful a word processor is. Windows includes a text editor called Notepad which is shown in Figure 1.23.

The Microsoft® Word display consists of three main areas:

- menus and toolbars which provide you with access to the word processor controls (e.g. Standard, Formatting and Drawing toolbars)
- the working area where you enter your words to create documents

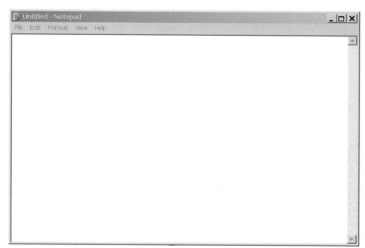

Figure 1.23 Microsoft® NotePad

- the status bar (reading from left to right) shows:
  - Page 1 – the page you are on (e.g. the first page)
  - Sec 1 – the section of the document you are on
  - 1/1 – shows you that you are looking at the first page of your document which is one page long
  - At 2.5 cm – this tells you that you are entering text that will be 2.5 cm below the top of the page when it is printed
  - Ln 1 – you are entering text into the 1st line of your document
  - Col 1 – you are entering text in the first character position of the document

Exercise 10

Creating a document

1 Open Microsoft® Word by clicking on the `Start` button, highlighting the `All Programs` option to open a menu of options and single clicking on `Microsoft® Word`. The application will open (Figure 1.22). Maximise the window using the control buttons in the top right-hand corner of the window.

2 On the first line of the work area you will see a flashing upright line. This is called the cursor and indicates where any text or numbers that you enter will appear on the screen. Press any letter or number on the keyboard. You will see your selected character appear and the cursor move one space to the right, indicating where the next character will be entered. To remove your character press the backspace key. This is marked with a left-pointing arrow and will delete any character to the left of the cursor. There is another delete key which removes characters to the right of the cursor. This is located in the bottom right of the keyboard below the number pad.

3 Move the mouse pointer around the display and you will see that it changes shape. It is no longer shaped liked an arrow when it moves across the work area but is like the letter I.

4 Using the keyboard type:

My name is .... I live in .... and I am .... years old.

Fill in the blanks with your own details – name, town/city and age.

To enter a capital letter (upper case character) you need to hold down the shift key and then press the letter of your choice. If you want to enter everything in upper case press the Capitals Lock (i.e. Caps Lock) key once. To return to lower case, press Caps Lock again. For the current exercises you only need to enter single upper case letters.

5 If you make a mistake then you can remove it using the backspace key.

6 When you have entered the text then move your mouse pointer until it is immediately in front of 'I live in ....' and then single click. You will see the cursor move to this new position. This is how you move the cursor using the mouse, although there are other ways such as by using the arrow keys on the keyboard.

7 If you press the enter key then the text will be broken into two parts as shown below.

continued

My name is ....

I live in .... and I am .... years old.

The Enter key inserts a new line, but if you continue typing text the words will automatically go to the next line when you reach the end of the previous one. This is called text wrapping. If you hold down any key you will see the character appear many times and wrap around when it reaches the end of a line.

8 If you single click on the menu item File (Figure 1.24) a menu will drop down. This provides a number of standard features which, if you click on them, give you access to useful functions such as:

- New – creates a new document

- Open – opens an existing document so that you can read it and amend it if you wish

- Save – allows you to save your document to the computer's store on the hard disk, on a floppy disk or on another storage medium

- Save As – allows you to save an existing file under a different name

- Print – allows you to print your document on a connected printer

- Exit – an alternative to using the Close button

You will notice that the menu covers part of the text you have entered but will disappear if you click your mouse anywhere outside of the menu area or when you select an option. Above the Exit option is a list of files (e.g. C:\..\Chapter One File Management an...). These are the most recent documents that have been opened in Microsoft® Word. You can access them by clicking on them.

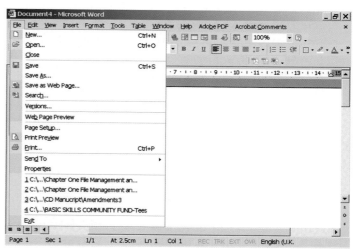

Figure 1.24 Microsoft® Word file menu

9 Close Word by selecting the File menu and the Exit option unless you want to progress immediately to Exercise 11.

Printing

Printers provide you with the means to output your computer work to produce letters, reports and other paper documents. There are several different types and three widely available types are:

- monochrome laser printer
- monochrome and colour inkjet printer
- colour laser printer

A laser printer uses magnetic toner to produce text and images on paper whereas inkjet printers work by squirting small drops of ink onto the page. They can provide both black and white and colour printing. Laser and inkjet printers are widely used in the work place and at home. Colour printers are more expensive than monochrome ones but the price of colour inkjets is now in reach of most computer users.

Printers are manufactured in a variety of sizes and shapes. Two key features of any printer are the on-switch and the paper holder. The on-switch can be positioned in a range of locations including the back corners, front panel and the sides of the printer. In a similar way, the paper can be fed into a pull-out drawer or pushed into an opening. Each manufacturer has their own design and it is important to study the printer's manual before using it.

Exercise 11

Printers

1 It is important to familiarise yourself with the printer you are going to use, so in this exercise you are going to explore your printer.

2 First make sure it is not connected to the power supply. Inspect the printer and see if you can locate the on-switch and where the paper is loaded.

3 Remove the paper and inspect it. In most cases the paper is A4 size and is loaded as a block. Replace the paper carefully. When you load paper it is useful to fan the edges of the block since this will help stop it sticking together. A problem with all printers is that the paper will sometimes jam inside (rather like a photocopier).

4 Connect the printer to the power supply and switch it on. Each printer will start in its own individual way but you are likely to hear some noise and see control lights flash. If you are using a large laser printer it will have a display panel and you will probably see a message appear, such as Warming Up. When the printer is ready, this message will change (e.g. Ready). Smaller laser and inkjet printers might have only a few lights. Inspect the labels near the lights and you may see error, paper and data lights. The meaning of the lights being illuminated depends on the type and model of your printer.

5 Observe the printer's start up process.

6 Some printers have a demonstration or test function. This is indicated by a button labelled Demo or Test. If your printer provides this function press the button and see what happens. Often a short document will be printed. In some cases this provides background information about the printer.

7 Once you are confident that you know how to switch the printer on and load the paper, switch the printer off if you are not going to use it.

Create, save and print a document

1 Open Microsoft® Word by clicking on Start , highlighting the All Programs option to reveal a menu of options and single clicking on Microsoft® Word . The application will open (Figure 1.22). Maximise the window using the control buttons in the top right-hand corner of the window if the display does not fill the screen.

2 When the application is open you will notice that in the work area there is a small flashing vertical line in the top left-hand corner. This is called a cursor and it is here that your text will appear when you begin to enter it.

3 Type the following:

This is a short passage to help me understand how to create, save and print a document. The keyboard has many keys to enter text and numbers. The number keys are 1, 2, 3, 4, 5, 6, 7, 8 and 9. The symbol keys are $=-/\#.,:@?!£\&\%+*$.

Observe the movement of the cursor and how the text wraps around at the end of each line. Remember to use the shift key to access symbols on the top of keys and to insert upper case letters.

4 Once you have created a document you can save it as a file by selecting the File menu and the Save option. The Save As window (dialog box) opens (Figure 1.25). This shows a view of a folder called Documents and Settings in which is stored a variety of folders (i.e. Administrator, Alan, Alanc, All Users, Christine and Peter).

To save your work you need to enter a file name in the box File name and then click on the Save button. Windows® inserts a a file name based on the text you have entered (i.e. This is a short passage to help me understand how to create). You can use this name or enter a new one by clicking in the File name box and entering a name. You may have to delete the automatic name. Your file will then be saved in the Documents and

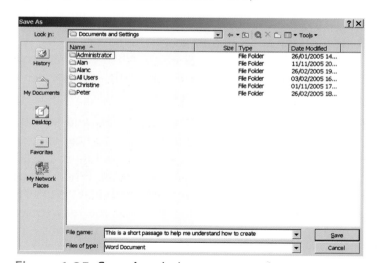

Figure 1.25 Save As window

Settings folder. If you would like to save your file elsewhere you have to change the name in the Look in box. You change this box by clicking on the down arrow button at the end of the box, and a list of other choices where you can store your file appears (Figure 1.24).

In many of the exercises you are instructed to save your file to a floppy disk. However, you are free to save them to any drive or folder.

5 Notice that below the file name box is another called Files of type. This allows you to save your file as a particular file format. Since you are saving from the Microsoft® Word application, it automatically defaults to Word Document.

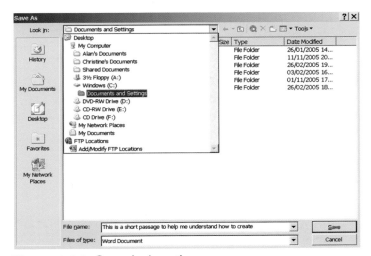

6 Insert a floppy disk into the drive. Enter your file name as Document, select Save in as 3½ Floppy (A:) and click on the Save button. You will hear the disk drive and

Figure 1.26 **Save As locations**

see the mouse pointer turn into an hour glass for a few moments. This tells you that Windows® is working on a task.

7 If you now change your document by adding more text and want to update your saved file all you need to do is select the File menu and option Save. The Save As window will not appear since the system assumes you want to update your file Document stored in the same place (i.e. floppy disk).

8 Add extra text in order to test saving again. Your passage should now read:

This is a short passage to help me understand how to create, save and print a document. The keyboard has many keys to enter text and numbers. The number keys are 1, 2, 3, 4, 5, 6, 7, 8 and 9. The symbol keys are $=-/\#.,:@?!£\&\%+*$. This is extra text to test saving again.

9 Select the File menu and the Save option. You may hear the drive start up but the Save As window will not appear. It is good practice to save your document early and then update it at regular intervals. Some applications can be set to save your work automatically every few minutes. However, you should establish the habit of saving at regular intervals. There are few things worse than losing all your work due to a problem with the computer or an electricity failure because you have not saved your work for a few hours.

(Microsoft® Word can automatically save your work – select the Tools menu, Options item to reveal the Options window. Choose the Save tab and consider the choices).

10 Another useful feature of saving in Windows® is that you can save the same document many times under different names. If you select File menu and the Save As option then the Save As window will appear and you can choose to save the document again under another name and in another folder. In this case save your document as Document2 on the floppy disk. You should see the original Document file (Figure 1.27).

11 You can repeat this operation as many times as you like and it is useful as a means of keeping an original document while revising its contents for another purpose (e.g. using

continued

a letter to the electricity company as a template for one to the gas supplier).

12 Having created a document you can print it by selecting the File menu and the Print option. A Print window will appear and you can print immediately if your printer is connected by clicking on the OK button. This will print your document using the printer's default settings. These are the standard settings which establish factors such as the number of copies, which pages to print if your document is longer than a single page, orientation of the paper (i.e. portrait or landscape) and quality of the printing. In many cases the defaults produce a perfectly acceptable printed document.

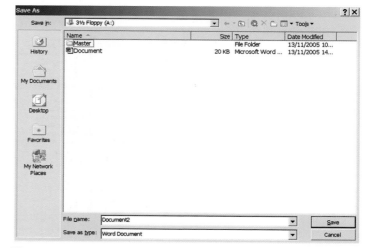

Figure 1.27 Saving several files with different names

13 Print your short document using the default settings. Repeat the printing actions until you are confident you understand the process.

14 Close Microsoft® Word by selecting the File menu and the Exit option.

Spell Checking

Microsoft® Word provides you with a function to check your spelling and grammar. This is carried out by selecting the Tools menu and Spelling and Grammar option. This opens the Spelling and Grammar window. In the window are displayed mistakes and suggested corrections that you are asked to decide on. You can choose to ignore them or accept the change.

The Spell Checker is often selected to work automatically when you are creating a document. In this case the word processor underlines words and phrases with either red or green lines. Red indicates a spelling mistake while green shows a grammatical error.

Spell checkers have limitations. They can only detect spelling mistakes. If you have used the wrong word but spelt it correctly then it will not be identified (e.g. see and sea; fill and full, and so and sow). It is therefore important not to rely only on the spelling checker but also to proofread your documents.

Retrieving a file

Once you have saved a file, you can use the application you used to create it to retrieve it in order to print extra copies or change its contents.

Exercise 13

Retrieving a file

1 Open Microsoft® Word by clicking on Start, highlighting All Programs and single clicking on Microsoft® Word. The application will open. Maximise the window using the control buttons in the top right hand corner of the window if the display does not fill the screen. Insert your floppy disk into the drive.

2 Select File menu and Open option. This will reveal the Open window. Choose 3½ Floppy (A:) disk by using the down arrow button at the end of the Look in box. This should reveal the files stored on your floppy disk (Figure 1.28).

3 Highlight the file you want to retrieve by single clicking on it. Click on the Open button and you will see the contents of the file appear in the Microsoft® Word working area.

4 Close the application by selecting the File menu and the Exit option.

5 Repeat this exercise until you are confident that you can retrieve files.

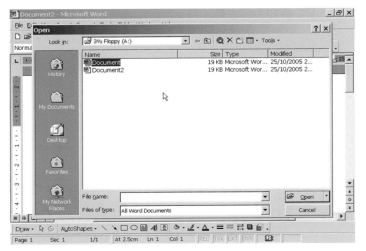

Figure 1.28 **Open window**

Exercise 14

Introducing editing

1 Load Microsoft® Word by selecting the Start button, highlighting the All Programs option and clicking on the Microsoft® Word item or by double clicking on the Microsoft® Word icon on the desktop.

2 Using the keyboard, type:

Titan is the largest satellite of Saturn and was discovered by Christiaan Huygens in 1655. It is a large moon with a radius of 2575 km and is the largest moon in the solar system. Titan has a nitrogen and methane-rich atmosphere. This makes observing the surface of the satellite difficult. The Voyager spacecrafts used a variety of methods to investigate Titan. These suggest that Titan has an atmospheric pressure greater than the Earth and possibly has methane clouds which rain ethane.

3 Observe that the text starts a new line when it needs to without your doing anything. This is called word wrapping. If you have been trained as a typist it can often be difficult to stop yourself trying to create a new line.

4 Move your mouse pointer to the start of the text on the T of Titan. Click there and you will see that the cursor (flashing line) has moved to the start of the text. If you enter text now it will appear at the cursor. This is the way you insert text into a document. If you press the Enter key you will create a new line. Press the Enter key twice and using the up arrow key on the keyboard move up the two lines you have just created. Enter the word Titan and you will have added a heading to your passage. The Enter key is sometimes known as the Return key.

The text will look similar to Figure 1.29. Do not worry if in your work area you are not able to get the same number of words per line as in the example. This is a result of the settings within the word processor which you can change later.

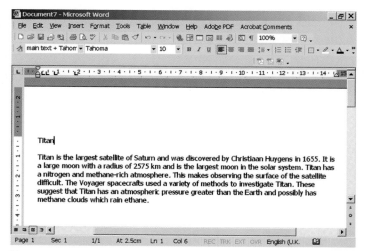

Figure 1.29 Text

5 When entering text you will sometimes make a mistake. It is therefore important to always proofread any text that you enter in order to remove errors.

6 There are two main ways to remove or delete text. Using the above example, the cursor should be flashing at the end of Titan. If you press the Backspace key then the cursor moves left and deletes the last character. If you continue to tap the key, you can delete your entry.

7 The other way to remove text is to use the Delete key which is located in the bottom-right corner of the keyboard near the number pad. The Delete key works by removing the characters to the right of the cursor.

8 Enter Titan again to replace your heading.

9 We will now save this passage on to a floppy disk as the file Titan. This procedure is the same as in Exercise 12 (i.e. insert a floppy disk into drive A: and select the File menu and click on the Save option to open the Save As window).

10 You can close Microsoft® Word now by clicking on the File menu item and selecting the option Exit. An alternative way is to click on the Close button on the top right-hand corner of the application window.

Manipulating text

In Exercise 14 you typed a short passage and saved it to your floppy disk. Microsoft® Word and other word processors provide you with tools to insert, delete, move and replace text. There are three tools called Cut, Copy and Paste which are especially useful. They are available on the

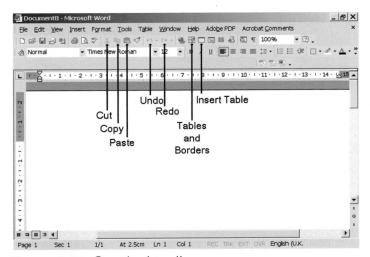

Figure 1.30 Standard toolbar

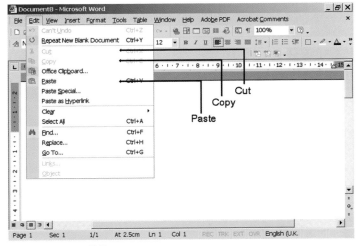

Figure 1.31 Edit menu

standard toolbar (Figure 1.30) and on the Edit menu (Figure 1.31). You can choose either option.

The three tools operate in similar ways:

The first step is to highlight the text you want to manipulate. To do this, you move your pointer to the start of the text you want to work on and click, holding down the mouse button and moving the pointer over the words that you want to manipulate. You will see them highlighted (i.e. the background colour changes). When you have highlighted all the words you need, release the mouse button. If you have made an error simply click the mouse away from the highlighted area and the highlighting will disappear so you can try again.

An alternative way of highlighting a line or a paragraph is to move the pointer into the page margin next to a line of text and it will change into an arrow shape. If you click the mouse when the pointer is arrow-shaped then the whole line will be highlighted. If you hold down the left button when the pointer is arrow-shaped then as you move the pointer you will continue to highlight the text. In this way you can highlight a whole passage.

If you click on the Copy tool or the menu option, the text you have highlighted will be copied to a special area of the computer's memory – the Clipboard. You can now paste it in another part of the passage. This process does not change the original text. You add the copied text by pointing to where you want to place it and clicking there. The cursor is now at the new location. If you then click on the Paste tool or the menu option, the highlighted text is inserted into the new location. You can see that the Copy and Paste tools work together. You cannot paste until you have copied.

The Cut tool or the menu option works in the same way but with the difference that when you select Cut, the highlighted text is removed.

An alternative to Cut is to highlight the text, release the left mouse button then hold it down again. You can then drag the words to a new location using the mouse pointer.

A common error when moving text is to leave behind a full stop or comma. It is always important to check that you have copied or cut the text you intended and have not left behind any parts of it.

The standard toolbar contains two important tools for when you make an error – Undo and Redo (Figure 1.30). If you make a mistake you can reverse it by clicking on Undo . If you make an error when using undo then you can turn the clock back with Redo . We will practise these functions in the next exercise along with Cut, Copy and Paste.

Printing

Printing documents is an important function of a word processor. However, it is important to always proofread your documents to ensure they are free of mistakes before printing them. Microsoft® Word offers a range of functions linked to printing, including an option to preview your text as a printed document without wasting any paper. Within the File menu, Print Preview opens up the window shown in Figure 1.32. This allows you to check if the document is presented in the way that you want it to be. When you have completed the preview, click on the Close button to return to the document.

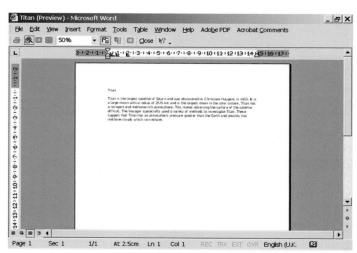

Figure 1.32 Print Preview

When you are ready to print, click on the File menu then choose the Print option to open the Print window (Figure 1.33).

You must first select the printer on which your document is to be printed. This is shown in the Printer area at the top of the window in the box entitled Name . The Microsoft® Windows® operating system allows you to link several printers to a

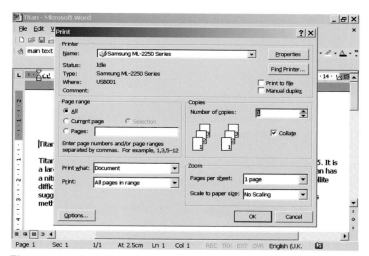

Figure 1.33 Print

single stand-alone computer. The list of printers is shown when you click on the down arrow next to the Name box. You select your printer by clicking on it.

You can choose what you want to print.

- All – whole document
- Current page – only the page on which your cursor is flashing
- Pages – you enter the page range you want to print (e.g. 23–34)
- Number of copies – how many copies you want to print

When you are ready you click on the OK button to start the printer.

Exercise 15

Manipulating and printing text

1 In Exercise 14 you saved a file called Titan. We are now going to load this file into Microsoft® Word.

2 Load Microsoft® Word either by selecting the Start button, highlighting the All Programs option and clicking on the Microsoft® Word item or by clicking on the Microsoft® Word icon on the desktop.

3 You can load a file by single clicking on the File menu item to open up the menu which has an option called Open. Click on Open and a window called Open will appear (Figure 1.28). An alternative approach is to click on the open icon on the standard toolbar (Figure 1.30).

4 The Look in box tells you what drive the window is looking at. You need to aim it at the 3½ Floppy (A:). You do this by clicking on the small button with the down arrow at the end of the Look in box. A menu will appear. Click on the 3½ Floppy (A:) option and the details of the Titan file will appear in the main working area. To open the file, click once on the file to highlight it and then on the open button on the right-hand side of the window. An alternative way is to double click on the Titan file. In either case the text of the file should now appear in the working area of Microsoft® Word.

5 Enter the following text as new paragraphs below the previous text.

The Voyager spacecraft were not simply on a mission to survey Titan. They were taking advantage of the outer planets (e.g. Jupiter, Saturn, Neptune and Uranus) being aligned in the 1970s so that it was possible to visit several in one space trip. Two Voyager spacecraft were launched a few weeks apart in 1977.

The Voyager-1 was to fly past Jupiter, Saturn and their moons while Voyager 2 was to visit Jupiter, Saturn, Uranus and Neptune and their moons. Both spacecraft had two cameras and took thousands of digital photographs of the outer planets and their satellites. The pictures were sent to Earth as radio signals containing the digital information.

6 Practise using the Undo and Redo icons so that you become familiar with how they work.

7 Practise using the Delete and Backspace keys. Remember that the Delete key removes text to the right while the Backspace key removes text to the left.

8 When you are confident about Undo, Redo, Delete and Backspace then attempt these tasks:

a) Highlight

The Voyager spacecraft were not simply on a mission to survey Titan.

This is achieved by positioning the mouse pointer immediately in front of the 'The' and holding down the left mouse button then moving the pointer over the sentence until it is all highlighted (i.e. background changes colour). You will see the sentence gradually highlight as you move over the text. Remember, do not forget to highlight the full stop.

b) Copy

With the sentence highlighted then click on the Copy icon. (If you place your mouse pointer over the copy icon you will see it animate and a small label will appear telling you it is the copy icon. This works with all the icons to help you identify their different functions.) You can also copy the text using the Edit menu which includes the Cut, Copy and Paste functions. When you click on Copy nothing will change and the sentence will remain highlighted.

c) Paste

To paste the text you have copied (i.e. the sentence highlighted) you need to move the mouse pointer to where you want to copy the text to. In this case move your pointer to the end of the passage and click once and you will see the cursor flashing in the new position and the highlighting will disappear. Now click on the Paste icon and you will see the sentence appear at the end of the passage (Figure 1.34).

9 If you click on the Undo icon the pasted text will be removed and you can practise pasting again. Continue copying and pasting until you feel confident.

10 Now try the Cut function.

a) Highlight the sentence below:

The pictures were sent to Earth as radio signals containing the digital information.

Figure 1.34 Paste

b) Cut

Click on the Cut icon and the sentence will disappear. You have not lost the text. It is simply saved to a special area of the memory called the Clipboard. Copied text is also saved here. Normally you can only paste the last item you have cut or copied. The clipboard does hold up to twelve items but to paste them you need to use the clipboard toolbar (select the Edit menu and then click on Office Clipboard to reveal the Clipboard window). Figure 1.35 shows the contents of the clipboard).

c) Paste

Position your cursor at the location you would like to

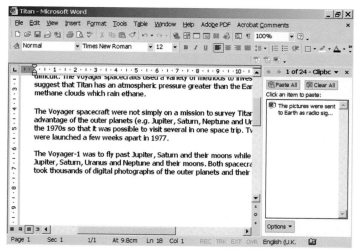

Figure 1.35 Clipboard

paste the cut text to by clicking once. If you click on the Paste icon then the text will now appear at the new position.

An alternative to using Cut is to employ the drag and drop technique. If you highlight the text you want to move and then click on it and hold down the mouse button you can drag the text to a new position. The pointer changes during the move to provide a guide bar to accurately position the text.

11 Practise using the Copy, Cut and Paste functions. If you use Undo, Redo, Delete and Backspace functions you will be able to return to the original passage.

12 Practise using the drag and drop technique. If you use the Undo function you will be able to return to the original passage.

13 When you have finished save your text to the floppy disk. The file should be called New Titan.

14 Print your text after proofreading it and checking its appearance using the Print Preview option in the File menu.

15 You can close Microsoft® Word now by clicking on the File menu item and selecting the option Exit. An alternative way is to click on the Close button on the top right-hand corner of the application window.

Tables

Microsoft® Word can help you to insert tables of information into your document. The Table functions are located in the Table menu. If you highlight the Insert option then a menu is revealed which includes the Table option. If you select the Table option then the Insert Table window appears. This allows you to chose the number of rows and columns your table will contain. Figure 1.36 shows the Insert Table window.

Alternatively you can select the Insert Table icon on the Standard toolbar. This opens a grid of rows and columns. You need to highlight the number of rows and columns that you want in your table by moving your pointer over the cells.

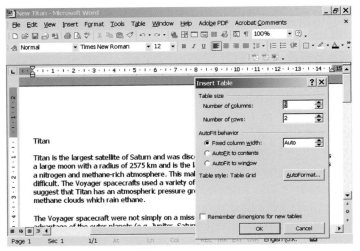

Figure 1.36 Insert table

Borders and shading

Microsoft® Word provides you with functions to enclose your documents or parts of them in a wide variety of borders. You can also shade your text to make it stand out. These functions are designed to help you produce quality documents but overuse of them can lead to the opposite effect. Shading is effective if the contrast between the text and background colours is sharp but if the colours chosen do not sufficiently contrast then the text can be difficult to read. Readability depends to a large extent on the degree of contrast between the colours.

The Borders and Shading option can be found in the Format menu and when it is selected the Borders and Shading window is opened (Figure 1.37). Across the top are three tabs – Borders , Page Border and Shading . The first tab provides a variety of ways of enclosing text while the third offers ways of shading text (Figure 1.38).

Alternatively you can select the Tables and Borders icon on the Standard toolbar.

Headers and footers

On many documents you will have noticed that at the top and bottom are standard words which appear on every page (e.g. authors name, date and page numbers). These are called the headers and footers. You will sometimes be asked to add them as part of your assessment tasks in order to identify the work as your own.

If you select the View menu and the Header and Footer option then an

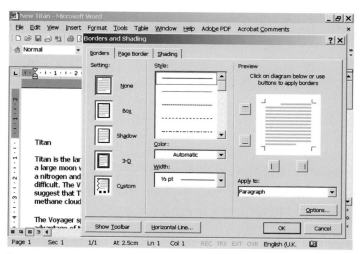

Figure 1.37 Borders and shading

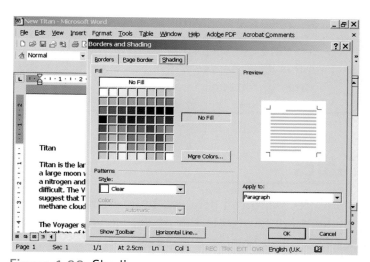

Figure 1.38 Shading

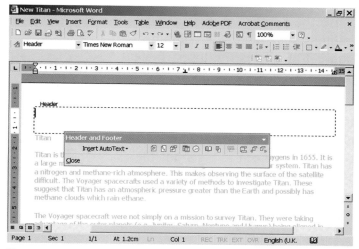

Figure 1.39 Header and Footer

area enclosed in a dashed line will appear at the top and bottom of your page with a toolbar containing a range of tools (Figure 1.39). Your page of text has a faded appearance. You can enter text from the keyboard into the dashed area or use the tools to insert items (e.g. date and filenames).

The tool Insert AutoText provides a range of items that you can enter into the header or footer such as Author, Page and Date.

Bullets and numbering

Microsoft® Word provides a variety of ways of producing lists. You can have many different sorts of bullets and numbers using the Bullets and Numbering option within the Format menu. This displays the Bullets and Numbering window (Figure 1.40) which has four tabs across the top – Bulleted, Numbered, Outline Numbered and List Styles. The first offers you a choice of different bullets and if you select the Pictures button in the bottom right corner then more graphic bullets are offered. The second tab offers a selection of numbers including alphabetical and employing brackets. The third tab provides access to more complex numbering and bullet systems and the fourth offers a range of list styles.

Alternatively you can choose the Numbering and Bullets icons on the Formatting toolbar.

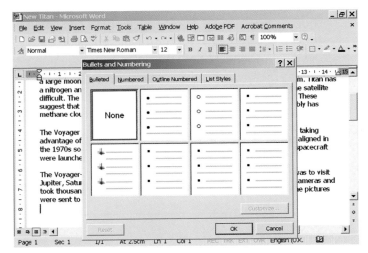

Figure 1.40 Bullets and Numbering

Word count

When writing, you will often want to achieve a specific length of document. If you are studying then assignments are often limited to a precise length (e.g. no more than 1000 words). Microsoft® Word lets you count the words within a document by selecting the Tools menu and the Word Count option. This opens the Word Count window. Figure 1.41 shows the number of pages, words, characters and lines for the whole document or a highlighted section. If you highlight a section, the word count will focus only on that area.

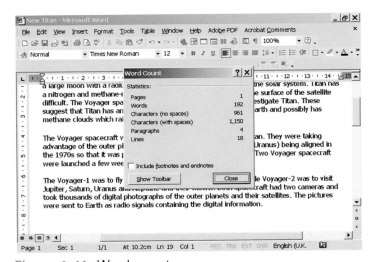

Figure 1.41 Word count

Tables, bullets, borders and shading

1 In Exercise 15 you saved a file called New Titan. We are now going to load this file into Microsoft® Word.

2 Load Microsoft® Word either by selecting the Start button, highlighting the All Programs option and clicking on the Microsoft® Word item or by clicking on the Microsoft® Word icon on the desktop.

3 You can load a file by single clicking on the File menu item to open up the menu which has an option called Open. Click on Open and a window called Open will appear (Figure 1.28). An alternative approach is to click on the open icon on the standard toolbar (Figure 1.30).

4 The Look in box tells you what drive the window is looking at. You need to aim it at the floppy disk. You do this by clicking on the small button with the down arrow at the end of the Look in box. A menu will appear. Click on 3½ Floppy (A:) and the details of the New Titan file will appear in the main working area. To open the file, click once on the file to highlight it and then on the open button on the right-hand side of the window. An alternative way is to double click on the New Titan file. In either case the text of the file will now appear in the working area of Microsoft® Word.

5 Enter the introductory text and table below at the end of the passage (select the Table menu, highlight the Insert option and click on the Table option).

The four main moons of Saturn are shown below.

Moons	Size (radius)
Titan	2600
Rhea	760
Iapetus	730
Dione	560

6 Highlight the table and select the Format menu and the Borders and Shading option to display the window. Select the triple line style. Notice that the preview changes to show you what effect it will have on the table. Figure 1.42 shows the table with triple line style applied.

7 Explore some other borders for the table. Try highlighing a paragraph and enclosing it in a border.

8 Highlight the title Titan and select the Borders and Shading window then the Shading tab. Choose a colour to shade the title. I selected red. Now highlight the second paragraph and shade it another colour. I selected yellow.

9 An alternative way of displaying the information about the four largest moons of Saturn is a list. Highlight the table and select the Table menu, highlight the Delete option and

click on Table . The table will be removed. Place your cursor one line below – The four main moons of Saturn are shown. Now select the Format menu and the Bullets and Numbering option to open the window. Choose the Bulleted tab and any of the bullets that you prefer. After the bullet enter the name of the moon and then press return. A new bullet will appear on the line below. Figure 1.43 shows the results of the bullets.

10 Now save your file with the name New Titan Extra.

11 The next step is to give the new document a header and footer. Select the View file and the Header and Footer option. The header dashed area and the toolbar will appear. Click on the Insert AutoText down arrow and a list of options will appear. Select the Author, Page, Date item. You should see that they appear in the header (Figure 1.44). Now scroll down the page and you will see a dashed area at the bottom for the footer. Click inside the area and select Insert AutoText and choose Filename : New Titan Extra.

12 The next step is to use the Word Count function to measure how many words are in your passage. Finally check your document for errors by proofreading it.

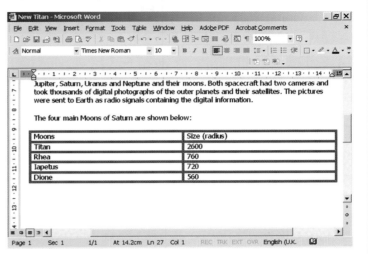

Figure 1.42 Triple line style

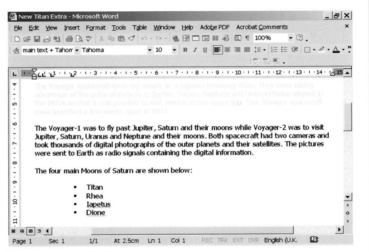

Figure 1.43 Bullets

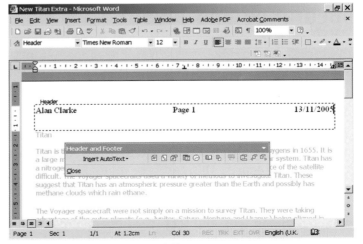

Figure 1.44 Headers and Footers

File management and e-document production

37

continued

13 When you have finished, save your file on to the floppy disk and print your document (remember to use Print Pre<u>v</u>iew to check before printing).

14 You can close Microsoft® Word now by clicking on the <u>F</u>ile menu item and selecting the option E<u>x</u>it. An alternative way is to click on the Close button on the top right-hand corner of the application window.

Replacing words and phrases

Obviously you can replace a word or phrase by simply deleting what you wish to replace and entering the new word or phrase. However, Microsoft® Word provides an automatic way to find and replace a word or a phrase. This is available within the <u>E</u>dit menu (Figure 1.31) as the R<u>e</u>place option. If you select this option by clicking on it then the window shown in Figure 1.45 will appear.

Type the text you want to replace in the Fi<u>n</u>d what box and the replacement text in the Replace wi<u>t</u>h box. The function will search for the text and either automatically replace it throughout the document (Replace All) or allow you to select which ones to change (Replace). You can just search for the text in the Fi<u>n</u>d what box by clicking on the <u>F</u>ind Next button.

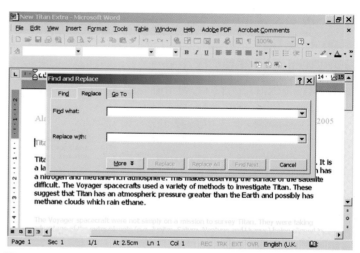

Figure 1.45 Replace

Appearance and layout

Word processors (e.g. Microsoft® Word) have many functions that allow you to change the layout and presentation of text. These include altering the margins, changing the line spacing, aligning (justifying) the text and emphasising words, phrases or whole passages. When you enter a passage of text there is no need to get the appearance right first time since these functions let you change it until you are satisfied.

Many organisations have a house style or a standard way of presenting their letters, documents and reports. This can take many forms but often it involves the use of a limited number of fonts and character sizes, leaving a space after each comma, two spaces after a full stop and using only main headings and one layer of sub-headings. This is intended to provide a common look and feel to all documents from an organisation. If you begin working for a new organisation it is important to know if they employ a house style.

Margins

The margins of a word processor document are controlled by the Page Setup item under the File menu. If you click on File and then on Page Setup, the window shown in Figure 1.46 will be opened.

Figure 1.46 shows you that you can change all four margins (i.e. Top, Bottom, Left and Right). You change the settings for each margin by clicking on the up or down arrow buttons. As you change the margin you can see the overall effect on your document by watching the Preview area. The changes take effect as soon as you click the OK button. If you make a mistake you can always use the Undo icon to reverse the changes.

The Page Setup window also provides access to functions that allow you to select the orientation of the the page. Figure 1.46 shows the choice between landscape and portrait orientation of the page. You select the orientation by clicking on your choice.

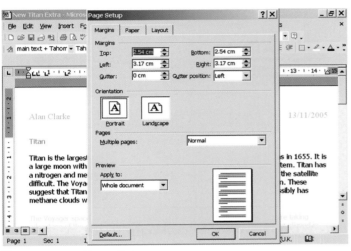

Figure 1.46 Page Setup

Line spacing

Word processors let you adjust the line spacing of your document, for example you could double space either a single paragraph or a whole document. The line spacing functions are provided within the Paragraph option of the Format menu. When you click on the Paragraph option, the window shown in Figure 1.47 will appear. Towards the middle of the window you will see the Line spacing box which, if you click on the down arrow at the end of the box, will display a range of options. These are selected by clicking on the one you want. When you enter text it will follow the new line spacing. To change existing text you need to first highlight the material you want to alter.

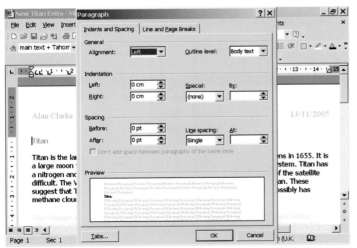

Figure 1.47 Paragraph

Tabs and indents

When you are writing you may want to indent text (e.g. at the start of a new paragraph) to provide emphasis or provide a visual clue for your readers. The Paragraph window (Figure 1.47) provides you with the means of controlling indents.

The Tab key on the keyboard allows you to indent text. The size of a tab (i.e. single press of the key – called a tab stop) is set by the Tabs option within the Format menu which opens the tab window. This controls size and justification of tabs. Figure 1.48 shows the Tab window.

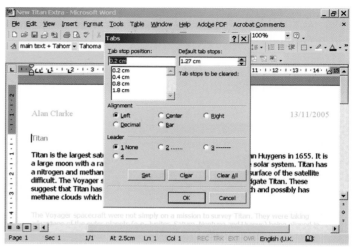

Figure 1.48 Tabs

Inserting a new paragraph

To add a new paragraph break you need to position the cursor by clicking with the mouse pointer at the desired position and then press the Enter key twice. The first key press moves the start of the new paragraph to the next line while the second press inserts a blank line between the paragraphs.

Emphasise text

Microsoft® Word provides you with a range of tools to emphasise your words. These include:

- changing the font and character size of your text
- emboldening your words
- underlining your words
- changing your text into italics

These functions are available on the Formatting toolbar (Figure 1.49) and also in the Format menu (Figure 1.50) within the Font item. If you select one of the toolbar options it will change to indicate that it is active and that everything you now enter is in the emphasised form (e.g. underlined). You need to click on the option a second time to deselect it. It can also be used to change existing text. The normal process of changing text, from a single character to a

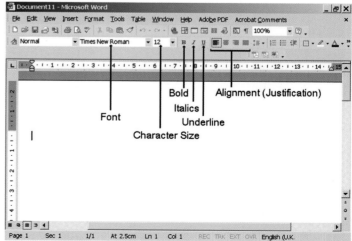

Figure 1.49 Formatting toolbar

whole document, is to highlight your selection and then choose the function's icon or menu option.

Alignment

There are four ways of aligning a document. These are:

- Left – the left text edge is parallel with the margin and the right is ragged
- Right – the right text edge is parallel with the margin and the left is ragged

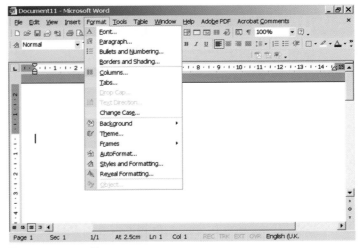

Figure 1.50 Format menu

- Centred – text is aligned down the centre of the page with both edges ragged
- Justified – both left and right text edges are parallel with the margins

Alignment functions are provided in the Paragraph option (Figure 1.47) of the Format menu (Figure 1.50) and on the Formatting toolbar (Figure 1.49). If you select one of the toolbar options it will change to indicate it is active and then everything you now enter will be in new line alignment (e.g. centred). You need to click on the option a second time to deselect it. The process can be used to change existing text by highlighting the section and selecting the desired alignment icon or menu option.

Exercise 17

Appearance and layout

1 Load Microsoft® Word either by selecting the Start button, highlighting the All Programs option and clicking on the Microsoft® Word item or by double clicking on the Microsoft® Word icon on the desktop.

2 Enter the passage below in Times New Roman and character size 12.

(Hint – select the font and character size from the Formatting toolbar before entering text.)

Invasion of Russia

In 1812 Napoleon invaded Russia with one of the largest armies that had ever been assembled. Over 600,000 men had been brought together from all parts of Europe that formed the French Empire. Italians, Dutch, Belgians, Germans and Frenchmen marched across the frontier and the vast majority never returned. It was 700 miles to Moscow and the army had to march across a desolate landscape of forest and marsh where villages were days apart.

In past campaigns French armies had relied upon living off the countries they had attacked. Russia was not a rich land and a large force would not be able to subsist from pillage. The French knew that they could not use their old tactics so they had gathered stores to transport into Russia. Each soldier was heavily loaded with flour, bread, rice and biscuits to last many days. The army staff had planned to transport huge quantities of supplies to last through the normal fast and furious French assault to knock out the Russian armies.

Napoleon's army entered Moscow less than three months later having fought several major and minor battles but it had not destroyed the Russian army. In past campaigns the occupation of the capital city had followed the destruction of the opposing army. It was not long before the French army had to retreat through winter weather with a supply system that had completely failed.

3 Save the passage on your floppy disk with the filename Invasion (there is a Save icon on the Standard toolbar – a picture of a floppy disk – or select the File menu and the Save option). It is good practice to save your text as soon as you can and then to update the file as you make changes. When you select Save later you will not be shown the Save As window since the application assumes that you simply want to update your original file. If you want to save the altered text as a different file you need to select the Save As option in File menu. The procedure is then the same as you earlier undertook for saving a new file.

The Save As option also serves the purpose of allowing you to change the file name of your document. This is useful if you want to create a master document for a whole series of publications or if you want to keep copies of the document at the different stages of its development.

4 Select the File menu and the Page Setup option to change the margins of your documents so that:

- left and right are 3 cm

- top and bottom are 3.5 cm

5 Change the line spacing to 1.5 by highlighting the text and selecting the Format menu and the Paragraph option.

6 Change the title Invasion of Russia so that it is in the Arial font and in character size 14 and embolden the text (i.e. highlight the text, choose the Arial font, the character size and bold option on the Formatting toolbar).

7 Change the alignment of the title to centred (i.e. highlight the title and select the Center icon on the Formatting toolbar).

8 Change the alignment of the rest of the passage to justified. Highlight the text and select the Justify icon on the Formatting Toolbar.

9 Insert a new paragraph at

Each soldier was heavily loaded with flour, bread, rice and biscuits to last many days.

Position your cursor before 'Each' and press Enter twice to break the text and insert a blank line between the paragraphs.

10 Remember to save your finished text and print the document (select the File menu, Print Preview and the Print icon). Check that the text is correct and correct any errors.

11 Close Microsoft® Word by selecting the File menu and the Exit option or use the Close button on the top right-hand corner of the window).

Templates

Many organisations base their correspondence and other documents on templates. These are standard documents in which the structure and layout is determined centrally. Users enter the content of the document but the rest is predetermined. This is to allow the organisation to present a consistent look and feel to the wider world. It allows the quality of documents to be more easily maintained.

Templates can be created to meet any document need such as:

- Letters
- Faxes
- Reports
- Minutes of meetings

To create a template you need to select the File menu and the New option to reveal the New Document area to the right of the work area. Select the General Templates item in the New from template section. This will open the Templates window. This has many tabs across the top. If you choose Letters & Faxes then a range of templates provided by Microsoft® Word are displayed (Figure 1.51). You

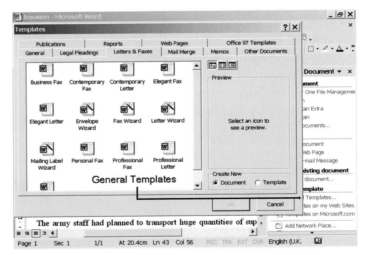

Figure 1.51 Template

can also create your own by selecting a document, clicking on the Template button in the area Create New in the bottom right-hand corner of the window and on the OK button. You can amend the templates provided by Microsoft® Word or create new ones.

Changing a password

Computer security is extremely important for both office and home users. In the office, making sure systems are secure through the use of passwords is important for protecting data from unauthorised access. At home, although you may not have data that you wish to keep secret, good security protects against misuse, be it accidental or malicious. Viruses are a continuous threat to all computers so that it is vital to ensure access to them is controlled. It requires a major effort to remove a virus infection and can result in a considerable loss in data, waste a large amount of your time and require technical assistance to remove. It is now established practice to maintain virus protection systems and an important part of this is to regulate access through passwords.

Microsoft® Windows® and many other suppliers offer a wide range of security systems. Whatever security software you use it is important to understand the need to use original passwords and to change them regularly. Try not to use your name or anything obvious. Good practice is to pick a word at random from a dictionary and add some numbers either within or at the end of the word, or to use a completely random series of numbers and letters.

To change your Windows® password you need to access the Control Panel. This involves clicking on the Start button and clicking on Control Panel to reveal the Control Panel window. In this window there is an icon called User Accounts (shown as two people). When you click on this icon it will open the User Accounts window (Figure 1.52). This allows you to:

- Change an account
- Create a new account
- Change the way users log on and off

Each user has their own account. If you click on Create a New Account

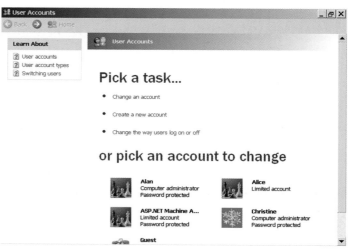

Figure 1.52 User accounts

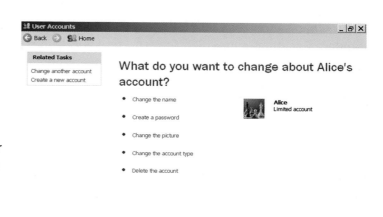

Figure 1.53 Alice's account

Figure 1.54 Create password

then you can add a new user to the computer system by following the sequence of choices. Alice is a new user and if you click on her name then her User Account appears (Figure 1.53) which allows you to create her password (Figure 1.54).

Other Control Panel options

The Control Panel provides ways of changing system settings. You can adjust:

- the sound volume of your system by selecting the Sounds and Audio Devices icon to display the Sounds and Audio Devices Properties window
- the date and time of the system by selecting the Date and Time icon to reveal the Date and Time Properties window

You can alter various other settings such as adjusting the display, mouse, keyboard and printers.

Screen prints

Windows provides you with a standard function to capture an image of the screen display (i.e. a screen print). This is available from the keyboard by pressing the PrtScr key. You can then open a blank document and use the Paste option to insert the image into a document. As part of the New CLAiT assessment you will occasionally be asked to use screen print to provide evidence of your work. It is therefore worth practising.

Safe working practice

There are a number of straightforward actions you can take to reduce the risk of injuring yourself when you are using a computer. One of the key problems is Repetitive Strain Injury (RSI) in which, by using the computer incorrectly, you place a strain on your body (e.g. hands, wrists and arms) which may result in permanent harm.

Some straightforward good practices include:

Space

It is important to give yourself plenty of space. You must have plenty of room for your legs and body. There should be enough space around the computer for your papers and books so that you can reach them without stretching. You can use a paper stand to hold your papers to help you copy text without turning. You should be comfortable. Even a tiny need to twist or turn your body can be harmful over a long period.

Breaks

It is good practice to take regular breaks away from the computer.

Chairs

Your chair should be adjustable so that you can alter the height and backrest. It should support your lower back. Your feet should either be placed squarely on the floor or on a foot rest with your knees slightly higher than the chair to ensure good circulation of blood. Again it is important to be comfortable.

Your eyes should be aligned slightly below the top of the monitor and you should be positioned about 45 cm from the display.

Reduce strain

When you are using the computer you must avoid placing any strain on hands and wrists by:

- keeping your wrists straight while typing (e.g. by using a rest)
- not resting on your wrists
- typing gently without excessive force
- taking frequent breaks and avoiding typing for long periods

Light

Computer monitors are very susceptible to reflection. It is therefore important to position your screen so it does not reflect light from the sun or the room lights. You will probably need to experiment. Monitors and other types of screen are normally designed to allow you to change their angle and their brightness and contrast.

Cables

Because computers often have a large number of cables near them to link them to other equipment, there is always a risk of tripping over them. It is good practice to inspect the general area around your computer to identify and remove any risks.

Shortcuts

You may have observed that when you are using Microsoft® Windows® or an application some of the menu options have a letter underlined. This is a keyboard shortcut. They provide you with an alternative way of selecting the option other than clicking on the option with the mouse pointer. You press the Alt key and, holding it down, press the letter that is underlined (e.g. File). This has the same effect as clicking on the option. It is useful if you are entering text as you can therefore select the option without taking your hands away from the keyboard.

Help

Microsoft® Windows® has a help function, accessed by selecting the Start button and clicking on the Help and Support option. The Help and Support Center window will

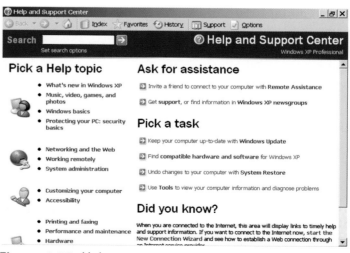

Figure 1.55 Help

appear (Figure 1.55). This provides help with many topics (e.g. What's new in Windows® XP) and ways of gaining assistance. You may wish to explore the topics. Click on the options which will reveal sub-topics and so on. You can return to the original display by clicking on the Back button in the left-hand top corner.

More practice

Activity 1

1 Load Microsoft® Word either by selecting the Start button, highlighting the All Programs option and clicking on the Microsoft® Word item or by clicking on the Microsoft® Word icon on the desktop.

2 Enter the passage below in Tahoma font and character size 10 by selecting the font and character size from the Formatting toolbar before entering text.

3 Set the margins as follows (File menu, Page Setup and Margins tab):

Left and right – 4 cm
Top and bottom – 3 cm

The page orientation should be portrait.

For many people guinea pigs are the perfect pet. They are small friendly animals who rarely bite and are easy to keep healthy. Guinea pigs are rodents and are not from Guinea so the name is a little misleading. They actually originate from Peru. There are several different breeds including Selfs which are smooth haired animals, Himalayans, Abyssinians and Crested.

Guinea pigs are herbivores. They need to be given fresh vegetables every day since they cannot make their own vitamin C. Their teeth grow all the time so they need to be given food which they need to grind so that their teeth do not get too long. Dry food is available which has been enriched with vitamin C. Guinea pigs are enthusiastic about their food and will tell you when they are hungry. They will talk to you when you are late just to remind you they like their food on time.

Guinea pigs can be kept indoors or outdoors. If they are in an outside hutch they need to be secured against both the cold and the local cats. A frosty night can leave pigs very distressed while they have few defences against cats. Indoor animals need the opportunity to exercise in the open air in a run or other secure enclosure. All guinea pigs love eating grass.

4 Create a header by selecting the View menu and the Header and Footer option. Enter your own name as the header and add a date to the footer and the file name Guinea Pig.

5 Once you have entered the text, carefully check it for mistakes and use the spell checker (Tools menu and Spelling and Grammar option) to ensure it is free from spelling mistakes. Save the passage on your floppy disk as a file called Guinea Pig by selecting the File Menu and then Save.

6 Insert a title 'Guinea Pig – Cavies' separated by one blank line from the rest of the passage in Arial font and character size 14. (Use the mouse to move the cursor, select the font and character size from Formatting toolbar before entering the title.)

7 Underline the title by highlighting the text and selecting the Underline icon from the Formatting toolbar.

8 Insert a new paragraph so that it becomes the third one.

These little animals enjoy each other's company so should be kept together. Female pigs are called sows and males are boars. The young animals are born with their eyes open and will be running around their hutch soon after birth. They are suckled by their mothers but will soon eat vegetables and can be separated from them within a few weeks.

9 Change the line spacing to double (by highlighting the passage, selecting the Format menu and the Paragraph option).

10 Change the alignment of the passage to Left (by highlighting the text and selecting the Align Left icon on the Formatting toolbar).

11 Replace 'guinea pigs' with 'guinea pigs (cavies)' throughout the passage – you should find six occurences (use the Edit menu and the Replace option). Proofread your final document to ensure it is free from mistakes.

12 Save your changed file (File menu and Save option or Save icon on the Standard toolbar).

13 Print your document by selecting the File menu, the Print Preview and Print options (or the print icon from within Print Preview).

14 Close Microsoft® Word (by selecting the File menu and the Exit option or click on the close button).

Activity 2

1 Create a folder called Hobbies on your floppy disk by clicking My Computer, choosing 3½ Floppy (A:), selecting the File menu, New and Folder options. Enter the name Hobbies to replace the New Folder title.

2 Create a sub-folder called Pets in the folder Hobbies by opening the folder and selecting File menu, New and Folder options. Enter the name Pets to replace New Folder title.

3 Create another sub-folder called Extra in the folder Hobbies.

4 Rename the folder Hobbies as your name (i.e. Alan Clarke) by highlighing the folder, selecting File menu and the Rename option.

5 Copy the file Guinea Pig from Activity 1 into the sub-folder Pets (highlight the file and Copy and Paste).

6 Delete the sub-folder Extra (highlight the file and select the Delete option from the File menu).

7 Take a screen print of the folder with your name (i.e. Alan Clarke) by pressing the Shift and PrtSc keys.

8 Take a screen print of the file Guinea Pig in the sub-folder Pets.

9 Paste your screen prints into a Microsoft® Word document.

10 Add a header and footer to your document and enter your name and date in the footer.

11 Save the document with the file name Screen Print to your floppy disk.

12 Print the document.

13 Close your files.

The screen print method is sometimes required as part of the assessment process to provide evidence that you have completed the tasks.

Activity 3

1 Load Microsoft® Word by selecting the Start button, highlighting the All Programs option and clicking on the Microsoft® Word item or by clicking on the Microsoft® Word icon on the desktop.

2 Enter the table below in Times New Roman font and character size 12 by selecting the font and character size from the Formatting toolbar before entering text.

3 Set the margins as follows (File menu, Page Setup and Margins tab):

Left and right – 2 cm
Top and bottom – 4 cm

The page orientation should be portrait.

Event	Team A Points	Team B Points
100 metres	10	2
200 metres	6	6
110 hurdles	0	12
400 metres	4	8
800 metres	2	10

4 Once you have entered the text, carefully check it for mistakes and use the spell checker (Tools menu and Spelling and Grammar option) to ensure it is free from spelling mistakes.

5 Embolden the titles Event, Team A Points and Team B Points.

6 Centre the headings Team A Points and Team B Points.

7 All the remaining text and numbers should be left aligned.

8 Save the table on your floppy disk as a file called Results by selecting the File menu and Save .

9 Print your table by selecting the File menu, the Print Preview and Print options (or the Print icon from within Print Preview).

10 Close Microsoft® Word (by selecting the File menu and the Exit option or click on the Close button).

SUMMARY

1 **What is a computer?** A computer consists of two main components: hardware and software.

2 **Hardware:** The physical elements of the equipment that you can see when you look at a computer. These include a monitor, main box (containing Central Processing Unit), printer, keyboard and mouse.

3 **Software:** The instructions that controls the hardware. Software is divided into two main types: operating systems and applications.

4 **Serial, parallel and USB ports:** Ports are the means of connecting peripheral equipment to the main computer.

5 **DVD and CD–RW drives:** These are different types of drives which allow disks to be used with a computer. DVDs allow the computer to read very large amounts of information which are stored on the disc. DVDs are often used to hold the contents of an entire movie. CD–RW drives allow you to save information onto a special type of CD-ROM and to read the information stored on the disc.

6 **Memory stick:** A portable device that allows you to store files and folders by plugging it into a computer's USB port. They are also called flash and pen drives and even a dongle.

7 **Mouse:** The mouse enables you to carry out a series of actions including single clicking with left and right mouse buttons, double clicking and dragging and dropping.

8 **Keyboard:** The keyboard allows you to enter text and numbers into computer applications.

9 **Window controls:** In the top right-hand corner of the window are three control buttons. These are minimise, maximise and close.

10 **Storing files:** Information is stored on disks (i.e. floppy and hard disks) in the form of files which are placed in folders to help organise them. Files have different formats depending on the nature of the information they store (e.g. documents and images).

11 **Windows Explorer:** Explorer provides the functions to search the disks for files and folders. Other functions include deleting and renaming files.

12 **Search:** Click on the Start button and Search option to reveal the Search Results window.

13 **Accessories:** Windows® contains several applications which come bundled with the operating system. These include WordPad (word-processing), Paint and Calculator.

14 **Load Microsoft® Word:** Open Microsoft® Word either by clicking on the Start button, highlighting All Programs and single clicking on Microsoft® Word option or double clicking on the Microsoft® Word icon on the Windows® desktop.

15 **Insert text:** You must position the cursor where you need to insert the text. Move your mouse pointer to the new position and click there. The cursor will appear as a flashing line and you can now enter your text.

16 **Save**: Select the File menu and the Save option. The Save As window (dialog box) opens. Select location (Look in box) and name your file (File name box) then click on the Save button.

17 **Save As**: Select the File menu and the Save As option. The Save As window opens. Select location (Save in box) and name your file (File name box) then click on the Save button.

18 **Save a file on a floppy disk**: Insert a floppy disk into drive A: and click on the File menu and the Save option to reveal the Save As window. Select the drive (3½ Floppy (A:)) and enter a file name.

Having saved a file once, you can update it by clicking on the File menu and Save without the Save As window appearing again. It simply overwrites the original file.

An alternative is to click on the Save icon on the Standard toolbar to update the file.

19 **Close**: Click on the File menu item and the Exit option or click on the close button in the top right-hand corner of the application window.

20 **Delete text**: You have two different keys which both work from the position of your cursor.

Backspace key – this removes text, character by character to the left of the cursor position

Delete key – this removes text, character by character to the right of the cursor position

There is also Undo and Redo. Undo removes the last action you have undertaken while Redo carries out actions removed by Undo.

21 **Move text**: Highlight the text you want to move. Select either the Copy or Cut icons on the Standard toolbar or alternatively the Edit menu and the Cut or Copy options. Reposition the cursor at the place you want to move the text to and then select the Paste icon on the Standard toolbar or the Edit Menu and the Paste option.

22 **Drag and drop**: Highlight the text. Click on it and hold down the mouse button. Drag the text to the new position using the mouse. The pointer changes during the move to provide a guide bar to position the text accurately.

23 **Tables**: Use the Table menu, highlight the Insert option and Table option to open the Insert Table window.

24 **Borders and shading**: Select the Format menu and the Borders and Shading option to open the window with three tabs (Borders , Page Border and Shading) across the top.

25 **Headers and footers**: Use the View menu and the Header and Footer option.

26 **Bullets and numbering**: Use the Format menu and the Bullets and Numbering option.

27 **Word count**: Use the Tools menu and the Word Count option.

28 **Replace text**: Use the Edit menu and the Replace option to open the Replace window. Enter the text you want to replace in the Find what box and the replacement text in the Replace with box.

29 **Change margins**: Use the File menu and the Page Setup item to open the window which controls the four margins (i.e. left, right, top and bottom).

30 **Orientation**: Select the File menu and Page Setup option. This presents you with the choice between landscape and portrait orientation of the page.

31 **Line spacing**: Use the Format menu and the Paragraph option. The Paragraph window will open with the Line spacing function box.

32 **Alignment**: Select the Format menu and the Paragraph option or the Formatting toolbar.

Select one of the toolbar options (Align Left, Align Right, Centered or Justify). It will change to show it is active and then everything you now enter will be in the new alignment. You need to click on the option a second time to deselect it.

To change existing text, highlight it and then select the alignment icon or the menu option.

33 **Printing**: Select the File menu, click on the Print option and the OK button.

34 **Retrieve**: Select the File menu and the Open option. This will reveal the Open window. Choose the disk by using the down arrow button at the end of the Look in box and select the file to be retrieved.

35 **Change password**: Select the Start button and click on Control Panel to reveal the Control Panel window. Double click on the Users and Passwords icon.

36 **Safe working practice**: The straightforward issues to reduce the risk of harm are sufficient space, regular breaks, eliminating strain and reducing light reflections.

37 **Shortcuts**: Press the Alt key and, holding it down, press the letter that is underlined (e.g. Edit).

38 **Print screen**: Press the Alt and PrtSc keys. Paste the image of the screen into a Word document by opening a new document and selecting the Edit menu and Paste option.

39 **Help**: Select the Start button and click on the Help and Support option.

40 **Spell and grammar checker**: Select the Tools menu and Spelling and Grammar option. This opens the Spelling and Grammar window.

The Spell Checker can be set work automatically so that spelling mistakes are undelined in red while green shows a grammatical error. It is always important to proofread text and not to rely only on the spell checker to identify mistakes.

Chapter 2

Unit 2

Creating spreadsheets and graphs

This chapter will help you to use spreadsheets and charts and graphs applications. You will be able to:

- identify and use a spreadsheet, including charts and graphs, correctly
- use an input device to enter and edit data accurately
- insert, replicate and format arithmetical formulas
- use common numerical formatting and alignment
- manage and print spreadsheets, charts and graphs
- develop pie charts, line graphs and bar/column charts
- select and present single and comparative sets of data
- set numerical parameters and format data

Assessment

This unit does not assume any previous experience of spreadsheets. However, it may be useful to have studied Unit 1: File management and e-document production. You will be assessed through a practical realistic assignment which is designed to allow you to demonstrate your knowledge and skills against each objective. Your tutor can provide you with more guidance.

Spreadsheet applications

Figures 2.1 and 2.2 show Microsoft® Excel® XP. Figure 2.1 shows Microsoft® Excel® with the New Workbook task pane open. The task pane is intended to help you undertake some frequent tasks in this case to open an existing workbook (spreadsheet) or start a new one. If you prefer to have the task pane closed you need to select the Close button in the top right-hand corner of the task pane or select the View menu and the Task Pane option to remove the tick icon next to the option. To open the task pane then repeat the operation (i.e. View menu and Task Pane option to insert the tick).

Figure 2.2 shows that Microsoft® Excel® XP is similar to other Microsoft® Office applications in that it comprises a menu and toolbars (e.g. Standard toolbar), work area and a status bar at the bottom of the display. On the top right-hand corner are the three control buttons – Minimise,

Maximise and Close which are displayed in all Microsoft® application windows. However, there are some differences which are:

1 The work area is divided into a grid of rows and columns to form many individual cells. The active cell illustrated in Figure 2.2 is in row 1 and column A and is known as A1. When you are developing formulas it is important to identify particular cells and this is done by stating the column and row intersection.

2 At the bottom of the work area are tabs indicating Sheet 1, Sheet 2 and Sheet 3. These show which worksheet is being used and Micosoft® Excel® allows you to group sheets together to form a workbook. Figure 2.2 shows that Sheet 1 is being displayed.

3 Beneath the formatting toolbar is a row called the Formula Bar which shows A1 at the left-hand end followed by a grey area with the f_x symbol. A1 indicates the active cell and therefore changes as this moves. After the f_x symbol, any formulas which are in the active cell are displayed. We will discuss formulas later in this chapter.

There are several ways of loading an application such as Microsoft® Excel®. The two most common are using:

- the Start button
- the Microsoft® Excel® icon on the Microsoft® Windows® desktop

In the bottom left-hand corner of the Microsoft® Windows® desktop is a button called Start. This allows you to access various applications and standard features of the operating system. If you single click on Start, a menu will pop up. If you place the mouse pointer over the All Programs item it will become highlighted (i.e. the background will change colour) and a new menu will appear alongside. If you click on the item shown as Microsoft® Excel® then the application will load. In a similar way if you double click on the Microsoft® Excel® icon shown on the desktop then Excel® will similarly load.

The exercises included in the chapter are intended to help you understand how to use spreadsheets, graphs and charts. They are simplified examples that are not intended to be tutorials on accountancy but explanations of Microsoft® Excel®.

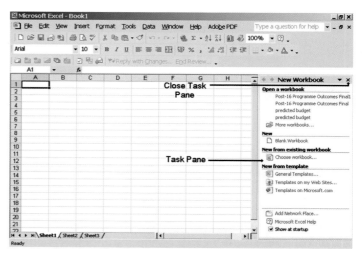

Figure 2.1 Microsoft® Excel® XP with task pane open

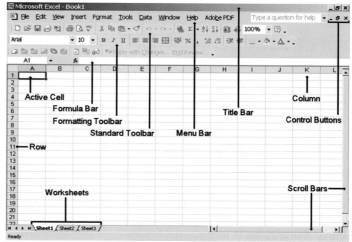

Figure 2.2 Microsoft® Excel® XP features

Exercise 18

Load and use Microsoft® Excel®

1 Load Microsoft® Excel® using either the All Programs menu or the Microsoft® Excel icon on the desktop.

2 Enter the table of information below to form your first spreadsheet. It shows a simple breakdown of the costs of operating the Acme Newsagent. Position your pointer in cell C3 and you will see the cell is highlighted by its borders becoming emboldened. Now enter Acme Newsagent. Repeat this entering Newspapers in B8, Groceries in B9, Stationery in B10, Wages in B11, Total in B12, Costs in C6, Overheads in D6 and Total Costs in E6. Now add the numeric cost data to form the column of figures in column C in rows 8, 9, 10 and 11.

Acme Newsagent			
	Costs	Overheads	Total Costs
Newspapers	12000		
Groceries	10000		
Stationery	8000		
Wages	6000		
Total			

3 To select an individual cell you need to click within it and it will be highlighted. However, you can also select a whole row or column. To select a row or column click in the letter (e.g. A) or number (e.g. 1) which is at the end of the row or the top of the column, respectively. The row or column will then be highlighted. To remove the highlighting you need to click in another part of the sheet.

4 If you make a mistake when entering text or numbers then you can delete the characters using the Backspace key. However, if you have moved to a new cell then you can either overwrite your original entry by clicking on the cell with the error and entering the correct text or numbers or edit the text as it appears on the formula bar. If you highlight the cell which contains the error you will see its contents appear in the formula bar and you use your mouse pointer to position your cursor in order to amend the text.

5 This table is perhaps a little crowded so you need to separate the rows with a blank row. Microsoft® Excel® allows you to insert new rows and columns. To insert a row, click on Groceries to tell Microsoft® Excel® where you want to insert the row (it is inserted above the row the cursor is in) and on the Insert menu (Figure 2.3) click the Rows item. A new row will be inserted between Groceries and Newspapers.

6 Now add a row between Groceries and Stationery, between Stationery and Wages, and, finally, between Wages and Total.

7 Insert a column of information by highlighting column F and and then select the Insert menu (Figure 2.3) and then the Columns item. A new column will be created. Enter headings 'Income' in cell G6, and 'Total Profit' in cell H6 and the information shown in Figure 2.4. The menus in all Microsoft® Office applications are sometimes presented in a shortened form ending with two arrows. If you click on the arrows the reminder of the menu options are displayed.

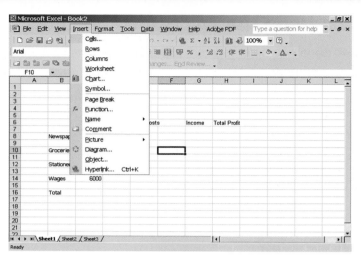

Figure 2.3 Insert menu

8 Save the spreadsheet you have created on to a floppy disk. This procedure is the same in all Microsoft® Windows® applications – you save a spreadsheet, database or graphic image in exactly the same way. Insert a floppy disk into drive A: and click on the File menu item and a menu will open showing a list of options. Select Save and a window will open.

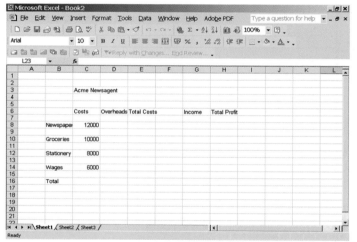

Figure 2.4 Spreadsheet

9 Click in the box File name and enter A:\Acme Newsagent. Now click on the Save button on the right of the window. You have now saved the table as a file called Acme Newsagent. You may hear drive A: work during this process.

10 It is possible to save the spreadsheet again under a different file name so that you have two identical files. Because they have different file names, they are treated as individual files. In order to do this you need to select the File menu and the option Save As.

11 You can close Microsoft® Excel® by clicking on the File menu item. A menu will appear with a list of options. At the bottom of the list is the option Exit. If you click on Exit then Microsoft® Excel® will close. An alternative way is to click on the Close button in the top right-hand corner of the application window.

New

On occasions you will want to start a new spreadsheet once you have completed the one you have been working on. This is achieved by selecting the **File** menu and the **New** option. This opens the New Workbook task pane (Figure 2.1) which is divided into a number of sections. These provide access to many standard templates for spreadsheets. Select the Blank Workbook option. A new blank spreadsheet will appear.

Delete, clear and hide

Microsoft® Excel® provides three useful options linked to deleting the contents of cells, rows and columns. These are:

- **Delete** (Figure 2.5)
- **Clear** (Figure 2.5)
- **Hide** (Figure 2.6)

The first step in using the options above is to identify the row, column, cell or area of the spreadsheet by highlighting or placing the mouse pointer in the cell or row or column. The **Edit** menu provides access to the **Delete** and **Clear** options. If **Delete** is selected, then a small Delete window appears providing different options for removing the item. Delete permanently removes the item and adjusts the spreadsheet layout. If **Clear** is selected, then another menu of options appears (e.g. if **All** is chosen the contents of the selected area are removed but not the spreadsheet structure/layout).

The difference between Delete and Clear is that Delete removes the contents and the spreadsheet structure, while Clear simply removes the contents. **Clear** also provides some extra options such as removing the formatting of an entry while leaving contents behind. You would probably use **Clear** to amend an area in the heart of a spreadsheet and **Delete** if you wanted to start again.

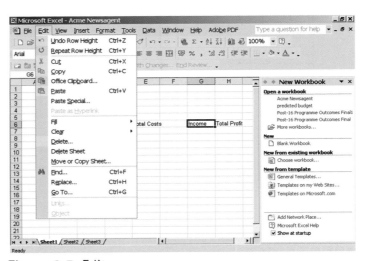

Figure 2.5 Edit menu

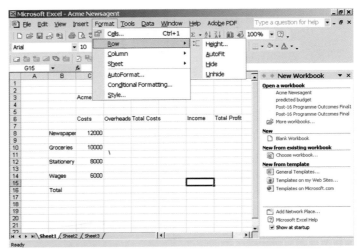

Figure 2.6 Format menu

The Hide function is accessed by selecting the Format menu, then the options Row, Column or Sheet (Figure 2.6). Again you identify the area you want to hide by highlighting or placing the mouse pointer in the particular row or column. By selecting Hide, that area of the spreadsheet will disappear. It can be returned by selecting the Unhide option. Hide does not delete the items, it only hides them from view: useful if you do not want to disclose confidential information.

Exercise 19

Delete, clear and hide

1 Load Microsoft® Excel® using either the All Programs menu or the Microsoft® Excel® icon on the desktop.

2 Enter the table of information below to form your first spreadsheet. It shows a family budget:

	January	February	March
Food and drink	300	320	270
Clothes	80	75	145
Travel	160	400	140
Leisure	60	110	95
Services	25	42	67
Council Tax	105	105	105

3 Save the spreadsheet you have created on to a floppy disk. Insert a floppy disk into drive A: and click on the File menu item and a menu will open showing a list of options. Select Save and a window will open.

4 Click in the box File name and Enter A:\Budget. Now click on the Save button on the right of the window. You have now saved the table as a file called Budget. You may hear drive A: work during this process.

5 If you make a wrong choice while working with the spreadsheet you can retrace your steps by using the Undo option in the Edit menu. This is also useful when you want to explore the effects of different options without making any permanent changes.

6 Explore the three options Delete, Clear and Hide. Highlight the February column (i.e. from the February title to 105) and then select the Delete option on the Edit menu. This opens a another menu with four options – Shift cells left is the default setting. Don't change the default just click on OK and notice what happens. You should observe that the column is deleted and the gap between January and March closes (i.e. the structure of the spreadsheet is removed).

7 Now select the Edit menu and Undo Delete and the column will reappear.

8 Highlight the February column again and select the Edit menu and highlight Clear to reveal a menu with four options. Click on All. Observe what happens. The content disappears but the gap between January and March does not close (i.e. the structure is not removed).

9 Now select the Edit menu and Undo Clear and the content will reappear.

10 Select the Highlight February cell and select the Format menu and highlight the Column option to reveal a menu of five choices. Select the Hide option. Observe what happens. The column disappears and a line of highlighting is left between January and March.

11 Now select the Format menu and highlight the Column option to reveal the menu of options. Select the Unhide option and you will see the column reappear.

12 Explore the three options using Undo or Unhide to return to the original spreadsheet until you understand the different effects of Delete, Clear and Hide.

13 You can close Microsoft® Excel® now by clicking on the File menu item and a menu will appear with a list of options. At the bottom of the list is the option Exit. If you click on Exit then Microsoft® Excel® will close. An alternative way is to click on the Close button on the top right-hand corner of the application window

Spreadsheet formulas

Figure 2.7 shows a spreadsheet of the costs and income of the Acme Newsagent. This spreadsheet employs a number of formulas to:

- add up columns and rows of figures
- calculate overheads
- calculate the total profit of the business

Formulas are used by spreadsheets to calculate numerical values. They allow you to add up columns of figures to produce a total, subtract the contents of different cells, multiply, divide and undertake more complex calculations. One of the most important features of a spreadsheet is that you can build formulas within the sheet to calculate almost anything.

The mathematical operators used in Microsoft® Excel® are:

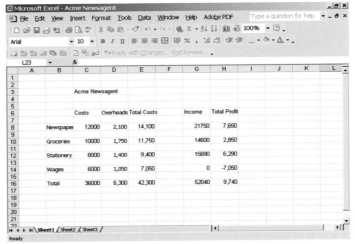

Figure 2.7 Acme Newsagent spreadsheet

- + add
- - subtract
- * multiply
- / divide

Brackets are also important because they tell Microsoft® Excel® to calculate anything in the brackets first before going on with the remaining parts of the calculation.

Formulas are based on giving each cell a reference (e.g. A1, D12, M7, etc.) made up of the column letter and the row number.

Example

B8   Column B and Row 8

In Figure 2.7 you can see the column letters and row numbers. Cell C8 (Column C and Row 8) contains the number 12 000. To calculate overheads (i.e. contents of D8) of the newspapers this number needs to be multiplied by 0.175 which represents the current rate of overheads (17.5% or 0.175). The formula is C8*0.175 (i.e. contents of cell C8 multiplied by the overhead rate). By using a formula referring to the cell's unique address C8 then each time the number placed in the cell changes the new value of overheads is automatically calculated.

Example

C8 = 12000   D8 = 2100 (Overheads)
C8 = 8000   D8 = 1400 (Overheads)
C8 = 4000   D8 = 700 (Overheads)

It is possible to have formula based on the actual number so that our example overhead formula could be 12000 * 0.175. This would give the correct value but each time the cost of newspapers changed you would also need to change the formula.

Figure 2.7 shows four examples of formulas. These are:

1 Cell D8   =C8*0.175

Overheads on newspapers are the cost of the newspapers (Cell C8) multiplied by 0.175 which produces 17.5% of the cost (the current rate of overheads). To avoid confusion with the letter x, spreadsheets use the symbol * as the multiplication sign.

2 Cell E8   =C8+D8

To produce the total cost of newspapers requires the cost of the papers (C8) to be added to the Overheads (D8).

3 Cell H8   =G8-E8

Total profit is income minus cost, so the profit on newspaper sales is the total income from the newspapers (cell G8) less their total cost (cell E8).

4 Cell C16   =SUM(C8:C14)

To total or add up a column or row of figures, the Microsoft® Excel® spreadsheet provides a standard function called SUM. This function means that all the contents of cells between C8 to C14 are added together (i.e. C8+C9+C10+C11+C12+C13+C14).

These four examples show that a spreadsheet is able to add, subtract and multiply the contents of any cell or combination of cells.

It is also possible to divide the contents of any cell. If we want to know what the profit was likely to be in a quarter (three months) we could divide the total profit (cell H16) by 4 (H16/4). The use of brackets tells Microsoft® Excel® to calculate anything inside them first. This is important since it changes the result.

Example

If C8 = 5 and D8 = 8   then C8+D8/2 = 9   but (C8+D8)/2 = 6.5

Replication

Formulas can be copied to new locations in a similar way to other Microsoft® Office applications. However, there is an important difference in that in most cases when you copy a formula to a new location it changes to allow for the new position in the spreadsheet. However, before you replicate a formula check that it is correct or you will be spreading an error across the spreadsheet.

Example

Formula to total three cells A1+A2+A3 and is in cell A5.

Copy the formula to B5 and the formula will change to B1+B2+B3 so that it carries out the same function but in the context of the new row.

Copying in a spreadsheet is called replication to show this change in formulas. In order to replicate data or a formula then highlight the area or cell to be copied and then use the Edit menu and the Copy option. Use the Paste option to copy the data or formula to the new location.

Exercise 20

Formulas

1 In Exercise 18 you saved a file called Acme Newsagent and we are now going to load this file into Microsoft® Excel®.

2 Using either the Start and All Programs menu or the Microsoft® Excel® icon methods, load Microsoft® Excel®.

3 You can load a file by single clicking on the File menu item to open up the menu which has an option called Open. Click on Open and a window called Open will appear.

4 The Look in box tells you which drive the window is looking at. You need to aim it at drive A:. You do this by clicking on the small button with the down arrow at the end of the Look in box. A menu will appear. Click on 3½ Floppy (A:) and the details of Acme Newsagent will appear in the main working area. To open the file, click on the file once to highlight it and then on the Open button on the right-hand side of the window. An alternative way is to double click on the Acme Newsagent file. In either case the content of the file should now appear in the working area of Microsoft® Excel®.

5 The first step is to enter a formula to calculate the Overheads on the Costs. Overheads are 17.5% of the costs so if you multiply costs by 0.175 you will calculate the Overheads. Enter =C8*0.175 into cell D8. To enter the other Overheads amounts you can use a technique called replication. Highlight cell D8 by single clicking on the cell and clicking on the copy icon on the Standard toolbar or the Edit menu and the Copy option. Now click on the cell you want to copy the formula to (e.g. D10) by highlighting the cell and clicking on paste on the Standard toolbar or the Paste option in the Edit menu. The formula is copied into the new cell but will change to adapt to its new location so it will now read =C10*0.175. Paste the formula into D12 (=C12*0.175) and D14 (=C14*0.175).

6 The second step is to enter the formula to total the costs and overheads. Microsoft® Excel® provides a standard function called SUM, available on the Standard toolbar (Figure 2.8). You highlight both cells C8 and D8 by clicking on C8 and holding down the left mouse button then dragging the pointer over D8 and E8 and releasing. The three cells should now be highlighted. By clicking on the SUM icon

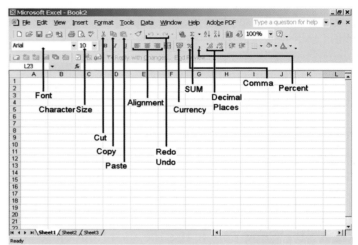

Figure 2.8 **Standard and formatting toolbars**

on the toolbar you will see the formula appear in E8 (=SUM(C8:D8)). Repeat this action for rows 10, 12 and 14. This will produce formulas in E10 (=SUM(C10:D10)), E12 (=SUM(C12:D12)) and E14 (=SUM(C14:D14)).

7 Now enter the formula to calculate Total profits. This is equal to Income minus Total Costs. In cell H8 enter =G8-E8 and then replicate the formula in H10, H12 and H14. If you make a mistake you can delete all the formula by highlighing the area (i.e H10 to H14) and selecting the Delete key or the Edit menu and the Delete option. It does not matter that you are deleting some blank cells. It will not have any effect.

8 Now total each column using the SUM function (i.e. highlight C8 to C16 and click on the SUM button to enter the formula in cell C16 =SUM(C8:C15)). Replicate the formula in D16, E16, G16 and H16.

9 Save the new file on your floppy disk as file A:\Acme Newsagent Formula. Select the File menu and the Save As option which will reveal the Save As window and you can save the file under the new name. If you select the Save option you will overwrite your original file. The Save As function allows you to save files under different names.

10 Close Microsoft® Excel® by selecting the File menu and the Exit option or click on the Close button on the top right-hand corner of the application window.

Presentation

Microsoft® Excel® provides the normal presentation options that are available in many Microsoft® Office applications. You can therefore:

- change or select fonts (Figure 2.8) and character size (Figure 2.8) using options on the Formatting toolbar
- embolden, italicise and underline text using options on the Formatting toolbar
- align (justify) text (align left, align right and centre text – Figure 2.8) using options on the Formatting toolbar
- change the format of numerical data (Figure 2.8) using options on the Formatting toolbar
- change the width and depth of rows and columns (Format menu – Figure 2.6)

These presentation options work in a similar way to other Microsoft® Office products. You can either select the option (e.g. font) before you enter text or numbers or change the option later. You change the formatting by highlighting the area that needs to be changed (e.g. cell, row or column) and then selecting the desired option.

Spreadsheets have extra formatting options to allow numerical information to be presented in a variety of ways. These include (Figure 2.8 – Formatting toolbar):

- Currency – to display numerical information with a £ sign in a currency format
- Percent – to display data in percentage style
- Comma – formats numbers with commas in appropriate places
- Decimal places – increase and decrease the number of decimal points shown

An alternative approach to changing the formatting is to use a pop-up menu that appears if you right click on the item or highlighted area you want to change. This opens a menu (Figure 2.9) with the option Format Cells which, if selected, opens a window of format options (Figure 2.10). This allows you, among other options, to change the format of numbers (i.e. decimal points, currency, etc.) by selecting the Number tab or using the Font tab to select fonts, character size, bold, italics and underline.

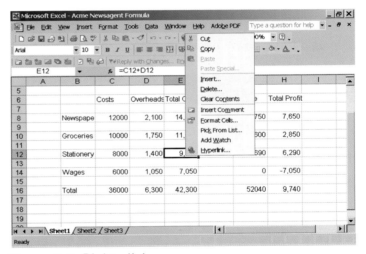

Figure 2.9 Right click menu

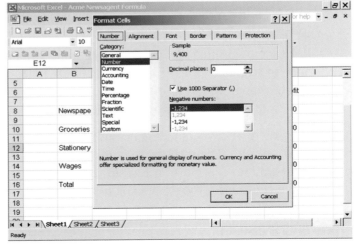

Figure 2.10 Format cells

Calculation

When you change data in a spreadsheet it will recalculate other values that are dependent upon the item. This may be carried out automatically so it can be confusing if you are unaware that it has happened.

The calculation takes account of the true value of the item, not simply what is displayed. If the display has removed or limited the number of decimal places then the values displayed will reflect the formatting. However, the calculation will be based on the actual value with all decimal places. The example below shows that this can be confusing faced with a spreadsheet calculation that adds 20 to 34 to produce 55. This looks wrong if you have forgotten that actual values typed in were 20.2 and 34.4 and that by selecting no decimal places you rounded up the result (i.e. 54.6 becomes 55 when rounded up).

Example

Actual value

20.2 plus 34.4 = 54.6

Excel® spreadsheet format without any decimal places

20 plus 34 = 55 (the decimal value is rounded up to the next whole number)

Exercise 21

Formatting

1 In Exercise 20 you saved a file called Acme Newsagent Formula and we are now going to load this file into Microsoft® Excel®.

2 Using either Start and the All Programs menu or the Microsoft® Excel® icon load Microsoft® Excel®.

3 You can load a file by single clicking on the File menu item to open up the menu which has an option called Open . Click on Open and a window called Open will appear.

4 The Look in box tells you what drive the window is looking at. You need to aim it at drive A:. You do this by clicking on the small button with the down arrow at the end of the Look in box and a menu will appear. Click on 3½ Floppy (A:) and the details of Acme Newsagent Formula will appear in the main working area. To open the file, click on the file once to highlight it and then on the Open button on the right-hand side of the window. An alternative way is to double click on the Acme Newsagent Formula file. In either case the content of the file should now appear in the working area of Microsoft® Excel®.

5 The title of the worksheet is not prominent. Enhance Acme Newsagents by selecting a new font and a new character size. Highlight the title then click on the arrow button on the Font box (Formatting toolbar) and a list of fonts will appear. You select one by single clicking on the item. Explore the fonts until you find one that you like. Now select the character size by using the down arrow next to the size box (the title must still be highlighted). Another list will appear from which you can choose a size. Pick one that emphasises the importance of the title.

continued

6 The headings of the rows and columns need to be emboldened. Highlight the row or column and click on the Bold icon on toolbar. Now centre the row headings by highlighting them and selecting the Center alignment icon.

7 Some of the headings are too wide for their columns. The columns can be adjusted by placing the mouse pointer over the row or column headings edge on the line that divides the row or column. The mouse pointer will change shape (i.e. double headed cross arrows) and if you hold down the left mouse button you can drag the column wider or narrower. Use the same technique to adjust the height of the rows. An alternative approach is to use the Format menu (Figure 2.6)

8 Adjust the column widths so that the headings fit the columns better.

9 In a spreadsheet it is important to be able to format the numerical data. In the Acme Newsagents example we are dealing with money so the data should be formatted as currency. This is achieved by highlighting the data and clicking on the Currency icon on the toolbar. Observe the change – a pound (£) sign will be added and a decimal point and two zeros added to show pence. If the result is too wide for the column then a series of hash marks (i.e. ####) will be shown.

10 The example worksheet does not have any data which include pence so we could remove the decimal point. Highlight the numerical data and click on the Decrease Decimal icon (Formatting toolbar – Figure 2.8). Click twice on the icon to remove the two digits after the point. Experiment with adding decimal places using the Increase Decimal icon, but finish with a display without decimal places (i.e. no pence). Figure 2.11 shows the final spreadsheet.

11 Save the new file on your floppy disk as file A:\Acme Newsagent Presentation. Select the File menu and the Save As option which will reveal the Save As window and you can save the file under a new name. If you select the Save option you will overwrite your original file. The Save As function allows you to save files under different names.

12 Close Microsoft® Excel® by selecting File menu and the Exit option or click on the Close button in the top right-hand corner of the application window.

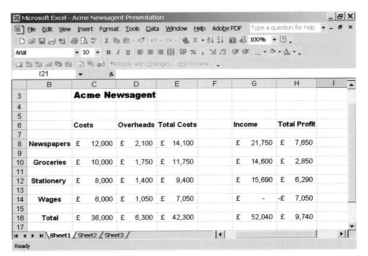

Figure 2.11 Acme Newsagent spreadsheet

Creating spreadsheets and graphs

65

Page setup

Microsoft® Excel® provides a range of functions to allow you to select the overall appearance of the page presenting the worksheet. These let you select the orientation of the page. There are two options: portrait or landscape. Figure 2.12 compares the two orientations and illustrates that you can set the four page margins at the top, bottom, right and left of the page.

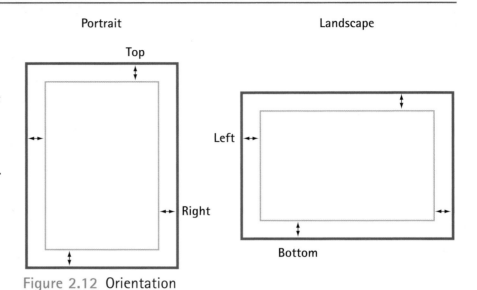

Figure 2.12 Orientation

To select orientation and margins you need to choose the File menu and Page Setup to reveal the Page Setup window (Figure 2.13). This has four tabs across the top. They are:

- Page
- Margins
- Header/Footer
- Sheet

Each tab provides access to a number of options. The Page tab (Figure 2.13) offers you the means to:

- choose orientation (i.e. landscape and portrait)
- scale the sheet to fit the paper
- select the paper size
- print the sheet
- preview what the sheet will look like when printed

The Margins tab (Figure 2.14) offers you the means to:

- set all four page margins (i.e. left, right, top and bottom)

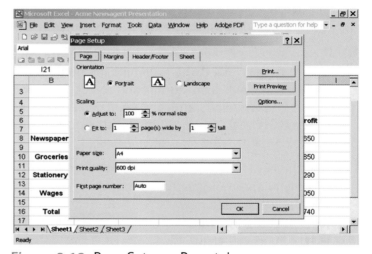

Figure 2.13 Page Setup – Page tab

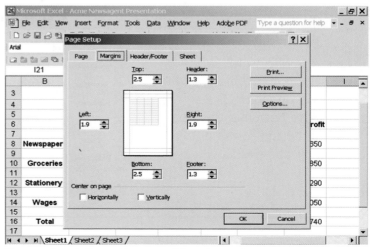

Figure 2.14 Page Setup – Margins tab

- set the size of the header and footer
- centre the sheet
- print the sheet
- preview what the sheet will look like when printed

The Header/Footer tab (Figure 2.15) offers you the means to:

- enter a header
- enter a footer
- enter custom headers and footers (i.e. date, filename and page number)
- print the sheet
- preview what the sheet will look like when printed

The Sheet tab (Figure 2.16) offers you the means to:

- choose how the sheet is printed including if the gridlines and row and column headings appear
- print the sheet
- preview what the sheet will look like when printed

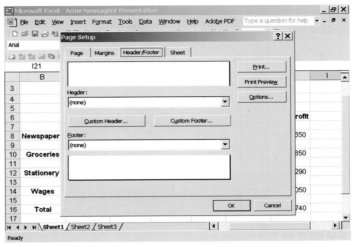

Figure 2.15 Page Setup – Header/Footer tab

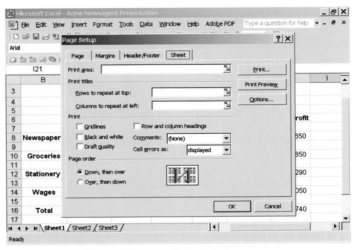

Figure 2.16 Page Setup – Sheet tab

Find and replace

You will occasionally need to change an entry in a spreadsheet. You can obviously do this by deleting what you wish to replace and entering a new item. However, Microsoft® Excel® provides an automatic way to find and replace an entry. This is available within the Edit Menu as the Replace option. This is very useful if you need to make several identical changes since it removes the risk of making a mistake in entering the replacement. A related function is the Find option in the Edit menu which will locate an entry. This is useful in large or complex spreadsheets.

Exercise 22

Presentation

1 Load Microsoft® Excel® using either the All Programs menu or the Microsoft® Excel® icon on the desktop.

2 Set the page orientation to landscape using the File menu and Page Setup option.

3 Enter the table of information below to form your first spreadsheet. It shows the operating costs of three different cars.

	January	February	March	April	May	June	Total
Model A	88	93	90	89	92	96	
Model B	102	108	101	99	105	111	
Model C	65	71	70	64	67	64	
Total							

4 Create a header using the File menu and Page Setup option. Use Custom header button to enter your name and insert an automatic date.

5 Save the new file on your floppy disk as file A:\Operating Costs. Select the File menu and the Save option which will reveal the Save As window and you can save the file.

6 Use the SUM function to calculate the total for January column.

7 Replicate the formula to display the total for all the months (i.e. February to June).

8 Use the SUM function to calculate the total for the Model A row (i.e. January to June).

9 Replicate the formula to display the total for all the remaining Models (i.e. Models B and C).

10 Insert the rows Model D and E between Model C and Total. Enter the information below:

	January	February	March	April	May	June
Model D	128	132	138	126	129	135
Model E	35	39	31	37	41	33

11 Insert a new column, Price, before January.

	Price
Model A	12235
Model B	14679
Model C	8980
Model D	17568
Model E	6950

12 Replicate the total formula to rows Model D and E and Column Price.

13 Develop a formula to calculate the mean price of the five car models (i.e. divide total of the prices by 5). Figure 2.17 displays the spreadsheet.

14 Save the file on your floppy disk as file A:\Operating Costs.

15 Close Microsoft® Excel® by selecting the File menu and the Exit option or click on the Close button in the top right-hand corner of the application window.

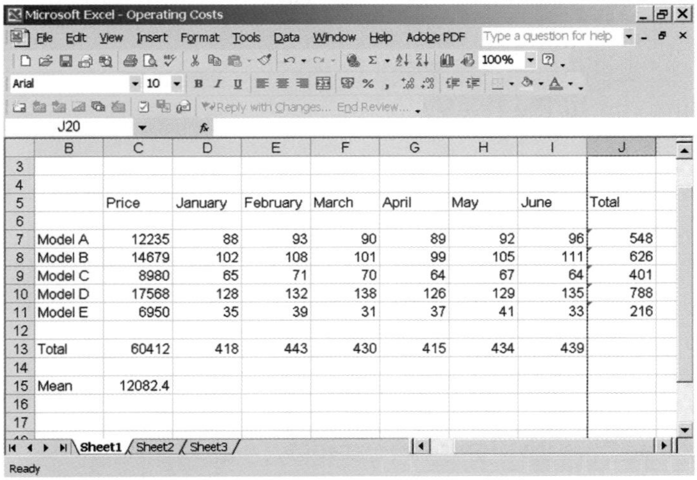

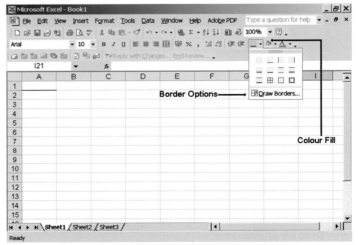

Figure 2.17 Operating costs totals

Borders and shading

Borders and shading can be added to spreadsheets to improve their appearance and highlight key aspects. This is important if you are preparing numerical information for your manager or a client. People often judge quality on appearance so even if you have developed a sophisticated mathematical model, if it is poorly presented it may be regarded with suspicion.

Microsoft® Excel® offers the borders function on the formatting toolbar which if selected opens a small window with a variety of options. These are shown in Figure 2.18. You can choose to enclose a whole sheet, draw an individual line or provide borders around each cell. This allows you to select the areas of the sheet you want to emphasise.

On the Formatting toolbar next to the Borders icon is the Fill Color function with which you can add colour shading to the sheet. When you chose Fill Color it will reveal a pallete of colours. Both Borders and Fill Color operate by highlighting the area you want to format and then choosing the type of border or colour you want. If you highlight a row and select red then you will see that the row gains a red background colour.

Printing

It is important to be able to print out a sheet or workbook. Microsoft® Excel® offers a range of functions linked to printing. These include previewing your sheet as a printed

Figure 2.18 Borders

document. Within the <u>File</u> Menu, <u>Print Pre<u>v</u>iew</u> opens up a window shown in Figure 2.19. This lets you check if the printed sheet is presented in the way that you want it to be. When you have completed the preview, click on the <u>Close</u> button to return to Microsoft® Excel®. If you want to print the spreadsheet immediately there is a <u>Prin<u>t</u></u> button to link you to the Print window.

Usually, the default is to print in portrait mode, that is, with the narrow edge of the paper at the top so that when you preview your sheet you may discover that it flows over two pages. If you would prefer it to be presented on a single page, you need to change the default to landscape (i.e. the long edge across the top). This can be carried out from the <u>Print Pre<u>v</u>iew</u> window by selecting the <u>Setup</u> button, which opens the Page Setup window. Select Landscape by clicking on the <u>Landscape</u> radio button and then clicking on the <u>OK</u> button to confirm the change. When you print now it will be in landscape mode. The example shown in Figure 2.19 would be printed in Portrait since we did not change the default.

When you are ready to print then click on the <u>File</u> menu and the <u>Prin<u>t</u></u> option. The window shown in Figure 2.20 appears. You are presented with a number of options which people initially may find puzzling.

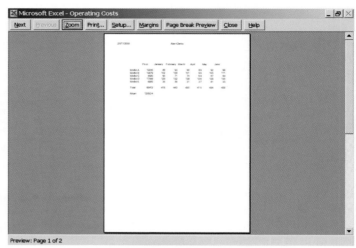

Figure 2.19 Print preview

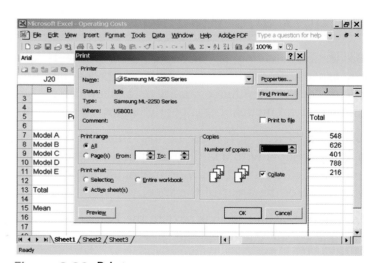

Figure 2.20 Print

1 You must first select the printer on which your spreadsheet is to be printed. This is shown in the Printer area at the top of the window in the box entitled <u>Name</u>. Microsoft® Windows® operating system allows you to link many different printers to a single stand-alone computer. The list of printers is shown when you click on the down arrow next to the <u>Name</u> box. Select your printer by clicking on it. The printer shown is the default printer.

2 You need to decide how much of the document you want to print (Print range). The choices are:
   - <u>All</u> – whole document (the default setting)
   - <u>Pages</u> – you enter the page range you want to print (e.g. 23–34)

3 You can select what to print (Print what). The choices are:
   - <u>Selection</u> (a highlighted area of the sheet)

- Acti<u>v</u>e sheet(s) (whole sheet) (the default setting)
- <u>E</u>ntire workbook (multiple related sheets)

4 You can select how many copies to print with the Number of <u>c</u>opies scrollbar.

When you are ready, click the OK button to start the printer. If you change none of the settings, the default ones will be used.

When printing a spreadsheet, it is important to decide whether you want to include the gridlines or not. This has to be set in the Page Set<u>u</u>p option of the <u>F</u>ile menu within the Sheet tab. The Gridlines checkbox must be clicked, which will put a tick in the box. Gridlines will be inserted in the spreadsheet printout. Another important option is to print the sheet showing the heading. This can be achieved through the Page Set<u>u</u>p option within the Sheet tab. The Row and co<u>l</u>umn headings checkbox must be clicked, which will put a tick in the box (Figure 2.16).

In some cases you will want to print the formulas rather than their results. Select the <u>T</u>ools menu and the <u>O</u>ptions item. This opens the Options window. Click on the View tab and look for the Window options section and the Formulas checkbox. You need to click in this box. A tick will appear and then you can click on the OK button to confirm the change. You should notice that you can also select options for printing rows and column headings and gridlines. This is an alternative way to using the Page Setup function.

To return to printing with the actual numbers or without gridlines you will have to repeat the operation and click once more in the Fo<u>r</u>mulas and Gridline boxes. This will remove the ticks. Confirm the change by clicking on the OK button.

When you choose to print the formulas, your spreadsheet format will change to accommodate their different lengths. It will change back when you deselect this option.

As part of your assessment you will need to be able to print a spreadsheet showing the formulas.

Exercise 23

Borders, shading and printing

1 In Exercise 22 you saved a file called Operating Costs and you are now going to load this file into Microsoft® Excel®.

2 Using either Start and the All Programs menu or the Microsoft® Excel® icon on the desktop load Microsoft® Excel®.

3 You can load a file by single clicking on the <u>F</u>ile menu item and then the <u>O</u>pen option to display the Open window.

4 The Look in box tells you what drive the window is looking at. You need to aim it at drive A:. You do this by clicking on the small button with the down arrow at the end of the Look in box and a menu will appear. Click on 3½ Floppy (A:) and the details of Operating Costs will appear in the main working area. To open the file, click on the file once to highlight it and then on the Open button on the right-hand side of the window.

continued

An alternative way is to double click on the Operating Costs file. In either case the contents of the file should now appear in the Microsoft® Excel® working area.

5 Insert a new row to form a new top line of the sheet and then insert a new column to the left of the Model column. This is to allow you to enclose the whole area in a border.

6 Highlight the whole area containing the data you have entered. Select the Borders function and explore the different options. Use the Undo function (Edit menu) to return your sheet to its original state. When you are confident that you understand the different options highlight the whole area and choose the option that provides a border around each cell (Figure 2.21).

7 Highlight the top row of the sheet (i.e. Price to Total) and select the Fill Color function and choose the colour red. The top row should now have a red background colour (Figure 2.21).

8 Create a header (i.e. select the File menu and Page Setup at the Header/Footer tab entering your name and automatic date).

9 Save the file on your floppy disk as file A:\Operating Costs Borders. Select the File menu then the Save As option which will reveal the Save As window and you can save the file.

10 Print the sheet in landscape orientation showing the data with gridlines but without row and column headings (i.e. Select File menu and Page Setup with Sheet tab (alternatively select Tools menu and Options). Ensure that the sheet prints onto a single page.

11 Print the sheet in landscape orientation showing the formulas (select Tools menu and Options item) with gridlines and row and

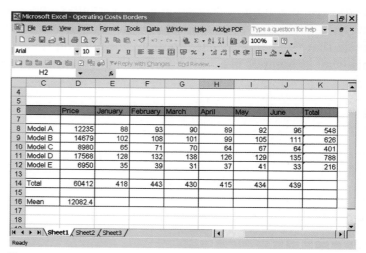

Figure 2.21 Borders and Shading

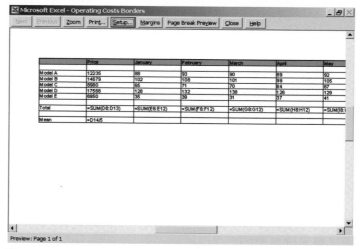

Figure 2.22 Displaying Formulas

continued

column headings (i.e. select File menu and Page Setup with Sheet tab). Ensure that the sheet prints on to a single page.

12 Figure 2.22 displays the formulas in Print Preview.

13 Close Microsoft® Excel® by selecting File menu and the Exit option or click on the Close button on the top right-hand corner of the application window.

Graphs and chart applications

When presenting numerical information, it is sometimes difficult even for highly numerate people to understand the relationship between the different elements. However, if you can convert the information into visual images then it is far easier to see the trends and relationships. There are several forms of visual representations such as pie charts, line graphs and bar or column charts. Microsoft® Excel® has a number of functions to turn numerical information into graphs and charts. There are other applications which allow you to model live data, that is, systems which take data as it is created (e.g. output from a processing plant) and show it in the form of a chart or a graph. These charts and graphs continuously change because the data they are modelling is altering all the time. This type of continuous output is often printed on a special printer called a plotter. Microsoft® Excel® graphs and charts are, in comparison, static representations of data.

Nevertheless, if the spreadsheet information changes then you can produce new graphs and charts. These allow you to monitor the information visually and are useful if you produce a monthly spreadsheet of sales figures, salary costs or staff absences. Charts and graphs also provide opportunities to compare numerical information.

Spreadsheets allow you to create models of information so that you can see the consequences of changes (e.g. price rises, decreased costs, changes in interest rates and pay increases). These changes can also be converted into graphs and charts to help you analyse the changes and their effect on other factors. A visual presentation of data (i.e. a graph or chart) may enable you to identify effects which are not easy to see in a table of numbers.

Figure 2.17 shows a comparison of the running costs of five models of cars. Although the table helps you to see the relationships, visual representation adds another dimension, assisting people to identify connections between the models that may not be otherwise obvious.

Pie charts

A pie chart is used to represent numbers as slices of a circle so that the size of each slice is

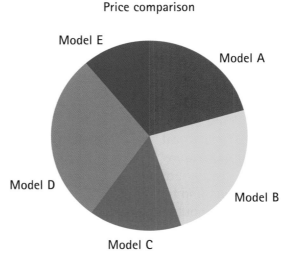

Figure 2.23 Price comparison

proportional to the whole. In Figure 2.23, the pie chart shows the comparison of the price of the five models.

Line graphs

A line graph helps you to compare different factors. The graph in Figure 2.24 compares the running costs of the five models over six months.

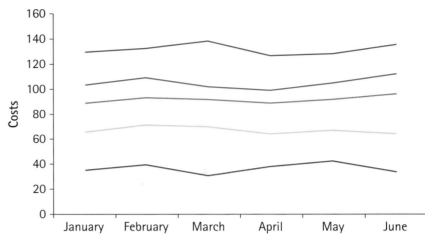

Figure 2.24 Running costs – Line chart

Column charts

A column chart represents numbers as columns of different height. Figure 2.25 shows the column chart for the running costs of the five models.

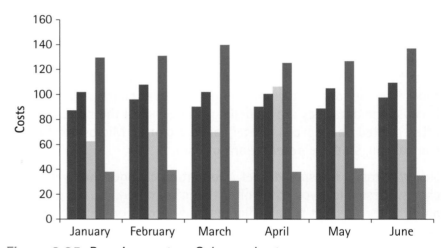

Figure 2.25 Running costs – Column chart

Bar chart

A bar chart is similar to a column chart except that the data is represented as bars rather than columns. Figure 2.26 shows a bar chart comparing the running costs of the five models.

Comparison

Figures 2.23, 2.24, 2.25 and 2.26 are based on the same numerical information (Figure 2.16) in the form of pie, line, column and bar charts. You should

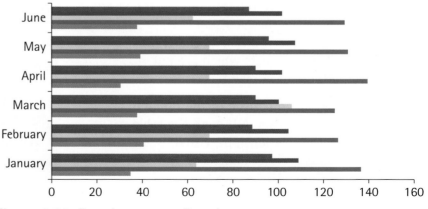

Figure 2.26 Running costs – Bar chart

review and compare the different visual presentations. How effective do you feel the displays are in showing the information? You need to consider what purpose the different forms of charts and graphs serve.

Creating a chart

Microsoft® Excel® contains a range of functions to present numerical information in the form of graphs and charts. These are available within the Chart function of the Insert menu. Alternatively you can select the Chart icon on the Standard toolbar (Figure 2.27).

The first step is to insert data into the spreadsheet in the normal way. Highlight the data and select the Insert menu and then Chart or alternatively the Chart icon. This opens up the Chart Wizard (Figure 2.28). On the left-hand edge is a list of Chart types from which you choose the type of chart or graph you wish to use. This is done by clicking once on the one you select. On the right-hand side of the window the charts will change to show you examples of your chosen chart. Again you need to select the example you want to use. This is achieved by a single click. A description of the chart is given below the examples. If you want to see what your actual chart will look like then you click on the Press and Hold to View sample button holding the left mouse button down. When you release the mouse button then the chart will disappear.

At the top of the Chart Wizard window you will see that it states that it is step 1 of 4. Figure 2.28 shows step 1 of the process. You move between the steps by clicking on the Next button. The second step is shown in Figure 2.29 which illustrates a column chart. The data range is shown in this display as =Sheet1!$E$8:$J$12. This may look confusing but if you ignore the $ signs it reads Sheet 1 E8:J12, that is,

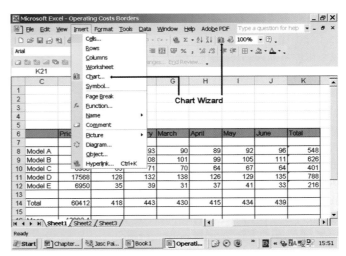

Figure 2.27 Chart function

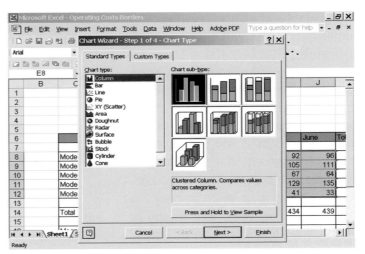

Figure 2.28 Chart Wizard – Step 1

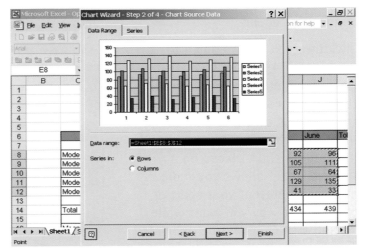

Figure 2.29 Chart Wizard – Step 2

the data is drawn from sheet 1 and the area E8 to J12.

It is vital to check that the Wizard has used the correct data range. It does not always get the range right and therefore your chart will be wrong. You should check the data range is correct each time you create a graph or chart. Each exercise will ask you to check your data range. In the middle of the window is an area called Series in. This offers two options, Rows and Columns. If you change the option you will see the chart change. It is worth considering the two options to identify which one serves your purpose best.

When the Next button is clicked again the display will change to step 3 (Figure 2.30). This dialog box allows you to label your chart. You can enter an overall title for the chart or graph, label the axes of the graphs and add a legend. The options available in step 3 will depend on the chart or graph you have selected. For example, a pie chart does not have axes so there is no point in providing options to label them. The legend is essentially an explanation of the colour coding of the chart. In this case it is needed since five colours are employed. You can use Step 3 to remove the legend.

Click the Next button again to display step 4 (Figure 2.31). This dialog box determines whether the chart is placed on a new sheet or as an additional object in an existing sheet (e.g. a chart placed alongside the data). A chart placed on a separate sheet allows you more freedom to present your chart or graph in the way you want while placing a chart alongside its related data helps to illustrate inter-

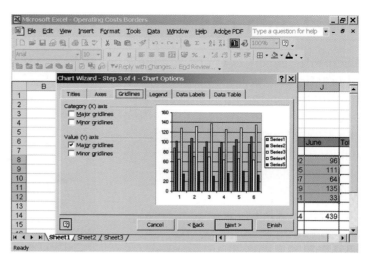

Figure 2.30 Chart Wizard – Step 3

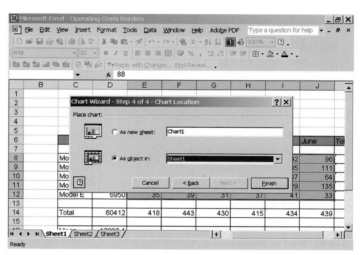

Figure 2.31 Chart Wizard – Step 4

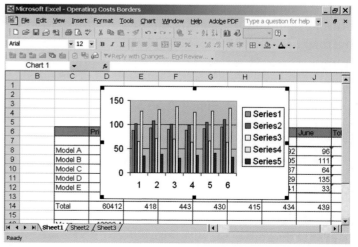

Figure 2.32 Column chart

relationships. The exercises will ask you to create your graphs or charts on a separate sheet. However you may wish to experiment with the other option. Once you have made this decision you can complete the process by clicking on the Finish button. At each step you can return to the previous step by clicking on the Back button. This allows you to correct errors.

On clicking the Finish button the chart or graph appears. Figure 2.32 displays the Column chart overlaying the related data. It can be dragged around using the mouse so that the data and the chart can be seen side by side.

To create the titles and labels for your charts and graphs requires that you understand the terms. Figure 2.33 displays the main titles and labels. The only one missing is the data label since it was not appropriate for this particular chart. You can add data labels to your charts. In Figure 2.33 you could show the value (i.e. the X-axis value, e.g. 100) against the actual column.

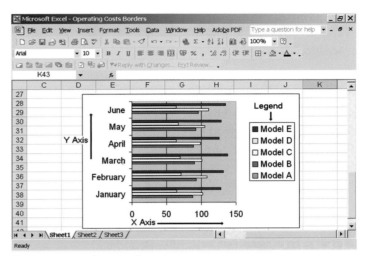

Figure 2.33 Parts of a chart

Editing a chart or graph

Once you have finished a chart or graph you can move it around the display, adjust its size and change the layout. This is done by single clicking on the chart. The chart's surrounding rectangle (enclosure) changes to show small black squares in each corner and the middle of the lines (Figure 2.32). These are called handles. If the pointer is clicked within the chart's enclosure and the mouse button held down and dragged then the whole chart can be moved to a new location. If the same approach is used with individual objects within the chart they too will be enclosed in a rectangle (Figure 2.34). You must click on the chart object itself, not on the surrounding white space. The objects can then be dragged to a new position within the chart's overall enclosure.

The mouse pointer changes shape when dragging the chart enclosure to new positions and when the mouse is being used to change the shape and size of the chart. If you place the mouse over the small black squares (handles) either in the middle of the lines or on the corners then they change to double-headed arrows and by holding down the mouse pointer you can drag the side or corner of the enclosure to expand the chart or push the line in to reduce the chart's size.

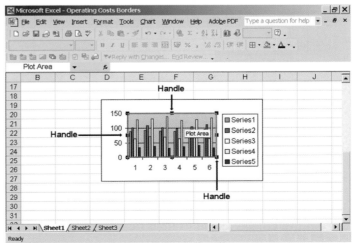

Figure 2.34 Editing a chart

Once you have created a chart you can still make changes and amend it by right clicking on the enclosure. This reveals a menu of options, shown in Figure 2.35. This is the Format Chart Area menu which allows you to access the options available during the Chart Wizard process and edit the chart or graph.

If you right click on the individual chart objects different menus of options appear such as Format Legend , Format Plot Area , Format Data Series and Format Axis .

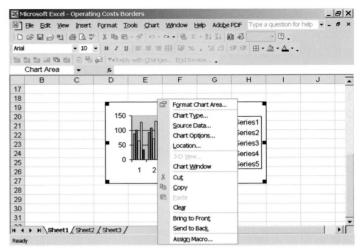

Figure 2.35 Format Chart Area menu

Exercise 24

Creating a column chart

1 Load Microsoft® Excel® using either Start and the All Programs menu or the Microsoft® Excel® icon on the desktop.

2 Enter the table of information below. It shows a simple breakdown of the sales of motor cars over a six month period.

January	35,000
February	47,500
March	21,000
April	32,900
May	16,000
June	34,780

Start your sheet in cell A1 (with January) with the sales information in B1 (35,000) so that the table covers the area A1 to B6.

3 Highlight the table (i.e. A1 to B6) by clicking once in A1 and holding down the mouse button, dragging the pointer to B6. The whole table will be highlighted and you can then release the button.

4 Select the Chart Wizard (i.e. Insert menu and Chart option). Explore the options of Column, Bar, Line and Pie charts by clicking on each in turn and then considering the different options and their descriptions.

5 Finally select Column Chart type and the default sub-type, which is in the top left-hand corner. Using the Press and Hold to View sample button review the chart. Remember that you must hold down the left mouse button to see the chart. If you release it, the image will disappear.

6 Select the Next button to move to Step 2 and review the data range to ensure it is correct. Click on the Next button again to move to Step 3.

7 In Step 3 select the Title tab and enter:

   Chart title – Car Sales

   Category (X) axis – Months

   Value (Y) axis – Income (pounds)

8 In Step 3 of the Wizard select the Legend tab and remove the tick from the Show legend radio button. In this case there is no need for a legend since there is only one set of data.

9 Click on the Next button to move to Step 4. Select As new sheet and enter the Car Sales Column Chart. When you are ready, click on the Finish button. The chart will appear on a separate sheet from the data it relates to (Figure 2.36).

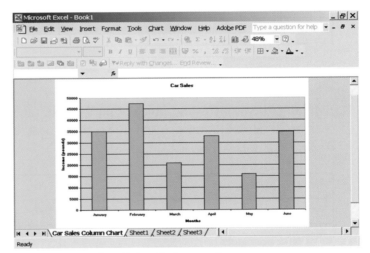

Figure 2.36 **Car Sales Column chart**

10 Save the spreadsheet you have created on to a floppy disk. This procedure is the same in all Microsoft® Windows® applications so you can save a spreadsheet, database or graphic image in exactly the same way. Insert a floppy disk into drive A: and click on File menu item and a menu will open showing a list of options. Select Save and a window will open.

11 Click in the box File name and Enter A:\Car Sales Column Chart. Now click on the Save button on the right of the window. You have now saved your chart as a file called Car Sales Column Chart. You may hear drive A: work during this process.

12 You can now close Microsoft® Excel®. Click on the File menu item and a menu will appear with a list of options. At the bottom of the list is the option Exit . If you click on Exit then Microsoft® Excel® will close. An alternative way is to click on the Close button on the top right-hand corner of the application window.

Exercise 25

Creating a line chart/graph

1 Load Microsoft® Excel® using either Start and the All Programs menu or the Microsoft® Excel® icon on the desktop.

2 Enter the table of information below. It shows a breakdown of the travel expenses claimed by an employee of a large company.

	Mileage	Subsistence	Other
April	230	85	56
May	450	120	32
June	80	16	6
July	167	45	14
August	144	23	7

Start your sheet in cell C8 (with April) with the final item of Other (i.e. 7) in F12 so that the table covers the area C7 to F12.

3 Highlight the months and mileage part of the table entered (i.e. C8 to D12) by clicking once in C8 and holding down the mouse button, dragging the pointer to D12.

April	230
May	450
June	80
July	167
August	144

4 Select the Chart Wizard (i.e. Insert menu and Chart option). Explore the Column, Bar, Line and Pie charts by clicking on each in turn and then considering the different options and their descriptions.

5 Finally select Line Chart/Graphs type and the default example. Using the Press and Hold to View sample button review the chart. Remember that you must hold down the left mouse button to see the chart. If you release it the image will disappear.

6 Select the Next button to move to Step 2 and review the data range to ensure it is correct. Then click on the Next button again to move to Step 3.

7 In Step 3 select the Title tab and enter:

Chart title – Expenses

Category (X) axis – Months

Value (Y) axis – Claim (pounds)

8 In Step 3 select the Legend tab and remove the tick from the Show legend radio button. In this case there is no need for a legend since there is only one set of data. Select the Gridlines tab and tick the Category (X) axis Major gridlines box and the Value (Y) Axis Major gridlines box. Watch the addition of gridlines.

9 Select the Next button to move to Step 4. Select As new sheet and enter Expenses Graph. When you are ready click on the Finish button. The chart will appear on a separate sheet from the data it relates to (Figure 2.37).

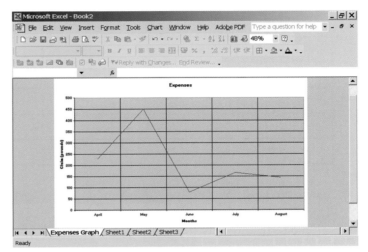

Figure 2.37 Expenses graph

10 Save the spreadsheet you have created on to a floppy disk. This procedure is the same in all Microsoft® Windows® applications. You can save a spreadsheet, database or graphic image in exactly the same way. Insert a floppy disk into drive A: and click on the File menu item. A menu will open showing a list of options. Select Save and a window will open.

11 Click in the box File name and Enter A:\Expenses Graph. Now click on the Save button on the right of the window. You have now saved your graph as a file called Expenses Graph. You may hear drive A: work during this process.

12 You can now close Microsoft® Excel®. Click on the File menu item and a menu will appear with a list of options. At the bottom of the list is the option Exit. If you click on Exit then Microsoft® Excel® will close. An alternative way is to click on the Close button on the top right-hand corner of the application window.

Exercise 26

Creating line graphs/charts – non-continuous data

1 In Exercise 25 you created a line chart for the mileage expenses for a company. This exercise offers you the opportunity to repeat the exercise and create two additional line charts for subsistence and other expenses. This involves selecting data that is not continuous.

continued

2 Load Microsoft® Excel® using either the Start and All Programs menu or the Microsoft® Excel® icon on the desktop.

3 Highlight the months and subsistence parts of the table by first clicking once in C8 and holding down the mouse button, dragging the pointer to C12 and releasing. Now hold down the Ctrl key and click in the E8 cell and holding down the mouse button, drag the pointer to E12. You should now have:

April	85
May	120
June	16
July	45
August	23

4 Select the Chart Wizard (i.e. Insert menu and Chart option). Select the Line Chart/Graph type and the default example. Using the Press and Hold to View sample button review the chart. Remember that you must hold down the left mouse button to see the chart. If you release it the image will disappear.

5 Select the Next button to move to Step 2 and review the data range to ensure it is correct. Then click on the Next button again to move to Step 3.

6 In Step 3 select the Title tab and enter:

Chart title – Expenses Subsistence

Category (X) axis – Months

Value (Y) axis – Claim (pounds)

7 In Step 3 select Legend and remove the tick from the Show legend radio button. In this case there is no need for a legend since there is only one set of data. Select the Gridlines tab and tick the Category (X) axis Major gridlines box and the Value (Y) Axis Major gridlines box. Watch the addition of gridlines.

8 Select the Next button to move to Step 4. Select As new sheet and enter Subsistence Expenses. When you are ready click on the Finish button. The chart will appear on a separate sheet from the data that relates to it.

9 Save the spreadsheet on the floppy disk with the file name Expenses Graph.

10 Now repeat the process but produce a line chart of the months and other expenses data. This will allow you to practice working with non-continuous data.

11 Highlight the months and other parts of the table by first clicking once in C8 and holding down the mouse button, dragging the pointer to C12 and releasing. Now hold down the Ctrl key and click in the F8 cell and holding down the mouse button, drag the pointer to F12. You should now have:

April	56
May	32
June	6
July	14
August	7

12 Create a new line chart for this data.

13 When you have completed both charts close Microsoft® Excel® by selecting the File menu and Exit option. Alternatively click on the Close button in the top right hand corner of the application.

Exercise 27

Creating a pie chart

1 Load Microsoft® Excel® using either Start and the All Programs menu or the Microsoft® Excel® icon on the desktop.

2 Enter the table of information below. It shows the number of books borrowed, by type, from a small branch library.

Library Books	
Romance	126
Historical	34
Crime	87
Contemporary	12
Factual	95

Start your sheet in cell D4 (with Romance) with the final item of expenditure (i.e. 95) in E8 so that the table covers the area D4 to E8.

3 Highlight the library data (i.e. D4 to E8) by clicking once in D4 and holding down the mouse button, dragging the pointer to E8.

4 Select the Chart Wizard (i.e. Insert menu and Chart option). Explore the options of Column, Bar, Line and Pie charts by clicking on each in turn and then considering the different options and their descriptions.

continued

5 Finally select Pie Chart type and the default example which is in the top left-hand corner. Using the Press and Hold to View sample button review the chart (remember that you must hold down the left mouse button to see the chart. If you release it the image will disappear).

6 Select the Next button to move to Step 2 and review the data range to ensure it is correct and then click on the Next button again to move to Step 3.

7 In Step 3 select the Title tab and enter:

Chart title – Library Books

8 In Step 3 select the Legend tab and change the placement of the legend to the left by clicking on the appropriate radio button.

9 In Step 3 select the Data Labels tab and select Value by clicking the tick box. This will display the value of each sector on the Pie chart.

10 Select the Next button to move to Step 4. Select As new sheet. The chart will appear on a separate sheet (Figure 2.38). This chart has a legend which is appropriate since it is important to know what each colour relates to. In this pie chart we have also added data labels (i.e. the value of each segment).

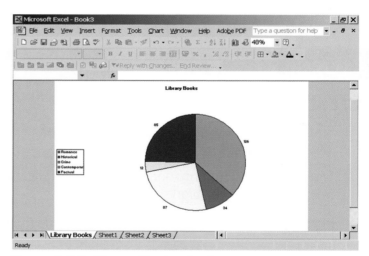

Figure 2.38 Library Books chart

11 Save the spreadsheet you have created on to a floppy disk. This procedure is the same in all Microsoft® Windows® applications. You save a spreadsheet, database or graphic image in exactly the same way. Insert a floppy disk into drive A: and click on the File menu item and a menu will open showing a list of options. Select Save and a window will open.

12 Click in the box File name and enter A:\Library Books. Now click on the Save button on the right of the window. You have now saved your chart as a file called Library Books. You may hear drive A: work during this process.

13 You can close Microsoft® Excel®. Click on the File menu item and a menu will appear with a list of options. At the bottom of the list is the option Exit. If you click on Exit then Microsoft® Excel® will close. An alternative way is to click on the Close button in the top right-hand corner of the application window.

Comparative charts and graphs

Displaying a single set of data can be important but charts and graphs are very useful when comparing several sets of information. In Exercise 25 you created a line graph (Figure 2.37) showing the relationship between months and mileage claimed. The spreadsheet (Expenses Graph) included data on subsistence and other claims. It is possible to produce a chart comparing these different elements.

Exercise 28

Comparison

1 Load Microsoft® Excel® using either Start and the All Programs menu or the Microsoft® Excel® icon on the desktop.

2 Load Expenses Graph by single clicking on the File menu to show the Open option. Click on Open and a window called Open will appear.

   The Look in box tells you which drive the window is looking at. You need to aim it at drive A:. You do this by clicking on the small button with the down arrow at the end of the Look in box. A menu will appear. Click on 3½ Floppy (A:) and the Expenses Graph will appear in the main working area. To open the file, click on it once to highlight it and then on the Open button on the right-hand side of the window. An alternative way is to double click on the Expenses Graph file. In either case the spreadsheet and chart will appear in the working area of Microsoft® Excel®.

3 The spreadsheet is on Sheet1 so click on the tab to locate it. Highlight the whole table of data (i.e. C7 to F12). This includes the row and column headings.

4 Select the Chart Wizard (i.e. Insert menu and Chart option). Select the Bar Chart type and the default example which is in the top left-hand corner. Using the Press and Hold to View sample button review the chart (remember that you must hold down the left mouse button to see the chart. If you release it the image will disappear).

5 Select the Next button to move to Step 2 and review the data range to ensure it is correct. Then click on the Next button again to move to Step 3.

6 In Step 3 select the Title tab and enter:

   Chart title – Comparing Expenses

   Category (X) axis – Months

   Value (Y) axis – Amount (pounds)

7 In Step 3 select Legend and explore the placement of the legend (top, bottom and right) by clicking on the appropriate radio buttons.

8 Select the Next button to move to Step 4. Select As new sheet and enter Comparing Expenses. When you are ready click on the Finish button. The chart will appear on a separate sheet from the data it relates to (Figure 2.39). The three coloured bars represent the different parts of the expenses claim.

9 Save the spreadsheet you have created on to a floppy disk. This procedure is the same in all Microsoft® Windows® applications. You save a spreadsheet, database or graphic image in exactly the same way. Insert a floppy disk into drive A: and click on the File menu item and a menu will open showing a list of options. Select Save As and a window will open.

10 Click in the box File name and enter A:\Comparing Expenses. Now click on the Save button on the right of the window. You have now saved your chart as a file called Comparing Expenses. You may hear drive A: work during this process.

11 Now repeat the process (remember that the data is on Sheet 1) but select a line graph instead of a bar chart. Call the new graph Comparing Expenses2. Figure 2.40 shows the line graph. Compare the bar chart with it and decide which you feel provides the more useful image. Try to identify which one helps you compare the three sets of data.

12 Save the spreadsheet you have created on to a floppy disk. This procedure is the same in all Microsoft® Windows® applications. You save a spreadsheet, database or graphic image in exactly the same way. Insert a floppy disk into drive A: and click on the File menu item and a menu will open showing a list of options. Select Save As and a window will open.

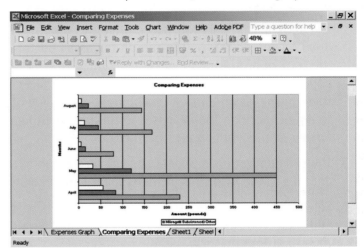

Figure 2.39 **Comparing Expenses – Bar chart**

13 Click in the box File name and enter A:\Comparing Expenses2. Now click on the Save button on the right of the window. You have now saved your chart as a file called Comparing Expenses2. You may hear drive A: work during this process.

14 You can close Microsoft® Excel® now. Click on the menu item and a menu will appear with a list of options. At the bottom of the list is the option Exit. If you click on Exit then Microsoft® Excel® will close. An alternative way is to click on the Close button on the top right-hand corner of the application window.

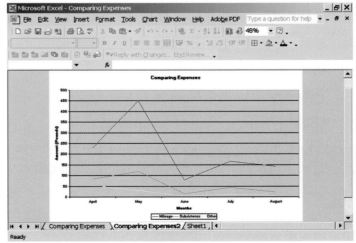

Figure 2.40 **Comparing Expenses2**

Axes and upper and lower limits

With any chart and graph it is important to be able to set the axes because these provide you with the scale against which to judge the display. Microsoft® Excel® provides functions to edit the scale. If you click on the corner of your axes then a handle will appear. Double clicking on the value axis (notice a small label appears to help you identify the axis) will open up the Format Axis window (Figure 2.41).

To change the scale you enter new values in the boxes within the Scale tab. The range is set by changing the Minimum and Maximum values.

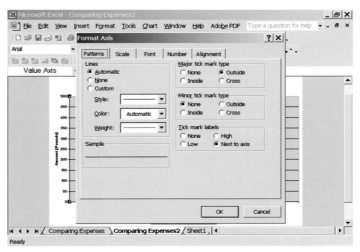

Figure 2.41 Set axes

Editing line graphs

Line graphs rely on the colour and thickness of the lines to distinguish them from the background. This is especially important when they are printed. The lines can be edited in a similar way to changing the scale of the axes. Double click on the line and the Format Data Series window will appear. Alternatively single click on the line to reveal the handles and then right click to reveal a menu with the option Format Data Series which, if selected, will display the Format Data Series window (Figure 2.42). To change the colour, thickness or style of the line you need to select from the options revealed by clicking on the down arrow alongside the options.

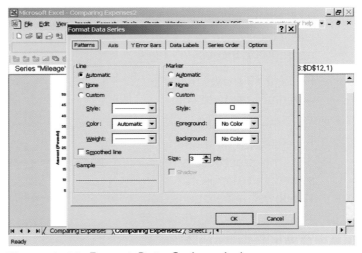

Figure 2.42 Format Data Series window

Exercise 29

Edit graph

1 Load Microsoft® Excel® using either Start and the All Programs menu or the Microsoft® Excel® icon on the desktop.

2 Load Comparing Expenses by single clicking on the File menu to show the Open option. Click on Open and a window called Open will appear.

3 The Look in box tells you which drive the window is looking at. You need to aim it at drive A:. You do this by clicking on the small button with the down arrow at the end of the Look in box. A menu will appear. Click on 3½ Floppy (A:) and Comparing Expenses will appear in the main working area. To open the file, click on it once to highlight it and then on the Open button on the right-hand side of the window. An alternative way is to double click on the Comparing Expenses file. In both cases the spreadsheet and graph will appear in the working area of Microsoft® Excel®.

4 The graph is on Comparing Expenses2 tab so click on it to display it.

5 Change each of the lines to improve their visibility. Double click on each line to open the Format Data Series window and explore the Style, Color and Weight options within the Patterns tab. Chose the options that you prefer.

6 Change the scale of the Y-axis to 0 to 500 and the major unit to 100 by clicking on the axis to reveal the handles and then right click to show a short menu with the Format Axis option. When this is chosen it will open the Format Axis window. Alternatively double clicking the axis will open the Format Axis window. Change the values in the option boxes and confirm the changes by clicking on the OK button.

7 Change the character size of the title, Y-axis, X-axis labels and legend lables by double clicking on them to reveal appropriate menus and tabs.

Figure 2.43 shows the outcomes of these changes.

8 Save the spreadsheet you have created on a floppy disk. This procedure is the same in all Microsoft® Windows® applications. You save a spreadsheet, database or graphic image in exactly the same way. Insert a floppy disk into drive A: and click on the File menu item and a menu will open showing a list of options. Select Save As and a window will open.

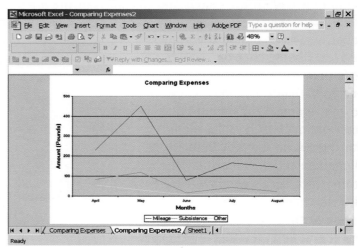

Figure 2.43 Comparing Expenses changes

9 Click in the box File name and enter A:\Comparing Expenses ammended. Now click on the Save button on the right of the window. You have now saved your chart as a file called Comparing Expenses amended. You may hear drive A: work during this process.

10 You can close Microsoft® Excel® now. Click on the File menu item and a menu will appear with a list of options. At the bottom of the list is the option Exit. If you click on Exit then Microsoft® Excel® will close. An alternative way is to click on the Close button on the top right-hand corner of the application window.

Printing a chart

Charts are visual representations of data so it is appropriate to print them in order that they can be distributed. Colour is also employed to distinguish between the different components; it is useful to provide coloured printouts whenever possible. If you do not have access to a colour printer then it is important to check that the colours you are using are clear when reproduced using different shades of grey. You can do this by using the Print Preview option in the File menu. If your computer is connected to a colour printer the preview will be in colour but if your printer is black and white only, then the preview will use different shades of grey.

To print a chart you need to select the File menu and then the Print option. Figure 2.44 shows the Print dialog box. The dialog box is divided into different areas. Printer shows the printer that your computer is connected to, Print range allows you to select All or a page range, Copies allows you to print multiple copies of the chart and Print what allows you to select which sheet to print (i.e. active sheet or the whole workbook). The Preview button allows you a final check to see if your chart is correct.

When your chart has been included in the sheet with the data (i.e. selected as Object within sheet at Step 4 in Chart Wizard) you can print the chart with the sheet data. This is obviously useful since you show the visual representation alongside the numerical information. However, there are also occasions when you need to print the chart separately. In order to print the chart or graph you need to highlight it and then select the File menu and Print option. The Print window will show in the Print what area with the Selection option selected (i.e. button filled). Alternatively you can choose the File menu and Print Preview option to review the Chart or Graph. The chart or graph can be printed directly by selecting the Print button to open the Print window. Figure 2.45 shows the Print Preview of the Comparing Expenses bar chart when the computer is linked to a colour printer.

Figure 2.44 Print

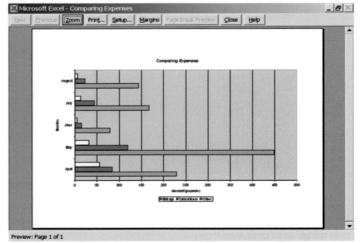

Figure 2.45 Printing a chart or graph separately

Exercise 30

Printing

1 Load Microsoft® Excel® using either Start and the All Programs menu or the Microsoft® Excel® icon on the desktop.

2 Load Car Sales Column Chart by single clicking on the File menu to show the Open option. Click on Open and a window called Open will appear.

3 The Look in box tells you which drive the window is looking at. You need to aim it at drive A:. You do this by clicking on the small button with the down arrow at the end of the Look in box. A menu will appear. Click on 3½ Floppy (A:) and Car Sales Column Chart will appear in the main working area. To open the file, click on it once to highlight it and then on the Open button on the right-hand side of the window. An alternative way is to double click on the Car Sales Column Chart file. In either case the spreadsheet and graph will appear in the working area of Excel.

4 The graph is on the Car Sales Column Chart tab so click on it to display it.

5 Change the Y-axis scale to 0 to 60000 by double clicking on it to open the Format Axis window and entering the new scale.

6 Add the data value to each column by double clicking on the bars to open the Format Data Series window and selecting the Data Labels tab and the Value radio button. Click on the OK Button to include the changes.

7 Save the revised chart as the file Car Sales Column Chart Revised by selecting the File menu and the Save As option on your floppy disk.

8 Using Print Preview look at the chart to check what Car Sales Column Chart Revised will look like when printed (Figure 2.46).

9 Print the chart on a single sheet by selecting the Print button to open the Print window. Click the OK button to print the chart.

10 You can close Microsoft® Excel® now. Click on the File menu item and a menu will appear with a list of options. At the bottom of the list is the option Exit. If you click on Exit then Microsoft® Excel® will close. An alternative way is to click on the Close button on the top right-hand corner of the application window.

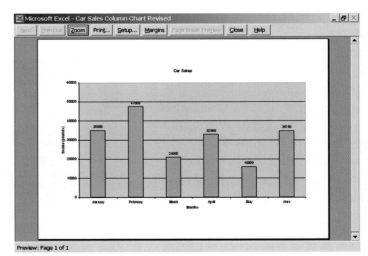

Figure 2.46 Print Preview

More practice

Activity 1

1 Load Microsoft® Excel® using either Start and the All Programs menu or the Microsoft® Excel® icon on the desktop.

2 Enter the table of information below to form a spreadsheet with two decimal places for cost and price. It shows a production plan of an engineering company called Tames Engineering. (Do not enter the information under potential profit. This shows how to calculate the formula).

	Volume	Cost	Price	Potential Profit
Nuts	6,000,000	0.03	0.04	(Price minus Cost) x Volume
Bolts	2,300,000	0.07	0.09	(Price minus Cost) x Volume
Bar	2,560,000	3.45	4.95	(Price minus Cost) x Volume
Sheet	2, 76,000	12.87	15.32	(Price minus Cost) x Volume
Plate	2, 17,000	36.80	39.50	(Price minus Cost) x Volume
Total				

3 Insert formulas to calculate potential profit, total volume and total potential profit (remember to replicate your formulas). You need to check if your formulas are correct. Once they are, you can change your numerical data many times with confidence that the calculations will be accurate.

4 Create a header and enter your name and an automatic date.

5 Improve the appearance of the sheet by:
   - Adding a title – Tames Engineering in Tahoma, size 14 and bold
   - Centring all the column headings and changing their font size to 14 and making them bold
   - Changing the column widths of Volume and Potential Profit so that they fit
   - Embolden all the row headings and change their fonts to 14.

6 Change the format of the Cost, Price and Potential Profit columns to currency.

7 Reduce decimal places in the Potential Profit column to nil.

8 Print your spreadsheet, showing gridlines and both formulas and actual values.

9 Investigate the effect on Potential Profit if you reduce prices to 0.035, 0.08, 4.70, 14.85 and 38.50, respectively. A key advantage of spreadsheets is that they allow you to model what will happen if you make changes to increase output or prices, or if costs change.

10 Print your spreadsheet showing gridlines and actual values.

11 Investigate what happens to the spreadsheet if you set the cost column to show only one decimal place. What you should observe is that the cost of Nuts appears to be 0.0 while the profit remains the same. This is because the formulas operate on the

real value not on what is presented. Change the cost column back to two decimal places.

12 Save the spreadsheet you have created with the file name Tames Engineering.

13 Close the file and exit Microsoft® Excel®.

Activity 2

1 Load Microsoft® Excel® using either Start and the All Programs menu or the Microsoft® Excel® icon on the desktop.

2 Enter the table of information below to form a spreadsheet with two decimal places. It shows the sales forecast of a printer, Jones Printing.

	April	May	June	Total	Price	Cash Flow
Books	6,000	7,500	5,600		1.84	(Total multiplied by Price)
Journals	11,000	9,890	7,600		0.37	(Total multiplied by Price)
Stationery	4,300	7,600	5,500		0.11	(Total multiplied by Price)
Catalogues	5,600	2,300	4,500		0.45	(Total multiplied by Price)
Total						

3 Insert formulas in Total (April+May+June) and Cash Flow (Total multiplied by Price) rows as well as totals for April, May, June, Total and Cash Flow columns (remember to replicate your formulas). You need to check that your formulas are correct. Once they are, you can change your numerical data many times with the confidence that the calculations will be accurate.

4 Create a header and enter your name and an automatic date.

5 Improve the appearance of the sheet by:
  - Adding a title Jones Printing in Arial, size 16 and bold
  - Changing all the column headings to centred Times New Roman, changing their font size to 14 and making them bold
  - Emboldening all the row headings and changing their fonts to Times New Roman, character size 14
  - Changing the column width of Cash Flow and the row headings so that they fit

6 Change the format of Price and Cash Flow columns to currency.

7 Print your spreadsheet showing gridlines and both formulas and actual values.

8 Investigate the effect on Cash Flow of increasing volumes during June to 6,000, 8,000, 6,000 and 5,000, respectively. A key advantage of spreadsheets is that they allow you to model what would happen if you made changes.

9 Print your spreadsheet showing gridlines and actual values.

10 Save the spreadsheet you have created on a floppy disk with the file name Jones Printing.

11 Close the file and exit Microsoft® Excel®.

Activity 3

1 Load Microsoft® Excel® using either Start and the All Programs menu or the Microsoft® Excel® icon on the desktop.

2 Open the spreadsheet file called Jones Printing that contains information about the sales of products.

3 Create a line graph showing the sales of the products during April, May and June.

4 Display the months along the X-axis.

5 Give the graph the title Jones Printing.

6 Call the X-axis Months.

7 Call the Y-axis Sales.

8 Use a legend to identify each line. Make sure each line is easily identified. Select the position of the legend.

9 Create the graph on a full page on a sheet separate from the source data. Figure 2.47 shows the result.

10 Create a header and enter your name and automatic date.

11 Save your graph as a file called Jones Printing Sales Graph

12 Print a copy of your graph

13 Close your file and exit Microsoft® Excel®.

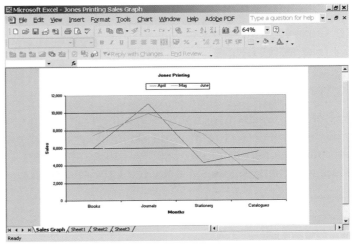

Figure 2.47 Jones Printing sales graph

Activity 4
Graphs and charts

1 Load Microsoft® Excel® using either Start and the All Programs menu or the Microsoft® Excel® icon on the desktop.

2 Enter the table of information below to form a spreadsheet. It shows the opinions of people by age.

Opinion polls by age					
	18 to 25	26 to 35	36 to 50	51 to 65	over 65
Sample A	11	23	35	6	7
Sample B	17	45	12	3	1
Sample C	4	15	22	32	21
Sample D	27	39	31	24	16
Sample E	3	11	17	9	3

3 Create a header and enter your name and an automatic date.

4 Create a column chart to compare the results of the opinion poll. Display the age ranges along the X-axis.

5 Give the chart the title Opinion Poll, call the X-axis Samples and the Y-axis Number.

6 Use a legend to identify the colours of each sample. Position legend so that it is visible.

7 Create the chart on a full page on a sheet that is separate from the source data. Figure 2.48 shows the result.

8 Save the file with the name Opinion Poll Chart.

9 Print a copy of the chart.

10 Close your file and exit Microsoft® Excel®.

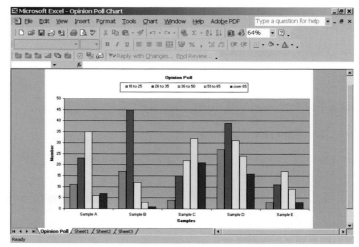

Figure 2.48 Opinion Poll chart

Activity 5

It is most important to practise creating charts and graphs. The following examples are provided to help you refine your skills. In each case, create the sheet and produce an appropriate chart or graph. Explore editing the chart by moving it, altering its shape and changing the axis scales. Finally print the chart.

Example 1	Population
Town A	23,000
Town B	46,000
Town C	106,000
Town D	213,000
Town E	11,000

Example 2	Household Expenditure
Family 1	9,700
Family 2	11,870
Family 3	29,450
Family 4	17,600
Family 5	5,600
Family 6	31,700
Family 7	12,150

Example 3	Comparisons – Internet users				
	1997	1998	1999	2000	2001
Education	1.2	1.4	1.9	2.7	3.5
Business	2.1	3.15	4.65	7.2	11.7
Home	0.2	0.3	0.45	0.7	1.35

Example 4	Comparisons – Rainfall				
	January	February	March	April	May
Area 1	12	15	17	11	9
Area 2	4	3	5	8	14
Area 3	7.5	9	8	7	6
Area 4	22	17	19	20	21
Area 5	16	18	23	15	18

In this chapter you have created a variety of spreadsheets, graphs and charts. They are a useful resource to provide you with many opportunities to practise your skills.

SUMMARY

1 **Load Microsoft® Excel®**: Select the Start button, highlight the All Programs menu and click on the Microsoft® Excel® item or double click on the Microsoft® Excel® icon on the desktop.

2 **Close Microsoft® Excel®**: Select the File menu item and the Exit option or click on the Close button on the top right-hand corner of the application window.

3 **New**: Select the File menu and the New option. This opens the New Workbook task pane which is divided into a number of sections. These provide access to many standard templates for spreadsheets. Select the Blank Workbook option. A new blank spreadsheet will appear.

4 **Enter text or numerical data**: Click on the chosen cell and enter text or numbers from the keyboard.

5 **Open Task Pane**: Select the View menu and the Task Pane option. To close the Task Pane repeat this operation or click on the Close icon in top right-hand corner of task pane.

6 **Delete, close and hide**: Select the Edit menu and either the Delete or Clear options. Each will provide you with a range of choices. Select the Format menu and one of the options Row, Column or Sheet and the Hide option. The Unhide option is also available.

7 **Undo**: Select the Edit menu and the Undo option.

8 **Insert rows and columns**: Select where the row or column should be inserted and then the Insert menu and either the Rows or Columns item.

9 **Delete rows or columns**: Select the row or column to be deleted by clicking in headings and then chose Edit menu and the Delete option.

10 **Cell references**: Each cell has a unique reference which is made up of the column letter and row number (e.g. A7, P16 and F12).

11 **Enter formulas**: Formulas are used to calculate numerical values (e.g. total columns of figures).

Formulas start with = sign (e.g. =F5-F9)

Mathematical operators
+   add
-    subtract
*   multiply
/   divide

A standard function (SUM) adds together the contents of a highlighted row or column of numbers (e.g. SUM(C3:C6) =C3+C4+C5+C6).

Brackets – operations inside brackets are carried out first.

12 **Change presentation**: Highlight the item and select the font, character size, embolden, italics, underline and align text icons from the Formatting toolbar.

Numerical formatting is again based on highlighting the item or area and then selecting the icon from the Formatting toolbar:

- Currency – to display numerical information with a £ sign in a currency format

- Percent – to display data in percentage style

- Comma – formats numbers with commas in appropriate places

- Decimal points – increase and decrease the number of decimal points shown

- Change the width and depth of a row

Place the mouse pointer over the row or column heading edge until the pointer changes shape. Hold down the left mouse button and drag the edge to widen or narrow the row or column.

or

Right click on the chosen item or highlighted area to reveal a pop-up menu. Select the Format Cells option to open a Format Cells window.

13 **Page Layout**: Select the File menu and the Page Setup option.

14 **Headers and Footers**: Select the File menu and the Page Setup option to open the Page Setup window. Choose the Header/Footer tab.

15 **Borders**: Select the Borders icon on the Formatting toolbar.

16 **Preview printing**: Select the File Menu and the Print Preview option.

17 **Printing**: Either select the Print button within the Print Preview window or Select the File menu, the Print option and the OK button.

18 **Print gridlines**: Either select the File menu, the Page Setup option, the Sheet tab, click in the Gridlines box and the OK button or Select the Tools menu, the Options item, the View tab, click in the Gridlines box and the OK button.

19 **Print Formulas**: Select the Tools menu, the Options item, the View tab, click in the Formulas box and the OK button.

20 **Print Row and Column headings**: Either select the File menu, the Page Setup option, the Sheet tab, click in the Row and column headings box and the OK button or Select the Tools menu, the Options item, the View tab, click in the Row and column headings box and the OK button.

21 **Open the Chart Wizard**: Insert data into the spreadsheet. Highlight the data then select the Insert menu and the Chart option.

22 **Column, bar, line and pie charts**: At the left-hand edge of the Chart Wizard is a list of Chart types. Click once on the type of chart. On the right-hand side of the window are displayed examples of your chart. Select the example with a single click and a description of the chart is given below the examples.

23 **Preview charts**: Click on the Press and Hold to View sample button holding the left mouse button down. If you release the mouse button then the chart will disappear.

24 **Data range**: The second step of the Chart Wizard shows the data range in the form of =Sheet1!$B$8:$C$14. Removing the $ signs, the data range is Sheet1 B8:C14.

It is crucial to check that the chart or graph is based on the correct data range.

25 **Titles, legends and labels**: Step 3 of the Chart Wizard provides options depending on the type of chart being developed.

26 **Correct errors**: Use the Back button to move back through the Chart Wizard steps.

27 **New sheet**: Step 4 of the Chart Wizard provides you with the options to present your graph or chart on a new sheet or as an additional object in an existing sheet (e.g. the one containing the data it relates to).

28 **Change display**: Single clicking on the chart will reveal handles which allow you to move and change the size of the chart using the mouse.

29 **Edit chart**: Right click in the chart. The Format Plot Area menu will appear allowing you to access the options available during the Chart Wizard process and make any changes.

30 **Alter axes**: Double clicking on the value axis (a small label appears to help you identify the axis) will open up the Format Axis window. The Scale tab allows you to change the scale of the chart axes.

31 **Save a file on a floppy disk**: Insert a floppy disk into drive A: then click on the File Menu and Save . Select drive (Floppy (A:)) and enter the file name.

Having saved a file once, you can update it by clicking on the File menu and Save without the Save As window appearing again. It simply overwrites the original file.

32 **Find and Replace**: Select the Edit menu and then Replace or Find .

Unit 3

Database manipulation

This chapter will help you to:

- identify and use database software correctly
- use an input device to enter data in an existing database and present and print database files
- create simple queries/searches on one or two criteria and sort data
- produce appropriate predefined reports from databases using shortcuts
- present data in full, sorted alphabetically and numerically

Assessment

This unit does not assume any previous experience of using a computer. You may find it useful to have completed Unit 1: File management and e-document production. You will be assessed through a practical realistic assignment which is designed to allow you to demonstrate your knowledge and skills against each objective. Your tutor can provide you with more guidance.

New CLAiT syllabus

New CLAiT does not require you to create a database table. You must only be able to add and edit its contents and query them. This chapter nevertheless offers you the opportunity to create small straightforward databases and then to practise adding and editing their contents. This is useful if you are planning to extend your studies to CLAiT Plus, which does require students to develop a database or if you are studying on your own without any access to a database.

If you do not want to create a database (i.e. undertake the extra tasks) then the databases are available from the supporting website (www.hodderclait.co.uk) and you are free to download them. We suggest that you download and save them on to a floppy disk.

Exercises which are not part of the New CLAiT requirements are marked as OPTIONAL.

Database applications

Microsoft® Access is a database creation application. You can use it to design databases for your own personal use (e.g. records of your video collection) or for an enterprise (e.g. customer information). In this chapter you will learn how to create a table of information in which information can be entered, stored and presented. A database can have one or many tables depending on the complexity of the system. In our exercises, we will concentrate on a single table, which is the basic building block of more extensive databases.

Figure 3.1 shows the opening display of Microsoft® Access. The application window resembles other Microsoft® Office applications in that it is divided into:

- menu and toolbars at the top of the display
- a working area in which to develop the database
- a status bar at the bottom of the window
- a New File task pane on the right side of the display

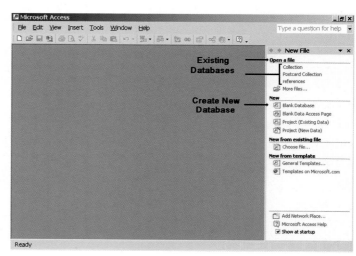

Figure 3.1 Microsoft Access

The New File task pane offers a range of options including:

- Open a file section
- a Blank Database option

The Open a file section shows a list of files that represent existing databases that you have recently opened. You can open them now by clicking on them. The Blank Database option opens a new database for you to create.

Spreadsheets versus databases

While both spreadsheets and databases create tables of information and so appear very similar, there are considerable differences between them.

A database can be designed so that:

- data can be continuously changed in an efficient and effective way without the operator needing to know about the structure of the database
- data held in the database can be presented in many different ways to meet a wide range of information needs
- data held in a database can be searched to locate any combination of data that it contains and the results of the search can be presented in a wide variety of ways

Microsoft® Access provides:

- Forms – these offer different ways of entering, editing and viewing information
- Queries – these allow you to answer any questions you may have about the data contained in the database
- Reports – these enable you to present information combining data from several tables or from a single one

Tables

The key feature of a database is a table. Figure 3.2 shows a Microsoft® Access table. Tables are groups of records. A record is a group of related fields, a field being a single item of the record, e.g. name, organisation and telephone numbers.

In Microsoft® Access there are various different types of field which include: text, number, yes/no (i.e. can only contain a yes or a no), memo (i.e. a longer piece of text), date/time, currency (i.e. money), autonumber (i.e. automatically numbers the records in a table) and hyperlink (i.e. links to a website). The number fields can be used as part of your calculations.

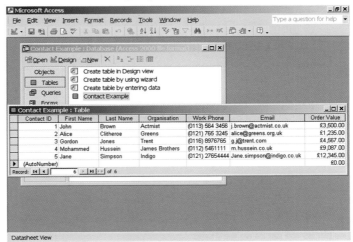

When you are creating a database table, you need to define the type of each field within the records. In Figure 3.2 first name, last name, organisation, works telephone and email are all text fields whereas Order Value is a currency field. The table illustrated is called Contact Example.

Figure 3.2 Microsoft Access table

Creating a new database – optional

The first step in creating a database is to consider the information you may want it to contain. The example below shows the information that you might want to include in a staff holiday record table.

Example
Name – individual's name (i.e. text field)
Team – which team the individual works in (i.e. text field)
Staff Number – pay number (i.e. number field)
Holiday – number of days holiday entitlement (i.e. number field)
Taken – number of days taken (i.e. number field)

Name	Team	Staff Number	Holiday	Taken
Singh	Personnel	23	25	12
Brown	Computers	35	30	15
Jones	Production	41	25	10
Carr	Sales	44	35	25
Patel	Computers	17	25	18
Scott	Personnel	14	30	20
Jenks	Production	51	30	14

This table of information consists of seven records with each record composed of five fields.

Optional Exercise 31

Creating a database table

1 Load Microsoft® Access by selecting Start , highlighting the All Programs menu and clicking on the Microsoft® Access item or click on the Microsoft® Access icon on the desktop.

2 Microsoft® Access will load (Figure 3.1). Select the Blank Database option within the New File task pane. The File New Database window opens to enable you to save your new database (Figure 3.3).

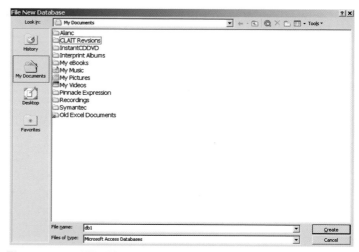

You need to select a drive or folder in which to store your new database as a file. If you click on the arrow button next to the Look in box, you can select 3½ Floppy(A:). Next you need to give the

Figure 3.3 File New Database

file a name. Insert the name Holidays in the File name box and click on the Create button (Figure 3.3). You will have saved your blank database as a file called Holidays on your floppy disk. The Holidays database window is now shown (Figure 3.4).

3 The Holidays database window shows three options with the Tables object on the left-hand side selected:

  – Create table in Design view

  – Create table by using wizard

  – Create table by entering data

Double click on Create table in Design view and the table window opens (Figure 3.5).

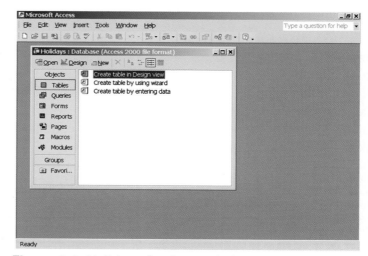

Figure 3.4 Holidays database window

4 You need to insert your field names and their types. If you enter Name in the Field Name box and click in the corresponding Data Type box, a small down arrow will appear revealing a list of types. Select Text . Click in the next Field Name box then enter Team. Complete the table, as shown in Figure 3.5.

5 When you enter a type, observe that, in the Field Properties pane at the bottom of the window, the Field Size shows a value (e.g. 50) with a text type and Long Integer with a number type. The value 50 indicates the number of characters that the field can store while a Long Integer is a whole number (i.e. no decimal places). If you wanted to show real numbers (i.e. with decimal places) then you

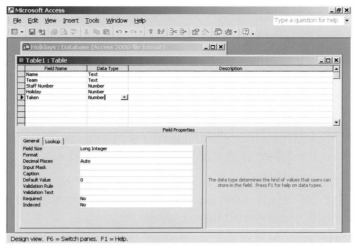

Figure 3.5 **Design View**

would need to click in the Long Integer box to produce a down arrow which, when clicked, gives you other options. In this case all our numbers are whole.

6 Close the window and you will be prompted to save your table. Indicate that you want to save the table and the Save As window will now appear allowing you to name your table. Call it Records and click on the OK button.

7 A warning message will now appear asking you to define a primary key. In this case you do not need to define one so click on the No button. A primary key is a unique number which allows different tables to relate to each other.

8 You can now see the Holidays database window but with an extra item added – Records (Figure 3.6).

9 Double clicking on Records allows you to begin entering the data. We will return to this table to enter the data later. Close the window by clicking on the Close button in the top right-hand corner of the Holidays database window.

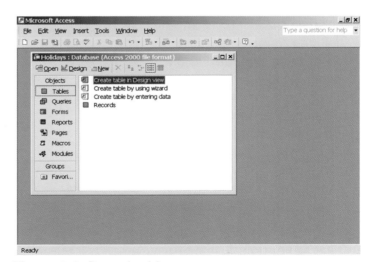

Figure 3.6 **Record table**

10 Close Microsoft® Access by clicking on Close button in

top right-hand corner of the main application window or select the File and the Exit option, unless you wish to carry on immediately with the next exercise.

The Holidays database is available on the supporting website (www.hodderclait.co.uk) if you would like to undertake this exercise without completing Exercise 30 (i.e. creating a database table).

Entering data

1 Insert your floppy disk into your drive. Load Microsoft® Access by selecting Start, highlighting the All Programs menu and clicking on the Microsoft® Access item or click on the Microsoft® Access icon on the desktop.

2 Microsoft® Access will load (Figure 3.1). In the New File task pane, Open a file section will be the Holidays file. Double click this item and the Holidays database window will be displayed (Figure 3.6).

3 Double click on Records and a blank table will appear. Using the example, complete the records, moving between the fields by clicking in each box. Alternatively use the arrow keys, Tab key or Enter key to move between fields.

4 When you have completed the table check each entry against the original data. It is vital that the data in a database is correct since you will use this data later and often base decisions on it. If you find an error, click into the field box to move the cursor into the box, and delete the mistake and insert the correct entry. Figure 3.7 shows the completed table.

5 If you move your mouse pointer between row or column headings you will see it change shape into an arrow (pointing to the right in the row heading and down in the column heading). If the pointer goes over the edge of a heading it changes into cross arrows. By holding down the left mouse button you can drag the column wider or row higher when the arrow's pointer is shaped as cross arrows.

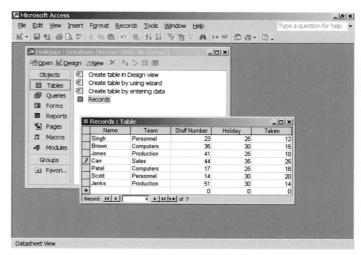

Figure 3.7 Records table

The down or right pointing single arrow will select (highlight) the row or column if clicked.

6 You now need to save the completed table. This is straightforward since it is saved automatically by closing the window. Click on the Close button in the top right-hand corner of the window.

7 Close Microsoft® Access by selecting the File menu and the Exit option.

Editing data

Microsoft® Access has several tools to assist you with adding, deleting, amending and inserting records. You can insert new records (i.e. rows) and fields (i.e. columns). If you left click with the pointer shaped as an arrow the row or column is highlighted (i.e. the pointer is over the column or row heading). By then clicking the right mouse button, a menu appears. Figure 3.8 illustrates the menu that appears when a row (i.e. a record) is highlighted. OCR New CLAiT requires that you are able to add and delete a record (i.e. a row).

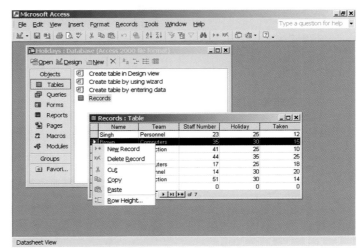

Figure 3.8 Right button menu

To alter a single field, click into the field and delete the entry before entering the new content. If you have a large database and a number of changes to make then it is more efficient to use the Replace or Find functions in Microsoft® Access rather than change each one separately. In the example we have been working on you might want to change a team's name (e.g. from Personnel to Human Resources). You could do this by going through all the records and manually changing them one by one. This is both time consuming and also likely to produce errors. The more efficient way is to select the Edit menu and the Replace option to open the Find and Replace window.

Exercise 33

Editing data

1 Insert your floppy disk into your drive. Load Microsoft® Access by selecting Start, highlighting the All Programs menu and clicking on the Microsoft® Access item or click on the Microsoft® Access icon on the desktop.

2 Microsoft® Access will load (Figure 3.1). In the New File Task Pane, Open a file section will be the Holidays file. Double click this item and the Holidays database window will be displayed (Figure 3.6).

3 Double click on Records and the holiday data will appear.

4 The records need to be amended.

Carr has been transferred to Production. Change the Team field by clicking in the field, delete Sales using the Delete key and enter Production.

Jenks has left the company so this record needs to be deleted. Position the mouse pointer over the row heading and when the pointer has changed into an arrow, click on the right mouse button. The menu (Figure 3.8) will appear. By clicking on Delete Record you will remove the Jenks record. You may see a message appear asking if you are certain that you want to delete a record. Click on Yes to remove the record.

A new person has joined the company so you need to insert a record for Simba. The record is:

– Simba, Sales, 178, 25, 0

If you click in the bottom empty line of the table in the Name field you can begin to enter the new record. You move between fields by clicking or pressing the Tab or Enter keys.

5 When you have finished entering the new record and amending the others, carefully check the table. It is vital that databases contain no errors or the information you extract from it will be flawed. Figure 3.9 shows you the final table.

6 You now need to save your changes. Close the table by clicking on the Close button in the top right-hand corner of the table window. Your changes will be saved automatically.

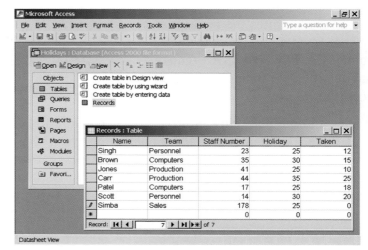

Figure 3.9 Amended table

7 Close Microsoft® Access by selecting the File menu and the Exit option.

Printing

An important aspect of all computer applications is the ability to print information. Microsoft® Access provides you with the functionality to print a table. This is available from the File menu and the Print option, which reveals the Print window and you can print using the default settings by clicking on the OK button.

The Page Setup option in the File menu opens the Page Setup window which has two tabs: Margins and Page. Within Margins, you can

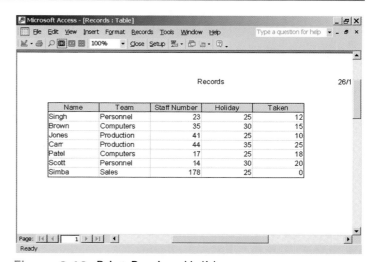

Figure 3.10 Print Preview Holidays

adjust the four margins and print using the Print Headings option. Within Page you can choose the orientation of the page (i.e. either portrait or landscape).

Print Preview in the File menu allows you to check the appearance of the printed document before you print it. Figure 3.10 shows the Print Preview window of the Holiday table. If you are content with the appearance, you can print it immediately by clicking on the Print icon and then on the OK button on the Print window which will then appear. Notice that the mouse pointer has changed into a magnifying glass which allows you to make the image larger or smaller.

Sorting, searching and querying

With a database, you can store a large amount of data and access it in any way you need to. Microsoft® Access lets you sort, query (i.e. question) and search the data to give you information.

Sorting lets you reorder the data and present it in a new sequence. You can sort the records into alphabetical, numerical or date order. This is useful if you want a list of the holidays information presented in the order of Staff Number, alphabetically by the name of the employee or the date of starting work. You can sort in ascending or descending order.

A, B, C and D – ascending or D, C, B and A – descending
or
1, 2, 3 and 4 – ascending or 4, 3, 2 and 1 – descending

Searching is the term used for finding a particular piece of data within the database. By selecting the Edit menu and the Find option, you reveal the Find and Replace window which enables you to search the table for a particular field of data. This is useful if, say, you want to find those employees who had not taken any holiday, those who had 25 days holiday entitlement and so on.

Exercise 34

Simple sorting (alphabetically and numerically)

1 Insert your floppy disk into your drive. Load Microsoft® Access by selecting Start, highlighting the All Programs menu and clicking on the Microsoft® Access item or click on the Microsoft® Access icon on the desktop.

2 Microsoft® Access will load (Figure 3.1). In the New File task pane, Open a file section will be the Holidays file. Double click this item and the Holidays database window will be displayed (Figure 3.6).

3 Double click on Records and the holiday data will appear.

4 Highlight the Taken column by placing your mouse pointer over the column heading until the mouse pointer changes to an arrow. Click on the left mouse button and the column will be highlighted.

5 With the Taken column highlighted, you can sort the data in the column using the Ascending and Descending icons on the toolbar. Figure 3.11 shows the records sorted with the Taken column sorted ascending (i.e. low to high).

6 Explore sorting this table using these icons and print each option (e.g. numerical ascending and descending). Select the File Menu, the Print option and the OK button.

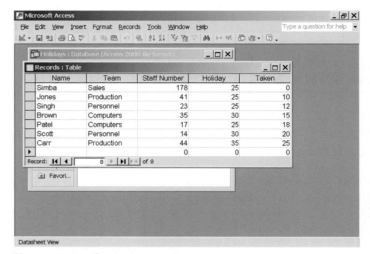

7 Experiment with alphabetical sorting using the Name column and again print each option. Figure 3.12 shows the Name column records sorted by ascending name.

8 Compare your printouts.

Figure 3.11 **Sorted records**

9 Close the table by clicking on the Close button in the top right-hand corner of the table window. You will be asked if you want to save the changes you have made (i.e. save the new format of your table). In this case click on the Yes button so that the new layout of the table is preserved.

10 Close Microsoft® Access by selecting the File menu and the Exit option unless you wish to continue with the next exercise which you will start at step 3.

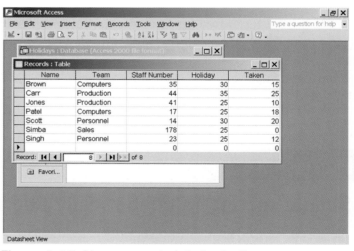

Figure 3.12 **Name sorted alphabetically**

By using the Microsoft® Access functions, you can sort or search the database at any time but in each case you need to enter your requirements. These are useful for individual questions that you are unlikely to want to repeat. However, Microsoft® Access also provides a way of saving useful searches or sorts by using a Query.

Exercise 35

Creating a query

1 Insert your floppy disk into your drive. Load Microsoft® Access by selecting Start , highlighting the All Programs menu and clicking on the Microsoft® Access item or click on the Microsoft® Access icon on the desktop.

2 Microsoft® Access will load (Figure 3.1). In the New File task pane, Open a file section will be the Holidays file. Double click this item and the Holidays database window will be displayed (Figure 3.6).

3 Select the Queries button in the list of Objects on the left-hand side of the window. Figure 3.13 shows the new view. Double click on Create query in Design View . A new window will open with an overlaid window called Show Table (Figure 3.14). Click on the Add button in this window with the Records table highlighted. A small window will appear headed Records within the Query1 window.

4 Click on the Close button on the Show Table window to reveal Figure 3.15, the Query window.

5 In the Query window, a small box (Records) will have been added that shows the fields making up the Holidays table. The cursor will be flashing in the first Field box and a small down arrow will be shown at the end of the same box. Click on the down arrow and a list of the Records fields will appear. Select Name by clicking on it. Name will appear in the first box. Move to the next box (to the right) and repeat the operation selecting Team this time and so on, until all five fields have been chosen.

6 In the Table row you will see the name of the table, Records, appear.

7 The third row is called Sort. If you click in any of the boxes you will see a down arrow appear which if you

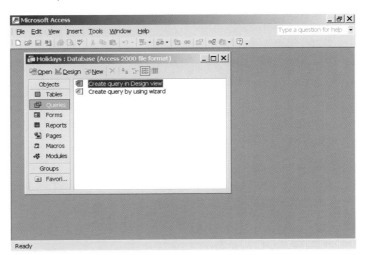

Figure 3.13 Queries

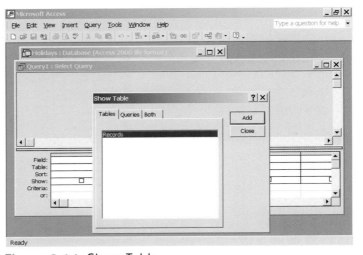

Figure 3.14 Show Table

click on it reveals a list showing Ascending, Descending or Not Sorted. You can sort the table in this query in any way you choose. Let's create a new sort. Select the Holiday column Sort box and select Descending. The query will sort the data table into the number of days of holiday from highest to lowest.

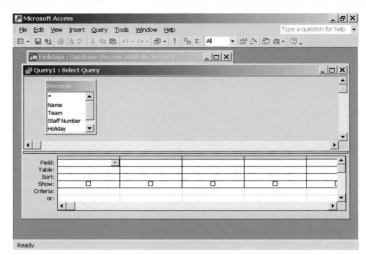

Figure 3.15 Query1: Select Query

8 We can now save this query by selecting the File menu and the Save As option. The Save As window will appear and you need to enter Holiday Entitlement in the box entitled Save Query then click on the OK button.

9 We could now close the query window by clicking on the Close button but instead we are going to create another query. First remove the sort from Holiday by clicking on the down arrow in the Holiday Sort field and selecting Not Sorted.

10 In the Show field you will have noticed that there is a tick in each field. This indicates that when the query is run, the contents of this field will be shown. If you click on the tick, it will disappear and then that field will not be shown. The tick is replaced by clicking again in the tick box.

11 The query you are going to create will show the holiday records of all people working in the Production team.

12 In the Criteria field on the Team column enter Production. When you click away from this field, you will see Production enclosed in inverted commas (i.e. "Production"). If you make a mistake when entering Production then the query will not find any information since it cannot match the fields – your entry must be exact.

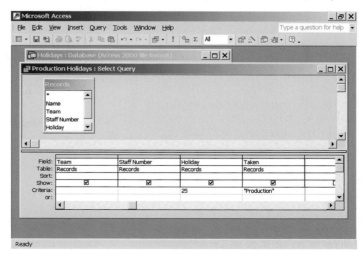

13 Save this query by selecting the File menu and the Save As option. Then enter Production Holidays as the name of the query and click the OK button.

14 Again, you could close this window but we will extend

Figure 3.16 Production holidays 25 days Query

continued

this query by adding a second criterion. In the criteria field on Holiday enter 25. In this case the number is not enclosed in inverted commas. Your query will show all the Production employees who have 25 days holiday entitlement. Figure 3.16 shows the final query.

15 Save this query by selecting the File menu and the Save As option and entering Production Holidays 25 days as the name of the query. Then click on the OK button.

16 Close the window by selecting the Close button in the top right-hand corner of the window. You will now see Figure 3.17 which shows the three saved queries. To run a query double click it. Try the three queries to see if they are producing the results you desire. The results of the query are removed by clicking on the close button.

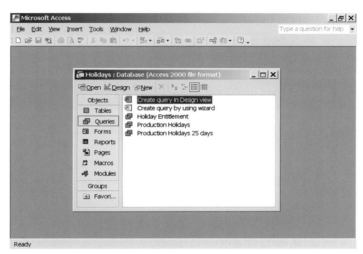

Figure 3.17 Three queries

17 If you find that the query is producing the wrong outcomes you can amend it by single clicking the query to highlight it and then by clicking on the Design button on the toolbar. This will open the query to allow you to make the required changes.

18 When each query is run, print the results by selecting the File menu, the Print option and the OK button.

19 Compare each printout and think about the queries you have created.

20 Close the Database window by selecting the close button and then close Microsoft® Access by selecting the File menu and the Exit option.

Search criteria

In the last exercise we used numerical criteria. It is possible to qualify the numerical criteria using the following symbols:

>   greater than
<   less than
>=   greater than or equal to
<=   less than or equal to
<>   not equal to

These symbols are available on the keyboard.

>   greater than (hold the Shift key down and then press full stop key)

<   less than (hold the Shift key down and then press the comma key)

>=   greater than or equal to (hold the Shift key down and then press the full stop key, release the keys and press the equals key)

<=   less than or equal to (hold the Shift key down and then press the comma key, release the keys and press the equals key)

<>   not equal to (hold the Shift key down, press the comma key and then the full stop key)

In your exercise you used the criteria of selecting records for Production employees with 25 days holiday entitlement. With these symbols you could vary these criteria to select employees with less than 25 (i.e. <25), more than 25 (i.e. >25), greater than or equal to 25 (i.e. >=25), less than or equal to 25 (i.e. <=25) and not equal to 25 (i.e. <>25).

Exercise 36

Using numerical criteria

1 Insert your floppy disk into your drive. Load Microsoft® Access by selecting Start, highlighting the All Programs menu and clicking on the Microsoft® Access item or click on the Microsoft® Access icon on the desktop.

2 Microsoft® Access will load (Figure 3.1). In the New File task pane, Open a file section will be the Holidays file. Double click this item and the Holidays database window will be displayed (Figure 3.6).

3 Select the Queries button in the list of Objects on the left-hand side of the window. Double click on Create query in Design View. A new window will open with an overlaid window called Show Table. Highlight Records and click on the Add button on Show Table.

4 Click on the Close button on Show Table window (Figure 3.14).

5 In the Query window a small box (Records) will have been added which shows the fields that make up the table. The cursor will be flashing in the first Field box and a small down arrow will be shown at the end of the same box. Click on the down arrow and a list of the table fields will appear. Select Name by clicking on it. Name will appear in the first box. Move to the next box and repeat the operation selecting Team this time and so on until all five fields have been chosen.

6 You are going to create a query that will identify the holidays for staff with a Staff Number less than 40 and who have taken more than 5 days holiday.

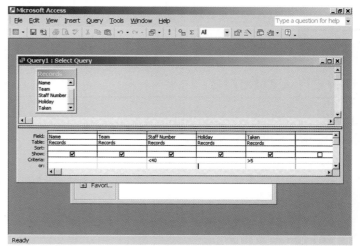

Figure 3.18 Two numerical criteria

7 Click in the Staff Number criteria field and enter <40 and then click in the Taken criteria field and enter >5. Figure 3.18 shows the selections.

8 Save this query by selecting the File menu and the Save As option then enter Staff Numbers as the name of the query and click the OK button.

9 Close the window by clicking on the Close button in the top right-hand corner of the window.

10 Run the new query and check the results that it produces. Amend if necessary. Figure 3.19 shows the result of running the query.

11 Print the results of your query (select the File menu, the Print option and the OK button).

12 Close the Database window by selecting the Close button and then close Microsoft® Access by selecting File menu and the Exit option.

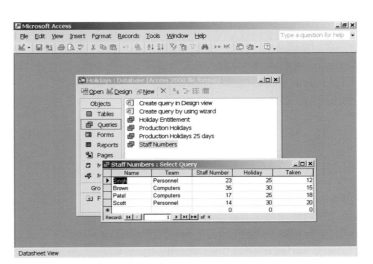

Figure 3.19 Staff Numbers query

Reports

If you need to print out the results of a query or to display records from tables, the report function lets you do this. On the left-hand side of the database window is the Reports button which will change the display to show two options:

- Create report in Design View
- Create report by using wizard

Clicking the second option (Create report by using wizard) (Figure 3.20) shows the first step of the Report Wizard. You can create a report based on either a database table of information or the results of a query. You can present the chosen information in both cases. The fields are shown in the left-hand column (Figure 3.20). The fields that you

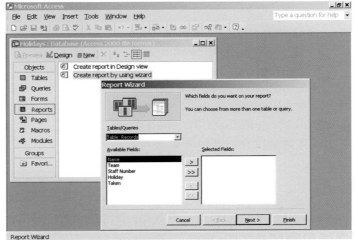

Figure 3.20 Holidays database Reports Wizard – Step 1

want to appear in the report need to be selected by highlighting them and selecting the single arrow button pointing to the right. The item is transferred into the right-hand column. If you want all the fields in the report then click on the double arrow button. The process of selection can be reversed using the arrow button pointing to the left which removes the chosen fields.

Once you have selected your fields, click on the Next button and a new display appears providing you with the option to group your data. Figure 3.21 shows the grouping display.

Having made your selections, click again on the Next button which allows you to sort the data. This is followed by options to choose the layout and page orientation of the report, select the style of the report from a set of templates and finally to name the report so that you can find it again. The final options also allow you to preview the report.

If you make a mistake then you can retrace your steps by using the Back button or use the Modify the report's design option on the final display (Figure 3.25). Figures 3.22 to 3.25 show the Wizard steps.

With any printed report it is important that the data is displayed in full with records and headings completely shown. Your readers can easily be confused by only a partial display and you will be judged on the quality of the output rather than the excellent design of your database.

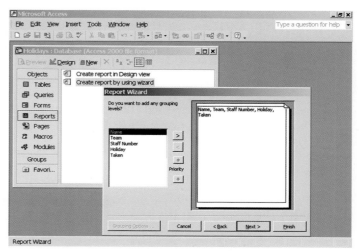

Figure 3.21 Data grouping

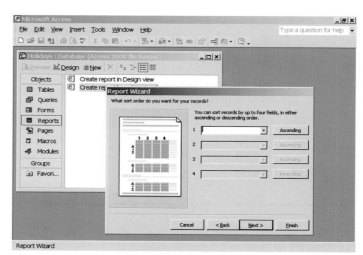

Figure 3.22 Sort data

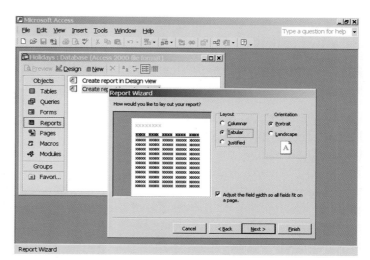

Figure 3.23 Layout and orientation

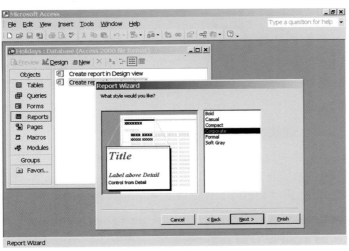

Figure 3.24 Style

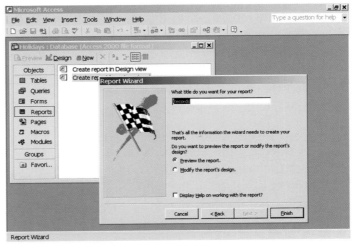

Figure 3.25 Preview Report

Exercise 37

Report

1 Insert your floppy disk into your drive. Load Microsoft® Access by selecting Start,
   highlighting the All Programs menu and clicking on the Microsoft® Access item or click
   on the Microsoft® Access icon on the desktop.

2 Microsoft® Access will load (Figure 3.1). In the New File task pane, Open a file section
   will be the Holidays file. Double click this item and the Holidays database window will be
   displayed (Figure 3.6).

3 Select the Report button in the list of Objects on the left-hand side of the window and
   the Create Report by using wizard option. This will open the Report Wizard window.

4 Select the query Staff Numbers and all the fields in the query by using the double arrow
   button. Check that all the fields have been transferred and then click on the Next
   button. There is no need to select any groupings so click on Next.

5 Select the sort on Name so that the report is presented in descending order of staff names (i.e. Z to A) and then click on Next.

6 Select the Tabular layout and Landscape orientation and then click on Next.

7 Select the Formal style and then click on Next.

8 Give the report the title Report Staff Numbers, select the Preview the report radio button and then click on the Finish button. The report will be shown since you have selected preview. Figure 3.26 shows the resulting report. It is important to check that you have displayed the data in full with complete field headings.

9 Print the report (select the File menu, the Print option and the OK button), check the contents are correct and that the data is printed in full.

10 Close the Database window by selecting the Close button and then close Microsoft® Access by selecting the File menu and the Exit option.

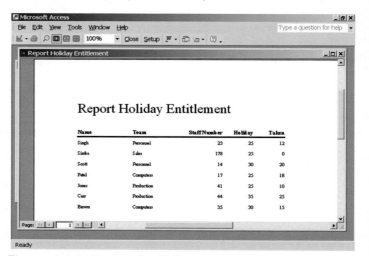

Figure 3.26 Report Staff Numbers

More practice

Activity 1
Creating a table – Optional

1 Load Microsoft® Access by selecting Start, highlighting the All Programs menu and clicking on the Microsoft® Access item or click on the Microsoft® Access icon on the desktop.

2 Microsoft® Access will load (Figure 3.1). Select the Blank Database option within the New File task pane. The File New Database window opens to enable you to save your new database (Figure 3.3).

You need to select a drive or folder in which to store your new database as a file. If you click on the arrow button next to the Look in box you can select 3½ Floppy (A:).

Next we need to give the file a name. Insert the name Customer Accounts in the File name box and click on the Create button. You will have saved your blank database as a file called Customer Accounts on your floppy disk.

3 The Customer Accounts database window shows three options with the Tables object on the left-hand side selected:
- Create table in Design view
- Create table by using wizard

– Create table by entering data

Double click on Create table in Design view and the table window will open.

4 You are going to create the table below:

Customer Accounts

Name – company name (Text)
Address – address of the company (Text)
Contact – name of company customer contact (Text)
Credit – credit limit of the company (Currency)
First Order – date of the first order from the company (Date/Time)
Size – size of the first order (Number)

Name	Address	Contact	Credit	First Order	Size
Deans	London	Anne	2500	01/10/90	500
Big Shop	Birmingham	Keith	1500	13/02/92	750
Mint	Sheffield	Jane	1000	26/06/96	250
Gordons	London	Stephanie	3000	19/08/95	250
Youngs	Manchester	David	2000	30/04/94	900
Palmers	Sheffield	Peter	3000	07/11/96	750

This table of information consists of six records with each record comprising six fields.

You need to insert your field names and their types. If you enter Name in the Field Name box and click in the corresponding Data Type box, a small down arrow will appear revealing a list of types. Select Text then click in the next Field Name box and enter Address. Complete the table – Contact, Credit, First Order and Size. Both Credit and Size are Currency type. First Order is Date/Time type.

5 When you enter a type you should observe that in Field Size a value (e.g. 50) will appear with a text type and Long Integer with a number type. The value 50 indicates the number of characters that the field can store while a Long Integer is a whole number (i.e. no decimal places).

6 Close the window and you will be prompted to save your table. Indicate that you want to save the table and the Save As window will now appear allowing you to name your table call it Accounts and click on the OK button.

7 A warning message will now appear asking you if you need a primary key. In this case you do not need to define one, so click on the No button. The table window reappears and you should close it by clicking on the Close button in the top right-hand corner of the table window. You can now see the Customer Accounts database window but with an extra item added – Accounts.

8 You can now enter the data by double clicking on Accounts. Enter the text to produce Figure 3.27.

9 When you have completed the table, check each entry against the original data. If you find an error, click in the field box to move the cursor into the box. Delete the mistake and insert the correct entry.

10 Explore sorting the information using the Ascending and Descending icons on the toolbar. Sort the Name, Credit and First Order Fields. This will show you how to sort alphabetically, numerically and by date.

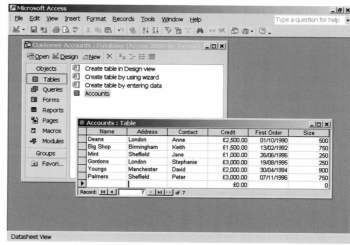

Figure 3.27 Accounts table

11 Close the window. The completed table will be saved automatically.

12 Click on the Close button in the top right-hand corner of the window.

13 Close Microsoft® Access by selecting the File menu and the Exit option.

Activity 2

The database Customer Accounts is available on the supporting website (www.hodderclait.co.uk) if you would like to undertake this exercise without creating the database.

Queries

1 Insert your floppy disk into your drive. Load Microsoft® Access by selecting Start, highlighting the All Programs menu and clicking on the Microsoft® Access item or double click on the Microsoft® Access icon on the desktop.

2 Microsoft® Access will load (Figure 3.1). In the New File task pane, Open a file section will be the Customer Accounts file. Double click this item and the Customer Accounts database window will be displayed.

3 Select the Queries button in the list of Objects on the left-hand side of the window. Double click on Create query in Design view. A new window will open with an overlaid window called Show Table. Click on the Add button on Show Table and then on the Close button.

4 In the Query window a small box (Accounts) will have been added which shows the fields that make up the Accounts table. The cursor will be flashing in the first Field box and a small down arrow will be shown at the end of the same box. Click on the down arrow and a list of the Customer Account fields will appear. Select Name by clicking on it. Name will appear in the first box. Move to the next box and repeat the operation selecting Address this time. Repeat the process adding contact, credit and size fields.

5 You are going to create a query based on two criteria. These are:

Customers in London
Customers who have a Credit limit greater than or equal to £2500

6   Click in the criteria box of Address and enter London.

7   Click in the criteria box of Credit and enter >=2500

8   Save this query by selecting the File menu and the Save As option then enter Location and Credit as the name of the query and click on the OK button.

9   Close the window by selecting the Close button in the top right-hand corner of the window. You will now see that the Customer Accounts window shows the query. Double click on the query to see if it produces the desired results (Figure 3.28). The results of the query are removed by clicking on the Close button.

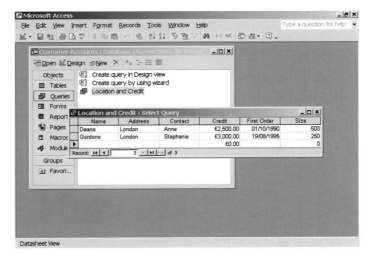

10 If you find that the query is producing the wrong outcomes then you can amend it by single clicking the query to highlight it and then on the Design button

Figure 3.28 Location and Credit query results

    on the toolbar. This will open the query to allow you to make the required changes.

11 When the query is run, print the results by selecting the File menu, the Print option and the OK button. Check that the data is displayed in full.

12 You are now going to design a query to identify all customers who first placed an order on or after 30/04/94. The Customer Accounts database window should be displayed.

13 Select the Queries button in the list of Objects on the left-hand side of the window. Double click on Create query in Design view. A new window will open with an overlaid window called Show Table. Click on the Add button on Show Table and then on the Close button.

14 In the Query window a small box (Accounts) will have been added which shows the fields that make up the Accounts table. The cursor will be flashing in the first Field box and a small down arrow will be shown at the end of the same box. Click on the down arrow and a list of the Customer Account fields will appear. Select First Order by clicking on it. First Order will appear in the first box. Move to the next box and repeat the operation selecting Name this time. You simply want to identify the names of the customers.

15 You are going to create a query based on one criterion:

    Customers who have placed orders on or after 30/04/94

16 Click in the criteria box of First Name and enter >=30/04/94.

17 Save this query by selecting the File menu and the Save As option then enter First Order as the name of the query and click on the OK button.

18 Close the window by selecting the Close button in the top right-hand corner of the window. You will now see that the Customer Accounts window shows the new query.

Double click on the query First Order to see if it produces the desired results (Figure 3.29). The results of the query are removed by clicking on the Close button.

19 If you find that the query is producing the wrong outcomes then you can amend it by single clicking the query to highlight it and then on the Design button. This will open the query to allow you to make the required changes.

20 When the query is run, print the results by selecting the File menu, the Print option and the OK button. Check that the data is displayed in full.

21 Close the Database window by selecting the Close button and then close Microsoft® Access by selecting the File menu and the Exit option.

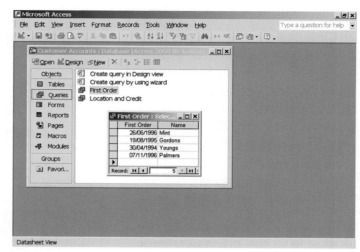

Figure 3.29 First Order results

Activity 3
Reports

1 Insert your floppy disk into your drive. Load Microsoft® Access by selecting Start, highlighting the All Programs menu and clicking on the Microsoft® Access item or double click on the Microsoft® Access icon on the desktop.

2 Microsoft® Access will load (Figure 3.1). In the New File task pane, Open a file section will be the Customer Accounts file. Double click this item and the Customer Accounts database window will be displayed.

3 Select the Report button in the list of Objects on the left-hand side of the window. Double click on Create report by using wizard. The Report Wizard window will open. Select the table: Accounts.

4 Select all the fields by clicking on the double arrow and transferring them to the right-hand column and then click on the Next button.

5 There is no need to group fields so click on the Next button.

6 Sort (i.e. A–Z) by Size and then click on the Next button.

7 Select the Tabular layout and the Landscape orientation and then click on Next button. Remember that you need to display the data in full.

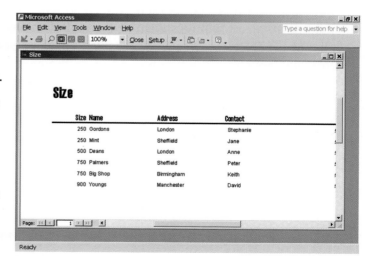

Figure 3.30 Size report

8 Choose the Compact style and then click on the Next button.

9 Give your report the title Size and select Preview. Click on the Finish button.

10 The report will appear for you to check (Figure 3.30). It is important to check that the data is displayed in full.

11 When the report is run, print the results by selecting the File menu, the Print option and the OK button.

12 Close the Database window by selecting the Close button and then close Microsoft® Access by selecting the File menu and the Exit option.

Activity 4

The Collections database is available on the supporting website (www.hodderclait.co.uk) if you would like to undertake the adding, editing and query tasks. If you are interested in creating the Collecting database, consider the instructions below:

Create the Postcard Collecting database

Category – different groups of cards
Type – specific types of cards
Date – date first cards published
Condition – physical condition of card
Price – price paid for card
Value – current market price
Location – album card stored in

Add data to the database

Category values are Glamour, Message, Liverpool and Modern

Category	Type	Date	Condition	Price	Value	Location
Glamour	Barribal	12/03/88	Mint	£8	£10	A
Glamour	Nanni	23/01/79	Good	£4	£5	B
Glamour	Other	01/12/92	Poor	£1	£1	B
Message	Davies	24/08/94	Very Good	£1.50	£1.50	C
Message	Other	13/06/93	Good	£0.75	£1	C
Liverpool	Tunnel	07/09/92	Good	£2	£1.50	D
Liverpool	Centre	17/11/93	Poor	£3	£2	A
Liverpool	Suburbs	03/04/91	Poor	£5	£6	B
Liverpool	Other	29/01/90	Poor	£2	£1	C
Modern	Political	22/07/91	Mint	£0.75	£0.25	D
Modern	Royalty	11/05/90	Mint	£0.50	£0.50	E
Modern	Cricket	20/12/90	Very Good	£1	£1.25	F
Modern	Football	14/02/89	Very Good	£0.60	£1	G

The table is shown in Figure 3.31.

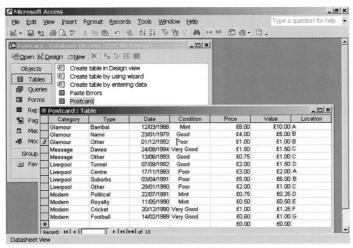

Figure 3.31 Postcard Collection

Activity 5

1 Open the Postcard Database.

2 Change the orientation of the page to portrait.

3 Print the Postcards Table showing all the information and field names.

4 Close the table and rename the table Postcards Your Name (e.g. Postcards Alan Clarke).

5 Open the Postcards Your Name table.

6 Change the condition of Liverpool Centre to Good from Poor.

7 Delete the Modern Cricket record.

8 Insert the following new records:

Message, American, 11/05/91, Very Good, £1, £1.50, C

Message, Europe, 16/11/97, Poor, £0.75, £0.90, C

Modern, Space, 23/09/99, Mint, £0.35, £0.50, F

Modern, Ships, 02/02/02, Mint, £0.50, £1.00, G

Carefully check that the information has been entered accurately. Correct any mistakes.

9 Save the table as Postcards Your Name. Figure 3.32 shows the table.

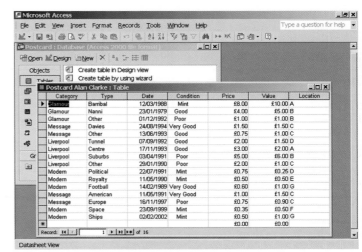

Figure 3.32 Postcards Alan Clarke

10 Change the page orientation to landscape and print all the table information with field headings. All the information should be visible.

11 Create the following Queries:

- Query to sort the records by ascending value
- Query to find records with a price less than £2
- Query to find all the records in location A with a value greater than £5

Check the accuracy of the queries.

Print each query result.

Save all the queries.

12 Create the following Reports (data should be displayed in full):

- Report to present postcards with a value greater than £5 showing the category, type and date purchased only
- Report to present all postcards in the table sorted in order of value (Figure 3.33)

13 Check the accuracy of the reports and that the data is displayed in full.

14 Print the reports.

15 Close the database.

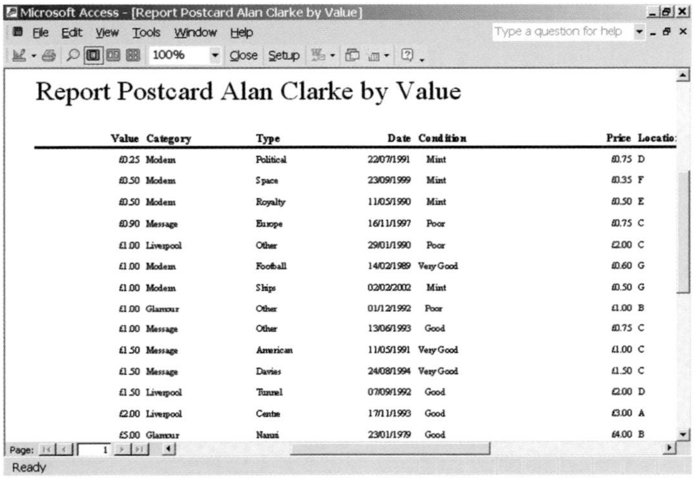

Value	Category	Type	Date	Condition	Price	Locatio
£0.25	Modern	Political	22/07/1991	Mint	£0.75	D
£0.50	Modern	Space	23/09/1999	Mint	£0.35	F
£0.50	Modern	Royalty	11/05/1990	Mint	£0.50	E
£0.90	Message	Europe	16/11/1997	Poor	£0.75	C
£1.00	Liverpool	Other	29/01/1990	Poor	£2.00	C
£1.00	Modern	Football	14/02/1989	Very Good	£0.60	G
£1.00	Modern	Ships	02/02/2002	Mint	£0.50	G
£1.00	Glamour	Other	01/12/1992	Poor	£1.00	B
£1.00	Message	Other	13/06/1993	Good	£0.75	C
£1.50	Message	American	11/05/1991	Very Good	£1.00	C
£1.50	Message	Davies	24/08/1994	Very Good	£1.50	C
£1.50	Liverpool	Tunnel	07/09/1992	Good	£2.00	D
£2.00	Liverpool	Centre	17/11/1993	Good	£3.00	A
£5.00	Glamour	Nanni	23/01/1979	Good	£4.00	B

Figure 3.33 Value report

Activity 6

The Trip database is available on the supporting website (www.hodderclait.co.uk) if you would like to undertake the adding, editing and query tasks. If you are interested in creating the Trip database, consider the instructions below:

Create the Trip database

Date – the date of the different bus trips
Name – people who have booked a place
Start – time of the start of journey
Return – time bus returns
Destination – final destination of bus trip
Cost – cost of trip

Add data to the database

Date	Name	Start	Return	Destination	Cost
03/05/05	William Hall	8.00	20.00	Harrogate	£25
03/05/05	Jane Hall	8.00	20.00	Harrogate	£25
18/05/05	Gordon King	7.30	22.00	Durham	£32
23/05/05	Lorna Alena	9.15	23.30	Lancaster	£27
12/06/05	Shubhanna Aris	6.00	22.30	Birmingham	£23
19/06/05	Eva Garcia	7.45	19.00	Northampton	£18
23/07/05	Harry Jones	8.30	21.00	Leicester	£15
07/08/05	Linda Brown	9.30	23.30	Warwick	£28

The Trip Customer table is shown in figure 3.34.

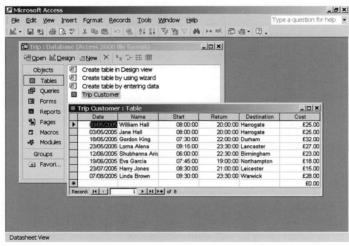

Figure 3.34 Trip Customer

Activity 7

1 Open the Trip Database.

2 Change the orientation of the page to portrait.

3 Print the Trip Customer table showing all the information and field names.

4 Close the table and rename the table Trip Customer Your Name (e.g. Trip Customer Alan Clarke)

5 Open the Trip Customer Your Name table.

6 Change the date of the trip to Warwick from 07/08/2005 to 09/09/2005.

7 Delete the trip to Northampton record.

8 Insert the following new records:

20/09/2005	Silvia Lewis	7.00	21.30	Shrewsbury	£35
25/09/2005	Jill Morris	8.15	20.00	Wolverhampton	£21
02/10/2005	Peter Jolly	9.30	21.00	Derby	£15
12/10/2005	Keith Smith	8.30	23.30	Burton	£20

Carefully check that the information has been entered accurately. Correct any mistakes.

9 Save the table as Trip Customer Your Name.

10 Change the page orientation to landscape and print all the table information with field headings. All the information should be visible.

11 Create the following Queries:

   ■ Query to sort the records by ascending cost of trip
   ■ Query to find records with trip costing more than £20

Check the accuracy of the queries.

Print each query result.

Save all the queries.

12 Create the following Reports (data should be displayed in full):

   ■ Report to present the trip records sorted alphabetically by customer name
   ■ Report to present records of trips costing more than £20

13 Check the accuracy of the reports and that the data is displayed in full.

14 Print the reports.

15 Close the database.

SUMMARY

1 **Load Microsoft® Access**: Use either the Start button and the All Programs menu or double click on the Microsoft® Access icon on the Windows® desktop.

2 **Close**: Click on the File menu and the Exit option or click on the Close button in the top right hand corner of the application or other window.

3 **Create a database – optional**: Load Microsoft® Access and select the Blank Database option within the New File task pane. The File New Database window opens to enable you to save your new database.

Select a drive or folder in which to store your new database as a file. If you click on the arrow button next to the Look in box you can select floppy disk.

Give the file a name. Insert the name in the File name box and click on the Create button. Your database is now saved.

The Database window is now revealed with three options with the Table object on the left-hand side selected:

- Create table in Design view
- Create table by using wizard
- Create table by entering data

Double click on Create table in Design view and the table window opens.

Insert your field names and their types.

You will be prompted to save your table when you close the window.

4 **Enter data**: Load Microsoft® Access. Double click on the database of your choice in the list displayed in task pane. The database window will appear.

Double click on the table of your choice and the blank table will appear. Complete the records, moving between the fields by clicking in each box. Alternatively use the arrow keys, Tab key or Enter key to move between fields.

Check each entry against the original data.

To amend a single field, click on the field, delete its incorrect content and then re-enter the data.

5 **Delete a record**: Highlight the record by positioning the mouse pointer over the row heading until the pointer changes shape. Click the left mouse button. Right click in the highlighted row, the menu will appear and you select Delete Record.

6 **Add a record**: Click on the blank row at the bottom of the table and insert data, moving between fields using the Tab or Enter keys or by clicking in the next field.

7 **Create a query**: Select the Queries button in the list of Objects on the left-hand side of the database window. Double click on the Create query in Design view option. A new window will open with an overlaid window called Show Table. Click on the Add button on Show Table and then on the Close button.

In the Query window a small box shows the fields that make up the table. The cursor will be flashing in the first Field box and a small down arrow will be shown at the end of the same box. Click on the down arrow and a list of the table fields will appear. Select the field which will then appear in the box. Move across the boxes, entering the chosen fields.

Enter criteria in appropriate boxes.

Sort data by clicking in the sort boxes. Select the down arrow and choose Ascending, Descending or not sorted.

8 **Save a query**: Save the query by selecting the File menu and the Save As option. Then enter the name of the query and click the OK button.

9 **Printing**: Select the File menu and the Print option. This reveals the Print window and you can print using the default settings by clicking on the OK button.

or

Select the File menu and Print Preview to check the appearance of the printed document before you print it. Click on the Print icon and then on the OK button in the Print window.

10 **Report**: Select the Reports button in the list of Objects on the left-hand side of the database window. Double click on the Create report by using wizard. The window Report Wizard will appear. This will guide you through a series of choices about the content and presentation of your report. This includes saving the report so it can be used again.

Unit 5

Creating an e-presentation

This chapter will help you to:

- identify and use presentation graphics software correctly
- set up a slide layout
- select fonts and enter text
- import and insert images correctly
- use the drawing tools
- format slides and presentation
- re-order slides and produce printed handouts
- manage and print presentation files

Assessment

This unit does not assume any previous experience of using a computer. However, you may find it useful to have completed Unit 1: File management and e-document production. You will be assessed through a practical realistic assignment which is designed to allow you to demonstrate your knowledge and skills against each objective. Your tutor can provide you with more guidance.

Presentation applications

Microsoft® PowerPoint® is a presentation application. It provides the resources to create presentations in the form of overhead projector slides, computer presentations and handouts. It is used extensively in both business and education. A sales manager may develop a presentation to persuade customers to buy a new product, a teacher may use it as a visual aid to make a subject more understandable and a manager may employ the application to explain changes in the organisation.

This chapter is based on Microsoft® PowerPoint® XP and Figure 5.1 shows the Microsoft® PowerPoint® interface. It is an application with many functions to assist in producing exciting and interesting presentations by providing a wide range of templates, graphic images and text tools.

When you load Microsoft® PowerPoint® it starts with a display divided into four areas. These are:

- toolbars and menu bar
- a blank slide occupying the work area
- New Presentation task pane on the right of the display – this provides access to recently created presentations (Open a presentation section) and assistance with developing new presentations (New section)
- Tabs pane on the left of the display which provides two different ways of gaining an overview of the presentation you are creating

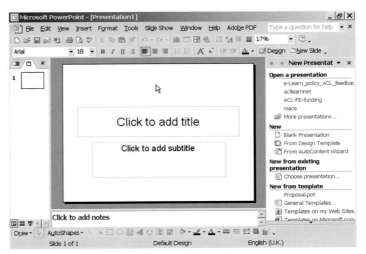

Figure 5.1 Microsoft® PowerPoint®

New blank presentation

We are going to create a new blank presentation so we need to click on the Blank Presentation option in the New Presentation task pane, New section. The display will change replacing the New Presentation task pane with the Slide Layout task pane (Figure 5.2). This provides a variety of layouts that you can use to design your slides. When the pointer is placed on a layout then a small label will appear giving you the name of the layout. You can select a layout either by clicking on the layout so that it appears in the work area or by clicking the down arrow box which, if clicked, opens a menu of options including Insert New Slide .

Figure 5.2 shows the title layout which is used to begin a presentation. At the moment the slide is transparent. Microsoft® PowerPoint® provides you with a variety of tools to add background colours and an overall design to your slides. These are available within the Format menu and Slide Design option. When you select this option the Slide Layout task pane will be replaced with the Slide Design task pane (Figure 5.3).

The Slide Design task pane offers three different sets of designs:

- Design Templates – different layouts for the slides
- Color Schemes – different combinations of colours for the slides
- Animation Schemes – different animations for the slides

When you select one of the options the section below changes to show

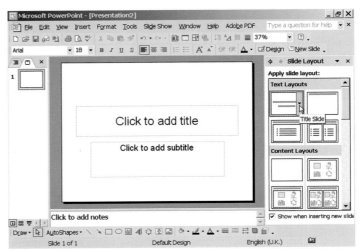

Figure 5.2 Blank presentation

the different choices. In Figure 5.3 the Design Template option has been chosen so the area is a scroll box with a variety of designs. To select a design you click on it and you will see it appear in the working area.

Once you have established the design of the slides you can then add the text that forms the message of your presentation. The title template offers you two text boxes in which you can add text. These are the title and subtitle. After clicking in the boxes, you simply enter text from the keyboard.

A presentation consists of several slides. Once you have completed the title slide, you then need to add a new blank slide. This is done by selecting the Insert menu and then the New Slide option (Figure 5.4). This will insert a new slide into the work area, in this case, a Title and Text slide (Figure 5.5). However, you can change this slide by choosing a new layout from the Slide Layout task pane that also appears when a new slide is inserted. The design of the new slide (e.g. background colours) remains the same as the first slide. It is important in any presentation that the slides are consistent, as this helps the audience to understand the presentation. If each slide is different, with multiple designs and colours employed, there is the danger that the people watching the presentation will be distracted from the message.

The new slide text layout is chosen in the same way as previously discussed (i.e. click on the selected layout), allowing you to present information in several different ways and to include illustrations in the slide. Some options are:

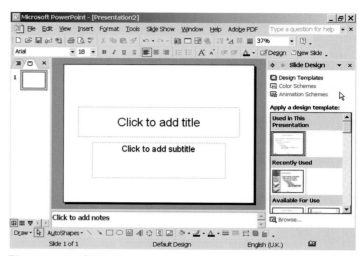

Figure 5.3 Slide design

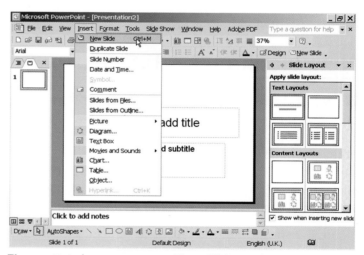

Figure 5.4 Insert menu – New Slide option

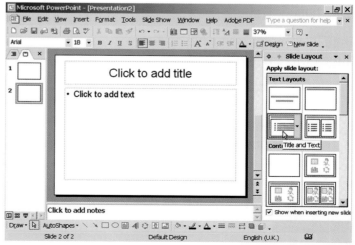

Figure 5.5 New slide

- title and text in a single rectangle
- title and text presented in two parallel rectangles
- title and text in one rectangle with a chart or other image in another

Each layout shows the text or image areas enclosed in a rectangle. These are called placeholders and can either be transparent (i.e. no border) or enclosed in a border.

The rest of the presentation can be developed in this way by adding slides one by one. Microsoft® PowerPoint® lets you edit your slides so it is possible to develop a presentation rapidly by outlining each slide and then completing the presentation later.

Although New CLAiT does not require you to use Microsoft® PowerPoint®'s more advanced features, the application does provide the means of animating slides so that your text can appear to fly onto the slide from almost any direction. The transition from one slide to the next can be made interesting by a variety of means. Some of these features are available in the Slide Show menu.

Organisations tend to develop standard house styles for all presentations carried out by their staff. Organisations have often produced their own design templates including features such as company logos and colour schemes. It is useful to find out if your employer has a house style since you will be expected to follow it and also it may save you a lot of preparation time.

Exercise 41

Creating a presentation

1 Load Microsoft® PowerPoint® using either the All Programs menu or the Microsoft® PowerPoint® icon on the desktop.

2 Select the Blank Presentation option from the New section of the New Presentation task pane. This will open the Title Slide layout. Select the Format menu and Slide Design option to open the Slide Design task pane. Explore the different design templates and select the Blends design template. Enter CLAiT 2006 as the title.

3 Create a second new slide using the Insert menu and New Slide option. A Title and Text layout will appear. Enter the following bullet points:

   - Level 1 Qualification

   - Certificate – 3 Units

   and the Title – CLAiT 2006. You can insert new bullet points by pressing the Enter key at the end of the previous line (e.g. after entering Qualification).

   If you make a mistake and identify it immediately you can delete the text by using the Backspace key. If you do not notice it until the slide is finished then click in the text where the error is. This will move the cursor to the location and you can now delete or insert text at this position.

   An alternative way of dealing with mistakes is to use the Undo button on the Standard toolbar (Figure 5.6). If you place the cursor over the Undo or Redo icons then a message will appear to help you identify them. Undo removes the last action you have carried out. You can use Undo repeatedly so that you can remove several actions. You can effectively undo the undo action by using the Redo button on the Standard toolbar. Practise using Undo and Redo.

To move to another slide you can use the scroll bar on the right of the display or click on the slide list to the left-hand side of the display. Practise by returning to the first slide and then to the second one.

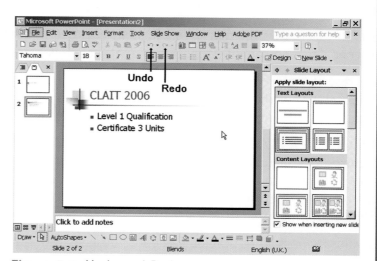

Figure 5.6 Undo and Redo

4 Create a third slide using the Insert menu, entering the following bullet points under the same title of CLAiT 2006:

– Mandatory unit

– Optional units

5 Create a fourth and final slide, entering the following bullet points under the same title of CLAIT 2006:

– Thank you

– Insert your name

Figure 5.7 shows the final slide within the Microsoft® PowerPoint® work area. Notice that on the left-hand side of the display there is an overview of the four slide presentation you have created.

6 It is important to check your presentation for spelling mistakes to avoid embarrassing yourself when you show your slides. To check your slides select the Tools menu and the Spelling option. If you have entered the text correctly then a message 'The spelling check is completed' will

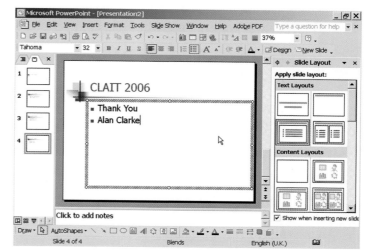

Figure 5.7 Final slide

appear. If the check reveals mistakes they will be shown within the Spelling window and alternative spellings will be offered for you to choose from.

7 Save the presentation you have created on to a floppy disk. This procedure is the same in all Microsoft® Windows® applications – you save a presentation, spreadsheet, database or graphic image in exactly the same way.

 – insert a floppy disk into drive A:

 – click on the File menu item and a menu will open showing a list of options.

 – Select Save and a window will open.

8 Click in the box File name and Enter A:\CLAIT 2006. Click on the Save button on the right of the window. You have now saved your presentation as a file called CLAIT 2006. You may hear the drive A: working during this process.

9 To run the slide show you have created select the View menu and then click on the Slide Show option. The presentation will fill the screen and you can move between slides by clicking the left mouse button. When the presentation is over you will return to Microsoft® PowerPoint®. Alternatively select the Slide Show menu and the View show option.

10 You can close Microsoft® PowerPoint® now by clicking on the File menu item and a menu will appear with a list of options. At the bottom of the list is the option Exit. An alternative way is to click on the Close button in the top right-hand corner of the application window.

Editing your presentation

As with other Microsoft® Office® applications, you are able to add, delete and replace parts of your presentation using functions such as:

■ Cut, copy and paste (Figure 5.8)

■ Search and replace (Figures 5.9)

Cut, copy and paste work by using the mouse pointer to highlight the text or object you want to edit. Highlighting is undertaken by clicking the mouse pointer at the chosen location and holding down the left mouse button while dragging it over the text or object. The text is shown to be highlighted by the background darkening. When the selected text is highlighted you can release the mouse button. To cut or

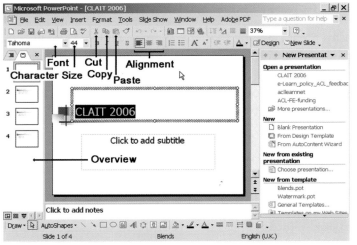

Figure 5.8 Standard toolbar – Cut and Copy

copy the highlighted area you click on the Standard toolbar icon (Figure 5.8). These functions are also available on the Edit menu (Figure 5.9).

The Cut function removes the highlighted area completely and you can then move it to a new location by using the mouse pointer. A new location is selected by positioning the pointer and clicking. The new position is identified by the cursor being moved (i.e. in the same way as the cursor is moved in Microsoft® Word). Now click on the Paste

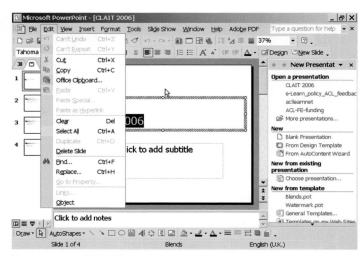

Figure 5.9 Edit Menu

option or icon and the cut section is placed back into the presentation. The Copy function operates in the same way except that the original highlighted area is not removed.

Cut and Copy are very useful functions since a key element in any presentation is consistency. These functions allow you to ensure quickly and effectively that identical elements are present on all slides (e.g. titles, company logos, etc.).

Presentations often consist of many slides and if you need to change some text on every slide it can be a long and tedious process. Microsoft® PowerPoint® provides a way of finding a particular section of text of any length and replacing it with an amended phrase. This is not only fast but also free from errors such as spelling mistakes caused by having to enter replacement text from the keyboard.

Search and replace is available as an option on the Edit menu called Replace. A window will appear (Figure 5.10) with two text boxes. Click in the top box and enter the words you wish to find then click in the lower box and enter the words you want to replace them with. There are also two options shown by the tick boxes in the bottom left-hand corner of the window:

- Match case
- Find whole words only

Match case means that the search will locate only these phrases that are identical in case (e.g. capitals) to the text entered in the window. Find whole words only restricts the search to matches that are entire words, otherwise the search finds words that are parts of longer words (e.g. a search for car will match with carton, care and handcart). This option is important if you are searching for a single word.

Once you have completed the two text boxes you can start the search by clicking on the Find Next button. The search starts from the location of the cursor and proceeds through the presentation. Whenever a match is located you have the choice of replacing it by clicking on the Replace button which changes that single entry. You then need to click on Find Next again to continue the search. An alternative is to click on Replace All which will change all the matches to the new text. Use this option only if you are completely certain that you want to change them all.

Slide order

An important function available in Microsoft® PowerPoint® is the ability to the change the order of the slides. This is provided in the View menu within the Slide Sorter option. When this is selected the display changes to show all the slides (Figure 5.11). Slides can then be dragged and dropped into a new order using the mouse pointer. Clicking on the slide you wish to move and holding down the left mouse button allows you to move to a new position.

If you highlight a slide with a single click you can also Cut, Copy and Paste slides using the functions on the Standard toolbar and within the Edit menu.

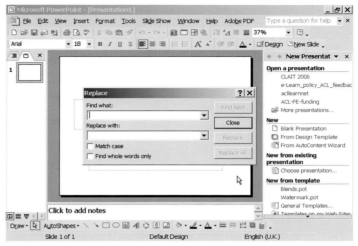

Figure 5.10 Replace

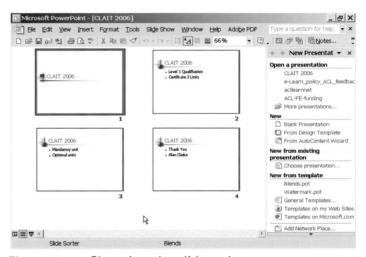

Figure 5.11 Changing the slide order

Exercise 42

Editing a presentation

1 Load Microsoft® PowerPoint® using either the All Programs menu or the Microsoft® PowerPoint® icon on the desktop.

2 In the New Presentation task pane in the Open a presentation section there should be a list of files. Double click on the CLAIT 2006 file shown in the list. The CLAIT 2006 presentation will be loaded, but remember to have your floppy disk inserted in the A: drive.

3 Using the Replace function in the Edit menu, change the title text from CLAIT 2006 to CLAIT 2006 Qualification on all four slides.

4 Using the Cut function, move the text Level 1 Qualification from the second slide to the subtitle box on slide one and amend the text by deleting the word Qualification.

5 Change the order of the slides by moving slide three to make it slide two.

6 Spell check the presentation. Figure 5.12 shows the revised presentation.

7 Save the presentation you have created on to a floppy disk. This procedure is the same in all Windows applications – you save a presentation, spreadsheet, database or graphic image in exactly the same way.

– insert a floppy disk into drive A:

– click on the File menu item and a menu will open showing a list of options.

– Select Save As and a window will open

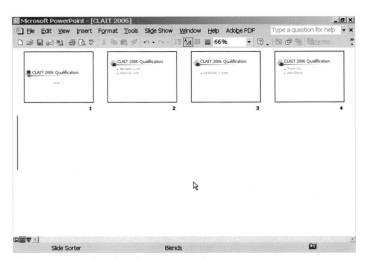

Figure 5.12 Revised presentation

8 Click in the box File name and Enter A:\CLAIT 2006 revised. Click on the Save button on the right of the window. You have now saved your presentation as a file called CLAIT 2006 revised. You may hear drive A: work during this process.

9 To run the slide show you have created, select the View menu and then click on the Slide Show option. The presentation will fill the screen and you can move between slides by clicking the left mouse button. When the presentation is over you will return to Microsoft® PowerPoint®. Alternatively select the Slide Show menu and the View show option.

10 You can close Microsoft® PowerPoint® now by clicking on the File menu item and a menu will appear with a list of options. At the bottom of the list is the option Exit. If you click on Exit then Microsoft® PowerPoint® will close. An alternative way is to click on the Close button on the top right-hand corner of the application window.

Enhancing your presentation

Microsoft® PowerPoint® has a variety of functions that allow you enhance your presentation. Many of these functions are similar to those available in other Microsoft® Office applications (e.g. Microsoft® Word) and include:

■ slide orientation

■ background colour

■ bold, italics and underline

- alignment
- bullet points
- change fonts and character size
- indent text (i.e. promote and demote text)
- insert graphics (i.e. pictures and charts)

Orientation

The orientation of the slides can be either landscape or portrait and is selected by using the Page Setup function in the File menu. This also allows you to choose the orientation for printing the handouts, overview and any notes.

Background

In a similar way you can apply a background colour to your slides through the Format menu and the Background option to open the Background window. This window lets you choose the colour of the background and apply it to all slides or to an individual one. Good practice is to have one consistent background through out the presentation.

Formatting

The Formatting toolbar (Figure 5.13) provides access to the functions that enable you to embolden text, write in italics, underline, align, change fonts and alter the size of characters. Microsoft® Office provides a wide range of fonts and character sizes. If you click on the small down arrow alongside the Font and Font Size boxes on the toolbar, a menu of options will drop down. Click on the selected option. You can do this before you enter text so that the words you enter will appear in the font and size of your choice or you can change the text you have already entered.

To change already entered text you must first highlight it and then make your choice from the drop-down menus. The font and size of your text is critical for an effective presentation since you are seeking to capture your audience's attention. The font must be attractive and interesting to the audience but must not distract from the message you are presenting. The size of characters must be selected carefully to ensure that the slides are visible from the back row, and it is useful to test your slides in the room. It is also important to check the legibility of your slides since colour combinations that appear very effective on the screen can be poor when projected or printed on to an overhead projector slide.

Promote and demote text

Microsoft® Powerpoint® provides tools to promote and demote text. This essentially means that you can

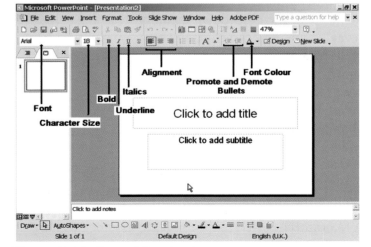

Figure 5.13 Formatting toolbar

structure your bullet points to enhance the main points and show the difference between main and subsidiary issues. By highlighting the text and selecting either the Promote or Demote icons on the Formatting toolbar you can add or remove an indent. This is the same as using the Tab key to indent your text.

These options offer you a variety of ways to emphasise your message and draw the attention of your audience to the critical points. Fonts, character size, bold, italics and underlining all make text stand out.

Alignment

Another useful function is alignment. You can align your text so that it is left, centre or right aligned. Left aligned means that the text starts parallel to the left margin and is uneven on the right edge (i.e. the normal way text is presented). Right aligned means that text is aligned parallel to the right margin and is uneven on the left. This is an unusual way to present text and is rarely used in a presentation. Centre aligned means that the text is centred down the middle of the slide. In presentations, centred is frequently used to draw the audience's attention to the words. Left is also used since it is the most readable way of presenting text.

In a similar way to the use of bold, italics and underline, you can select the alignment before entering the text by clicking on the icon on the Formatting toolbar or you can choose to change the alignment later. Highlight the words you wish to align and click on the appropriate alignment icon. You can align a single word, a sentence, a paragraph, a slide or indeed the entire presentation or you can combine all three ways.

Bullet points

An important device in a presentation is the bullet point list. This is a simple list of items beginning with a symbol (e.g. numbers or geometric symbols) to differentiate it from the rest of the text. It is useful since during a presentation you will be using the slides to indicate the key points of the topic which can be shown as individual bullet points.

Microsoft® PowerPoint® provides a selection of bullet points to choose from, accessed from the Format menu. By clicking on the Format menu item, the drop-down menu is revealed and you can click on the Bullets and Numbering option to show the Bullets and Numbering window. Figure 5.14 shows some bullet symbol options and the Picture button provides access to a wider variety. The Numbered tab reveals styles of numbering that can be used as bullets. You need to explore the wide range of options.

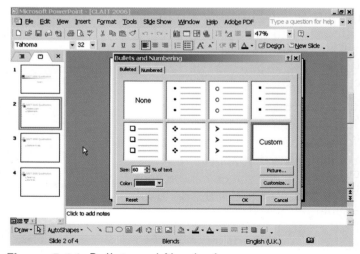

Figure 5.14 Bullets and Numbering

A Microsoft® PowerPoint® template assumes you are using bullet points so it will automatically provide lists. However, you can change the default setting by clicking on the Format menu, selecting Bullets and Numbering and choosing a bullet style. Your chosen style will then appear as you enter the text. However, you can alter the bullet at any time by highlighting the item and choosing a new style. You can change a single item or a whole list.

Illustrations

Pictures can make a presentation more interesting. Use the Picture options on the Insert menu to insert images at any point in your presentations. However, when you are selecting the layout of each slide there are several that include pictures.

To insert a picture into a slide you need to click on the Insert menu item, highlight the Picture option and a second menu will appear to the right of Insert. This provides you with various choices. Clip Art images are provided with Microsoft® PowerPoint® to help you design presentations. From File allows you to select images you have created yourself or have bought. We will consider only the Clip Art option.

By clicking on Clip Art you open a library of pictures to select from. Figure 5.15 shows you the Insert Clip Art pane that is initially displayed. This allows you to search for the clip relevant to a particular topic.

The pane display will change to show the results of your search (i.e. a series of images). To select a picture. You need to click on it, and a short menu of options will appear. The top option will place the image on your slide. However, at this point you may get an error message telling you the pictures are on another disk. This is the Microsoft® Office installation disk and if you have it, you need to place this disk in the CD-ROM drive.

Figure 5.15 Clip Art

The image will either be placed at the cursor or, if your slide has no cursor showing, in the middle of the slide (Figure 5.16). A frame surrounds the image and, if you move the mouse pointer over the image, it changes to a star shape. By holding down the left mouse button when it is over the image you can drag it around the slide and position it. You fix the image by releasing the mouse button and clicking away from the graphic. However, if you click on the graphic image again, the frame will reappear and you can move it to a new position.

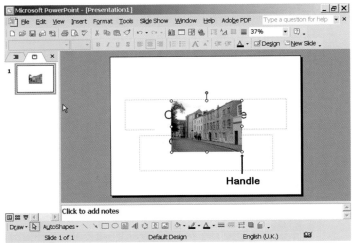

Figure 5.16 Position image

An alternative approach is to select a slide layout that includes pictures and to click on the clip art icon. The Select Picture window will appear which allows you to search for a clip art image and insert it in the way described above.

Lines and drawings

Microsoft® PowerPoint® offers functions that enable you to add lines and drawn shapes such as rectangles, ovals and autoshapes (i.e. many different outlines). These are available on the Draw toolbar. In addition you can shade objects or fill the shapes with colour using the Fill Color and Line Color functions. You can colour text, insert three-dimensional shapes and add special effects to text (i.e. WordArt). Figure 5.17 illustrates the Draw toolbar functions.

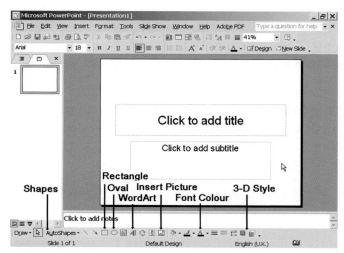

Figure 5.17 Draw toolbar

Exercise 43

Enhancing your presentation

1 Load Microsoft® PowerPoint® using either the All Programs menu or the Microsoft® PowerPoint® icon on the desktop.

2 In the New Presentation task pane in the Open a presentation section there should be a list of files. Double click on the CLAIT 2006 revised file shown in the list. The CLAIT 2006 revised presentation will be loaded, but you must have inserted your floppy disk which contains the presentation file.

3 During this exercise you are going to use the various Microsoft® PowerPoint® functions to enhance your presentation. The first step is to emphasise the titles on each slide and in particular on the opening one. On the initial slide, change the title font to Algierian (or another you feel has impact), the character size to 48 and embolden it. You need to highlight the title and then select the font, character size and the bold option. Once you have made your selections, simply click away from the highlighting to see the changes made. You may need to widen the text box to allow the title to appear on a single line.

4 Next change each title on the other slides to Algerian but with character size 44.

5 The slide bullet points were produced using the default options so you need to change them to a bullet symbol of your choice. Systematically highlight each list of bullet points and select another bullet symbol (i.e. Format menu, Bullets and Numbering option). It is worth exploring the different options to identify one you like and feel is appropriate.

6 Now change all the other text to a font and character size different from the title (e.g. Arial). Explore the different options until you find a font that looks good. Remember to highlight the text and use the font and character options on the Formatting toolbar.

7 Centre your bullet points (e.g. using the alignment icons on the Formatting toolbar) and check to see if you feel this is appropriate way of presenting the text. If you do not like the way it appears, change to left aligned.

8 Insert a graphic image on the opening slide to provide interest. Remember to move to this slide by using the scroll bar and then select the Insert menu, highlight the Picture option and click on Clip Art. Try to pick an image appropriate to the study of an information and communication technology qualification. Move the image around the slide until you place it in an appropriate spot.

9 While the image is enclosed within its frame, placing the mouse pointer over an edge will change its shape to a double-headed arrow (Figure 5.18). If you hold down the left mouse button you can change the shape of the picture. Try to alter the size of the image. You will need to pull the corner to avoid distorting the image.

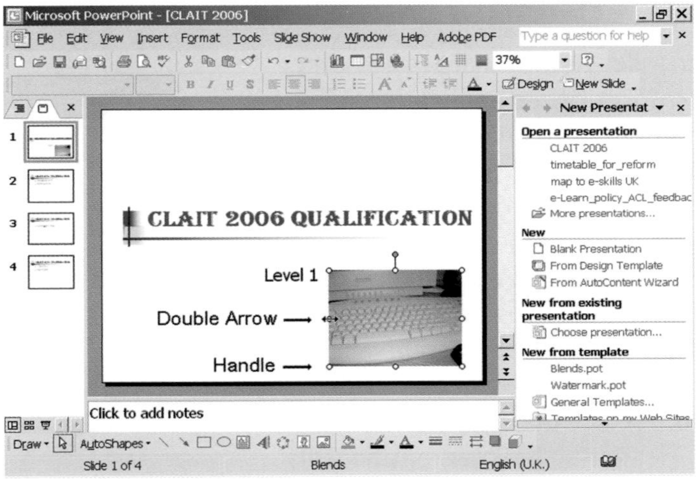

Figure 5.18 Inserting a picture

10 Change the background colour of all the slides (Format menu, Background option and Background window). Use the Preview option in the Background window to explore the different colours.

11 Spell check your presentation (Tools menu and Spelling option).

12 Save the presentation you have created on to a floppy disk. This procedure is the same in all Microsoft® Windows® applications. You save a presentation, spreadsheet, database or graphic image in exactly the same way:

- insert a floppy disk into drive A:

- click on File menu item and a menu will open showing a list of options

- select Save As and a window will open.

13 Click in the box File name and Enter A:\CLAIT 2006 revised2. Click on the Save button on the right of the window. You have now saved your presentation as a file called CLAIT 2006 revised2. You may hear drive A: work during this process.

14 To run the slide show you have created, select the View menu and then click on the Slide Show option. The presentation will fill the screen and you can move between

continued

slides by clicking the left mouse button. When the presentation is over you will return to Microsoft® PowerPoint®. Alternatively select the Sli<u>d</u>e Show menu and the <u>V</u>iew show option.

15 You can close Microsoft® PowerPoint® now by clicking on the <u>File</u> menu item and a menu will appear with a list of options. At the bottom of the list is the option E<u>x</u>it . If you click on E<u>x</u>it then Microsoft® PowerPoint® will close. An alternative way is to click on the close button on the top right-hand corner of the application window.

Headers and footers

You can add headers and footers to your slides in a similar way to other Microsoft® Office applications. This is very useful in a presentation since you can automatically date and number your slides as well as add any standard comments. As part of the assessment you will be asked to identify your slides by inserting your name and study centre number in the footer. To add a header and footer, select the <u>View</u> menu and the <u>Header and Footer</u> option. This reveals a window (Figure 5.19) in which the <u>Slide</u> tab provides you

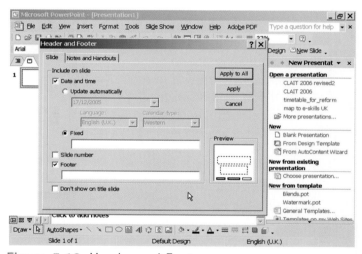

Figure 5.19 Header and Footer

with options to select the date and time which are automatically updated, number your slides and add text as a footer. The other tab, <u>Notes and Handouts</u>, lets you add headers and other footers to your handouts and notes.

Printing your presentation

So far, we have considered how to create a presentation which appears on the computer screen or which could be projected using a data or video projector. However, in many cases you will want to print your slides to provide a set of handouts or to be able to project them on an overhead projector (OHP), which involves printing them on transparencies. There are different types of transparencies depending on your printer (i.e. laser and inkjet). It is important to check that you are using the correct type since using the wrong one may result in poor slides or even damage your printer.

To print your slides you need to click on the <u>File</u> menu and the option <u>Print</u> . This will reveal the Print window (Figure 5.20). The Print window is divided into areas. These are:

- Printer – this shows you the name of the printer that will be used
- Print range – there are a variety of options which you select by clicking on the radio

buttons. The All option prints the whole presentation. Current slide prints only the slide being viewed at that moment. Selection prints the area of the slide which has been highlighted and Slides allows you to select some of the slides by entering their numbers in the text box alongside

- Copies – this allows you to print more than one copy and to collate them
- Print what – by clicking on the small down arrow at the end of the box, a list of options is revealed allowing you to print slides (transparencies), handouts, notes pages and outline view.

The different Print what options are:

- slides – prints the images on to transparencies and paper
- handouts – prints the slides on to paper so that each person in your audience has a copy of your presentation to take away
- notes pages – you can add notes to your slides so that the audience gets a copy of the slides and your speaking notes
- outline view – this is a list of just the text of the whole presentation. It is useful to help you check that you have not left out any important points

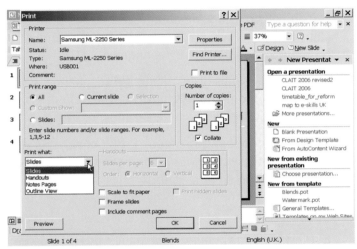

Figure 5.20 The Print dialog box

Exercise 44

Printing

1 Load Microsoft® PowerPoint® using either the All Programs menu or the Microsoft® PowerPoint® icon on the desktop.

2 In the New Presentation task pane in the Open a presentation section there should be a list of files. Double click on the CLAIT 2006 revised2 file shown in the list (Figure 5.21). The CLAIT 2006 revised2 presentation will be loaded, but you must have inserted your floppy disk which contains the presentation file.

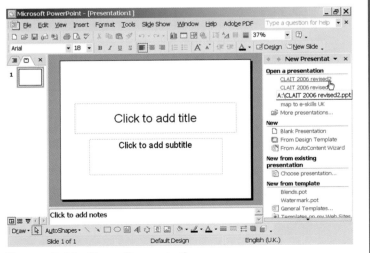

Figure 5.21 Open Presentation

continued

3 You are going to print your slides and produce audience notes (i.e. a handout).

4 Print your slides on to paper initially to check how they look.

Transparency film is quite expensive so it is worth checking before you waste it. Transparencies are loaded into the printer in the same way as paper but make sure you are using the correct type of transparency for the printer (e.g. inkjet or laser transparencies). It can damage your printer if you use the wrong type. Read the instructions on the transparency box as you may need to insert them in a particular way.

5 You will be using the default settings to print. Microsoft® PowerPoint® defaults to printing slides as landscape images but handouts, notes pages and outlines as portrait images. Defaults can be changed.

6 Print your slides (File menu, Print , change Print what to Slides (it may already be set to this option) and OK button). The default is to print all your slides so you do not need to change the Print range settings.

7 Print handouts (File menu, Print , change Print what to Handouts and OK button). The default is to print six thumbnail images on each page and therefore since your presentation comprises four slides, four thumbnail images of the slides will be printed. If you look to the right of the Print dialog box you will see how the thumbnails will appear.

8 Print the notes pages (File menu, Print , change Print what to Notes Pages and OK button). In this case your presentation is printed on four sheets with a copy of the slide at the top and a space below for any notes you may have added.

9 Print outline view (File menu, Print , change Print what to Outline View and OK button). The outline is printed on a single sheet.

10 Take a moment to consider the different printer outputs. You can close Microsoft® PowerPoint® by clicking on the File menu item and a menu will appear with a list of options. At the bottom of the list is the option Exit . If you click on Exit then Microsoft® PowerPoint® will close. An alternative way is to click on the Close button on the top right hand corner of the application window.

Master slides

There is a special type of slide called a Master Slide which allows you to define the fonts, character sizes, colour and layout that will be used throughout your presentation. This is very helpful in ensuring that you provide a consistent appearance to your slides. Anything you place on the master slide will appear on all the slides.

When you start a new presentation you create a master slide by selecting the View menu, highlighting the Master option and clicking on Slide Master . The master slide appears (Figure 5.22). In some cases a toolbar called Slide Master View will also appear – drag it towards the toolbars and you will see it join the other toolbars. To define fonts, click on an area and then change the font, character sizes and other features (e.g. insert picture). These features will be reproduced throughout the presentation.

Once you have defined your master, go ahead with designing each slide and you will see the standard features appear on each of them. If you want to make a change, then by altering the master slide you can change all the slides.

Exercise 45

Master slide

1 Load Microsoft® PowerPoint® using either the All Programs menu or the Microsoft® PowerPoint® icon on the desktop.

2 Select Blank Presentation from the New Presentation task pane.

3 Select the File menu and the Page Setup option to set the slide orientation to Landscape.

4 Select the View menu and highlight the Master option to reveal an additional menu. Select the Slide Master option to reveal the outline of the master slide (Figure 5.22). A toolbar called Slide Master View may appear. Drag it towards the toolbars and it will join them.

5 In order to change or add borders to the top text box you need to right click in the placeholder and select the Format Placeholder option. This opens the Format Autoshape window (Figure 5.23). Change the line colour to black by clicking on the down arrow at end of the color box and you will see that the title placeholder will be enclosed in a black rectangle.

6 You can amend the master layout by left clicking within the text placeholders. Change the text of the title area to Arial, character size 36 and bold. The title should be centred.

7 The first level bullet should be Arial, character size 24 and left aligned.

8 The second level bullet should be Arial, character size 20, left aligned and indented from the first level bullet. The bullets should be separated by one character space. Delete the other bullet levels.

9 Click in the footer and enter your name, automatic date and time. The slide number should be displayed on the bottom right of the slide (i.e. View menu and Header and Footer option).

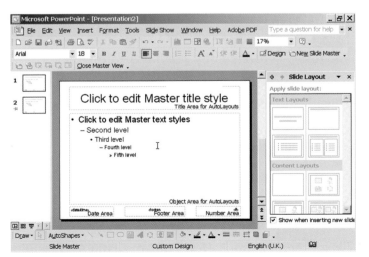

Figure 5.22 Master slide

10 Change the background colour to cyan by selecting the Format menu and the Background option to reveal the Background window. Click on the down arrow to reveal colours, select cyan then click on the Apply to All button. You will see the background colour change.

11 Save the presentation you have created on to a floppy disk. This procedure is the same in all Microsoft® Windows® applications: you save a presentation, spreadsheet, database or graphic image in exactly the same way:

   – insert a floppy disk into drive A:

   – click on File menu item and a menu will open showing a list of options.

   – select Save and a window will open.

12 Click in the box File name and enter A:\Master. Click on the Save button on the right of the window. You have now saved your presentation as a file called Master. You may hear drive A: work during this process.

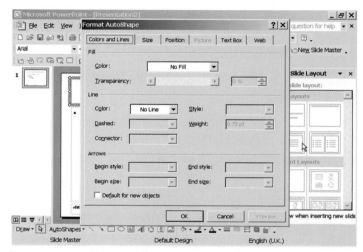

Figure 5.23 Format Autoshape window

More practice

Activity 1
Sell a product

1 Load Microsoft® PowerPoint® using either the All Programs menu or the Microsoft® PowerPoint® icon on the desktop.

2 You are going to develop a presentation to sell the Wireless Laser Printer (WLP). Microsoft® PowerPoint® is often used for sales presentations.

3 Create a master slide by selecting the View menu, highlight the Master option and choose the Slide Master option.

4 Select the Landscape orientation using the File menu and Page Setup option.

5 Select the font Tahoma, character size 40 and bold for the title placeholder at the top of the slide. Centre the title.

6 Select the font Times New Roman, character size 36 and italics for the first level bullet point. The bullets are left aligned. Delete the other bullet levels – this presentation only employs level 1 bullets. Choose a bullet character.

7 Enter your name, automatic date and time in the footer (<u>V</u>iew menu and <u>H</u>eader and Footer option). The slide number should be shown on the bottom right-hand side of the slide.

8 The background colour should be white (select the F<u>o</u>rmat menu and <u>B</u>ackground option).

9 Save the presentation using the file name Sales.

10 Create slide 1 by selecting the <u>V</u>iew menu and choosing the <u>N</u>ormal option. This will open the title template in the working area. Insert the title Wireless Laser Printer and select a clip art image below the title placeholder (i.e. <u>I</u>nsert menu and <u>P</u>ictures option).

11 Insert a new slide (<u>I</u>nsert, <u>N</u>ew slide and select a layout with title and text areas).

12 Insert Wireless Laser Printer on the title bar and then add the following bullets:

- No Cables
- Radio Communication
- Under £200

13 Insert a new slide (<u>I</u>nsert, <u>N</u>ew slide and select a layout with title and text areas).

14 Insert Wireless Laser Printer as the title and the following bullets in italics:

- 10 pages per minute
- 600 dots per inch
- Quiet operation
- Design life 100,000 pages
- 3 Year warranty

15 Insert a new slide (<u>I</u>nsert, <u>N</u>ew slide and select a layout with title and text areas).

16 Insert Wireless Laser Printer as the title and the following bullets in italics:

- Acme Printer Company
- 234 New Way, Birmingham
- Info@acmestar.co.uk
- Your name, Sales Representative

17 Spell check your presentation.

18 Save the presentation you have created on to a floppy disk with the file name Sales (<u>F</u>ile menu and <u>S</u>ave option).

19 Print your slides and a handout with all the slides on one page (<u>F</u>ile, <u>P</u>rint option and <u>OK</u> button).

20 To run the slide show you have created, select the <u>V</u>iew menu and then click on the Slide Show option. The presentation will fill

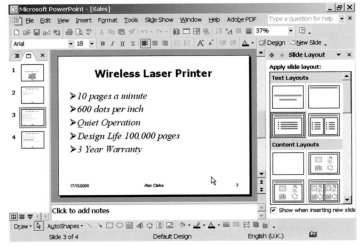

Figure 5.24 Sales presentation

the screen and you can move between slides by clicking the left mouse button. When the presentation is over you will return to Microsoft® PowerPoint®. Alternatively select the Slide Show menu and the View show option. Figure 5.24 shows slide 3.

21 You can close Microsoft® PowerPoint® now by clicking on the File menu item and a menu will appear with a list of options. At the bottom of the list is the option Exit. If you click on Exit then Microsoft® PowerPoint® will close. An alternative way is to click on the Close button in the top right-hand corner of the application window.

Activity 2
Amend a presentation

1 Load Microsoft® PowerPoint® using either the All Programs menu or the Microsoft® PowerPoint® icon on the desktop.

2 In the New Presentation task pane in the Open a presentation section there should be a list of files. Double click on the Sales file shown in the list. The Sales presentation will be loaded, but you must have inserted your floppy disk which contains the presentation file.

3 Change the orientation of the presentation from landscape to portrait (File menu and Page Setup option).

4 Change the text on slide 3 from 10 pages per minute to 25 pages per minute.

5 Add a line below the bullet point text on slides 2, 3 and 4 (Line icon on Drawing toolbar).

6 Save the presentation with the new file name Sales Revised (File menu and Save As).

7 Print the four slides as handouts with 4 slides on a page (File menu, Print option, Print what section and OK button).

8 Change the order of the slides so that slide 3 becomes slide 2 (View menu and Slide Sorter option). Figure 5.25 illustrates the process. Compare the appearance of the slides in portrait orientation with your earlier presentations in landscape.

9 Print the outline view of the presentation with your name as a footer for this printout (i.e. View menu, Header and Footer option and Notes and Handouts tab).

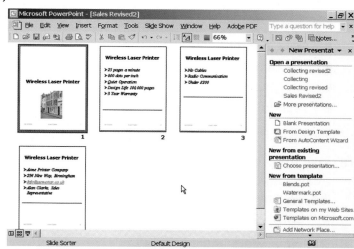
Figure 5.25 Order slides

10 Save the amended presentation as the file Sales Revised2 (File menu and Save As).

11 To run the slide show you have created, select the View menu and then click on the Slide Show option. The presentation will fill the screen and you can move between slides by clicking the left mouse button. When the presentation is over you will return to Microsoft® PowerPoint®. Alternatively select the Slide Show menu and the View show option.

12 You can close Microsoft® PowerPoint® now by clicking on the File menu item and a menu will appear with a list of options. At the bottom of the list is the option Exit . If you click on Exit then Microsoft® PowerPoint® will close. An alternative way is to click on the Close button in the top right-hand corner of the application window.

Activity 3
Explain a hobby

1 Load Microsoft® PowerPoint® using either the All Programs menu or the Microsoft® PowerPoint® icon on the desktop.

2 You are going to develop a presentation to explain why collecting postcards is interesting and fun. Microsoft® PowerPoint® is often used to explain a subject to an audience.

3 Create a master slide by selecting the View menu, highlight the Master option and choose the Slide Master option.

4 Select Landscape orientation using the File menu and Page Setup option.

5 Select the font Times New Roman, character size 44 and bold for the title placeholder at the top of the slide. Centre the title.

6 Select the font Arial, character size 36 and italics for the first level bullet point. The bullets are left aligned. Choose a bullet character. Delete the other bullet levels.

7 Enter your name, an automatic date and time in the footer (View menu and Header and Footer option). The slide number should be shown on the bottom right-hand side of the slide.

8 The background colour should be yellow (select the Format menu and Background option).

9 Save the presentation using the file name Collecting.

10 Create slide 1 by selecting the View menu and choosing the Normal option. This will open the title layout in the working area. Change the title layout by selecting the layout showing a title placeholder at the top of the slide and text placeholder below from the Slide Layout task pane on the right of the display. Insert the title Postcard Collecting and then add the following bullets to the text placeholder:

   ■ Postcards are over 100 years old
   ■ 1896 in Great Britain
   ■ Thousands of collectors
   ■ All ages and backgrounds
   ■ Many different themes e.g. local history

11 Insert a new slide (Insert , New slide) and select a layout with title and text areas. Insert Postcard Collecting in bold as the title and the following bullets:

   ■ Wide price range
   ■ From 10p to many pounds
   ■ Photographic to artist-drawn cards
   ■ Local history
   ■ Many books to explain the hobby

12 Insert a new slide (<u>Insert</u>, <u>New slide</u>) and select a layout with title and text areas. Insert Postcard Collecting in bold as the title and the following bullets:

- Many collectors fairs
- Postcard clubs
- Monthly magazine
- Dealers
- Websites

13 Insert a new slide (<u>Insert</u>, <u>New slide</u>) and select a layout with title and text areas. Insert Postcard Collecting in bold as the title and the following bullets:

- Visit the postcard display
- Ask any questions

14 Spell check your presentation. Figure 5.26 shows the first slide of the collecting presentation.

15 Save the presentation you have created on to a floppy disk:

- insert a floppy disk into drive A:
- click on <u>File</u> menu item and a menu will open showing a list of options.
- Select <u>Save</u> and a window will open.

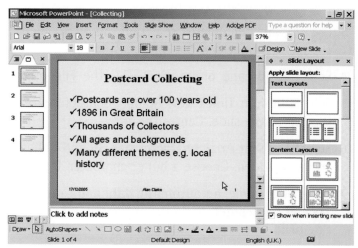

Figure 5.26 Collecting presentation slide 1

16 Click in the <u>File name</u> box and enter A:\Collecting. Click on the <u>Save</u> button on the right of the window. You have now saved your presentation as a file called Collecting. You may hear the drive A: work during this process.

17 Print your slides and a handout (<u>File</u>, <u>Print</u> option and <u>OK</u> button).

18 To run the slide show you have created select the <u>View</u> menu and then click on the <u>Slide Show</u> option. The presentation will fill the screen and you can move between slides by clicking the left mouse button. When the presentation is over you will return to Microsoft® PowerPoint®. Alternatively select the <u>Slide Show</u> menu and the <u>View show</u> option.

19 You can close Microsoft® PowerPoint® now by clicking on the <u>File</u> menu item and a menu will appear with a list of options. At the bottom of the list is the option <u>Exit</u>. If you click on <u>Exit</u> then Microsoft® PowerPoint® will close. An alternative way is to click on the <u>Close</u> button in the top right-hand corner of the application window.

Activity 4
Edit Collecting presentation

1 Load Microsoft® PowerPoint® using either the <u>All Programs</u> menu or the Microsoft® PowerPoint® icon on the desktop.

2 In the New Presentation task pane in the Open a presentation section there should be a list of files. Double click on the Collecting file shown in the list. The Collecting presentation will be loaded, but you must have inserted your floppy disk which contains the presentation file.

3 Demote bullet point two in slide 1 – *1896 in Great Britain* – Arial, 28

4 Demote bullet point four in slide 1 – *All ages and backgrounds* – Arial, 28

5 Demote bullet point five in slide 1 – *Many different themes e.g. local history* – Arial, 28

6 Demote bullet point two in slide 2 – *from 10p to many pounds* – Arial, 28

7 Save the presentation with the new file name Collecting Revised (File menu and Save As).

8 Print the four slides as handouts with 2 slides on a page (File menu, Print option, Print what section and OK button).

9 Change the order of the slides so that slide 3 becomes slide 2 (View menu and Slide Sorter option).

10 Print the outline view of the presentation with your name as a footer for this printout (i.e. View menu, Header and Footer option and Notes and Handouts tab).

11 Save the amended presentation as the file Collecting Revised2 (File menu and Save As).

12 To run the slide show you have created select the View menu and then click on the Slide Show option. The presentation will fill the screen and you can move between slides by clicking the left mouse button. When the presentation is over you will return to Microsoft® PowerPoint®. Alternatively select the Slide Show menu and the View show option.

13 You can close Microsoft® PowerPoint® now by clicking on the File menu item and a menu will appear with a list of options. At the bottom of the list is the option Exit . If you click on Exit then Microsoft® PowerPoint® will close. An alternative way is to click on the Close button in the top right-hand corner of the application window.

Other ideas

If you would like to practise then the following list of ideas for presentations might be useful. Design presentations to:

- introduce new employees to your workplace
- explain why you deserve a pay rise
- explain a hobby or interest (e.g. collecting postcards, keeping guinea pigs or walking)
- help new computer users understand the uses of information and communication technology
- help people new to the Internet to search for information

SUMMARY

1 **Load Microsoft® PowerPoint®**: Use either the `Start` button and the `All Programs` menu or double click on the `Microsoft® PowerPoint®` icon on Microsoft® Windows® desktop.

2 **Close**: Click on the `File` menu item and the `Exit` option or click on the `Close` button on the top right-hand corner of the application window.

3 **Save a file on a floppy disk**: Insert a floppy disk into drive A: and click on the `File` menu and `Save`. Select the drive (3½ Floppy (A:)) and enter the file name.

   Having saved a file once, you can update it by clicking on the `File` menu and `Save`, without the `Save As` window appearing again. It simply overwrites the original file.

4 **Start a new presentation**: Select the option `Blank Presentation` from the New Presentation task pane on the right of the display.

5 **Select new layout**: Select a layout by clicking on the desired layout in the Slide Layout task pane to reveal a menu. Select `Insert New Slide` from the menu.

6 **Delete text**: You have two keys (i.e. Backspace and Delete) which both work from the position of your cursor.

   Backspace key – this removes text, character by character, to the left of the cursor position.

   Delete key – this removes text, character by character, to the right of the cursor position.

   There is also undo and redo. Undo removes the last action you have undertaken, while redo carries out the actions removed by undo. Undo can be used to remove text that has just been typed.

7 **Select design template**: Select the `Format` menu and the `Slide Design` option to open the Slide Design task pane on the right of the display. Choose a design.

8 **Spell check**: Select the `Tools` menu and the `Spelling` option.

9 **Change Slide Order**: Select the `View` menu and the `Slide Sorter` option.

10 **Insert graphics**: If you have used a graphics template then you need to double click on the image area to access the clip art search window. Search for a suitable image.

   Select the `Insert` menu, highlight the `Picture` option to reveal another menu of options. Select the `Clip Art` item to open the Insert Clip Art pane.

   You may see an error message telling you the pictures are on another disk. This is the Microsoft® Office installation disk and you need to place this disk, if you have it, in the CD-ROM drive.

11 **Move the image**: Place the mouse pointer over the image and the pointer will change to indicate that the picture can be dragged by holding down the left mouse button.

12 **Change the font, character size and text characteristics** (bold, italics and underline): Highlight the text you want to change. Change the font and/or character size by selecting

the item in the drop-down list on the Formatting toolbar. Change the text characteristics (i.e. bold, italics and underline) by selecting the icon on the Formatting toolbar.

13 **Change the text alignment**: Highlight the text you want to change. Select the alignment option by clicking on the icon on the Formatting toolbar.

14 **Replace text**: Select the Edit menu and the Replace option. The Replace window appears. Enter the text you want to replace in the Find what: box and the replacement text in Replace with: box.

15 **Bullets**: Select the Format menu and the Bullets and Numbering option. The dialog box gives you a range of styles to choose from.

16 **Orientation**: Select the File menu and the Page Setup option.

17 **Background**: Select the Format menu and the Background option to open the Background window.

18 **Header and Footer**: Select the View menu and the Header and Footer option.

19 **Printing**: Select the File menu and the Print option.

20 **Masters**: Select the View menu, highlight the Master option and click on Slide Master, Handout Master or Notes Master.

Unit 8

Online communication

This chapter will help you use electronic communication to:

● identify and use email and browsing software

● navigate the World Wide Web and use search techniques to locate data on the Web

● transmit and receive email messages and attachments

Assessment

This unit does not assume any previous experience of using a computer. However, you may find it useful to have completed Unit 1: File management and e-document production. You will be assessed through a practical realistic assignment which is designed to allow you to demonstrate your knowledge and skills against each objective. Your tutor can provide you with more guidance.

What is the Internet?

The Internet is essentially a worldwide network linking millions of computers. It was initially developed to allow communication between research organisations and provides users with a range of services including:

■ Email (electronic mail)
■ the World Wide Web (WWW)

It is possible to send email messages anywhere in the world to anyone having an email account. It is like being able to send a postcard almost instantaneously. It is fast and efficient and many people regard email as one of the major benefits of the Internet.

The World Wide Web comprises an extremely large number of locations called websites which provide

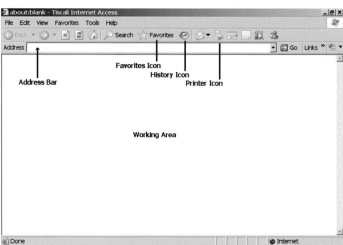

Figure 8.1 Microsoft® Internet Explorer

information about a subject or organisation using text, sound, video and graphics. These sites are located on computers scattered all over the world, linked by telecommunication networks (e.g. telephone lines and optical cables). The World Wide Web uses the Internet to offer information on almost every topic. Visiting websites is is known as surfing the Web and browsing websites.

To explore the World Wide Web you need to use a browser, which is an application designed to allow you to view websites. There are many browsers including:

- Microsoft® Internet Explorer (Figure 8.1)
- Netscape®
- Mozilla Firefox

There are other browsers, including ones developed to help visually impaired users to browse websites by reading the site contents aloud. Microsoft® Internet Explorer is probably the most widely used browser.

To send and receive emails requires access to an email application. Microsoft® Internet Explorer is linked to email software called Microsoft® Outlook® (Figure 8.2) which provides the functions that allow you to send and receive email. There are also a number of other email systems including those that operate from websites.

Figure 8.2 Microsoft® Outlook®

Accessing the World Wide Web

The process of accessing the World Wide Web depends on where you are trying to communicate from. If you are at a college or at work then it is probably very straightforward, involving simply loading the email application or browser. College or work networks are often linked to the Internet automatically. However, at home you will probably need to carry out the additional action of connecting to the Internet through an Internet Service Provider to which you have subscribed. Once you have made your connection, you can then load the browser or email application. If you have broadband (e.g. ADSL) at home then the process will be similar to college or work since many broadband systems offer a continuous link to the Internet although since there are a range of ways of configuring systems there may be differences depending on how the computer and broadband is set up.

Some hotels and other organisations offer wireless connections meaning that if you have a laptop that is wireless-enabled you can access the Internet and send emails through your account simply by being within their buildings. This is becoming increasingly common but arrangements vary and in some cases there are charges or you need to register to use the service.

Surfing the World Wide Web

To locate a particular website you need to know its address (or URL – Uniform Resource Locator). When this is entered into the Address bar and the Enter key is pressed, the browser searches for the website which is then displayed in the browser window.

Website addresses are unique and are structured in a similar way to a postal or street address. The address or URL for the BBC is http://www.bbc.co.uk. This comprises:

- http – Hypertext Transfer Protocol – this tells the browser how to transfer the web page across the Internet so you can view it
- www – World Wide Web
- bbc – host of the website
- co – company
- uk – United Kingdom

The general form is thus http://www.host.typeoforganisation.country. However, websites in the USA do not use a country suffix. Other codes for some organisations and countries are:

- .ac – university/academic
- .com – company
- .co – company
- .edu – educational institution
- .org – charity or not for profit organisation
- .gov – government
- .mil – military
- .net – network
- .be – Belgium
- .ca – Canada
- .dk – Denmark
- .nl – Netherlands
- .ch – Switzerland

Structure of a website

A website consists of a variety of pages each displaying content in the form of text and graphics. Some will also provide sound and video. The pages can vary in length and you often need to scroll them. Each page is linked to the others by hyperlinks which, when clicked on, allow you to jump around the site. A website can be designed so that almost anything can be linked to something else. Links exist to connect items of information within pages as well as between different pages. This can sometimes be confusing since you may feel you have jumped to a new page whereas you have only moved to a new part of the same page. Websites vary in size and can be very large and complex. Figure 8.3 illustrates links between web pages. There can be links such as:

- from an image to a text passage
- from a word to the top of a page

- from an image to another picture
- from the bottom of one page to the top of another
- between pages and within pages

Links may take the form of underlined words, of areas of the screen that change the shape of the mouse pointer when it passes over them or of buttons.

The standard address of a website (e.g. http://www.host.type.country) usually links to what is called the Home page of the site which is rather like the contents page of a book. It normally has links to the main parts of the site but it is also possible to link to individual pages within a website by extending the address (e.g. http://www.host.type.country/ nextpage/otherpages). This is useful when you want to direct people to a particular page but it can be confusing since by following a link you may suddenly find yourself in the middle of a new website. Links can be:

- between pages in a single site
- between pages in different sites
- within a single page

Figure 8.4 illustrates a structure of a simple website. This is presented as a series of layers but websites are often more complex than this with direct links from the home page to major parts of the site ensuring that you do not need to move through each layer. Although this is efficient, it is easy to get lost in a more complex website.

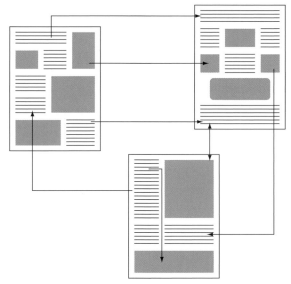

Figure 8.3 Links between web pages

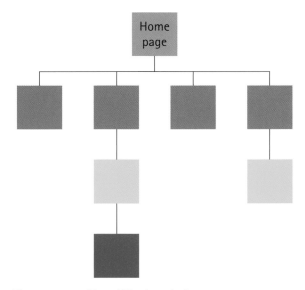

Figure 8.4 Simplified website structure

Exercise 57

Using the browser

Establish a connection to the Internet – this will depend on your location (i.e. home, work or college).

1 Using either the All Programs menu or by clicking on the Microsoft® Internet Explorer icon on the desktop, load the browser. The browser may appear either filling the entire screen or in a window. If you want to expand the window to fill the whole screen, use the Maximise button in the top right-hand corner of the window.

2 Enter http://www.bl.uk/ (this is the website of the British Library) in the Address bar and press Enter. It is vital to be 100% accurate when entering URLs since any mistake will result in your browser giving you an error message suggesting there is no website at that address. When the page appears in your browser, scroll down and view the content. This is the home page so you should be able to locate a menu of the contents of the site.

3 Try to locate the links to other pages. These will take the form of either underlined words, words in a different colour, areas that are highlighted when you move the pointer over them or the mouse pointer changing shape to become a hand.

4 Click on a link that looks interesting and watch what happens. You should see the page disappear and a new one take its place. Often the outline of the page will appear quickly but illustrations will take longer although a frame showing their location may be revealed almost at once. It takes time for the contents of a page to load. The length of time changes depending on the size of the page (i.e. pages containing many illustrations are slow to load), how many people are visiting the site at the same time (i.e. the site gives equal priority to all visitors so if thousands of people are using the site at the same time it will be slow) and the number of people using the World Wide Web (i.e. the more people, the slower the access).

5 Explore the new page and again jump from this to another and so on. Investigate the site and see what you can find.

6 After a few jumps to new pages, it may be difficult to remember the route you have taken. However, you can retrace your steps using the Back button on the toolbar which will move you back to the page you jumped from. You can return using the Forward button.

7 Use Back and Forward and observe what happens. You may notice that pages are faster to load in some cases since your computer has stored the contents of the page and can therefore quickly access it.

8 Explore the site until you are confident that you can recognise links, move between pages and use the Back and Forward buttons.

9 You can jump from one website to another from anywhere, so delete the British Library URL and enter http://www.thebritishmuseum.ac.uk/ in the address bar and press Enter.

10 Observe the new website appear. This is the home page of the British Museum website. Explore this site practising linking to new pages, locating links and retracing your path.

11 When you are confident about navigating sites, close the browser by selecting the File menu and the Close option or click on the window Close button on the top right-hand corner of the browser. You can exit the browser from any page within a site.

Searching a website

Unless the site is small or has limited links, locating precise content is quite difficult if you simply follow the links. A large, complex site can be difficult to use, so many have a facility to search for chosen topics. Figure 8.5 shows a site search facility or search engine that will allow you to locate any content within the site that matches your search words.

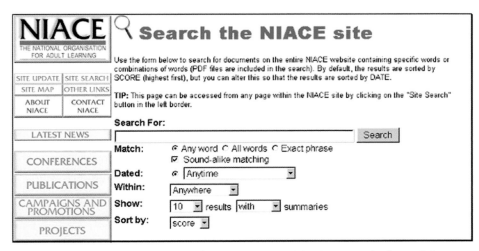

Figure 8.5 Site search engine (Reproduced with the permission of Atomz.com)

This search engine works in a similar way to many others in that you enter a word or words and it seeks to match them to content. In this case you are allowed to refine the nature of the match:

- Any words – any of the words you have entered match any word in the content
- All words – all the search words appear in the content in any order
- Exact phrase – the search phrase is matched exactly in the content
- Sound-alike matching – you can match with any words that sound like your search words

The search engine gives a score indicating the closeness of the match. In many cases, search engines give you a number of matches which you can review to see if they are correct. It is normal to start with a very wide search and then to refine it so that you do not get too many to review.

Exercise 58

Search a single site

1 Establish a connection to the Internet – this will depend on your location (i.e. home, work or college).

2 Load the browser using either the All Programs menu or by clicking on the Microsoft® Internet Explorer icon on the desktop. The browser may appear filling the

entire screen or in a window. If you want to expand the window to fill the whole screen, use the Maximise button on the top right-hand corner of the window.

3 Enter http://www.niace.org.uk/newsearch.htm in the address bar and press enter – this is the website of the National Institute of Adult Continuing Education (NIACE). This URL will jump you into the page on which the search engine is located.

4 Investigate the site search engine by trying a number of different searches.

5 Enter 'information and communication technology' with option Any word (click into the radio button alongside the option) and click on the Search button. A list of matches appears with a brief summary describing them to help you identify if it is the correct one. You can display matches without a summary by changing the 'with summary' option (click on the down arrow to select other options).

6 This search reported over 2000 matches and showed the top ten matches. You can change the number displayed by altering the Show option (click on the down arrow to select a new number). The number of matches you will find will be different since websites are always changing and developing.

7 If you scroll down to the bottom of the results page you will again find the search engine. Alternatively click on the Back button.

8 Search again for 'information and communication technology' with option All words and click on the Search button. The search engine reports the matches and again displays the top ten.

9 Search again for 'information and communication technology' with option Exact phrase and click on the Search button. The search engine reports the matches and again displays the top ten.

10 Search again for 'information and communication technology' with option Exact phrase, Dated within last 2 weeks and click on the Search button. The search engine reports the matches and again displays the top ten.

You will have noticed that the more restrictive your search options, the smaller number of matches.

11 Explore the search engine using different combinations of options until you are confident you understand how it works.

12 You can jump to the content matched by clicking on the link shown with each match (e.g. underlined and coloured words). You will have to do this frequently to check if it is what you are searching for. To return, use the Back button.

13 When you are confident about searching, close the browser by selecting the File menu then the Close option or click on the window Close button in the top right-hand corner of the browser.

Other opportunities to practise

There are a variety of ways that search facilities work on a website. If you would like to practise your search skills, try using the site search engines on:

- www.thebritishmuseum.ac.uk – The British Museum
- www.bl.uk – The British Library
- www.tate.org.uk – The Tate Gallery
- www.movinghere.org.uk – The Moving Here site

All four sites have powerful search facilities to help you locate information.

Searching the World Wide Web

There are millions of websites covering almost every subject. Many organisations provide search engines to help you locate content on the World Wide Web. They have indexed web pages so that you can search them by using key words. This is similar to searching a single website. However, while it is relatively easy to find the content on a single site using a site search engine, it is far more difficult on the World Wide Web because of the number of sites. World Wide Web search engines search for individual web pages rather than entire sites.

Search engines are essentially large databases of web pages that have been amassed automatically by the engine. This is carried out by using tools called spiders or robots which follow links between pages and index the pages they find. The index is directly related to the words presented on the web pages. When you enter your keywords for the information, you are searching the database and not the World Wide Web itself.

There are many search engines and although they all work in broadly similar ways, there are differences between them. They differ:

- in the range of search options they provide
- in how they present or rank the results of a search

There are two different types of search engine:

- individual
- meta

Individual search engines are essentially what we have been describing. A meta engine does not develop its own database but rather searches the databases of several other individual search engines. They are therefore very useful in finding more elusive content.

Another way of finding content on the World Wide Web is by using devices called directories. Directories are very different from search engines. While you search an engine using key words that you select as being related to what you are seeking, a directory provides you with categories to choose from. The contents of directories are chosen for you. The staff pick sites that they believe you will be interested in so they are in a sense making recommendations whereas a search engine leaves the whole choice to you. Directories are very quick to use while a search engine can take time to identify suitable pages. However, the categories available to you in a directory are limited to what have been identified as popular items (e.g. computers, shopping and holidays), but a search engine places no limits on categories you can search for.

There are many different search engines and directories. The list below shows some examples:

Alltheweb	http://www.alltheweb.com
AltaVista	http://www.uk.altavista.com/
Bigbook	http://www.bigbook.com
Chubba	http://www.chubba.com/
Excite	http://www.excite.com/
Google	http://www.google.com
	http://www.google.co.uk
HotBot	http://www.hotbot.com/
Looksmart	http://www.looksmart.com/
Lycos	http://www-uk.lycos.com/
Northern Lights	http://www.nlsearch.com/
Webcrawler	http://www.webcrawler.com/
Yahoo	http://www.yahoo.com
	http://www.uk.yahoo.com

Search engines can also be used to find individual email addresses. There are several that specialise in locating email addresses.

Bigfoot	http://www.bigfoot.com/
InfoSpace	http://www.infospace.com/
Whowhere	http://www.whowhere.com/
Yahoo People	http://people.yahoo.com/

Meta search engines include:

Dogpile	http://www.dogpile.com/
Metacrawler	http://www.metacrawler.com
Monster Crawler	http://www.monstercrawler.com
Lxquick	http://www.lxquick.com
Ask	http://www.ask.com

Searching is easy to do, but can be difficult to do well. Most search engines offer help in a variety of ways and it is useful to investigate these options. Different search engines operate in different ways so that undertaking an identical search using several will produce different results. The next two exercises are based on comparing the same search using two different search engines (i.e. Altavista and Google).

Exercise 59

Searching the World Wide Web – Altavista

1 Establish a connection to the Internet – this will depend on your location (i.e. home, work or college).

2 Load the browser by using either the All Programs menu or by double clicking on the Microsoft® Internet Explorer icon on the desktop.

3 Enter http://www.uk.altavista.com in the address bar and press Enter – this is the website of Altavista. If you would like to compare this search engine with a directory then visit

http://www.bigbook.com. Study the Altavista search engine and notice that there are options to search for images, audio, video and news.

4 Return to the Altavista home page, Web tab. We will try to locate a hotel in Edinburgh. So enter the word – hotels – into the box of the search engine and select the option which restricts the search to the United Kingdom (click on the radio button – a small circle which when you click on it inserts a dot in its centre to show it is active). Click on the Find button.

The results give several million pages matching the word hotels and also offering a number of sponsored matches about hotels.

5 This is not very useful as there are too many matches. Let's refine the search by adding the word Edinburgh. You should enter – hotels Edinburgh – select the UK option and click on the Search button.

6 The results of this search were still several thousand pages that match the words and also some sponsored matches relating to hotels in Edinburgh. However, the number of matches is significantly reduced.

7 Refine the search by joining the words with a plus sign – hotels+Edinburgh. The engine will now search for pages containing both words.

8 A final search involves enclosing the words in double inverted commas. This normally makes the engine search for pages in which the phrase "hotels Edinburgh" appears. Finally try to reverse the order of the words so enter "Edinburgh hotels".

9 You can jump to any matching web page by clicking on the link (underlined and coloured words) to check if it is what you are looking for. To return to the search engine, use the Back button. Explore the search engine by carrying out a search to find web pages that interest you (e.g. look for pages about a hobby, football team, government or places of interest).

10 When you are confident about searching, close the browser by selecting the File menu and the Close option or click on the window Close button in the top right-hand corner of the browser.

Exercise 60

Searching the World Wide Web – Google

1 Establish a connection to the Internet – this will depend on your location (i.e. home, work or college).

2 Load the browser by using either the All Programs menu or by clicking on the Microsoft® Internet Explorer icon on the desktop.

3 Enter http://www.google.com in the address bar and press Enter. This is the website of the Google search engine (Figure 8.6).

4 Notice that this search engine offers options to search for images, groups, news, Froogle and more. Explore the other options and see if you can find out what Froogle offers.

5 We will try again to locate a hotel in Edinburgh, so enter the word – hotels – into the search box. Click the Google Search button.

The result of the search are far from useful since there are far too many matches. Let's refine the search by adding the word Edinburgh. You should enter – hotels Edinburgh – and click on the Google Search button.

Figure 8.6 **Google search engine**

6 A third possible step is to modify the search by joining the words with a plus sign. The engine will search for pages containing both words: hotels+Edinburgh.

7 A fourth search is to enclose the words in inverted commas. This normally makes the engine search for pages that include the phrase "hotels Edinburgh".

8 A final way is to reverse the search words and enter "Edinburgh hotels".

9 Compare the results of the two searches and consider the effectiveness of different search approaches and search engines. It is useful to compare which pages each search engine identified in their top ten.

10 Explore the Google search engine by carrying out a search to find web pages that interest you (e.g. look for pages about a hobby, football team, government or places of interest).

11 When you are confident about searching, close the browser by selecting the File menu and the Close option or click on the window Close button in the top right-hand corner of the browser.

Exercise 61

1 Try searching for hotels in Edinburgh using Yahoo UK (http://uk.yahoo.com).

2 Search engines often provide other services. Try finding out what news and other services the different search engines offer.

Saving information

Browsers provide functions allowing you to save the contents of web pages, images and save the URL so you can return to the page and to print the page. All these functions require the browser to be accessing the chosen web page.

To print the page, select the File menu then the Print option, which will open the Print dialog box. Press the OK button in the Print dialog box and the web page will now be printed using the printer default settings. Web pages are quite often long, so printing a web page can produce several A4 sheets. Figure 8.7 shows the File menu.

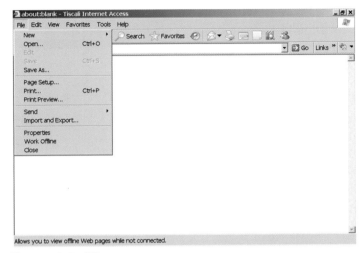

Figure 8.7 File menu

In a similar way, the contents of the web page can be saved by selecting the File menu and the Save or Save As options. This opens the Save dialog box. To save a web page as a file, you need to identify a folder in which to save it. This is done by clicking on the down arrow at the end of the Save in box to open a list of the drives and folders. To select one, single click on it. Once you have selected a folder you can name your file by clicking in the File name box and entering the name using the keyboard. The file can now be saved by clicking the Save button. The latest browsers allow you to save both the text and images unlike the earlier ones which only allowed you to save the text and left gaps where the pictures should be.

You can also save images by positioning the mouse pointer over the picture and right clicking. This will open a menu of options including Save Picture As... . If you select this option then a window called Save Picture will open that offers you the opportunity to select the file name (i.e. in the box at the bottom of the window called File name) and the file type (i.e. in the box

at the bottom of the window called Save as type). Usually this will be completed by the system identifying the file. It is often JPEG or GIF since these are widely used on websites. The window also allows you to choose where to save the file by using the Save in box at the top of the window.

Once you have found a useful website it is important to be able to find it again. Microsoft® Internet Explorer lets you save the URLs in a special area called Favorites. To store a URL, you need to be

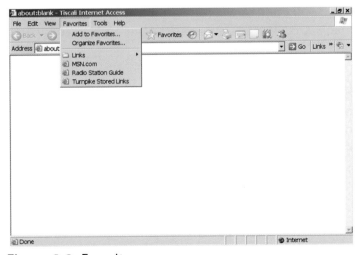

Figure 8.8 Favorites

accessing the chosen website. You then select the Favorites menu and the Add to Favorites option. Figure 8.8 shows a list of Favorites. To return to a Favorite website you simply click on it. You can organise your Favorites into folders, grouping related sites together.

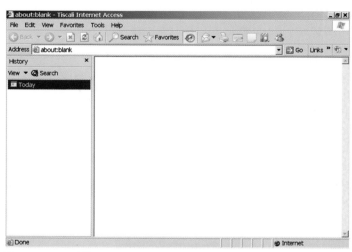

Figure 8.9 History

Another way of returning to a useful website is to use the browser's history records. Microsoft® Internet Explorer keeps records of sites visited. However, this record system is often set to keep the list of sites visited for just a short time so its main task is to allow you to return to a particular site after a session visiting many different websites. Figure 8.9 shows the History record open. It is accessed by clicking on the History button on the toolbar.

Microsoft® Outlook®

When you first start to use email it has a magical quality. You connect to the Internet, open your email application (e.g. Microsoft® Outlook®) and your emails arrive. What happens is that an email is addressed in the same way as a letter or postcard. This address directs the email to a location on the Internet, normally that of the Internet Service Provider who supplies your access to the Internet, where it is stored on a computer until you collect it. In some cases that may be your employer or college. Often as soon as you connect to the Internet and open your email application, the mail automatically arrives. However, sometimes you will need to request that the email is sent to you (often called downloading) or even establish a link to the Internet before accessing your messages. It depends on your situation.

An important issue to remember is that computer viruses are often distributed by email. You should always protect your computer system with up-to-date virus protection software. Most virus protection applications will allow you to set them so that all incoming and outgoing emails are checked. This is critical to protect your computer.

Microsoft® Outlook® is an email system that also offers many additional features to manage your activities (e.g. diary). You can access it from the All Programs menu or by clicking on the Microsoft® Outlook® icon on the Microsoft® Windows® desktop. This means you can use it independently from Microsoft® Internet Explorer. You do not need to be connected to the Internet in order to use Microsoft® Outlook® to read old emails, to write new emails or reply to one that you have received.

However, to send or receive new emails does require a connection to the Internet. Once you are connected then the emails you have created can be sent. This is like writing letters at home and having to walk to the postbox to post them. This process of writing or reading emails while not being connected is called 'working off-line'. This is important since it will save you the telephone charges associated with being connected.

Figure 8.2 shows you the major features of Microsoft® Outlook®. These are:

■ Inbox – this is the folder in which your email is stored when it is received; it is sometimes called the mailbox.

■ Outbox – this is the folder in which your emails are stored until they are sent (i.e. before you connect to the Internet).

■ Sent Items – this is the folder in which all your emails that have been sent are stored.

■ Deleted Items – this is the folder in which emails that have been deleted are stored. This is very useful to help rectify mistakes.

■ Drafts – this is the folder in which emails that are only partially written are stored.

■ Address book (Open book icon on toolbar) – this provides access to an electronic address book where email addresses can be stored.

Many of these functions are all shown on the left-hand side of the application in the small window marked Folders, with the exception of Address Book which is a toolbar button. Microsoft® Outlook® provides you with these features to ensure that emails are safeguarded and organised. However, you can also use standard Microsoft® Windows® file-saving methods to save emails as files in other folders. This is useful if the email relates to a particular topic and you have already created a folder for other files so that you can keep everything together.

Incoming mail is displayed in the Inbox which you access by clicking on the Inbox function in the Folders list or in the main work area (i.e. right-hand side of opening display). Figure 8.10 shows the Inbox. If you select an email by single clicking to highlight it you will see that the message appears in the window below. Microsoft® Outlook® offers a range of ways of showing messages and these are available in the View menu. To open the message so that it is displayed in a separate window you need to double click on it.

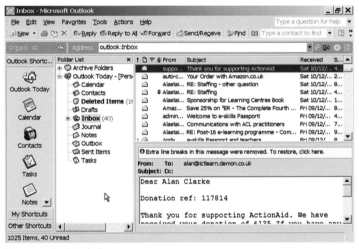

Figure 8.10 Inbox

To save an email in an external folder, highlight the message and select the File menu and the Save As option. This will open Save Message As window. This is identical to other Microsoft® Office applications. You need to:

■ Select the drive (e.g. floppy disk) using the Save in box down arrow

■ Select a file name using the File name box. Microsoft® Windows® provides you with a name based on the contents of the document but it is always best to name your own files to ensure you can remember them

If you have opened the message the process of saving to an external folder is the same.

You can also save your messages to a folder within the Inbox folder. In order to save your emails to an internal folder you must first create it. The first step is to highlight the Inbox folder within the folders list on the left of the display and then select the down arrow on the

New button on the toolbar. This will open a menu of options from which you should choose Folder to reveal the Create New Folder window (Figure 8.11). You enter the name of the folder you want to create and then click on the OK button. Your new folder is created within the Inbox folder. You could create it within any of the folders.

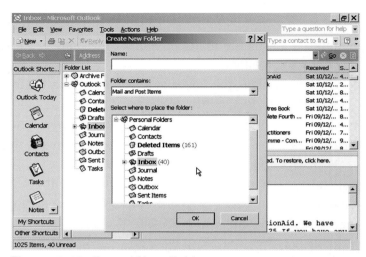

Figure 8.11 Create New Folder

Once you have started to use email you will rapidly have too many messages to remember them all. It is therefore critical to organise them in folders so you can find them later. Figure 8.12 shows a folder structure which organises the management of messages. Once you have saved a message it is important to remove it from the Inbox or you will quickly have a very long list of messages displayed. To delete an email simply highlight it and press the Delete key on the keyboard or select the Delete option in the Edit menu.

When you want to read a saved email you simply highlight the folder and you will see the saved messages appear in the message area. You are then able to select the message you want to read and it will open so you can view it. When you send emails they are automatically saved in the Sent Items folder.

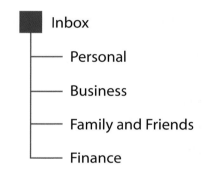

Figure 8.12 Email folders

Sending messages

To send a new email, click on the New button on the toolbar of Microsoft® Outlook®. This will open the email window (Figure 8.13). The layout of the message window guides you through how to write your message. You need to enter an email address, a subject and the contents of your message. You can also send copies of your message to other people. When you have completed your message, send it by clicking on the Send button. If you are connected to the Internet, the email will be sent immediately. If you are working off-line (i.e. you are not connected to the Internet) then the email is stored in the Outbox and the number stored will be shown in brackets next to the title Outbox.

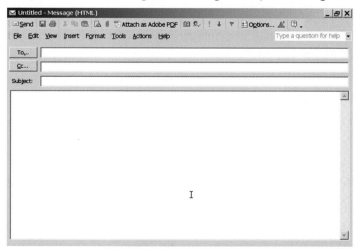

Figure 8.13 Sending an email

You should see the number increase by one when you click on the Send button. The email will be dispatched as soon as you next connect to the Internet.

Emails are normally short messages but other computer files such as spreadsheet, word-processor or presentation files can be attached. This allows far more detailed information to be communicated. Sales staff, for example, can send their expense claims as a spreadsheet file or managers can send their reports as word-processor files. These files are called attachments and they are easily added to the email using the Insert File button (i.e. shown by a paperclip).

Email is very useful in business in that mail carries the sender's details. It automatically gets assigned a date and time of creation so that messages can be more easily traced or kept in order. These features allow detailed records to be straightforwardly maintained. Equally important is that any emails you receive can be kept (e.g. in your folders).

The address of an email follows a standard convention. It is a combination of the user's name with a domain name (often the email's computer host or Internet Service Provider) joined by the @ symbol. Some examples of email addresses are:

- ajones@acme.co.uk
- alison.jones@acme.net
- jones@harry.org.uk
- a.jones@acme.com

Many organisations standardise email addresses so that if you know one email addresses you can work out other ones.

For example

You know one member of staff's email address is d.harrison@acme.co.uk then if you know another person is called James King then his email address may be j.king@acme.co.uk.

Exercise 62

Send an email

1 Load Microsoft® Outlook® using either the All Programs menu or by clicking on the Microsoft® Outlook® icon on the desktop.

2 Open a new message by selecting the New button on the toolbar to reveal the email window (Figure 8.13).

3 If you are studying OCR CLAIT 2006 as part of a class, ask your learning colleagues if you can send them an email or ask a work colleague for their address.

Enter the following text

    To: e-mail address of your colleague

    Subject: Practice email

    This is my first email and I would be grateful if you would reply to it so that I can see what happens.

    Name

continued

4 Before you send your email check that you have entered the address accurately. It must be 100% correct or it will not be delivered. If you send a message to an unknown address you will receive an error message saying that there is no such address. Often this is the result of a tiny error.

5 Click on the Send button as soon as you have completed the message. If you are not connected to the Internet you will see the message added to the Outbox (number in brackets will increase by one). If you are connected then the message will be sent immediately and a copy placed in the Sent Items folder. Check this folder and see if your message has been added.

6 If you are not connected to the Internet you should then connect and you will see your message sent. It should only take a moment or two.

7 Explore Microsoft® Outlook® by clicking on menus and buttons and investigating the different options. Observe the changes to the display.

8 When you are confident that you understand the layout of the application, close Microsoft® Outlook® by selecting the File menu and the Exit option or click on the window Close button in the top right-hand corner of the application window.

Receiving emails

Emails that have been sent to you will appear in the Inbox which you access by clicking on the Inbox folder in the Folders List or in the main work area (i.e. right-hand side of opening display). Figure 8.10 shows the Inbox. A list of emails is shown in the Inbox which presents you details of who the message is from, its subject and the date and time it was received. This information can be preceded by a symbol (e.g. a paperclip indicates an attachment and an exclamation mark, an important message). If you single click on a message it will be highlighted and its contents revealed in the box below the list. If you double click on the message then it will open fully (Figure 8.14).

When you receive an email you have a variety of options. You can:

■ read then delete the message (with the email highlighted or the message window open, select the Edit menu and the Delete option or press the Delete key)

■ read and save the message (with the email highlighted or the message window open select the File menu and the Save As option)

Figure 8.14 Open email

- read and reply to the original email sender (with the email highlighted or the message window open, click on the `Reply` button on the toolbar)
- read and reply to everyone who received the original email (i.e. copies) (with the email highlighted or the message window open click on `Reply to All` button on the toolbar)
- read and forward the message to someone else (with the email highlighted or the message window open, click on the `Forward` button on the toolbar and enter the email address of the person you want the message copied to)
- read and copy the message to a folder (with the email highlighted or the message window open, select the `Edit` menu and the `Copy to Folder` option. This allows you to place a copy of the message into one of the existing local folders or in a new local folder. This is useful in that within Microsoft® Outlook® you begin to create a filing system for your communications. Alternatively you could use `Save As` option we discussed earlier)
- read and copy the message to another person (with the email highlighted or the message window open, click on the `Reply` button on the toolbar. Enter the address of the person you want to copy your reply to in addition to the sender in the `Cc` box or delete the senders address and enter the address of the person you are copying the message to)
- print the message (with the email highlighted or the message window open, select the `File` menu and the `Print` option)

Emails are often printed and it is important always to print the email header. This shows the details of the sender, receiver, date sent and subject of the message. This allows you to trace the background to the message and to link it to other related items. It is quite common to print a series of messages to read and answer while travelling and then to send the answers when you return to the office. In order to avoid mistakes it is clearly vital to have the details on the printout. During the assessment for this chapter you will be required to print emails with the headers.

The process of deleting messages from your Inbox once you have acted on them is important since very quickly after starting to use email you are likely to have a vast number of old messages. It is vital that these are organised (e.g. saved into folders) or you will rapidly become confused by the mountain of correspondence.

Some of the emails you receive will be accompanied by attachments. If you look at the top line of the Inbox you will see a variety of headings – one is a paperclip. If you now look down the list of messages, if any have a paperclip it indicates a message with an attachment. These are files of information (e.g. word-processor files). To open an attachment double click on it and it will open, providing you have the appropriate application available on your computer. A Microsoft® Word file requires Microsoft® Word, a Microsoft® Excel® file requires Microsoft® Excel® and so on. If the appropriate application is not present then you will see an error message stating that it cannot identify the application. Once an attachment is open you can save or print it using its application. The appropriate application will be opened automatically by the attachment.

Viruses are frequently transmitted by email attachments. It is therefore important not to open an attachment unless you know who has sent you the message. Equally important is to have up-to-date virus protection software on your computer. Many virus protection systems allow you to check attachments automatically before opening them. It is good practice to check email attachments even if you know the sender. Some viruses automatically send email messages to spread their effects.

Netiquette

Many organisations have established codes of conduct for using email. Email messages are often informal and short making them easy to misunderstand. This has given emails a reputation for causing offense without intending to do so. Many people do not realise that the same laws apply to emails as do to letters (e.g. libel). These codes of conduct are called 'netiquette'. Netiquette rules vary but some widely used ones are:

- never send or reply to a message in anger
- always introduce your message (e.g. Dear... or Hi...)
- always end your messages (e.g. Best Wishes, etc)
- do not include items in an email that you would not send in a letter
- do not send any form of material that could cause offence

There are possibly other rules and it is important to find out what your employer's netiquette code is and to follow it.

Formatting email

Emails are often informal and can easily be misunderstood so it is important to consider how to format messages to make them clear. When creating a new message you can select from a range of formatting options by selecting the Format menu and a series of options including:

- Font
- Paragraph
- Background

The Font options allows you to select the font, style (i.e. underlined, italics or embolden) and character size. The Paragraph offers options to align your message left, right and centre as well as a bullet list, while the Background options offers the possibility of using a picture of your choice as a background for the message or changing the colour of the background.

This range of different options provides powerful ways of presenting your messages to give impact. However, the main purpose of any message is to ensure that the receiver understands it. It is therefore important not to overuse the different features since they can sometimes distract the reader from the message.

Exercise 63

Receiving emails

1 Load Microsoft® Outlook® using either the All Programs menu or by clicking on the Microsoft® Outlook® icon on the desktop.

2 Single click on the Inbox which will be highlighted and a list of emails received will be listed. Email messages that you have not opened are shown in bold. You will possibly find a reply to a previous email but even if no one has sent you a message, Microsoft® Outlook® usually shows a welcome email from the Microsoft® Outlook® team.

3 Single click on a message. You will see the content displayed. This is very useful if you are seeking to check your email rapidly.

4 Double click on a message and you will see the Message window open.

5 Click on the Reply button and a new window will appear (Figure 8.15) showing the original message but it reverses the sender and receiver. In the space above the original message you enter your reply. This enables both the original message and reply to be sent. If this email provokes a response, the email will have the original, the reply and the second reply. Emails can contain the whole communication.

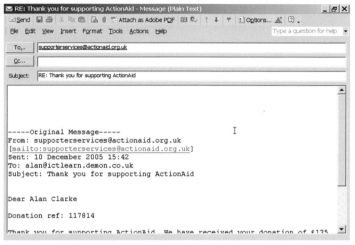

Figure 8.15 Reply

6 Enter a reply that is appropriate to the message you have opened. In my example, I might reply:

> Hi
>
> I hope the donation helps
>
> Keep up the good work
>
> Alan Clarke

7 Click on the Send button as soon as you have finished. If you are connected to the Internet your message will be sent. If you are working off-line then the message will be stored in the Outbox and you will see the number in the box increase.

8 Open the email again and this time, click on Reply to All and you will see the same window (Figure 8.15) open. This is because the original email was sent only to you. If the original message had been copied to other people then your reply would go to everyone. Close the window, select the File menu and the Close option or click on the Close button in the top right-hand corner of the window.

9 Open the email again and click on the Forward button. You will see the same window (Figure 8.15) open again but with a blank To line. This lets you send your message to another person. You can also add an extra message. To close the window, select the File menu and the Close option or click on the Close button in the top right-hand corner of the window.

10 Open the email again and click on the Reply button. You will see the same window (Figure 8.15) open again with the sender and receiver reversed. Delete the address in the To box and enter another address (perhaps another student if you are taking a course) and copy the email to the new person.

11 Repeat step 10 but instead of substituting the address in the To box, insert the address of the person you are copying to in the Cc box.

12 Compare the Reply, Reply All, Forward and Cc functions.

13 When you are confident that you understand the three functions, close Microsoft® Outlook® by selecting the File menu and the Exit option or click on the window Close button in the top right-hand corner of the application window.

Attaching files

Attaching files to an email can be very useful. You initially need to start a new email (click on the New button) which opens the Email window (Figure 8.13). To add an attachment, click on the Insert File button (i.e. paperclip) on the toolbar. This will open the Insert File window (Figure 8.16).

This window gives you access to all your saved files. To move around the different drives, use the drop down arrow next to the Look in box and then click on the selected folder or drive. When you have identified the file, double click on it or single click the file and then click on the Insert button. The attached file will appear in your message.

Electronic address book

An important function that Microsoft® Outlook® provides is the storage of email addresses. You can copy addresses from emails that are sent to you or enter new ones manually. Once you have created an entry in the electronic address book, you can send an email directly from it.

The address book can be opened by selecting the Address Book icon (i.e. an open book) on the toolbar. This opens the Address Book window (Figure 8.17). It will often open in a

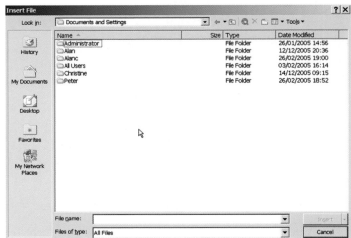

Figure 8.16 Insert File

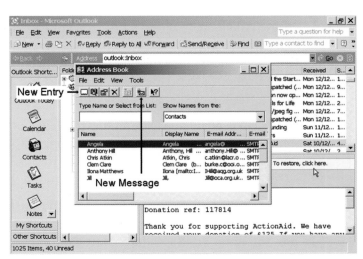

Figure 8.17 Address Book

small window which you will need to enlarge to full screen size by selecting the Maximise button in the top right hand corner of the window. You can enter new addresses by selecting the New Entry button which will open a new window with the options:

- New Contact
- New Distribution List

In New Contact you insert an individual address. New Distribution list allows you to create a group of email addresses so that by typing a single name you can send a message to everyone in the group. If you select the New Contact option then you will open the Properties window which resembles a paper address book where you can record names, addresses, email addresses, telephone numbers, etc.

A useful function provided by the Address Book is the ability to send an email from it. If you select the New Message button with an address highlighted, then the email window will open with the email address of the entry inserted (Figure 8.18).

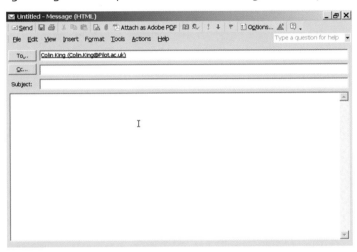

Figure 8.18 Send email

Exercise 64

Using an address book

1 Load Microsoft® Outlook® using either the All Programs menu or by clicking on the Microsoft® Outlook® icon on the desktop.

2 Click the Address Book icon to open the window (Figure 8.17). Click on the New Entry button to reveal the New Entry window and select the New Contact option and click on the OK button to open the Contacts window (Figure 8.19).

3 Add the following information to create a new record

   Bill Jones
   Acme
   11 New Way
   Newtown

   020 345 7896

   b.jones@acme.co.uk

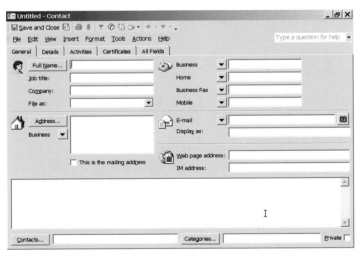

Figure 8.19 Contacts window

continued

When you have completed the entry, click on the Save and Close button and you will see the new entry in the Address Book.

4 Try entering the contact details and email addresses of some people you know. If you are using this book as part of a course, ask the other learners for their details. Practise until you are confident of adding new addresses. You can delete entries by highlighting them and selecting the File menu and the Delete option.

5 If you single click on an address it will be highlighted and by selecting the New Message button, you can send an email to this address. If you double click on an address, you can add more information to your record, such as the postal address.

6 Select an address and send a new email. An email window will appear with the address you have selected in the To box. Experiment with the different formatting options (e.g. fonts, character size, alignment and background colours) for presenting your email.

7 Explore the other Address Book functions until you are confident you understand what it can offer you.

8 Close the Address Book window by selecting the Close button on the top right-hand corner of the window or the File menu and the Close option.

9 Close Microsoft® Outlook® by selecting the File menu and the Exit option or click on the Close button on the top right-hand corner of the application window.

Web-based email

Another way of providing yourself with an email account, if you have access to the Internet, is through web-based email suppliers. To send or receive messages you must gain access to the World Wide Web. This has the advantage that you can access your messages from any computer in the world connected to the Internet, although it does have the disadvantage that you must be online to read or send messages.

Almost all the web-based services are free but you will find advertising related to both the sites you have to visit and in some cases the emails you send. In order to establish an account you normally only have to visit the site, complete some online forms, and choose a user name and password. Once this is done you are ready to send and receive email.

Some Internet Service Providers will offer you both a web-based account and one linked to your home computer. This gives you the opportunity of reading and replying to your mail when you are away from home.

Company policy and legislation

Although the World Wide Web provides a huge amount of useful information, it also contains offensive material, pornography and information which is incorrect. Many employers have established policies about the use of the World Wide Web. It is critical that you are aware of your organisation's policy.

Companies frequently forbid the use of the World Wide Web to access offensive material and in many cases it is a serious disciplinary offence to breach the policy. The legal position should also be considered. There have been several prominent court cases about using the World Wide Web to access pornography. It is important to be aware of both the law and access policy. In a similar way, learning centres, colleges and libraries which provide public access to the Internet also place restrictions on the use of the system.

Many organisations have also developed policies regarding the use of email which you should be fully aware of. In simple terms, it is always best to include in an email only material you would write in a letter. You are just as liable for what you write in an email as in a letter.

More practice

Activity 1
Locate a website

1 Access the website at www.movinghere.org.uk which is a website allowing people to learn more about migration to Great Britain. It contains a wealth of material. Figure 8.20 shows the home page today but since websites are dynamic, it is likely that it will have changed to some extent when you view it.

We would like to acknowledge The National Archive for their permission to use the screen capture of *Moving Here*.

Figure 8.20 Moving Here

2 Use the site search facility to locate information about stories from Ireland.

3 Save the page as a Favorite so that you can locate it again.

4 Print the web page.

5 On the printout of your web page write your name and the date you located it.

6 Use the links on the website to locate the gallery and return to the home page.

7 Save the Home page as a Favorite so that you can locate it again.

8 Print the Home page and write your name and the date you located it.

9 Close your browser when you have completed the task.

Activity 2
Searching the World Wide Web

1 Using a search engine of your choice, locate a picture of the Fighting Temeraire which is a famous painting by the artist J.M.W. Turner.

2 Use the links to find a page with a copy of the painting.

3 Save the page as a Favorite so that you can locate it again.

4 Print the web page.

5 Write your name on the printout and indicate the painting of the Fighting Temeraire.

6 Close your browser when you have completed the task.

Activity 3
Sending an email message

The website linked to this book (www.hodderclait.co.uk) has an email bin into which you can send emails but you will not get a reply.

1 Using Microsoft® Outlook® or another email editor, send an email message to a friend or colleague. Use the formatting options to present your message in an attractive and effective way.

Title: Practising email

Text: I am learning how to send emails. I would be grateful if you would email me and attach a picture file to the message. I have attached a file with an image.

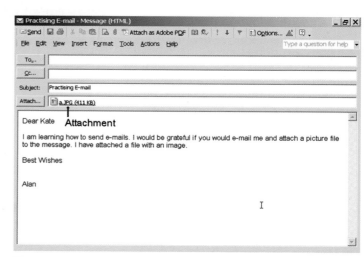

2 Attach an image file to the message (the images used in this book are available from the associated website if you do not have access to one). Figure 8.21 illustrates an example message.

Figure 8.21 Email with attachment

3 Check your message for mistakes.

4 Close Microsoft® Outlook® or your chosen email editor.

Activity 4
Replying to an email

1 Open your email system and access your Inbox to check if you have received any messages.

2 Open the message from your friend and read it.

3 Ensure that the attachment is checked for viruses.

4 Save the email attachment to a folder you have created.

5 Reply to the message.

   Many thanks for your help

6 Make sure your email system will save your reply.

7 Send your reply.

8 Close your email system.

Activity 5
Managing email

1 Open Microsoft® Outlook® or another email system and access your Inbox.

2 Create a series of folders to store your emails within the Inbox folder.

3 Create four folders for emails relating to work. They are:

- Proposals
- Confidential Matters
- Staff
- General

Figure 8.22 indicates the structure of the Inbox folders.

4 Close Microsoft® Outlook®.

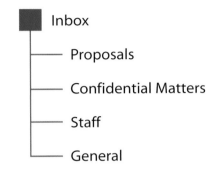

Figure 8.22 Email folders

Activity 6
Address Book

1 Open Microsoft® Outlook® or another email system and access your Inbox.

2 Open the Address Book and add the following new addresses.

Sheila Davidson
Unicorn Enterprises
234 High Road
Hatson

s.davidson@unicornenterprises.com

Janice Lord
Gold Ltd
Gordon House
Rose Street
Firstville

Janicelord@ltdgold.co.uk

Frank Stevenson
Philips plc
675 Lion Court
Kilston

FS@philplc.co.uk

3 Select an address and send a new email to them.

4 Close Microsoft® Outlook® or your chosen email editor.

Other ideas

- Send an email to a colleague with one of your files (one that you have created in another unit) attached.
- Search the World Wide Web for opportunities to shop for books, compact discs or videos.
- Search the World Wide Web for your favourite football, rugby or cricket team.
- Many websites provide you with the opportunity to email the developers with your feedback so take advantage of this to practise sending emails.
- Many television and radio programmes ask listeners and viewers to send them emails. This will give you an opportunity to practise your emailing.

SUMMARY

1 **Load Microsoft® Internet Explorer:** Use either the Start button and the All Programs menu or double click on the Microsoft® Internet Explorer icon on the Microsoft® Windows® desktop.

2 **Close Microsoft® Internet Explorer:** Click on the File menu item and the Close option or click on the Close button in the top right-hand corner of the application window.

3 **Load Microsoft® Outlook®:** Use either the Start button and the All Programs menu or double click on the Microsoft® Outlook® icon on Microsoft® Windows® desktop.

4 **Close Microsoft® Outlook®:** Click on the File menu item and the Exit option or click on the Close button in the top right-hand corner of the application window.

5 **URL (Uniform Resource Locator):** Website addresses are unique and consist of http (Hypertext Transfer Protocol), www (World Wide Web), the website host, a code to explain the type of organisation and a country code (e.g. http://www.bbc.co.uk).

   Perfect accuracy is essential.

6 **Links:** Links connect different web pages both within a particular website and to other websites. Links are indicated by underlined words, coloured text, the mouse pointer changing shape (i.e. from an arrow to an hand) or areas being highlighted by the mouse moving across them.

7 **Retracing your route:** Microsoft® Internet Explorer provides you with Back and Forward buttons. These allow you either to retrace your steps or to return along your route.

8 **Searching:** Complex websites often provide a means of searching for distinct pages. In a similar way there are search engines that will locate websites which relate to a user's interest. The search engines tend to operate by matching words which the users enter describing their interest. They match the words in different ways such as:

   - match with any words entered

   - match with all words entered in any order

   - match with the exact phrase entered

9 **Saving web addresses**: Microsoft® Internet Explorer lets you save URLs so that you can return to the website later. From the chosen website, select the Favorites menu and the Add to Favorites option to save the URL.

10 **Saving a web page**: Select the File menu and the Save option.

11 **Save an Image displayed on a web page**: Right click on the image to open a menu of options. Select Save Image As to open the Save Image window.

12 **Printing a web page**: Select the File menu and the Print option.

13 **Create a new email**: Select the New button on the toolbar of Microsoft® Outlook® and the Email window will be revealed. Enter your message and address, then click on the Send button.

    If you are connected to the Internet, the email will be sent immediately.

    If you are working off-line (i.e. you are not connected to the Internet) then the email is stored in the Outbox and the number of messages stored will be shown in brackets next to the title Outbox.

14 **Read a message**: Emails are stored in the Inbox. Clicking on the Inbox will reveal a list of messages. If you single click on a message, it will be highlighted and its contents revealed in the box below the list. If you double click on the message, then a new window will open, showing the message.

15 **Reply, Forward and Copy messages**: With the message window open, you can reply to the email, forward its contents to another person or copy the message to a folder.

    Reply – with the email highlighted or the message window open, click on the Reply or Reply to All buttons on the toolbar.

    Forward the message – with the email highlighted or the message window open, click on the Forward button on the toolbar and enter the email address of the person you want the message copied to.

    Copy the message to a folder – with the email highlighted, select the Edit menu and the Copy to Folder option. This allows you to place a copy of the message in one of the existing local folders or a new local folder.

16 **Attached files**: To open an attachment, double click on it and it will open providing you have the appropriate application available on your computer.

    To attach a file, start a new email (click on the New button) and click on the Insert File button (i.e. paperclip) on the toolbar. This will open the Insert File window from where you can select a file.

17 **Save and recall email addresses**: Select the Address Book icon (i.e. open book) to open the window. This offers a series of options that allow you to add, delete and send emails.

18 **Send an email using a saved address**: With the Address Book open, highlight the chosen address (single click), select the New Message button and a blank email will appear with the To line completed.

19 **Print an email**: With the email highlighted or the message window open, select the File menu and the Print option.

20 **Company policies and legislation**: It is essential to be aware of both your organisation's policy and the law relating to the use of the Internet.

Chapter 1

Unit 1

Integrated e-Document Production

This chapter will help you to:

- use a computer's system hardware and software safely and securely to create a variety of business documents

- use an input device to enter and manipulate data accurately from a variety of sources

- work with data files, using database and/or spreadsheet facilities to select and import data

- use mail merge facilities

- create, format and print a mail merge master document and mail merge documents

- create and print an integrated document, combining text, numeric and tabular data, an image and a chart

- format page layout and manipulate text according to a house style.

This chapter covers the content of unit 1 of the CLAiT Plus course, which is mandatory. There are no preconditions for studying this unit. However, its content does assume that you have the skills and understanding which are provided by the OCR Level 1 ICT course New CLAiT (e.g. Unit 1: File Management and e-Document Production).

Assessment

After studying unit 1, your skills and understanding are assessed during a three-hour practical assignment. This is set by OCR and marked locally. However, the marking will be externally moderated by OCR. This ensures that the standard is being applied correctly across the many different providers of OCR CLAiT Plus. If you are unsuccessful, you can be reassessed using a different assignment.

An alternative approach is for you to be assessed by either an OCR set scenario or a locally designed assignment.

Files and folders

All information stored on a computer is held in a file. Each file has an individual name and they are stored within folders. Folders are also sometimes called directories. Folders serve essentially the same function as paper folders do in filing cabinets, that is, they allow records to be stored in an organised and systematic way. Computer files need to be organised for similar reasons that paper files and records do. You need to be able to locate them so you can read, update (change), copy, remove, rename or move a file.

The Microsoft Windows® operating system provides a range of functions that allow you to:

- create and name folders (directories)
- open, close and save files
- delete files and folders
- move files and folders
- copy files and folders
- rename files and folders
- protect files
- print the file structure.

The file management application provided within Microsoft Windows® is called Windows® Explorer, shown in figure 1.1. This is opened by clicking on the Start button, then highlighting the All Programs option to open another menu. Highlight the Accessories item

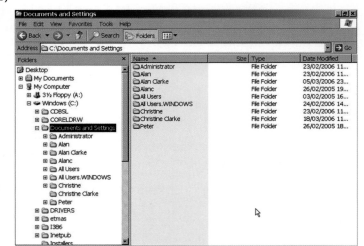

Figure 1.1 Windows® Explorer

to open a menu with the Windows® Explorer option. The Explorer's application window is divided into a number of areas. These are:

- title bar (e.g. Documents and Settings)
- menu bar
- toolbar
- address (i.e. the highlighted folder)
- folders (on the left-hand side of the display) – showing the structure of folders stored on the hard disk, floppy disk, CD-ROM or other storage media. The plus sign indicates that a folder has more folders stored within it. If you click on the plus sign, the structure will be opened up to show these folders. The revealed folders may also be shown with a plus sign, indicating further folders stored within the revealed ones
- contents of the folder (on the right-hand side of the display). This shows the files and folders stored within the highlighted folder.

The folders and files can be opened by double-clicking on them with the mouse pointer. The files will only open if an application which is able to read the file is present on the computer system. If no suitable application is identified by the system, a message will appear asking you to identify the correct application. When Microsoft Windows® is unable to locate a suitable application, it offers you the opportunity to select one in which to open the file.

Windows® Explorer functions

Windows® Explorer provides the tools to create new folders and to delete, rename, move, copy and save files and folders. These functions are available on the File (figure 1.2) and Edit menus. The Edit menu provides the Move, Cut, Copy and Paste options.

- ■ **New** – create a new folder in the folder currently being viewed in Windows® Explorer
- ■ **Delete** – deletes the file or folder highlighted in Windows® Explorer
- ■ **Rename** – allows you to change the name of the highlighted file or folder
- ■ **Cut** – allows you to cut a file or folder with the intention of moving it to a new location using the **Paste** option
- ■ **Copy** – allows you to copy a file or folder to a new location using the **Paste** option, but leaving the original file or folder unaffected.
- ■ **Paste** – allows you to place a copied or cut file or folder in a new location
- ■ **Properties** – this allows you to control who has access to specific files and folders and to archive files.

These functions enable you to control your files and folders. They allow you to administer them in a similar way to moving paper files and folders in a conventional filing cabinet. When you have hundreds of folders and thousands of files it is essential that you are able to control them. When you initially start a task it is natural to create a folder to store the files you create. Later you may need to move it so that it relates to folders and files that hold similar information.

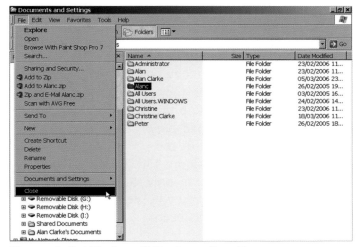

Figure 1.2 Windows® Explorer functions

Protect and secure files

All organisations and many individual activities rely on information technology (IT) to achieve their purposes. The main outcome of any IT activity is the file. It is therefore important to be able to protect files from unauthorised use, damage and loss. Microsoft Windows® XP provides several functions to control access and protect files. This includes controlling the operations that individual users can perform. Users are broadly divided into two groups:

- ■ administrators
- ■ limited.

Administrators are able to make changes to the computer system configuration. They are often senior or technical staff who have the skills to support other users. Limited users are only allowed to undertake their own activities. They are not authorised to carry out more extensive tasks.

Passwords are allocated so that when you log on to the system it knows

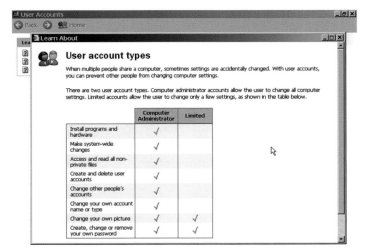

Figure 1.3 Types of user

what activities you are allowed to perform. Figure 1.3 shows what the two types of user are able to do.

Read-only

Some document files may need to be protected from unauthorised use, such as master documents which should not be changed. The Properties function allows you to designate a file as read-only, that is, computer users can read its contents but cannot alter it. A master file may contain the specification of a product, describe a standard business process or represent an agreement with a partner organisation. These types of document should only be changed as

part of an agreed process, so it is useful to designate them read-only.

In order to make a file read-only, you need to highlight it within Windows® Explorer, select the File menu and the Properties option to open the Properties window. Click on the General tab and the Read-only option is displayed towards the bottom of the window (figure 1.4). To make the selected file Read-only, click in the radio button and you will see a tick appear to show it has been enabled.

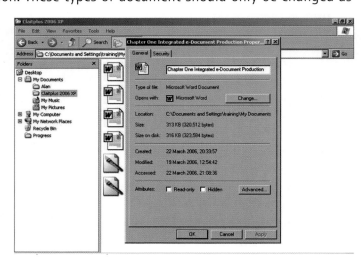

Figure 1.4 Properties

Archives

There are often files that come to the end of their lives but are important to keep. They may be records of projects, financial or other information that you may wish to refer to over a longer

period. These files need to be archived, which is basically a process of long-term storage.

Another useful function available within the Properties window is to create archive files. Again, you need to highlight the file or folder within Windows® Explorer and then select the Properties option in the File menu. In the General tab is a button labelled Advanced. If you click on it, the Advanced Attributes window opens (figure 1.5). This provides an option to create archive files by clicking on the appropriate radio button.

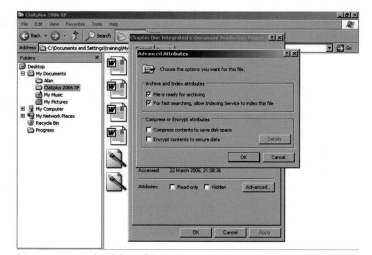

Figure 1.5 Archive files

Types of files

There are many different types of files; each is shown as a different icon (figure 1.6) or ending with a full stop and three letters that indicate the type of file and helps you to distinguish between them. Some examples are:

- .doc   – Microsoft Word® document
- .bmp   – bitmap image file
- .jpg/.jpeg   – image file
- .txt   – text document
- .htm   – hypertext markup document (i.e. a web page)
- .exe   – application file (i.e. an executable file)
- .ppt   – Microsoft PowerPoint® presentation (i.e. presentation graphics)
- .mdb   – Microsoft Access® database
- .xls   – Microsoft Excel® spreadsheet

Figure 1.6 shows a range of file icons, such as:

- Acme Newsagent – Microsoft Excel® file
- CLAiT 2006 – Microsoft PowerPoint® file
- Customer Accounts – Microsoft Access® file
- East Wolds – bitmap
- Document – Microsoft Word® file

Most files can be opened by double-clicking on them if a compatible application is available on the computer. An executable file is one which launches an application.

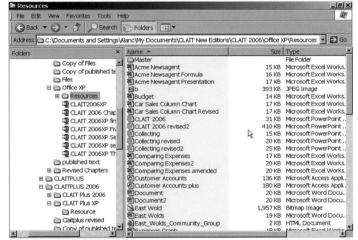

Figure 1.6 File icons

Printing a Window

If you wish to obtain a permanent record of a file structure or the contents of a window, Windows® provides a standard function to allow you to produce a printout of the contents. If you hold down the ALT key and then press the Print Screen (sometimes Print Scrn or PrtSc) key, a copy of the window contents is held on the Clipboard. This is a special area in the computer's memory used to store information. You can then paste the image into a document (e.g. in Microsoft Word®) and print it using the normal functions of the application. If you want to capture the contents of the whole display, you need only press the Print Screen key and then paste the image into a document.

You will be required to use the Print Screen option to capture images of your work as part of the assessment process. If you are asked to change a file into read-only, then the Print Screen function will allow you to show the Properties window as evidence that you have achieved the objective.

Entering data

When you apply for a bank account or credit card, or change insurance company, the forms you complete are often used to enter your information into the company's computer systems. Almost every organisation keeps records on its customers, clients, staff and suppliers. These all require people to enter data into the computer and many forms are now designed to assist the process.

Computer data can be used for a variety of purposes once entered into a system. It forms the basis for managers to make decisions which affect both the organisation and the individual or company the records refer to. If incorrect, a great deal of harm can potentially result. Many organisations check that both the input documents and the data entered are correct. Proofreading documents and screen displays is an important skill to master.

When inputting thousands of documents, even a small reduction in the quantity of data to be entered will make a substantial improvement to productivity. This is often achieved by encoding the data so that a single letter or code represents a chunk of information. For example:

- A means an overdraft limit up to £250
- B means an overdraft limit up to £500
- C means an overdraft limit up to £1000.

Spelling and grammar checkers

Applications can often assist you with checking the accuracy of your documents. Most modern word processors, spreadsheets and databases provide spelling and grammar checkers.

Microsoft Word® provides both. These are available in the Tools menu as the Spelling and Grammar option. This will check the document, starting from the position of the cursor, and work towards the end of the document before going back to the start. When the option is clicked, a dialog window (figure 1.7) appears and works through the document, stopping each time it locates what it considers an error. This can take several forms, such as:

- punctuation
- capital letter
- grammatical error
- spelling mistake.

You need to decide if you want to take the advice the checker is offering (i.e. use the Change button) or if you are going to ignore it (Ignore button). In some cases the checker will offer more than one answer and you need to choose which is correct or whether they are all wrong. When you make your decision the checker acts, then moves on, to stop when it finds another item that it considers to be incorrect. It will tell you when it has completed the whole document.

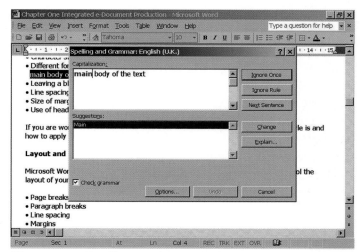

Figure 1.7 Spelling and grammar

Spelling and grammar checkers only suggest changes to you. You need to decide if you want to act on them. They may be wrong, so simply agreeing with the advice may add errors to the document. You must be sure that the change is correct. However, checkers are very good at locating typographical (data entry) errors.

You can set the spelling and grammar checker to work as you enter information. You select the Tools menu and the Options item to reveal the Options window. You need to choose the Spelling and Grammar tab, which allows you to configure both the checkers. When you enter information, the checkers underline items that they identify as a spelling mistake in red and grammar errors in green.

English date formats

The way dates are presented varies in different countries. For example, in Britain dates are shown as: day, month and year, while in the USA they are presented as month, day and year. Obviously there is room for confusion if they are mixed or used in an inappropriate way. In addition, there are several different formats for presenting English dates, such as:

- 13 February 1952
- 13/02/1952
- 13-02-52
- 13 Feb 52

Often, when you are entering dates, the format is specified and it is critical that you follow the specification. If you do not, it is likely that the application (e.g. the database) will not recognise the date format and thus will be unable to locate it. This will produce errors.

Font families

CLAiT Plus uses the term font families. There are two types, called Sans Serif and Serif. A serif type font has small projections on the ends of the characters, while a sans serif type font does not. You might say that serif fonts have more fancy characters or that sans serif fonts have plain characters.

The exercises sometimes use font names rather than families, so below are some examples of sans serif and serif.

Serif:
E Courier New
E Times New Roman

Sans serif:
E Arial
E Tahoma

Exercise 1

Data entry

1 Open Microsoft Word® by clicking on the Start button, highlighting All Programs and selecting Microsoft Word® or by double-clicking on the Word® icon on the Microsoft Windows® desktop.

2 Enter the data input sheet below:

Name: Janet Jenkins   Date: 12/01/02

Area: South-East

Visit – Order

Order taken during visit to Acme Engineering for period 1/04/02 to 30/06/02. Stock to be called off with delivery within 72 hours of request for stock.

Order
     Part No. 123   64
     Part No. 789   23
     Part No. 901   74
     Part No. 314   17

Discount 5% for volume purchase

Standards terms – payment of order within 30 days of delivery

3 Note the layout of the information, the standard format of the dates and the use of codes rather than describing the stock ordered (e.g. Part No. 123). There are several different ways of formatting dates and some applications will only accept particular ways, so it is important to get it right.

4 Systematically check your document against the input sheet to ensure that it is correct. If you find an error, move the cursor to the error by clicking once at the desired location. You can delete the mistake using either the backspace (deletes to the left) or delete (deletes to the right) key and entering the correction.

5 Check the spelling and grammar of the entry (select the Tools menu and the Spelling and Grammar option).

6 Insert a floppy disk into the drive and save your document by selecting the File menu and the Save option. This will reveal the Save As dialog window (figure 1.8). Change the Save in: box to Floppy (A:) by using the down arrow at

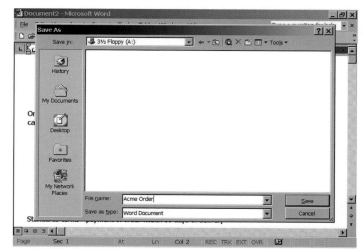

Figure 1.8 Save As

continued

end of box to show a list of options. Save the document as File name: Acme Order. When you are ready, click the Save button. You have now saved your document as a file called Acme Order.

7 Close Microsoft Word® by selecting the File menu and the Exit option (or continue with Exercise 2).

Amending documents

A key advantage of a computer application is that it allows you to amend your documents. Microsoft Office® applications let you delete, insert, copy and move information within a document. These functions operate in a similar way in all Microsoft Office® applications. They are available in the File and Edit menus. The functions operate in the following ways:

- Delete – insert the cursor before or after the word or phrase you need to remove and then use the delete or backspace key on the keyboard. The backspace key deletes to the left while the delete key works to the right. Alternatively, highlight the word or phrase and press the delete key to remove the selected items.

- Insert – place the cursor in the desired location and then enter the new information. This requires that you position the pointer at the new location and click the mouse button. In addition, on the keyboard is an insert key (labelled Ins). When this is pressed, any data entered from the keyboard will overwrite existing information. This occasionally happens by accident and can be confusing until you realise the key has been pressed. To cancel the key, press it again.

- Copy – highlight the word or phrase you want to copy and then select the Edit menu and click on the Copy option. Move the cursor to the location where you want to copy the information to and then select the Edit menu and the Paste option. The copied items will now appear at the new location and will also remain at their original place.

- Move – highlight the word or phrase you want to move and then select the Edit menu and click on the Cut option. The word or phrase will disappear. Move the cursor to the location where you want to move the information to and then select the Edit menu and the Paste option. The cut (moved) items will now appear at the new location.

Exercise 2

Amend a document

1 Insert your floppy disk into the drive.

2 Open Microsoft Word® by clicking on the Start button, highlighting All Programs and selecting Microsoft Word® or double-clicking on the Word® icon on the Microsoft Windows® desktop.

3 Open the file Acme Order by selecting the File menu and the Open option to reveal the Open dialog window. Change the Look in: box to Floppy (A:) using the arrow button at

the end of the box. This will reveal the files stored on the floppy in the central area of the window. Double-click on the file Acme Order or single-click to highlight it and then click on the Open button.

4 The document Acme Order will appear in the Microsoft Word® work area.

Figure 1.9 **Proofreading**

The figure shows a boxed document:

Name: Janet Jenkins   **Date:** 12/01/02

Area: South-East

Visit - Order

Order taken during visit to Acme Engineering for period 1/04/02 to 30/06/02. Stock to be called off with delivery within 72 hours of request for stock.

Order

Part No. 123	64
Part No. 789	23
Part No. 901	74
Part No. 314	17

Discount 5% for volume purchase

Standards terms - payment of order within 30 days of delivery

5 Figure 1.9 shows a printout of the input sheet after it has been proofread.

6 Make the changes indicated by the proofreading:

a) Insert a new paragraph between the sentence ending 'to 30/06/02' and sentence beginning 'Stock to be'.
b) Insert 24/ so that it reads 24/72 hours of request for stock.
c) Insert letters (2 tabs from numbers), as below:

Order
Part No. 123	64	A
Part No. 789	23	B
Part No. 901	74	C
Part No. 314	17	C

d) Indent the line starting with Order one tab.
e) Indent the line starting with Discount one tab.
f) Delete the letter 's' so that Standards now reads Standard.

7 Revised document should now look like this:

Name: Janet Jenkins   Date: 12/01/02

Area: South-East

Visit – Order

Order taken during visit to Acme Engineering for period 1/04/02 to 30/06/02.

Stock to be called off with delivery within 24/72 hours of request for stock.

```
     Order
     Part No. 123    64    A
     Part No. 789    23    B
     Part No. 901    74    C
     Part No. 314    17    C

     Discount 5% for volume purchase

     Standard terms – payment of order within 30 days of delivery
```

8 Save your revised document as file Acme Order Amended by selecting the File menu and the Save As option.

9 You have now amended the document in relation to the proofreading corrections. This has allowed you to practise deleting and inserting information. You now have the opportunity to practise copying and moving text around the document. Try:

   a) Reordering the list of parts so that they are presented in numerical order

```
e.g.  Part No. 123    64    A
      Part No. 314    17    C
      Part No. 789    23    B
      Part No. 901    74    C
```

Use the Copy, Cut and Paste functions to achieve this result.

   b) Using these functions to move and copy text until you are confident that you understand their use.

10 Close Microsoft Word® by selecting the File menu and the Exit option.

Proofreading symbols

Proofreaders employ a number of symbols to identify changes they are recommending. The symbols are written on the document and then other symbols are placed in the margin to explain the nature of the amendment. Figure 1.10 gives some examples of common symbols.

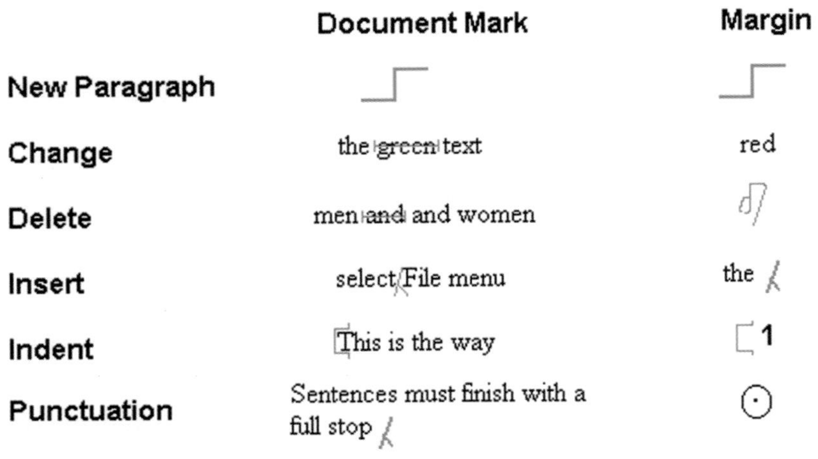

	Document Mark	Margin
New Paragraph	⌐	⌐
Change	the green text	red
Delete	men and and women	⌧
Insert	select File menu	the ∧
Indent	This is the way	⌐1
Punctuation	Sentences must finish with a full stop ∧	⊙

Figure 1.10 Proofreading Symbols

Creating a new document

One of the most useful computer applications is word-processing. Modern word processors, such as Microsoft Word®, provide users with functions to lay out documents precisely, including:

- margins, line spacing, page and paragraph breaks
- headers and footers
- bullet point lists.

Many organisations want to present a standard appearance to their clients and therefore adopt a defined house style for all their documents. This normally includes:

- font (e.g. Times New Roman)
- character size (e.g. 12)
- different fonts and character sizes for headings and the main body of the text
- leaving a blank line between each paragraph
- line spacing (e.g. 1.5)
- size of margins
- use of headers and footers (e.g. page numbers and date inserted).

If you are working within an organisation you need to understand what the house style is and how to apply it.

Layout and formatting functions

Microsoft Word® and many other word processors offer a number of functions to control the layout of your documents. These include:

- page breaks
- paragraph breaks
- line spacing
- margins.

Microsoft Word® will automatically start a new page when the old one is full. Page break is the means of starting a new page when the last one is not full. You are thus controlling the layout of the document. Page break is available in the Insert menu under the Break option.

There are several ways of indicating a new paragraph and you select them in Microsoft Word® by using the Format menu and the Paragraph option. Within this option you can also change the line spacing of the text, that is, the space you want to leave between the lines of text. If you are creating a document which will be proofread, then often you will double-space the text so that the proofreader has space to write notes on the document.

Margins are the spaces at the left, right, top and bottom of the document in which you are entering information. Microsoft Word® allows you to change all four margins in any way that you want, by using the File menu and the Page Setup option.

Page setup

When creating a document it is often useful to start by setting up the layout of the pages. You are free to alter this later if you change your mind. Once you have opened a new document, the layout can be established using the File menu and the Page Setup option. This opens the Page Setup dialog window (Figure 1.11).

Page Setup has several tabs on the top of the window which, if clicked, reveal windows providing more options. The Margins tab in the Page Setup window allows you to change the right, left, top and bottom margins of your documents and to preview how the changes affect the appearance of the document. You can also change the orientation of the page – portrait or landscape.

By clicking on the Paper tab, the options shown in figure 1.12 can be seen.

By clicking on the Layout tab, the options shown in figure 1.13 can be seen. Among the options are the ability to change the size of the header and footer. These are special areas at the top (header) and bottom (footer) of the document in which you can place information which will be repeated on all pages of the publication. Headers are often the place to put the title of the document, while footers may contain details of the author. In both locations you can insert automatic fields which change, such as page numbers.

Headers and footers

You can insert a header or a footer (or both), depending on the type of

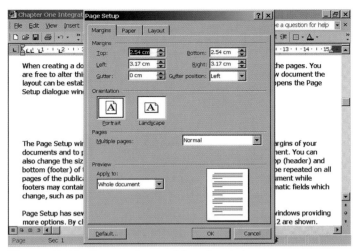

Figure 1.11 Page setup – Margins tab

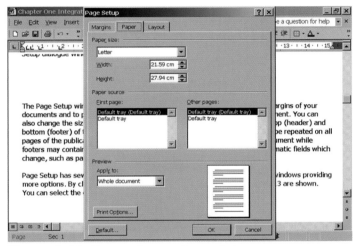

Figure 1.12 Page set up – Paper tab

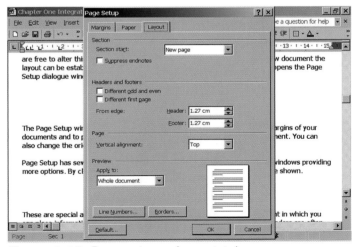

Figure 1.13 Page setup – Layout tab

document you are designing. The function is available on the View menu. Select the Header and Footer option, which opens a header area on your document and a toolbar providing extra options. If you scroll down the page you will find the footer area at the bottom of the page.

Once the header or footer area is visible (i.e. the area enclosed by a dotted line) you can enter text. This will appear at the cursor which you will see flashing in the top left-hand corner of the area. To insert a field within the area, click on the menu option of your choice (e.g. Insert Page Number). If you place your pointer over each option, a small label will appear to name the function. The menu has wider functionality, including providing access to the Page Setup dialog window. At the start of the menu is a button, Insert AutoText, that allows you to insert a range of information, including the author's name, the last date the publication was printed, and so on. Figure 1.14 shows many of the options to add extra information and fields to either the header or footer area.

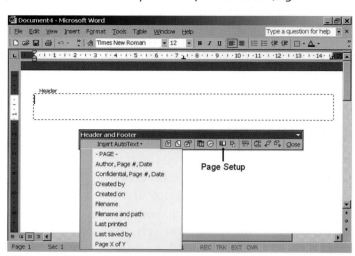

Figure 1.14 Header and footer options

Bullets and numbering

A useful way of presenting information is a list, which is easy to read and understand. Microsoft Word® provides you with the means of producing bullet point lists, which start with a symbol, letter or number so that the information is structured. They are accessed by selecting the Format menu and clicking on the Bullets and Numbering option. This opens the Bullets and Numbering window (figure 1.15).

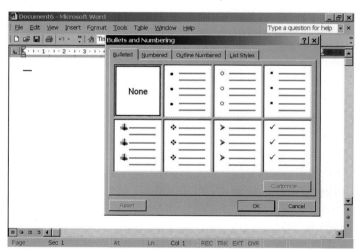

Figure 1.15 Bullets and numbers

Figure 1.15 shows some of the different bullet point options available. The window is divided into tabs. If you click on a tab (e.g. Numbered) you can see a range of other options, including numbered, aphabetical and indented lists. To select a bullet, you single-click to highlight it and then click on the OK button, or you double-click the selection.

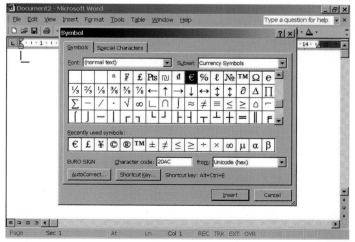

Figure 1.16 Special symbols

Special symbols

Microsoft Word® provides a wide range of special symbols which you can insert in your text. These are accessed by selecting the Insert menu and clicking on the Symbol option. This will open the Symbol window (figure 1.16), which provides access to a large number of symbols. These are selected by highlighting the symbol and then clicking the Insert button. The symbol is then inserted into the text at the cursor.

Search and replace

It is important in any word-processed document to be able to locate words or phrases in a document and replace them with an alternative. You could simply read through the passage and find each word or phrase and then replace it, by deleting the original words and entering the new ones from the keyboard. The problem with this type of approach is that it is easy to make errors (e.g. by incorrectly spelling the new word) or to miss one of the words you are seeking to change. Microsoft Word® provides you with a means to automate the process.

If you select the Edit menu and click on the Replace option, the Find and Replace window (figure 1.17) will appear. Enter the word or phrase you are seeking in the Find what: box, and then the words you are replacing them with in the Replace with: box. Start the process by clicking on the Find Next button. The function will search through the document until it locates a match. You then have the choice of replacing the words with your new selection. Clicking on the Find Next button will move the search through the document. This systematic approach will ensure no errors are made.

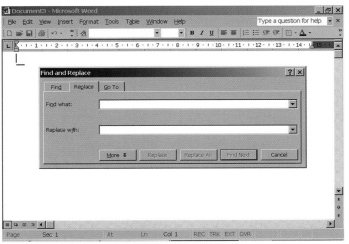

Figure 1.17 Find and Replace window

Widows and orphans

When creating a document there is always the risk that you will produce what are termed widows and orphans. These are isolated words or sentences. The page break may leave an isolated word or phrase on one page while the text it relates to is on another. This is poor presentation and Microsoft Word® provides you with a variety of ways to avoid it, including:

- Insert a page break to avoid leaving text behind which relates to the new page.
- Change the font or the character size so that the amount of text that can fit on a page is altered and may avoid widows and orphans.
- Change the line spacing so, again, the volume of text that fits on a page changes.

Microsoft Word® also offers an automatic way of minimising orphans and widows. This is available in the Format menu within Paragraph option. If you select the Line and Page Breaks tab it will open a window with the Widow/Orphan control option. Click in the associated radio button, which will insert a tick in the box. This adjusts the line spacing and page breaks to avoid widows and orphans.

House style

Word-processing enables almost everyone to write letters and other documents. This provides considerable flexibility to organisations, but it does make it difficult to ensure the quality of documents. Organisations have addressed the problem of quality by setting standards which are often called house styles. This normally sets a standard for:

- the layout for letters (e.g. position of address, date and size of margins)
- fonts
- character size.

This gives a standard look and feel to documents so that a minimum quality standard is established. Organisations often spend considerable effort developing a house style. They insist that all employees follow the standard.

Exercise 3 below is intended to help you practise laying out a document in accordance with a defined house style. The house style is:

Margins (left, right, top and bottom)	3 cm
Orientation	Portrait
Header	Text centred
Footer	Automatic date field and automatic page number – one line below date, both centred
Line spacing	Single
Body text	Times New Roman and size 12, left-justified
Bullet text	Times New Roman and size 12, left-justified
Tables	Times New Roman, size 12, left-justified Column headings, Times New Roman, size 12, bold and centred with gridlines

This house style should also be applied to Exercises 3, 4, 5 and 6.

Exercise 3

Layout

1 Open Microsoft Word® by clicking on the Start button, highlighting All Programs and selecting Microsoft Word® or double-clicking on the Word® icon on the Microsoft Windows® desktop.

2 Using the File menu and the Page Setup, set the four margins to 3 cm and both header and footer to 2 cm.

3 Enter the passage below, which includes using a bullet list, in accordance with the house style:

The Solar System consists of the Sun and nine planets which are in orbit around it. The Solar

continued

System began life 4,500 million years ago when the planets condensed out of an immense cloud of gas. The nine planets are:

- Mercury
- Venus
- Earth
- Mars
- Jupiter
- Saturn
- Uranus
- Neptune
- Pluto

In addition to the planets there are approximately 63 moons and many thousands of asteroids. Moons orbit the planets while the asteroids orbit the Sun. Asteroids vary in size from several miles across to simple lumps of rock. They are often irregular in shape and have strange orbits.

The planets are divided into two groups. Those planets which orbit close to the Sun (e.g. Mercury, Venus, Earth and Mars) are called the inner planets. Planets that are further away from the Sun such as Jupiter, Saturn, Uranus, Neptune and Pluto are called the outer planets.

4 Systematically check your document to ensure that it is correct. If you find a mistake, move the cursor to the error by clicking once at the desired location. You can delete the mistake using the backspace (deletes to the left) or delete (deletes to the right) keys and enter the correction.

5 Check the spelling and grammar of the entry (select the Tools menu and the Spelling and Grammar option).

6 Insert your floppy disk into the drive and save your document by selecting the File menu and the Save option. This will reveal the Save As dialog window. Change the Save in: box to Floppy (A:) by using the down arrow at the end of the box to show the list of options. Save the document as File name: Solar System. Click the Save button. You have now saved your document as a file called Solar System.

7 Now add a header and footer to the document. The header should read Solar System, in Arial font with a character size of 16. The title should be centred. The footer should show the page number centred on the page and one line below the date.

8 Save your document again by selecting the File menu and the Save option.

9 Close Microsoft Word® by selecting the File menu and the Exit option.

Indenting text

In any document you may wish to indent your text. There are several ways of doing this. The most straightforward is to use the tab key on the keyboard, which will indent the text. You can set the size of the tab by selecting the Format menu and the Tabs option, which will open the Tabs window (figure 1.18). In this window you can change the size of the tab and the alignment.

An alternative approach is to select the Format menu and click on the Paragraph option. This will reveal the paragraph window (figure 1.19) that allows you to set the size of the indent from both margins (i.e. left and right) and see the effects in the Preview window. The Special box provides access to indents for the first line, hanging or none. First-line indent will indent only the first line of each paragraph, while a hanging indent sets the whole paragraph except the first line to be indented. For example:

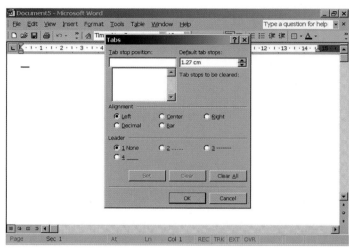

Figure 1.18 Tabs window

First line indent

Aaaaaaaaaaaaaaaaaaaaaaaaaaaaaaaaaaaaaaaaaaaaaaaaaaaaaaaaaaaaaaaaaaaaaaaaaaa aaaaaaaaaaaaaaaaaaaaaaaaaaaaaaaaaaaaaaaaaaaaaaaaaaaaaaaaaaaaaaaaaaaaaaaaaaaaa

Hanging indent

Aaaaaaaaaaaaaaaaaaaaaaaaaaaaaaaaaaaaaaaaaaaaaaaaaaaaaaaaaaaaaaaaaaaaaa
aaaaaaaaaaaaaaaaaaaaaaaaaaaaaaaaaaaaaaaaaaaaaaaaaaaaaaaaaaaaaaaaaaaa
aaaaaaaaaaaaaaaaaaaaaaaaaaaaaaaaaaaaaaaaaaaaaaaaaaaaaaaaaaaaaaaaaaaa
aaaaaaaaaaaaaaaaaaaaaaaaaaaaaaaaaaaaaaaaaaaaaaaaaaaaaaaaaaaaaaaaaaaa

The Paragraph window also enables you to set line spacing and control pagination.

A third method is to use the ruler at the top of the Microsoft Word® work area. If it is not visible you can reveal it by selecting the View menu and clicking on Ruler. By dragging the stops at the end of the ruler you can create first-line and hanging indents. It is possible to change the right indent or tab by dragging the right ruler stop.

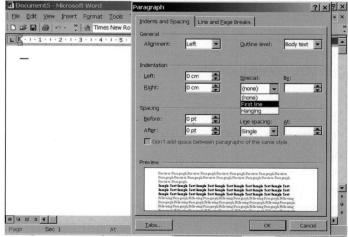

Figure 1.19 Paragraph window

Exercise 4

Indents

1 Insert your floppy disk into the drive.

2 Open Microsoft Word® by clicking on the Start button, highlighting All Programs and selecting Microsoft Word® or double-clicking on the Word® icon on the Microsoft Windows® desktop.

3 Open the file Solar System by selecting the File menu and the Open option to reveal the Open dialog window. Change the Look in: box to Floppy (A:) using the arrow button at the end of the box. This will reveal the files stored on the floppy in the central area of the window. Double-click on the file Solar System or single-click to highlight it and then click on the Open button.

4 The document Solar System will appear in the Microsoft Word® work area.

5 Experiment with the three alternative approaches to indenting your text. Try to indent the start of each paragraph and also to create hanging indents. Continue until you are confident you can use the alternative approaches.

6 There is no need to save your efforts.

7 Close Microsoft Word® by selecting the File menu and the Exit option. When you close without saving you will see a window appear asking you if you want to save. In this instance you do not, but on other occasions it may stop you making a mistake.

Tables

Microsoft Word® and many other word processors can present information in the form of a table. To insert a table into a document requires selecting the Table menu (figure 1.20), highlighting Insert and clicking on the Table option. This will open the Insert Table window (figure 1.21).

The Insert Table window allows you to set the number of rows and columns in the table and to set the size of each column. The features (e.g. size of columns, number of rows and columns) are altered using the up and down

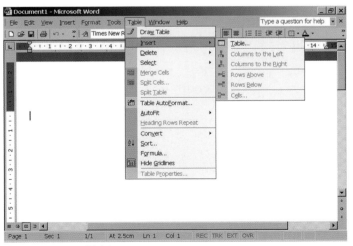

Figure 1.20 Table menu

arrows alongside the appropriate boxes. By clicking on the arrows, you can change the feature. Once you have set the parameters of the table you can insert the table by clicking on the OK button.

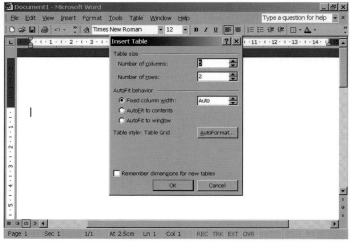

Figure 1.21 Insert Table window

Exercise 5

Tables

1 Insert your floppy disk into the drive.

2 Open Microsoft Word® by clicking on the Start button, highlighting All Programs and selecting Microsoft Word® or double-click on the Word® icon on the Microsoft Windows® desktop.

3 Open the file Solar System by selecting the File menu and the Open option to reveal the Open dialog window. Change Look in: box to Floppy (A:) using the arrow button at the end of the box. This will reveal the files stored on the floppy in the central area of the window. Double-click on the file Solar System or single-click to highlight it and then click on the Open button.

4 The document Solar System will appear in the Microsoft Word® work area.

5 You are now going to insert the table shown below into this document.

Planet	Year Length	Moons	Atmosphere
Mercury	88 days	None	None
Venus	225 days	None	Carbon dioxide
Earth	365 days	One	Nitrogen and oxygen
Mars	687 days	Two	Very thin
Jupiter	12 years	Sixteen	Gas planet
Saturn	29 years	Eighteen	Gas planet
Uranus	84 years	Seventeen	Gas planet
Neptune	165 years	Eight	Gas planet
Pluto	248 years	One	Thin

6 Insert this table at the end of your document by selecting the Table menu, highlighting Insert option and clicking on Table to reveal the Insert Table window. Set the table parameters to 10 rows and 4 columns. Text is added by clicking in the respective cells or by using the tab keys to move between the rows and columns.

7 Check the accuracy of your table and correct any errors by clicking in the appropriate cell.

8 Save your document by selecting the File menu and the Save As option. This will reveal the Save As dialog window. Change the Save in: box to Floppy (A:) by using the down arrow at end of the box to show the list of options. Save the document as File name: Solar System Table. When you are ready, click the Save button. You have now saved your document as a file called Solar System Table.

9 If you review the table you will see that the columns do not fit the information you have entered. To customise the widths of the columns you must highlight the columns you want to change. In this case, highlight them all by clicking in the Planets cell and holding down the mouse button, then drag the pointer down to the bottom right-hand corner of the table.

10 Select the Table menu and highlight the AutoFit option to reveal a range of options. Consider the different choices. Click on the AutoFit to Contents option. You will notice that your table changes. Figure 1.22 shows the table.

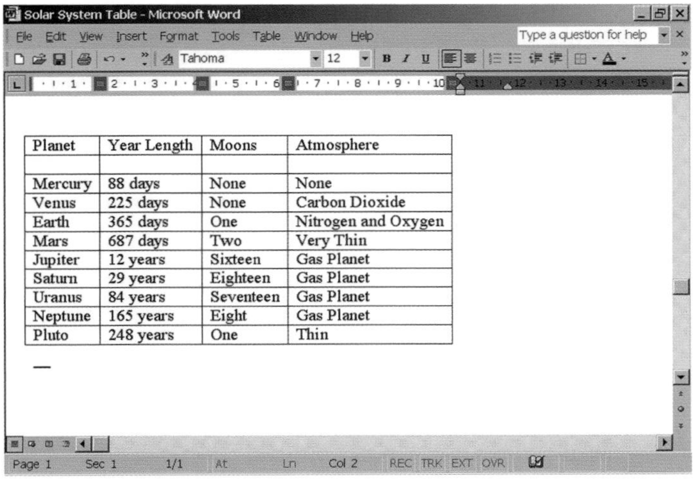

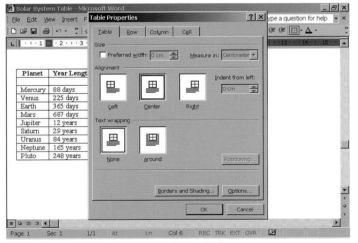

Figure 1.22 Table

11 You can change the appearance of the information within the table by highlighting the cells and selecting the option you desire, such as font, character size, bold, italics, change alignment (i.e. left, right and centre). Remember, your design is governed by the house style (see Exercise 3).

12 Centre and embolden the titles of the columns.

13 Change the font size of the whole table to 10.

14 You can align the table as well as the information it contains by using the Table menu and clicking on the Table Properties option. This will reveal the Table Properties window (figure 1.23). The window has a number of tabs, which will reveal tools to operate on rows, columns and cells.

Figure 1.23 Table Properties window

Integrated e-Document Production

203

15 Table tab allows you to align the whole table. Use it to centre the whole table.

16 Save your document again by selecting the File menu and the Save option.

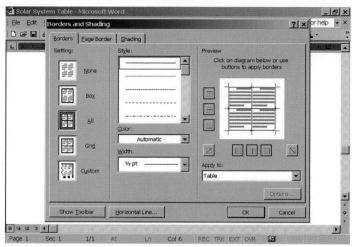

Figure 1.24 Borders and shading

17 The other tabs allow you to change the height of rows, width of columns and alignment of text in each cell. Explore the options but do not make any permanent changes (i.e. use the Undo and Redo options in the Edit menu). Continue your experiments until you understand the different options.

18 You can also change the borders and shading of your table by using the Format menu and the Borders and Shading option to reveal the Borders and Shading window (figure 1.24).

19 The Borders and Shading window enables you to change the borders of your table by using the Setting, Style, Colour and Width of lines. You can explore the different options since the Preview window shows you what your choices look like.

20 Highlight your table and, using the Borders and Shading window, select an attractive border.

21 Highlight your table and, using the Borders and Shading window and the Shading tab, select an appropriate shading colour (e.g. yellow). Figure 1.25 shows our table.

22 Save your document again by selecting the File menu and the Save option.

23 Print your document by selecting the File menu and Print option.

24 You can now practise using the Find and Replace function available within the Edit menu. Searching from the start of the document, locate the words 'Gas planet' and replace them with the word 'Gas giant'. You should find the phrase four times.

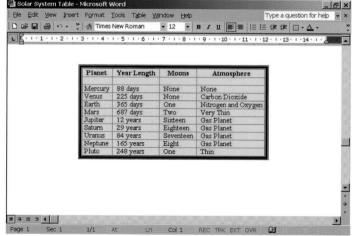

Figure 1.25 Revised table

25 There is no need to save the amended document since you are simply practising.

26 Close Microsoft Word® by selecting the File menu and the Exit option. When you exit without saving, you will see that a window appears to ask if you want to save. This is intended to prevent you losing data. In this case, you do not need to save, but sometimes you will, so always consider the question before making a decision.

Integrating documents

In the modern workplace you are often working with a variety of applications, such as word-processing, spreadsheets, charts and graphs and databases. It is useful to be able to import files from one application into another. Several integrated packages of applications, such as Microsoft Office®, provide tools to help you create an integrated document.

Microsoft Word® allows you to import files from other Microsoft Office® applications, to insert images from Clip Art collections and to add images you have created yourself. If you consider the options within the Insert menu you will see a variety of tools to import files into your document. In addition, you can simply use the Copy, Cut and Paste functions (i.e. Edit menu) to copy or move an image from one Microsoft Office® application and paste it into another.

The Picture option provides access to a range of functions to import images into your documents, including Clip Art, images stored as a file, WordArt, pictures scanned or photographed with a digital camera and charts produced in Microsoft Excel®.

Using the File option you can insert a file from another application to produce an integrated document. In many cases, Microsoft Word® will convert the file format into one with which it is compatible. However, some formats will not be accepted and you may see a warning message the first time you attempt to import a file, telling you that you need to install the file conversion software.

Warning Message
Microsoft Word® can't import the specified format.
This feature is not currently installed. Would you like to install it now?

To install the conversion program you need to insert the Microsoft Office® CD-ROM and click on the OK button, then follow the instructions on the screen.

Nevertheless, the Copy, Cut and Paste options are perhaps the most straightforward way of transferring resources between applications. You can copy a database table, spreadsheet or image and paste its contents into Microsoft Word® in the same way you can within an application.

The general process of importing images, charts, data or text using copy and paste is straightforward. In the original application (e.g. Microsoft Excel®, Access) highlight the sheet, table or data that you want to import and copy it using the Copy function, which is often available in the Edit menu. Now move to Microsoft Word®, or the application in which you are creating the integrated document, and use the paste function to insert the copied object. The copied image will appear at the cursor position in the document.

The different elements that you are integrating have probably been created without any intention of combining them. It is therefore important to be clear about how they need to be combined. If you have a specification then it is important to present the integrated document as it is specified. If you do not follow the specification, the required outcome will not be achieved.

The different components are likely to employ different fonts, character sizes and other layout features, and you may have to make changes so that the integrated document is effectively presented. In order to change the format of imported text or data, you need to highlight it and select the desired font and character size.

Images and charts will often need to be resized to fit into the combined document since they will have been produced for other purposes. In changing the size of an image or chart you need to ensure that its original proportions are maintained or the quality of the image will be reduced. When you import an image or chart it will appear in a rectangle, with small rectangles at each corner and at the midpoint of each side. If it does not, a single click on the image will enclose the image. This is the equivalent of highlighting it. If you place your mouse pointer on the enclosing small

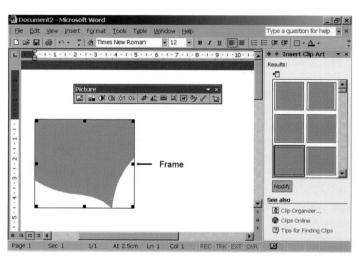

Figure 1.26 Clip Art

rectangles, the mouse pointer will change to become a double-headed arrow. If you hold down the mouse button you can reshape the image or chart by dragging the edge. In changing the shape you need to make sure that the proportions and quality of the image are maintained. You can also move the image or chart by placing the pointer in the centre of the image and holding down the mouse button, then dragging the whole image or chart to a new location. Figure 1.26 depicts inserting a Clip Art image into a Microsoft Word® document.

When you import a Microsoft Excel® spreadsheet into Microsoft Word® it will have a small rectangle with a star inside at the left-hand top corner. If you place your pointer on this square, it will change shape to a star, and by holding down the mouse button you can move the sheet to the location of your choice. At the bottom right-hand corner is a matching small square, which changes its shape to a double-headed arrow when you place your cursor on it. By holding down the mouse button you can resize the sheet.

Generic text and data files

Generic text and data files are ones which can be accessed by the majority of applications without their format needing to change. Earlier we discussed how to use the **File** option to import files into Microsoft Word®, which involves the conversion of the file format. Generic files do not normally need to have their files converted since they can be read by a large number of applications (e.g. word processors). A generic text file will often have the extension .txt.

A generic file can be imported using the **File** option within the **Insert** menu. When it appears, its format will often need to be amended (e.g. sentences broken up, extra spacings and gaps in the text). This is due to the limited formatting instructions contained in a generic file to make it compatible with many applications. Data files will sometimes be split across more than one page, owing to the position they are imported to. It is good practice to present data on a single page so that it is easier for the reader to understand.

When you are initially creating an integrated document you could begin by simply basing it on a generic text file. Microsoft Word® will open a generic text file in the same way it opens a Word® file. Select the File menu and the Open option. This will open the Open window. At the bottom of this window is a box called Files of type with a down arrow button, which, if clicked, provides a list of file formats. This should be All Files or Text Files so that the system can locate text files. When a text file is located, you can open it by either highlighting it and clicking on the Open button or by doubling-clicking the file. It will open within Microsoft Word®.

Printing an integrated document

The process of printing an integrated document is identical to printing any other. However, there is probably a greater need to check the appearance of the printed document since you are combining a number of resources into a single one. To preview prior to printing in Microsoft Word® you need to select the File menu and the Print Preview option. This will reveal the Print Preview window and show you how your integrated document will appear when printed. If you are satisfied, you can close the window, then select the File menu and the

Exercise 6

Integrated documents

1 Open Microsoft Word® by clicking on the Start button, highlighting All Programs and selecting Microsoft Word® or double-click on the Word® icon on the Microsoft Windows® desktop. A blank page will appear.

2 Enter the following text:

This is an example of a document combining different resources.

This should be in accordance with house style (see Exercise 3).

3 Leave three blank lines. Select the Insert menu and click on the File option to reveal the Insert File window. Using the down arrow button alongside the Look in: box change the folder to read your floppy disk. The files stored on the floppy disk will be shown in the central area.

4 Double-click on the Solar System Table.doc and it will be inserted into your new document.

5 Leave a blank line and again select the Insert menu, highlight the Picture item and click on the Clip Art option to reveal the Insert Clip Art pane on the right of the Microsoft Word® work area. You can search for a suitable image (e.g. astronomy) and a variety of thumbnail images will appear. If you place the mouse pointer over an image you want to insert, a button with a down arrow will appear. If you click on the button, a menu will be revealed (figure 1.27). If you select the Insert option, the chosen image will be inserted into the document. Select an image and insert it into your integrated document.

6   You may be presented with messages asking you to insert the Microsoft Office® installation disks if the Clip Art has not been installed on your computer.

7   Using the Insert menu and the File option, practise adding other resources to your document (e.g. Microsoft Excel® spreadsheet files). You may see messages that indicate you have to install extra facilities to convert the format of files. In order to do this, you will need the installation disks for Microsoft Office®. If you are not confident about carrying out this task, seek help before going on.

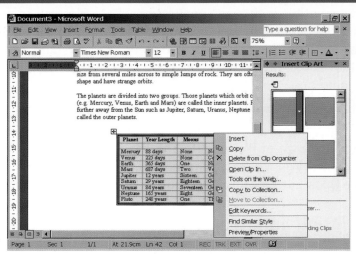

Figure 1.27 Insert Clip Art window

8   Save your document by selecting the File menu and the Save option. Name your file Integrated.

9   Preview your document in order to check its appearance when printed by selecting the File menu and the Print Preview option. Close the Print Preview window and either amend your document to correct any errors or print your document by selecting the File menu and the Print option.

10 Open a new blank document so that you can now practise importing text and data files, images and charts.

11 Select the Insert menu and the File option. This will open the Insert File window. In any order that you prefer, select text files, data files, charts and images and import them into your blank document. Continue to import until you are confident that you understand the process. Importing these files and images also provides an opportunity to format the integrated document. Practise your formatting skills again until you are confident. There is no need to save your changes.

12 Close Microsoft Word® by selecting the File menu and the Exit option. When you close without saving you will see that a window appears to ask if you want to save. This is intended to prevent you losing data. In this case, you do not need to save, but sometimes you will, so always consider the question before making a decision.

Print option to reveal the Print window. The document will be printed if you click on the OK button using the printer's default settings.

Mail merging

There are many occasions when you want to send the same document to a number of different people. Microsoft Word® provides a function called Mail Merge, with which you can automate the process. To carry out a mail merge you need to have a document and a source of information called a data source. The document is often a letter, while the data source contains the details about each person to whom it is going to be sent (e.g. names and addresses). The Mail Merge function lets you link the document and data source together to produce a series of customised documents (e.g. letters with each individual's address).

The Mail Merge function is accessed by selecting the Tools menu, highlighting the Letters and Mailings item to reveal a sub-menu with the option Mail Merge Wizard. Click on Mail Merge Wizard to open the Mail Merge task pane on the right of the work area (figure 1.28).

The Mail Merge task pane offers you a step-by-step method of undertaking a mail merge. The first step is to select the type of document you want to work with by clicking in the appropriate radio button. In figure 1.28 the letter has been chosen. At the bottom of the pane is the instruction Next: Starting Document. When you click on this instruction, the display changes to show figure 1.35. You select from the options and move on, clicking the instruction at the bottom. However, here you have an additional option of moving back one step. If you select Next, this changes the display to figure 1.29. The process is therefore to make selections from the options and to move on. Figures 1.30, 1.31, 1.32, 1.33 and 1.34 illustrate the method.

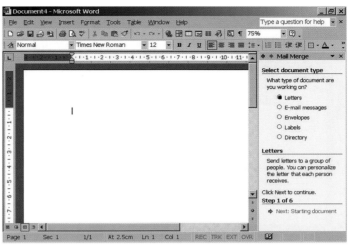

Figure 1.28 Mail Merge task pane

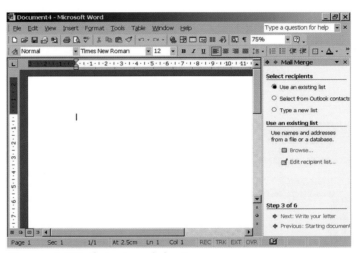

Figure 1.29 Select recipients

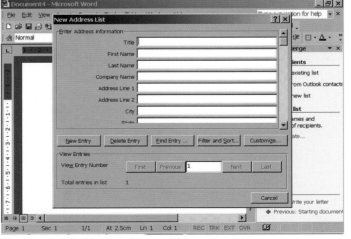

Figure 1.30 New Address List

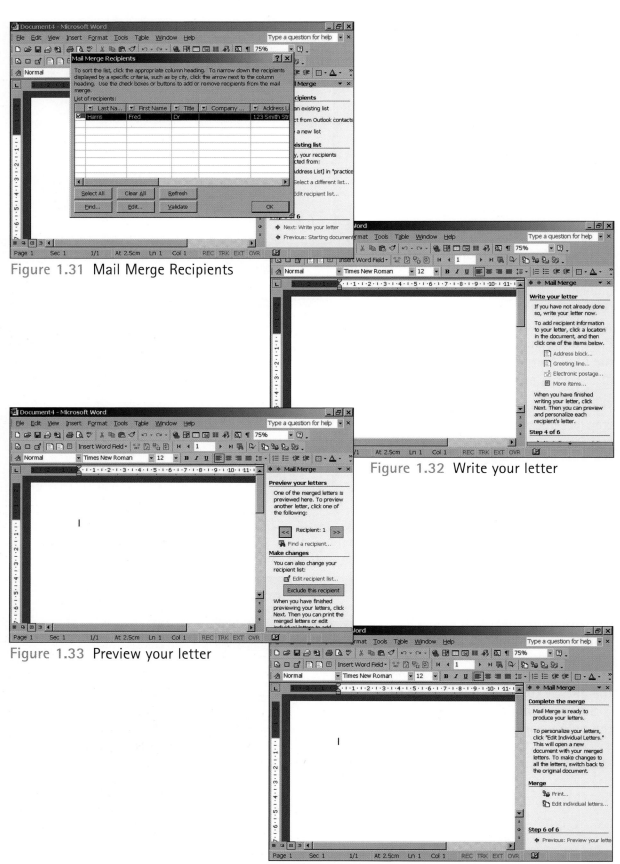

Figure 1.31 Mail Merge Recipients

Figure 1.32 Write your letter

Figure 1.33 Preview your letter

Figure 1.34 Complete the merge

Exercise 7

Mail merge

1 Open Microsoft Word® by clicking on the Start button, highlighting All Programs and selecting Microsoft Word® or double-click on the Word® icon on the Microsoft Windows® desktop. A blank page will appear.

2 In order to undertake a mail merge you need to have a standard letter or other document you want to customise for a variety of people. Enter the following text, which will form the basis of the merged document. Leave sufficient space at the start of the letter to enter the name and address of the recipient (six lines).

Dear

Invitation

I would like to invite you to the annual meeting of the Community Development Group. The meeting will consider the annual report of the organisation including the financial statement and agree the objectives for next year. It is important that members are able to attend in order to contribute to the group's plans.

Yours sincerely,

Gordon Donaldson
Chairman

3 Select the Tools menu and highlight the Letters and Mailings option to reveal a sub-menu. Click on the Mail Merge Wizard to open the Mail

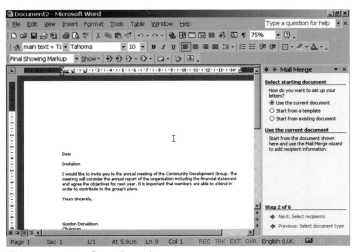

Figure 1.35 Starting document

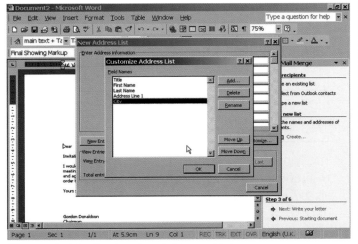

Figure 1.36 Customize Address List

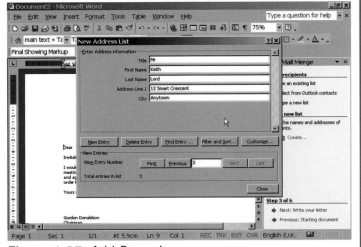

Figure 1.37 Add Records

Merge pane (figure 1.28). Choose the Letters option and click on Next: Starting document. The display will change (figure 1.35).

4 Select the option Use the current document and click on Next: Select recipients. If you need to, you can go back to the previous step by using the Previous: Select document type option. Select the Type a new list option and click on Create. The New Address List window will appear (figure 1.30).

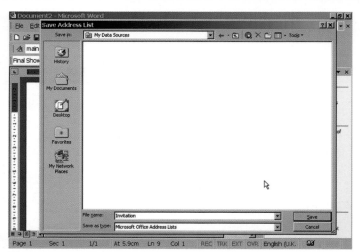

Figure 1.38 Save Address List

5 You are going to create three records, as shown in the table below:

Title	First Name	Last Name	Address1	City
Dr	James	Daniels	6 Long Street	Anytown
Ms	Karen	Brown	5 Short Road	Anytown
Mr	Keith	Lord	12 Smart Crescent	Anytown

The window asks you to enter details, but the first step is to customise the field headings to produce those you need. Click on the Customize button to open the Customize Address List. Use the Add, Delete, Rename, Move Up and Move Down buttons to produce a new data source. Figure 1.36 shows the Customize Address List window.

Once you have amended the address list, click on the OK button to open the New Address List window (figure 1.37) to enter the addresses of the recipients. When the three records have been added, click on the Close button. You will then be asked to save your new data. Figure 1.38 shows the Save Address List window. Save the list with the file name Invitation. Microsoft Word® XP saves the data in a folder called My Data Sources. When the list is saved (i.e. Save button selected), the Mail Merge Recipients window is opened (figure 1.45). When you are ready, select the OK button to close the window.

6 Now select the Next: Write your letter option. You need to insert into the letter the field names from the data source so that the application knows where to position the data. Click on the More items option to reveal the Insert Merge Field window (figure 1.40). This allows you to insert the fields by placing the cursor where you want the field in the letter, highlighting the field and clicking on the Insert button. Insert the fields in the letter.

Figure 1.41 shows the letter with the data fields added. You need to position the merged fields, allowing spaces between fields and adding any punctuation that is needed.

7 Now click on the option Next: Preview your letters to preview each merged letter (figure 1.42). It is important to check that the merged letters are correct.

You can use the arrow keys to move forward and backwards through the letters. The Exclude this recipient button lets you edit the merged letters.

8 Once you have checked the letters, you can click on the option Next: Complete the merge. Figure 1.43 shows the complete merge display. There are two options: Print, to send the letters to your printer and finish the task, or Edit individual letters. If you choose the second option then a new window (figure 1.44) will appear. This allows you to print all the letters, select a range or a single one. Explore the options and then select All.

9 Print the letters.

10 Word's Mail Merge facilities provide you with functions that allow you to query the information so that you can locate items. In this example we are going to find all the people receiving the letter who live in a particular location.

11 Query your data source to locate the recipients of the letter who live in Long Street. Select the Tools menu, highlight the Letters and Mailing option and click on Mail Merge Wizard. This opens the Mail Merge

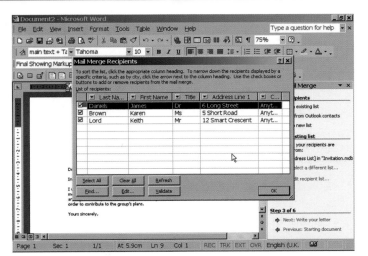

Figure 1.39 Mail Merge Recipients

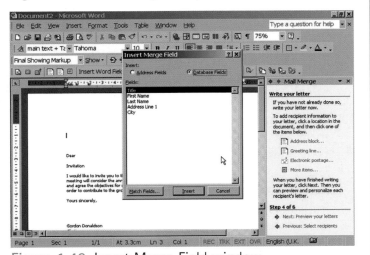

Figure 1.40 Insert Merge Field window

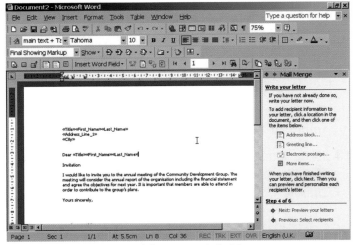

Figure 1.41 Letter with merged fields

recipients – Office Address List. Select Edit recipients list to open the Mail Merge Recipients List window. Next click on the Edit button to edit the address details, then choose the Filter and Sort button which opens the Filter and Sort window. In the Files box use the down arrow to select the Address Line 1 option. In the Comparison box again use the down arrow button to select the Contains option, and finally in the Compare to: box enter Long Street. Click on OK and the query will locate all the recipients living in Long Street.

12 You will have noticed that there are many more options. You can base your query on any of the fields and use a range of comparison options (e.g. equal to). In our example we only had one condition for locating the information, but you may have noticed that in the second line of the Filter and Sort window is an AND which allows you to develop complex queries (e.g. recipients living in Long Street with first name James). Explore the different options until you are confident.

13 Close Word by selecting the File menu and the Exit option.

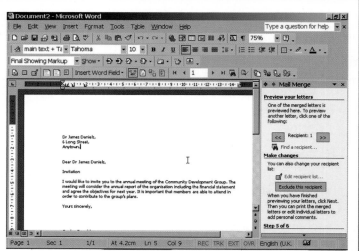

Figure 1.42 Preview merged letter

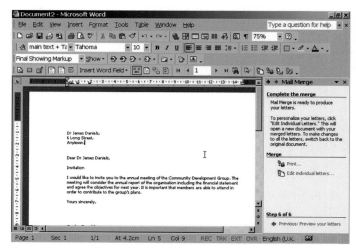

Figure 1.43 Complete the merge

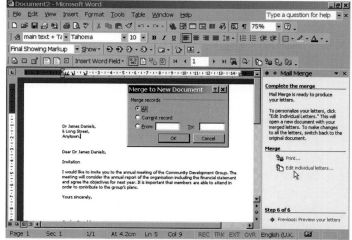

Figure 1.44 Edit individual letters

More practice

These exercises all refer to a set of related tasks that you might be asked to perform in a business or other form of organisation. They involve producing documents and related activities.

You are an admistrative assistant in the Countryside Timber Leisure Building Company. Your manager has asked you to prepare some sales literature. This consists of:

- a sales acknowledgement
- a direct sales letter
- an information leaflet.

This will involve you in producing a document that integrates text, graphics and data files.

You will need access to a set of resources, including:

- Timber Leisure Buildings (.doc file)
- Garden Shed product (.doc file)
- Contracts (Microsoft Word® data file)
- Specification (data file)
- CountryLogo (image file)

These are available on the Hodder Education website (www.hodderclait.co.uk).

Activity 1

The objective of this activity is to produce a sales acknowledgement, based on a mail merge document, sent to customers to acknowledge their order. You need to create a master mail merge document.

First Name	Last Name	Value	Contract
John	King	£1200	Garden Shed
Diana	Morris	£870	Broad Shed
Silvia	Francis	£657	Tool Bunker

1 Open Microsoft Word® and create a mail merge document
2 Enter the following text, leaving blank lines or paragraph space when they are shown. Insert the merged fields from the table below:

   Figure 1.45 shows the Customize Address List window, while figure 1.46 shows the Mail Merge Recipients.

Sales Acknowledgement

Countryside Timber Leisure Building Company

We would like to acknowledge receipt of your order for a {*insert Contract merge fields*}. This is being managed by {*insert Project Manager merge field*} who you should contact with any queries. The total cost of the order is {*insert Value merge field*}.

Yours sincerely,

{*insert your own name*}
Managing Director

3   Create a header and footer and enter your own name in the header.

4   Change the format of the sales acknowledgement so that it has:

- heading (i.e. Sales Acknowledgement) – centred and enboldened
- heading (i.e. Countryside Timber Leisure Building Company) – left-aligned and enboldened

Select a font, character size and margins to present the document in the most effective way.

5   Save the master document with the file name Acknowledgement. Figure 1.47 shows one of the merged acknowledgements.

6   Print the document.

7   Password (Sales1) protect the file from modification.

8   Save the file with the name Acknowledgement.

9   Close the file and exit Microsoft Word®.

Activity 2

During the assessment you will often be asked to take a screen print as evidence that you have completed a task. In this activity you will have an opportunity to practise this task.

1   Open Acknowledgement which you created in activity 1.

2   Use the screen capture facility to demonstrate that you have set password protection. Figure 1.48 shows what you should capture.

3   Print the screen capture.

4   Query your data source to locate the contract for a garden office. You need to select the Tools menu, highlight the Letters and Mailings option and click on Mail Merge Wizard. This opens the Mail Merge recipients – Sales Recipients. Select the Edit recipient list to open the Mail Merge

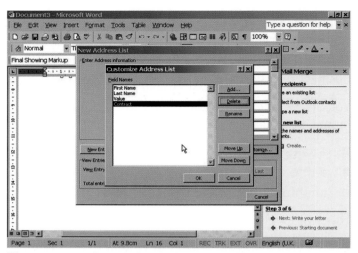

Figure 1.45 Customize Address List

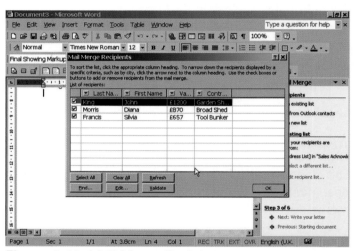

Figure 1.46 Mail Merge Recipients

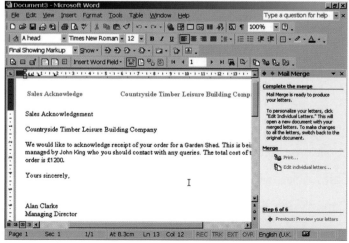

Figure 1.47 Acknowledgement

Recipients List window. Next click on the E̲dit button to reveal figure 1.49, then choose the Filter and S̲ort button, which opens the Filter and Sort window (figure 1.50).

5 Print the result.
6 Close the file and Microsoft® Word.

Activity 3

In this activity you are asked to create a sales letter. This will involve combining two files. The files are:

Timber Leisure Buildings

CountryLogo

1 Open the Timber Leisure Buildings document or enter it.

Dear
Timber Leisure Buildings

Do you have enough space? A cost effective solution to the problem of a lack of space to work, store equipment and garden furniture is a timber building. We can supply a wide range of building to meet your needs. These include:

Garden Office®
This building is available in several sizes and is designed to provide a room from which you can operate a business.

Tool Bunker
A problem that many people face is where to store garden and other tools. Our tool bunker provides a secure store for expensive items.

Broad Shed
For many gardeners a simple tool bunker is not sufficient. The broad shed is designed to offer a way of storing tools, furniture and sports equipment safely and securely.

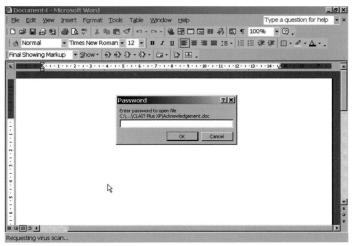
Figure 1.48 Password protection

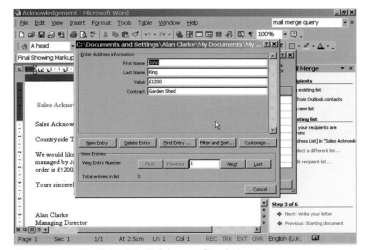
Figure 1.49 Edit Mail Merge Recipients

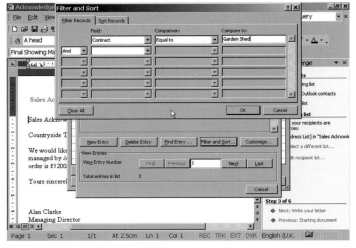
Figure 1.50 Filter and Sort

Please contact Countryside Ltd for more details of our products or visit us at our show site at Country First on the A46.

Yours sincerely,

Managing Director

2   Format Timber Leisure Buildings as follows:

> Paper size – A4
> Orientation – portrait
>
> Alignment – left
> Font – Tahoma
> Character size – 10
> Line spacing – single

3   Format the Timber Leisure Buildings headings as follows:

> Alignment – centred and emboldened
> Font – Times New Roman
> Character size – 14

4   Format the three other subheadings (i.e. Garden Office, Tool Bunker and Broad Shed) as follows:

> Alignment – left and emboldened
> Font – Times New Roman
> Character size – 12

5   Save the file as Direct Sales.

6   Insert the image CountryLogo in the top right-hand corner of the letter. You will need to resize the image, but it must not be distorted by the process. Figure 1.40 shows the document.

7   Add a header and footer to the document, then insert your name in the header and the automatic date in the footer.

8   Save the file as Direct Sales.

9   Close the file and Microsoft Word®.

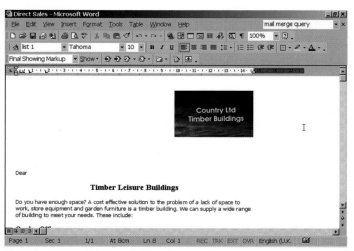

Figure 1.51 Direct Sales document

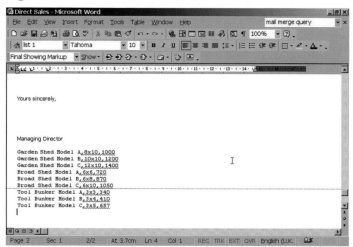

Figure 1.52 Imported table

Activity 4

The sales letter needs to include a table of the timber buildings' specifications and costs. These are provided as the data file in CSV format. This requires the file specification.

1 Open the Direct Sales document.

2 Insert the file Specification.csv below the last line in the letter, after 'Managing Director'.

3 The file will appear, as shown in figure 1.52. Each item of information is separated by a comma.

4 Format the imported information to form a table (Table menu and Convert option). Figure 1.53 illustrates the converted text.

5 Add a new row to insert three column headings, Product, Size and Cost, to the table. Format the table contents to Arial, with a character size of 12. Centre the table.

6 Embolden the column headings and centre them. Apply a shading of your choice to the heading (ie across the new row).

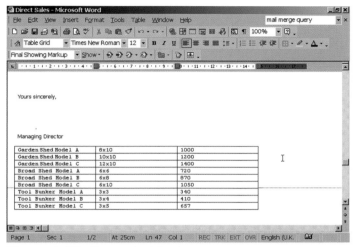

Figure 1.53 Converted text

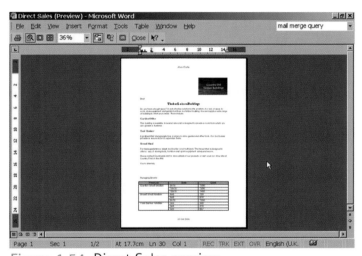

Figure 1.54 Direct Sales preview

7 Merge the cells in the left-hand column so that three new cells are produced (i.e. all Garden Office® cells togther, all Tool Bunker cells together and all Broad Shed cells together). Edit the new cells so that they read Garden Shed Models, Broad Shed Models and Tool Bunker Models).

8 Proofread the document and check you have carried out all the instructions.

9 Check that the layout of the letter is acceptable using the Print Preview function and print a copy of the letter. Figure 1.54 shows the letter in preview.

10 Save Direct Sales.

11 Close the file and Microsoft Word®.

Activity 5

This activity involves creating an information leaflet for the Garden Shed product. The basic text has already been produced and is available from the website or, alternatively, you can enter the text.

Garden Shed

The Garden Shed has been designed for the many people who need to work from home but have little space within their houses to establish an office. The building is available in three sizes:

- Version A, 8ft $\times$ 10ft at £1000
- Version B, 10ft $\times$ 10ft at £1200
- Version C, 12ft $\times$ 10ft at £1400

All models are constructed out of seasoned timber with an inner lining to provide sound and temperature insulation. The roof is constructed using a rubberised process to ensure that it is waterproof. The door and windows are provided with security locks to ensure that the building is safe.

The Garden Shed is provided as a flat pack so that you can assemble it yourself on a concrete base. Alternatively, we can construct the building for you. The costs are available on application to Country Ltd.

1 Open the file Garden Shed product in Microsoft Word®.
2 Format the whole document as Arial, size 10 and centre the headings as character size 12, emboldened.
3 Delete the phrase 'to ensure that the building is safe'.
4 Replace the word 'Version' with 'Model'. Make sure that the first letter is a capital.
5 Insert a copyright symbol at the bottom of the leaflet – © Country Ltd.
6 Spellcheck the document and proofread.
7 Insert a header with your name and a footer with an automatic file name.
8 Save the file as Garden Shed Revised.
9 Print a copy of your document,
10 Close the file and Microsoft Word®.

Activity 6

1 Archive all the source files: Timber Leisure Buildings, Garden Office® product, Contracts, Specification and CountryLogo.
2 Produce evidence that you have undertaken the archiving by using the screen capture function.
3 Print a copy of the screen capture.

SUMMARY

1 Files and folders

All information stored on a computer is held in a file. All files have an individual name and they are stored within folders. Folders can also be stored in other folders. Folders are sometimes called directories.

2 Open files

Files can be opened by double-clicking on them with the mouse pointer. The files will only open if an application which is able to read the file is present on the computer system. If the application is not present, Microsoft Windows® will display a window asking you to locate the appropriate application since the operating system cannot find it.

3 Windows® Explorer

Windows® Explorer provides you with the tools to create new folders and delete, rename, move, copy and save files and folders. These functions are available on the File menu and toolbar. To open Windows® Explorer, click on the Start button and highlight the All Programs option to open another menu. Highlight the Accessories item to open a menu with Windows® Explorer option.

4 Read-only

Highlight the file within Windows® Explorer, select the File menu and the Properties option to open the Properties window. Click on the General tab and in the Read-only radio button.

5 Archive files

Highlight the file or folder within Windows® Explorer and select the Properties option in the File menu. In the General tab is a button labelled Advanced . If you click on it, the Advanced Attributes window opens. This provides an option to create archive files by clicking on the appropriate radio button.

6 Types of files

There are many different types of files. File names normally end with a full stop and three letters (e.g. .doc). This indicates the type of file and helps you to distinguish between them. In addition, the icons show the type of file.

7 Print windows

Press the ALT key and then the Print Screen (sometimes Print Scrn) key. Paste the window image into a document (e.g. Microsoft Word®) and print the document using the normal functions of the application.

To capture the contents of the whole display you need only press the Print Screen key and then paste the image into a document.

8 Spelling and grammar checkers

In Microsoft Word® spelling and grammar checkers are available in the Tools menu as the Spelling and Grammar option.

Automatic checking can be set using the Tools menu and the Options item to reveal the Options window. Choose the Spelling and Grammar tab and configure both checkers. Spelling mistakes are underlined in red and grammar errors in green.

9 Save
Select the File menu and the Save option. This will reveal the Save As dialog window, which allows you to choose where to save your file (e.g. floppy disk) and to name it. After you have saved your file once it will be updated each time you click on the Save option.

10 Save As
Select the File menu and the Save As option. This will let you save your file under a new name or in a new location.

11 Page Setup
Select the File menu and the Page Setup option. This opens the Page Setup dialog window. You can choose the layout of your page (e.g. margins, orientation, size of headers and footers).

12 Headers and footers
Select the View menu and the Header and Footer option, which will open a header area on your document and a toolbar which provides extra options for the header. If you scroll down the page you will find the footer area at the bottom of the page, with the toolbar.

13 Bullets and Numbering
Select the Format menu and click on the Bullets and Numbering option. This will reveal the Bullets and Numbering window.

14 Special symbols
Select the Insert menu and click on the Symbol option. This will open the Symbol window.

15 Search and replace
Select the Edit menu and click on the Replace option to reveal the Find and Replace window.

16 Widows and orphans
Select the Format menu, the Paragraph option and the Line and Page Breaks tab. Click the Widow/Orphan control radio button.

17 Indent text
There are several ways of indenting text:

- Use the tab key on the keyboard. You can set the size of the tab by selecting the Format menu and clicking on the Tabs option, which will open the Tabs window.
- Select the Format menu and click on the Paragraph option. This will reveal the Paragraph window.
- Select the View menu and click on Ruler. By dragging the stops at the end of the ruler you can create first-line and hanging indents.

18 Tables
Select the Table menu, highlight the Insert option and click on the Table option. This will open the Insert Table window.

19 Change column widths

Highlight the columns you want to change. Select the Table menu, highlight the AutoFit option to reveal a range of options, and click on AutoFit to Contents.

20 Presentation of table contents

Highlight the content of the cells you want to change and select the option you desire, such as font, character size, bold, italics, alignment (i.e. left, right and centre).

21 Table alignment

Select the Table menu and click on the Table Properties option. This will reveal the Table Properties window, which has a number of tabs that contain tools to operate on rows, columns and cells.

- Table tab – allows you to align the whole table
- Other tabs let you change height of rows, width of columns and alignment of text in each cell.

22 Borders and Shading

Highlight your table, then select the Format menu and the Borders and Shading option to reveal the Borders and Shading window. This allows you to change the borders of your table by using the Setting, Style, Color and Width of lines options.

23 Layout and formatting

Select the Format menu and click on the Paragraph option to open the Paragraph window. This enables you to change alignment, line spacing and indentation.

24 Import charts, images, data and text

The Copy, Cut and Paste functions let you move charts, images, data and text between Microsoft Office® applications.

Alternatively, select the Insert menu and click on File option, or highlight the Picture option to reveal a sub-menu which enables you to choose an image from Clip Art or From File (i.e. a file stored on the computer).

25 Mail Merge

The Mail Merge function is accessed by selecting the Tools menu, highlighting the Letters and Mailing item to reveal a sub-menu with the option Mail Merge Wizard. Click on the Mail Merge Wizard to open the Mail Merge task pane on the right of the work area. The Mail Merge task pane offers you a step-by-step method of undertaking a mail merge.

Unit 2

Manipulating Spreadsheets and Graphs

This chapter will help you to:

- identify and use spreadsheet and graph software correctly
- enter, edit and manipulate data
- create formulae and use common functions
- format and present data
- link live data from one spreadsheet to another
- select and control data sources
- present data using graphs and charts
- format axes and labels
- format the presentation of graphs and charts
- use graphs to extrapolate information to predict future values
- use spreadsheets to solve problems and project results.

This chapter covers unit 2 (Manipulating Spreadsheets and Graphs). There is no precondition for studying this unit. However, its content does assume that you have the skills and understanding that are provided by the OCR Level 1 ICT course New CLAiT (e.g. Unit 2: Creating Spreadsheets and Graphs and Unit 1: File Management and e-Document Production).

Assessment

After studying unit 2, your skills and understanding are assessed during a three-hour practical assignment. This is set by OCR and marked locally. However, the marking will be externally moderated by OCR. This ensures that the standard is being applied correctly across the many different providers of OCR CLAiT Plus. If you are unsuccessful, you can be reassessed using a different assignment.

An alternative approach is for you to be assessed by an assignment set by OCR or designed by your centre. These assignments cover all the assessment objectives included in the unit. You will need to complete an OCR evidence checklist, explaining how each assessment objective has been covered.

Font families

CLAiT Plus uses font families in its assessments rather than font names. In chapter 1 font families are explained, along with how they relate to font names (see page 7). As you undertake each exercise, consider which font family the font you are using belongs to. For example:

Serif: Courier New and Times New Roman
Sans serif: Tahoma and Arial.

Spreadsheet applications

This chapter is based on Microsoft Excel® XP, which is a modern package that you can employ to create spreadsheets. It also provides you with the means of converting data from your spreadsheet into a graph or chart. Figure 2.1 shows the Microsoft Excel® application interface. Its main feature is a grid of columns and rows. This is the work area of the spreadsheet. The columns are designated with a letter (A, B, C, etc.), while the rows are numbered (1, 2, 3, etc.). The intersection of columns and rows produces a rectangular area called a cell. Each cell is known by the letter and number of its column and row (A1, B2, C3, etc.).

When you click in a cell it is highlighted. In figure 2.1, cell A1 is highlighted. You will also see that the highlighted cell reference is given at the left end of the formula toolbar. At the bottom of the grid, in the left-hand corner, three are tabs, called Sheet 1, Sheet 2 and Sheet 3. These allow you to move between three spreadsheets, which combined are called a workbook. The sheets are often related (e.g. sales figures for three different products).

To the right of the work area is the task pane, which you can switch off and on. This provides a range of options to help you undertake different tasks. When the application opens, the task pane offers options to help you create a new spreadsheet workbook. The task pane changes, depending on what you are attempting to do.

The work area is surrounded by an interface, which is broadly similar to many other Microsoft Office® applications. It has a menu bar and a number of toolbars providing access to the many different functions available within Microsoft Excel® to create, amend and manipulate spreadsheets.

The two main ways of loading Microsoft Excel® are:

■ Click on the Start button in the bottom left-hand corner of the Microsoft Windows® desktop. A

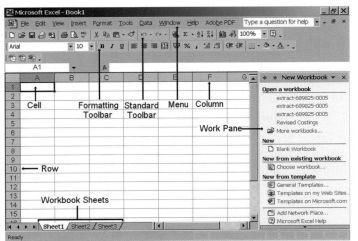

Figure 2.1 Microsoft Excel® XP

menu will pop up. If you highlight the All Programs item a new menu will appear alongside it. If you click on the item shown as Microsoft Excel®, the application will load.

■ Double-click on the Excel® icon shown on the desktop.

A variety of exercises are included in this chapter. Their prime purpose is to help you understand how to create and use spreadsheets. They are simplified representations of the world and are not intended to be tutorials on accountancy, but rather explanations of Microsoft Excel®.

The primary purpose of a spreadsheet is to analyse numerical information to assist an organisation's management. They may be used to consider the sales of a product, wage costs, overheads and many other issues. However, one key factor essential for all spreadsheets is numerical accuracy. Data entered must be correct and calculations need to be checked to ensure they are perfect. When creating a spreadsheet you must devote a lot of time to checking that all data and formulae are accurate.

Modelling

A key role for spreadsheets is to model information and enable you to explore what would be the result of a change. For example, you might create a spreadsheet showing the production costs of manufacturing a component. The spreadsheet would let you explore what would be the effect of changing the process (e.g. investing in a new machine which allows you to manufacture the component using half the workforce).

You could create a spreadsheet showing the relationship between sales staff and profit. You might explore the effects of increasing or decreasing the number of staff.

You might develop a spreadsheet showing the relationship between commission and sales volumes. This would allow you to consider the influence of changing the rates of commission.

Create a spreadsheet

To create a new spreadsheet requires that you understand the nature of the information you are going to model and how you want to present the spreadsheet.

The first step is to establish the structure or layout of the spreadsheet. This is important in that it will influence the way the information it contains is accepted. Senior managers will only act on the results of a spreadsheet if they are persuaded that it is quality work. A sheet that is well presented, with an effective structure, will go a long way towards demonstrating that it is worth considering. You can start a spreadsheet with an initial structure and then amend it later to improve its appearance.

The structure of a spreadsheet can be established using the Page Setup

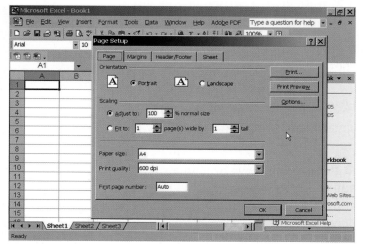

Figure 2.2 Page Setup

CLAiT Plus 2006 for Office XP

option, which is available from the File menu. If you click on the Page Setup option it will reveal the Page Setup window (figure 2.2). This is divided by a series of tabs into Page, Margins, Header/Footer and Sheet.

The Page tab lets you set the orientation of the sheet (i.e. portrait or landscape). It also provides access to the scaling feature, which lets you fit your spreadsheet on to a specified number of pages when you are printing it, by scaling the size of the sheet. For both options, click on the relevant radio buttons.

The Margins tab (figure 2.3) provides the means of changing the size of the four margins (i.e. top, bottom, left and right). The window demonstrates the orientation of the sheet and the four margins. Using the up and down arrows near each box you can increase or decrease the margins. The same display also allows you to set the size of the header and footer and, finally, to centre the sheet on the page either horizontally or vertically. This can improve the appearance of the spreadsheet.

The Header/Footer tab (figure 2.4) enables you to customise the information that heads and foots the sheet. By clicking on the Custom Header or Custom Footer buttons you will reveal the Header or Footer window (figure 2.5).

Headers and Footers

Using the Header and Footer windows, you can insert text which will appear at the top or bottom of the sheet. In addition, you can add a number of automatic fields that will change, depending on the sheet, when they appear (e.g. number of the page, new date and a change of file name). The font, character size and style of text can be changed using the text button. The other buttons allow automatic

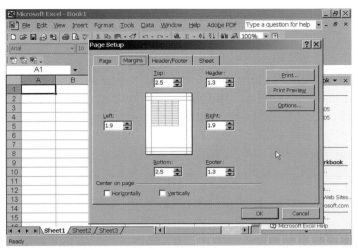

Figure 2.3 Margins tab

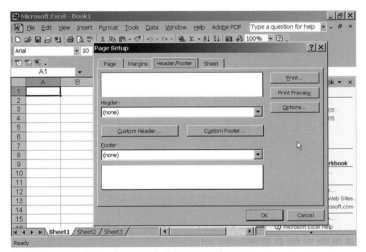

Figure 2.4 Header and Footer tab

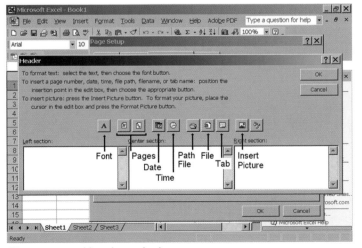

Figure 2.5 Header window

fields to be inserted. The text and automatic fields are inserted at the cursor in the left, right or centre of the header or footer.

Figure 2.5 shows the icons that appear on the Header window (and also on the Footer) and identifes their purpose. Place the cursor in your chosen location or highlight the text, and then click on the icon. The first icon allows you to format the text, while the remaining icons provide you with the means of inserting an automatic field into the header or footer.

Exercise 8

Create a spreadsheet structure

1 Load Microsoft Excel® using either the All Programs menu or the Excel® icon on the desktop. Close the Workbook task pane (button in right-hand corner).

2 Set the orientation of the sheet to landscape, margins to 2 cm – right and left, and 2.5 cm – top and bottom, and the header and footer to 1.5 cm (select File menu and Page Setup option).

3 Insert header to read: 'Sales Forecast' (Arial font and character size 14 bold, in the Center section)

4 Insert automatic fields in the footer:

File name – Left section
Page number – Center section
Date – Right section

5 Enter the table of information below to form your first spreadsheet. Start Item in cell B5. You can use any font and character size that you want to. I selected Arial, character size 10 for the headings and Tahoma, character size 10 for the items.

Item	January	February, etc. (all 12 months of the year)
Hand Tools		
Power Tools		
Wood		
Metal		
Fastenings		
Paint		
Wallpaper		
Electrical		
Garden		
Kitchen		
Garage		

6 Check that you have entered the data accurately and correct any mistakes. If you click in the cell which contains the error, you can amend the mistake by pressing the delete key and re-entering. Alternatively, the contents of a selected cell appear on the formula bar and can be edited if you click on the bar and then use the arrow keys and keyboard.

7 It is good practice to save your work early and update the file as you make changes and enhance the spreadsheet. Insert a floppy disk into the A: drive and select the File menu, then click on the option Save to reveal the Save As window. Change the Save in : box to select the floppy disk and add the file name Sales Forecast in the File name box. Click on the Save button. You will probably hear the floppy drive

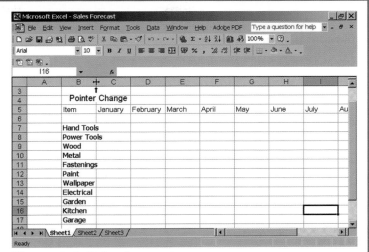

Figure 2.6 Sales forecast

and your spreadsheet will be saved as the file Sales Forecast. The top line of Microsoft Excel® will change to read 'Microsoft Excel® – Sales Forecast'.

8 You have probably noticed that some of your titles are too large for the cell in which they have been placed (e.g. Hand Tools, Power Tools and September). You can change the size of a column by placing the mouse pointer on the line between the two columns (its appearance will change – figure 2.6), and if you hold down the left mouse button, you can drag the column wider. Make columns B and K wider.

9 Check the appearance of your spreadsheet as a printed document by selecting the File menu and the Print Preview option. This will show you how the sheet will appear if printed. If the text is too small, click on the Zoom button. If it is then too big, click on it again. The preview will allow you to check the content and presentation of the header and footer, sheet and margins and orientation. If you click on the Setup button you can see the settings, and clicking on Margins will reveal them. Explore the different options and ensure you have produced the sheet accurately.

10 Save your sheet by selecting the File menu and clicking on the Save option. The Save As window will not appear since the application assumes you simply want to update your file stored on the floppy disk.

11 Close Microsoft Excel® by selecting the File menu item and clicking on the Exit option or by clicking on the Close button in the top right-hand corner of the application window.

Saving

You can choose to save a spreadsheet in a variety of formats. In the Save As window is a box called Save as type, and there is a down arrow at the side of this box. If you click on this button, a list of formats in which you can save your spreadsheet appears. They include:

■ Microsoft Excel® Workbook – current Microsoft Excel® 2000 format

- Web Page – your sheet is going to be presented on a website
- Microsoft Excel® 4.0 Work – older version of Microsoft Excel®
- other spreadsheet applications.

You need to select which format will serve your purpose. Do you want your work to be read easily on an earlier version of Microsoft Excel® or another application, presented on a website or simply used on Microsoft Excel® XP? The decision has consequences: if you save the sheet in the format suitable for an earlier version of Microsoft Excel® you may lose some presentation aspects or other features. If you are in doubt, you should save in the format of the current version of Microsoft Excel® (Microsoft Excel® Workbook).

Formulae

One of the key features of a spreadsheet is that it can undertake mathematical calculations. It can total columns of figures, add, subtract, multiply and divide the contents of cells. It can carry out complex mathematical operations using formulae which you can devise.

The mathematical operators used in Microsoft Excel® are:

+	add
–	subtract
*	multiply
/	divide
<	less than
<=	less than or equal to
>	more than
>=	greater than or equal to

Brackets are also important in that they tell Microsoft Excel® to calculate anything in the brackets first, before going on with the remaining parts of the calculation. A simple formula could be:

=B2+B3 – this means add the contents of cell B2 to the contents of cell B3
=B2-B3 – this means subtract the contents of cell B3 from the contents of cell B2
=B2/B3 – this means divide the contents of cell B2 by the contents of cell B3
=B2*B3 – this means multiply the contents of cell B2 by the contents of cell B3.

These simple operators can be used to produce more complex formulae and hence carry out complex mathematical actions. For example:

=(B2+B3)/4 – add the contents of cells B2 and B3 together and divide the total by 4
=(B2*10)-(B3/B2)-20 – multiply the contents of cell B2 by 10 and subtract from it the contents of cell B3 divided by the contents of cell B2, then subtract 20 from the total.

When a formula consists of several arithmetical operators (e.g. add, subtract, multiply or divide), Microsoft Excel® works them out according to a standard rule. It will work out multiplication and division first, and addition and subtraction second. If the formula contains multiplication and division or addition and subtraction, it works out the calculation from left to right. However, also remember that anything enclosed in brackets will be calculated first.

Standard formulae

There are a variety of standard functions available to Microsoft Excel® users. These include:

- SUM – this function totals the contents of a group of cells
- AVERAGE – this function produces the average of a number of values (e.g. a column of figures)
- COUNT – this function counts the number of entries in a group of cells that contain numbers
- COUNTA – this function counts the number of cells in a given range with any contents
- COUNTIF – this function counts the number of cells that are equal to a criterion in a range of cells (e.g. M2:M5 holds nails, screws, tacks, screws therefore COUNTIF(M2:M5, "screws")=2).
- MIN – this identifies the minimum value of the contents of a group of cells
- MAX – this identifies the maximum value of the contents of a group of cells
- SQRT – this function calculates the square root of a number (or the contents of a cell)
- IF – this allows you to set a condition so that an action is only carried out if it is satisfied, for example, IF (G4 >=50, "Pass", "Fail" – this means that if the contents of cell G4 are equal to or greater than 50 then the word Pass will appear). This could be the outcome of entering examination marks into a spreadsheet. If G4 is less than 50 then the word Fail will appear. The example shows that there are two outcomes of an IF function – one if the condition is true (i.e. Pass) and one if the condition is false (Fail). If you do not specify the false outcome, the word False will appear if the condition is not met. This can be confusing in some situations.

Here are some examples:

=SUM(A2:A8) – produces the total of the contents of the cells A2, A3, A4, A5, A6, A7 and A8

=AVERAGE (A2:A5) – produces the average of the contents of the cells A2, A3, A4 and A5 (i.e. (A2+A3+A4+A5)/4)

=COUNT (N11:N17) – counts the number of cells between N11 and N17 inclusive which contain numbers

=COUNTA (N11:N17) – counts the number of cells between N11 and N17 inclusive which hold content

=COUNTIF (N11:N17, "Car") – counts the number of cells between N11 and N17 inclusive which equal Car

=SQRT(A7) – if A7 is 25 the function produces the square root of 25, which is 5

=IF (A3>40, A3/10) – if the contents of cell A3 is greater than 40, then divide A3 by 10.

These functions involve identifying a list of cells. This is called the range of cells and can be selected by highlighting them on the spreadsheet, or by writing the first and last cell, separated by a colon, to designate that all the cells between the two are included. They are enclosed in brackets. At the beginning of the function an equals sign tells Microsoft Excel® to carry out the calculation.

A full list of all the functions can be accessed by clicking on the down arrow next to the Sum function button on the Standard toolbar. This reveals a list of functions and the button More Functions (figure 2.7). If you click on More Functions, you open the Insert Function window. If you highlight a function, its definition is given at the bottom of the window. Functions serve a wide range of purposes. Some are linked to mathematical operations, while others provide the means of testing logic (e.g. IF). The Insert Function window allows you to insert the function into the sheet, but you can also simply enter the function from the keyboard or double-click on the function in the list or window. When you enter a function, a new window will sometimes appear called Function Arguments. This allows you to enter any ranges or other information required by the function. However, in other cases the function will be entered with space for you to insert the range (figure 2.8).

Function Arguments asks you to set the parameters for the function. Figure 2.9 illustrates the window for the AVERAGE function. The window provides a short explanation of what is required. For some functions, the requirements are similar to AVERAGE in that a range of cell references is needed. In some cases, Microsoft Excel® will offer you a range, depending on the cell in which you are inserting the function. However, you should always check if it is correct.

The example below shows the use of functions and their mathematical values for a short column of figures (D6 to D9) in column D of a spreadsheet.

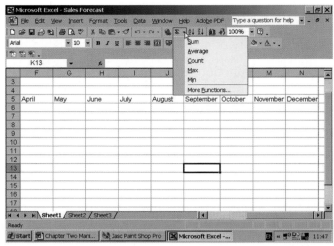

Figure 2.7 Functions

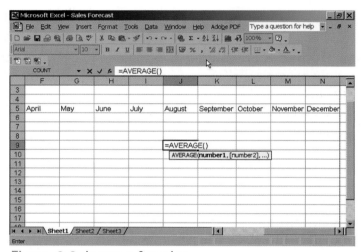

Figure 2.8 Insert a function

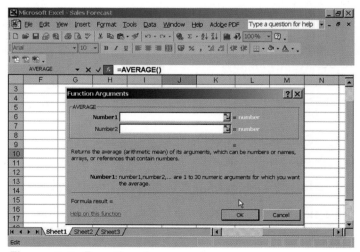

Figure 2.9 Function Arguments

Example:	Value	
D6	78	78
D7	56	56
D8	34	34
D9	56	56
D10	=AVERAGE(D6:D9)	56
D11	=MIN(D6:D9)	34
D12	=MAX(D6:D9)	78
D13	=SUM(D6:D9)	224
D14	=COUNT(D6:D9)	4
D15	=COUNTA(D6:D9)	4
D16	=COUNTIF(D6:D9,34)	1
D17	=SQRT(D9)	7.48

Name

Some of these functions you could design yourself (e.g. SUM (H3:H6) is the same as H3+H4+H5+H6). However, there is always the risk that you will make an error with your own formulae, and in many cases they require more information to be entered from the keyboard. The standard functions are a better guarantee of success.

An alternative approach to defining a range is to highlight the cell or cells and then to select the Insert menu and highlight the Name option to reveal a short menu. Click on the Define option to reveal the Define Name window (figure 2.10). The highlighted cells referenced are shown in the box at the bottom of the window. The name of the cells is entered into the top box. By clicking on the Add button you create the name, and you complete the task by clicking on the OK button. The group of cells is defined by the name.

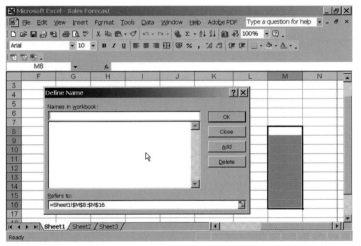

Figure 2.10 Name

To delete a name select the Insert menu, highlight the Name option and select the Define option to reveal the Define window. A list of the names is shown in the middle box. Highlight the name you want to remove and click on the Delete button.

Logical operators/functions

Using the IF function, you can ask questions of your data. It checks if a defined condition is true and then causes an action to take place. Its format is:

IF (Condition, true, false) – that is, if the condition is correct, then the true statement will take place. If it is not true, then the false statement will take place.

For example, you could establish a function so that if a sales person exceeded his target he would receive a bonus:

=IF(A10>55,B12*1.20,B12*0.95)

If cell A10 (containing the number of items sold) is greater than 55 (the sales target) then the contents of cell B12 (sales person's salary) is multiplied by 1.20 (i.e. salary is increased by 20 per cent). If the content of cell A10 is not greater than 55 then the contents of B12 are multiplied by 0.95 (i.e. salary is reduced by 5 per cent).

The IF function is not the only way of testing conditions. There are also three logical operators. These are:

OR   OR(condition1, condition2) This returns true if one or more of the conditions is true; otherwise it returns false.

NOT   NOT(condition) This reverses the value of the condition.

AND   AND(condition1 and condition2) This returns the value true if both the conditions are true; otherwise it returns the value false.

These operators are often useful when combined with the IF function.

In our earlier example, the salespersons only had to sell more than their target to achieve their bonus. If the conditions were that they had to sell more than the target for two consecutive periods, the formula would be:

=IF(AND(A10>55,A9>47),B12*1.20,B12*0.95)

A9>47 represents the sales target in the previous period.

The OR operator can also be used if the condition for receiving the bonus was to exceed the sales target in either period.

=IF(OR(A10>55,A9>47),B12*1.20,B12*0.95)

Logical operators can be confusing initially for many people, but can be very useful in carrying out complex tasks.

An important issue with formulae, which may seem obvious, but is often a source of confusion, is that if you change data on a spreadsheet and the data is used within a formula, then the value of the formula will also change. In complex spreadsheets with several interdependent formulae, a single change in data can lead to a series of changes across the sheet. This is the key advantage of a spreadsheet model in that you can see the effects of changes in data on outcomes. You can therefore explore different options (e.g. increase in price, a change in transport costs).

Error messages

In any mathematical calculation you can make an error, and Microsoft Excel® provides a number of messages to tell you about mistakes. These are:

This occurs when the formula or function produces a number greater than can fit in a cell.

#VALUE   The formula contains a mistake in one of its components (i.e. a cell or mathematical operator).

#DIV0!   This is a common error in that the formula involves division by zero. Often you have not entered a value into a cell which is being used to divide another value. You need to check to ensure all the cells have a value.

#NAME?	A meaningless term is included in the formula.
#N/A	This results from a formula requiring data from a cell which does not contain the information at that moment.
#REF!	The formula has an incorrect cell reference.
#NUM!	The formula contains an incorrect number.
#NULL!	The formula has an incorrect cell reference.

In all cases you need to check that the function is correct, you have specified the correct range of cells and that the cells have had the correct contents entered.

It is critical when constructing formulae that they are perfect. Once a spreadsheet is produced, its results are assumed to be accurate. An error in a formula will often be overlooked. When a formula is initially developed it should be checked carefully to ensure it is correct. An error in a formula may not be noticed once a spreadsheet is in use and its results may have a considerable influence on business decisions.

References

It is critical when using a spreadsheet to be able to specify which parts of the sheet you want to work on. This can be a single cell, which is shown by combining the column letter with row number (e.g. A4), or a groups of cells, which is shown by giving the first and last cells, separated by a colon. When a cell name or a range of cells is inserted into a formula or function it is called a reference. This means the formula or function is referring to the contents of that cell or range of cells. If the content changes, the value of the formula or function changes.

There are three types of reference:

- relative
- absolute
- named.

The relative reference is the normal one you encounter when you use Microsoft Excel®. If you move the cells (e.g. delete or insert rows or columns) then the reference in the formula changes to allow for the new position.

The absolute reference is one which remains unchanged no matter what happens. You create an absolute reference by using the $ symbol (e.g. SUM (A2:A5) is a relative reference, while SUM ($A$2:$A$5) is an absolute reference).

A mixed reference combines both relative and absolute references within the same formula or function (e.g. H5+$G$3).

References are especially important when you copy and paste blocks of your sheet. This is called replication and it automatically changes the relative references to allow for their new position. This is very useful if you want to copy formulae or functions, since they will be accurate in their new places. Replication can save a great deal of checking and changing, which would be needed if you had to undertake it manually.

When you highlight a cell, its reference is shown in the left-hand box of the formula bar. You can employ this reference name box to move to any cell of the sheet by entering its reference in the box and pressing enter.

Using the name box, you can give an individual cell, or group of cells, an individual name. Highlight the cell or area and enter the chosen name into the box and then press the enter key. If you enter this name into the reference box in future, the cell or area will be selected.

The four types of references can be combined in formulae to give you many different options. Named references allow you to specify a particular cell or group of cells within a formula. Relative references allow formulae to be replicated, therefore saving time and avoiding creating errors; while absolute references provide you with the option to use an unchanging reference. You can mix different types of reference to maximise the possibilities to solve particular problems or to meet different needs.

Replication and accuracy

Replication is the spreadsheet function that allows data and formulae to be copied to new areas of the sheet. If a formula employs relative references, the formula will change itself to conform to its new position. When you replicate formulae, sometimes zeros will be added to cells that do not contain any data. It is important to remove them to avoid errors, such as dividing by zero, when the formulae are calculated.

Replication has the advantage of ensuring that the formulae and data are accurately entered, as well as saving time. Numerical accuracy is vital to spreadsheets; in fact, perfection is required. Spreadsheets are concerned with modelling numerical data to predict trends, analyse data and identify outcomes. Organisational decisions will often be based on the spreadsheet analysis, so if the data is incorrect, the outcomes will also be wrong and thus will lead to poor decisions. It is therefore critical to the success of spreadsheets that the data is entered accurately. It is good practice to check data at all stages of entering to ensure it is correct.

References and formulae

The application of relative cell references is not difficult to understand. It obviously helps to copy formulae accurately from one part of a spreadsheet to another. However, absolute cell references are not so obvious. They are useful when you need to include standard values in formulae, so it is important to keep them in a single set of locations. If you were producing a spreadsheet to calculate export prices you might wish to include the exchange rates in a series of cells and then link to them through absolute references. In engineering you are often dealing with mathematical constants (e.g. density of iron), and in statistical calculations there are often constants that need to be used. These could all be placed in cells with absolute references.

Figure 2.11 illustrates formulae that use both absolute and relative references. The formulae have been replicated to show the changes to the relative references. The spreadsheet shows a simple calculation of the price of an export product. The euro exchange rate is located in cell D3.

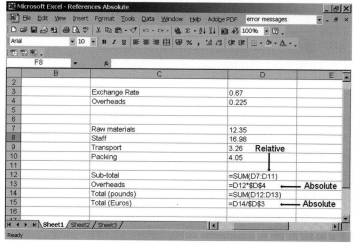

Figure 2.11 Formulae

Overheads are calculated on the basis of 22.5 per cent of the total cost (i.e. the sum of raw materials, staff, transport and packing costs). The cost in pounds is a simple total, while the cost in euros is the cost in pounds divided by the exchange rate.

Figure 2.12 shows the same calculation, but using a named reference instead of an absolute reference, and, once again, it has been replicated to illustrate the changes and the constants. A significant advantage of named references is that you can give them a meaningful name. In this example, 'exchange' will have a meaning to the people using the spreadsheet, whereas D3 will not. If it needs to be amended months or years after being created, it will be easier with a name, and the chance of making mistakes will be reduced.

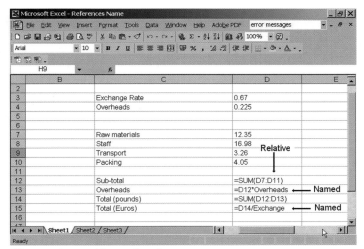

Figure 2.12 Named reference

Exercise 9

Entering data and creating formulae

1 Insert your floppy disk into the A: drive.

2 Load Microsoft Excel® using either the All Programs menu or the Excel® icon on the desktop. Open the file Sales Forecast by selecting the File menu, then clicking on the Open option to reveal the Open window. Change the Look in: box to select the floppy disk and the file name will appear in the work area. Double-click Sales Forecast or single-click it and then click the Open button. The spreadsheet will open in Microsoft Excel®.

3 Enter the data shown below.

Item	January	February	March	April	May	June	July	August	September	October	November	December
Hand Tools	12000	13500	12120	9890	10675	10950	11500	10125	10975	11100	10760	15600
Power Tools	32000	27540	27895	26450	26860	27125	27450	26875	24800	25230	25780	37800
Wood	15000	14760	13890	12300	12860	13200	12900	11500	11800	12700	13500	13250
Metal	2300	2150	1980	1875	2050	2300	1550	1250	2300	2100	2050	1950
Fastenings	4750	5050	4430	3675	3980	4100	3500	3250	3300	3400	3050	3100
Paint	17800	18230	16760	16980	19870	22345	20125	16500	17900	19500	18500	17500
Wallpaper	22900	23175	22980	21870	20760	19650	18900	17500	17900	19850	20300	23500
Electrical	14500	16800	15120	13870	14320	13760	13750	14100	13575	13900	14500	16750
Garden	2100	1900	2700	4500	5500	5700	7800	4600	3800	2800	1450	1900
Kitchen	3300	3760	3580	4125	4580	4875	5120	4980	4570	3900	4300	6700
Garage	7900	8800	5780	6750	6890	7200	7500	8000	6875	6800	6500	9100

4 Carefully check the accuracy of your data, since you are going to depend on it once you begin to calculate trends and other useful information. The validity of the calculations is totally dependent on the initial correctness of the data. It is worth spending a lot of time checking the entries.

5 Save your sheet by selecting the File menu and clicking on the Save option. It is good practice to save your work every few minutes.

6   You are going to total each monthly column and each item row. There are several ways of doing this, but the most straightforward involves using the AutoSum function on the Standard toolbar. Highlight the column from cell C7 to C18 and then click on the AutoSum icon on the toolbar and you will see the total of the column appear, 134,550. Click elsewhere in the sheet to remove the highlighting, and then on the total, and you will see the formula appear on the formula toolbar, =SUM(C7:C17).

7   Once you have successfully produced the total for the January column, you can replicate it to the other columns. Highlight C18, select the Edit menu and click on the Copy option, then Paste the contents to D18. If you highlight D18 you will see the formula =SUM(D7:D17). This shows you that in copying the formula the references have been changed to fit the new position. This is called replication and the references are relative. Repeat this process for the remaining columns.

8   Now total the first row (Hand Tools) by highlighting from C7 to O7 and clicking on the AutoSum icon on the Standard toolbar. This will produce the total 139,195 and the formula =SUM(C7:N7). If you highlight cell O7, you will see the formula appear on the toolbar. Edit the formula to make the references absolute =SUM($C$7:$N$7). Replicate (copy) this formula to cell O8 and you will notice that the new total is still 139,195 and the formula remains =SUM($C$7:$N$7). The absolute references are not changed by replication. Now use Undo to remove the formula and the changes that made the cell O7 formula absolute.

9   Replicate the formula =SUM(C7:N7) to O8 and the other rows. Total for Power Tools is 335,805 and formula =SUM(C8:N8).

10 Check the formulae are all correct and then save your sheet by selecting the File menu and clicking on the Save option.

11 Now total all the columns in cell O18 – the total is 1534975. If ####### appears it means that the number is too large to be shown in that cell. The formula is =SUM(C18:N18). Insert the name Total in B18 and O5.

12 Print your sheet by selecting the File menu and Print Preview. Figure 2.13 shows the appearance of the printout. It shows that the gridlines are missing and that some of the spreadsheet is absent. This is because it will be printed on a second sheet – Preview: Page 1 of 2 at left-hand bottom corner of figure 2.13.

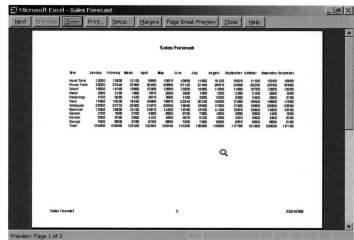

Figure 2.13 Print preview

CLAiT Plus 2006 for Office XP

13 To add the gridlines you need to select the Setup button in the print preview window to reveal the Page Setup window. Select the Sheet tab and click in the Gridlines and Row and column headings boxes so ticks appear. Click on the OK button when you are are finished and you will see the window disappear and a new print preview appear, showing gridlines and headings (figure 2.14). When you want to print the sheet,

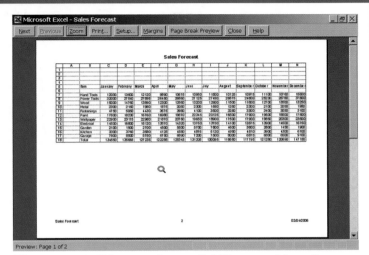

Figure 2.14 Print preview – Gridlines and headings

click on the Print button. To remove the options, repeat the actions and click in the ticked boxes to see the ticks disappear.

14 Print the sheet without gridlines or row and column headings, and then with them.

15 Save your sheet by selecting the File menu and clicking on the Save option.

16 Close Microsoft Excel® by selecting the File menu item and clicking on the Exit option or by clicking on the Close button in the top right-hand corner of the application window.

Printing

You can also print parts of a spreadsheet rather than the whole sheet by highlighting the section you require, selecting the File menu and the Print option. This will reveal the Print window. In the window is a section called Print what, with three options:

- Selection – print areas that are highlighted
- Active sheet(s) – print all the selected sheets
- Entire workbook – print all the sheets within the workbook.

Selection is a useful option if you are seeking to show changes and their effects.

There is a Preview button at the bottom of the Print window with which you can reveal the print preview and access the Page Setup to allow you to print gridlines and row and column headings. You can print the selection or whole sheet by clicking on the Print button in the preview window or by clicking the OK button in the Print window.

The printouts you have considered so far have shown the actual values of calculations. It is also useful to print out the sheet showing the formulae that are being used. This serves several purposes, not least that it is easier to check the accuracy of the formulae on a printout than on the screen.

To print the formulae you must select the Tools menu and the Options option. This will reveal the Options window (figure 2.15). In the View tab is a section called Window options. You can select to print the formulae by clicking in the Formulas box. This is also an alternative way of selecting Gridlines and Row & column headers. When you have made your choices, click on the OK button to enact them.

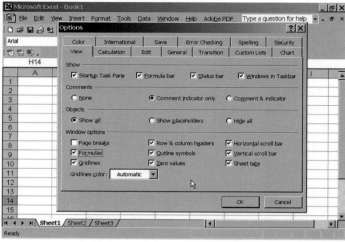

Figure 2.15 Options window

The formulae are now shown instead of their values, and if you select the Print Preview option you will see the spreadsheet showing them. It is useful when printing formulae also to print the row and column headers, since these allow you to interpret the references within the formulae.

Changing format

The Formatting toolbar (figure 2.16) provides a variety of tools to enhance the format of your spreadsheet. They all operate in a similar way. You highlight the cell or cells you need to change and select the appropriate tool from the toolbar. You can:

- change the font
- alter the character size
- embolden the entry
- change to italics
- underline the entry
- align the contents to the left, right or centre
- present the numbers as currency (e.g. £100,000.00)
- present the numbers as a percentage (e.g. 10000000%)
- present the numbers in a comma style (e.g. 100,000.00)
- increase or decrease the number of decimal places (e.g. 100,000 increased by two places becomes 100,000.00)

Spreadsheets are heavily concerned with numerical data and provide you with a variety of ways of formatting data (e.g. percentage, date, time, negative, currency, scientific and general). To select a particular format, you must initially highlight the cell or cells you want to change and then

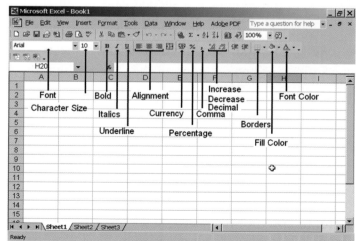

Figure 2.16 Formatting toolbar

select the specific icon from the toolbar. Formats are important since formulae will be designed to calculate values based on the format of the data. An important issue is that the format will control the appearance of the cell contents, but does not change their actual values, which are used in calculations.

For example, if a format has been chosen that limits decimal places to two, then 12.346 will be presented as 12.35, while when it is part of a calculation its actual value will be used, so that if the cell is multiplied by 10 its presented and actual value will be 123.46. However, this will appear to be wrong since 12.35 multiplied by 10 equals 123.50. This confuses many spreadsheet users.

If you enter a date or time in the correct way, Microsoft Excel® recognises it automatically as a date or time. Date formats that Microsoft Excel® accepts are shown by selecting the Format menu and the Cells option to reveal the Format Cells window. For example: 12-hour clock – 3.00pm; 24-hour clock – 15.00. In the Number tab, the Date and Time options show a list of accepted formats (e.g.12/12/2002 or 12 December 2002). Microsoft Excel® treats time as a number, so it is important to enter it correctly. Time can be entered in a 12- or 24-hour format. If you enter a 12-hour number, it must be followed by an 'a' or a 'p' to show if it is a.m. or p.m., respectively.

Microsoft Excel® can calculate time if the data is entered correctly. Date and times can be entered in a single cell providing they are separated by a space.

Borders

The appearance of a spreadsheet can be important in persuading people (e.g. senior managers) to accept its value as a useful business tool. To enhance the spreadsheet's appearance you have a variety of tools, including the Borders tool, with which you can enclose an individual cell, a selection of cells or the whole sheet within a border. Figure 2.17 shows the Borders tool options, available within the Formatting toolbar. When the icon is clicked, a small window of options appears. By clicking on an option you will add it to the cell, selection or whole sheet that you have highlighted.

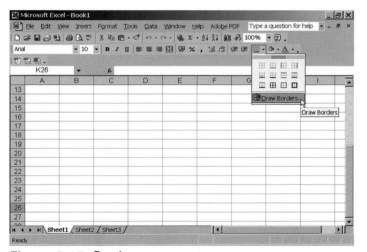

Figure 2.17 Borders

Enhancing the spreadsheet

1 Insert your floppy disk into the A: drive.

2 Load Microsoft Excel® using either the All Programs menu or the Excel® icon on the desktop. Open the file Sales Forecast by selecting the File menu, clicking on the Open option to reveal the Open window. Change the Look in: box to select the floppy disk and the file name will appear in the work area. Double-click Sales Forecast or single-click it and then click the Open button. The spreadsheet will open in Microsoft Excel®.

3 You can insert additional rows and columns. Click on the row 4 heading and you will see the entire row is highlighted. Click on the Insert menu and select the Rows option. A new row will be inserted and the spreadsheet will change.

4 Now change the character size of the columns headings (e.g. January, February) to 14, centred and embolden them. Highlight the cells and click on the Formatting toolbar options required. You will notice that they change in size and are too large for the column widths. Adjust the widths so that the headings are visible (i.e. January, February, August, September, October, November and December).

5 Now change the character size of the row headings (Items, Hand Tools, etc.) to 14 and embolden them. You will notice that they change in size and are too large for the column width. Adjust the width so that the headings are visible.

6 Now change the total row and column to currency (e.g. £ 100,000.00). Again, the change may be too large for the column width and you will need to make changes.

7 Now change the data by centring all the figures except the totals.

8 Save your sheet by selecting the File menu and clicking on the Save option. Figure 2.18 shows the appearance of the spreadsheet.

9 You are now going to calculate the monthly average for each item. In cell P8 insert =Average(C8:N8) – that is, the Average function and the range C8:N8, which are the monthly figures for Hand Tools. When you are finished, click elsewhere on the sheet to see the formula enacted. You should see the value appear.

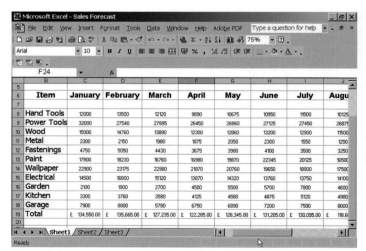

Figure 2.18 Enhancing spreadsheet

10 Replicate the formula for the other items and change their format to currency. You will need to change the column width to ensure everything is visible. In P6 enter the heading Average in character size 14 and embolden.

11 Print the whole spreadsheet, first showing the actual values of the calculations (using the File menu and the Print option), and then showing the formulae in full, using the Tools menu, Options option, View tab and Formulas box.

12 Highlight the headings across the top of your sheet (i.e. row 6). Select the border icon on the toolbar and click on the All Borders option (if you place your pointer over the options they will be named) and the row will be enclosed in a border.

13 Save your sheet by selecting the File menu and clicking on the Save option.

14 Print using the Selection option in the Print window, the headings enclosed in their border to show the changes you have made. You will need to highlight the headings.

15 An important thing to consider with any spreadsheet is the effect of changing some of the assumptions. If in our spreadsheet we decide to have a marketing campaign on selected products at Christmas, how would that impact on our national averages? Our public relations company has suggested the following new sales figures for December:

Power Tools: 65,000

Electrical: 38,000

Kitchen: 18,500

Enter these new values in the spreadsheet and see the averages and totals change. Are the changes significant? You could consider other predicted amounts. You might want to be more or less optimistic than the public relations company. When you enter the new data and click elsewhere, you should see the Calculated values updated. If this does not happen, click on the equals sign on the Formula taskbar and on the OK button in the window that appears. This will recalculate the formulae.

16 Print the outcomes of your changes, using the Selection option in the Print window. You will need to highlight the new sales figures for December and the new averages and totals.

17 Close Microsoft Excel® by selecting the File menu item and clicking on the Exit option or by clicking on the Close button in the top right-hand corner of the application window.

Hiding rows and columns

Within the Format menu are a number of functions which operate on cells, rows, columns and sheet. The Row and Column options reveal options to change the width of a column or the height of a row and to hide or unhide rows or columns.

It may not seem sensible to hide a row or column, but it is useful if, say, you want to show a customer the costs of a project without revealing confidential information.

Column widths

In earlier exercises you have adjusted the width of columns by using the mouse pointer to drag them. However, Microsoft Excel® provides you with the means to set exact column widths. To set widths, select the Format menu and click on Column to reveal a sub-menu with the option Width. Clicking on the Width option reveals the Column Width window. To change widths, enter a figure and then click the OK button. The function operates on the column or area of the sheet you have highlighted.

Orientation of text

When you enter text into a spreadsheet it is normally left-justified. To change its orientation, select the Format menu and click on the Cells option to reveal the Format Cells window (figure 2.19). The Alignment tab provides options to:

- align the text both horizontally and vertically (the options are available by clicking on the down arrow buttons at the end of the boxes)
- Wrap text – this allows you to enter multiple lines of text in a cell
- Shrink to fit – this reduces the size of text so that it fits into a cell
- Merge cells – this turns two or more cells in a single larger cell
- change the angle of orientation of the text (i.e. slope the text).

These functions work in the normal way (i.e. highlight your chosen cells and choose the desired options).

The other tabs provide extra functions. The Border tab provides an alternative way of selecting borders. The Number tab allows you to select the format of the figures, and the Font tab to choose different fonts, character sizes and the other functions available on the toolbar.

It is important to align spreadsheet data (columns of figures are normally shown perfectly aligned) so that readers can understand the information presented. Even small differences in the alignment can make

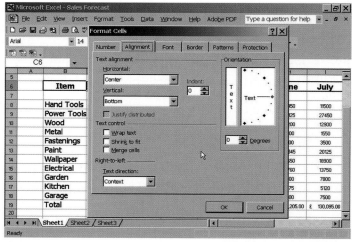

Figure 2.19 Format Cells window – Alignment tab

it difficult to understand a sheet of numbers. Often, important organisational decisions are based on spreadsheet analysis (e.g. signing contracts, setting prices, agreeing pay rises) – part of the decision is influenced by being persuaded that the information is accurate. This is certainly affected by the presentation. If a sheet is a mess it will not persuade managers to take key decisions. One that presents a quality image will help managers to accept the information it is offering. Microsoft Excel® provides the means to align data both vertically and horizontally so that you can produce high quality presentations.

Another useful device that is offered within the Format Cells window is the ability to merge cells. This is helpful when you want a title or label to cover more than one column or row.

Again, this is useful to develop a quality presentation of your information. The importance of a quality product should not be underestimated.

Sorting data

There are occasions when you want to sort your data into order, and Microsoft Excel® provides a straightforward way of sorting a column of data into either ascending or descending order. This function also operates on text, whereby the list is sorted alphabetically.

The sort functions are available on the Data menu or the Standard toolbar. The Sort functions on the toolbar allow you to sort on one column, while the function available from the Data menu enables you to sort on

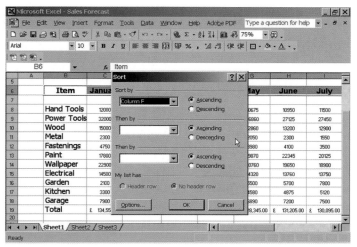

Figure 2.20 Sort window

more than one column of data. Select the Data menu and click on the Sort option to reveal the Sort window (figure 2.20). You can then select a series of columns to sort by and choose either ascending or descending order.

Autofilter

Filtering lets you focus only on items that meet a set criteria. With Microsoft Excel® you can filter a list to show only the rows that meet the criteria (e.g. a spreadsheet of employees could be filtered to show only staff employed in a particular team). One of the options in the Data menu is Filter. If this is highlighted, a new menu appears with the option AutoFilter. To use AutoFilter, make sure that the pointer is within the sheet (i.e. a cell is highlighted). When you select the option AutoFilter you will see that a button with a down-pointing arrow is added to top row of your spreadsheet (figure 2.21). If you select the down arrow button you will see a list of the unique items in the column (figure 2.21). If you choose an item, all the other rows

that do not match the item will be hidden. You have filtered the list to show only the items you wish to study.

The dropdown list also offers three other options:

- All – essentially, this removes the filter and shows the whole sheet of information.
- Top 10 – this allows you to filter against some numeric factor, such as the 6 products with the lowest value of sales or the 5 items with the highest profit. Top 10 is just a

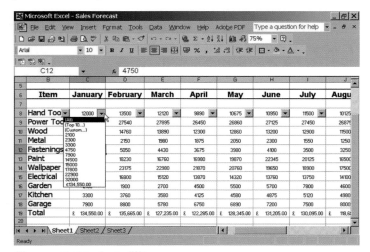

Figure 2.21 AutoFilter

name; it does not limit you to 10 items. When you select Top 10, a window appears enabling you to select the top or bottom, the number of items and items or per cent.

- Custom – this allows more complex filtering to be used.

Tracking changes

In many organisations, people work in teams and a spreadsheet may be used by a variety of people. A very useful feature of Microsoft Excel® and other modern spreadsheets is the ability to show changes that have been made. This is available by selecting the Tools menu, the Track Changes option and the Highlight Changes option, which, when clicked, will open the Highlight Changes window (figure 2.22).

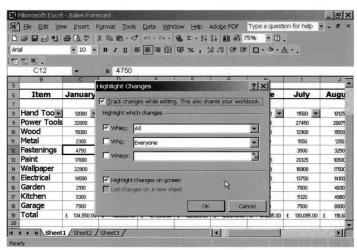
Figure 2.22 Highlight Changes window

You select the options by clicking in the boxes and a tick appears. When you then edit the spreadsheet, the changes are shown by the cells being enclosed by a coloured border. If the spreadsheet is printed, the changes are also shown.

Importing files

There are several ways of importing or opening information/data from other applications within Microsoft Excel®. The most straightforward is to use the Copy and Paste functions, which are available in all Microsoft Office® applications. An alternative is to use the Open option within the File menu. The file types which can be imported into Microsoft Excel® are shown in the Files of type box. It is often puzzling when you see files in a range of types. The type depends on the application software used to create it. This determines its purpose and what it is compatible with. Some generic file formats are designed to allow the file to be opened by a wide range of applications. An example of this is a text file shown by the extension .txt. The file you want to import is located using the Look in: box to identify the floppy disk, hard drive or folder. The files and folders are shown in the work area and are selected by either highlighting the file with a single click and then clicking on the Open button, or by double-clicking on the file.

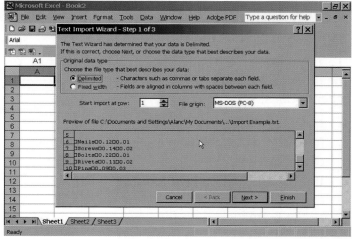
Figure 2.23 Wizard Step 1

The chosen file then needs to be converted into Microsoft Excel® format. To undertake this task, you are helped by a Microsoft Excel® Wizard, shown in figures 2.23, 2.24 and 2.25. The Wizard opens automatically when you try to import a file. If the file you have selected is not one of those that Microsoft Excel® can import, you will see an error message appear. This will say that the file format is not valid. A valid file will open the Wizard, but you may have to select the correct file in the Files of type box for the file you are importing.

Figure 2.23 shows the initial Wizard window, and this asks you to select if the file you are importing is delimited or fixed column width. The file can be seen in the scroll box for you to check. A delimited file is one in which the data is separated by commas or tabs, while a fixed width is one where the data is aligned into columns. When you have made your selection, click on the Next button to move to step 2 of the Wizard (figure 2.24).

Figure 2.24 illustrates how you define the delimiter used if your file is of this type. Click on the Next button when you have finished. Step 3 (the final step) of the Wizard gives you the opportunity to adjust the type of each column (figure 2.25).

By using the scroll box you can see the changes to the data and check how it will appear in a spreadsheet.

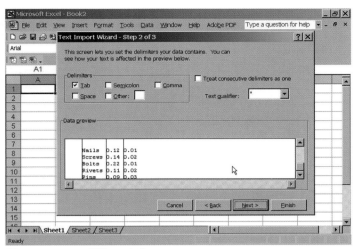

Figure 2.24 Wizard Step 2

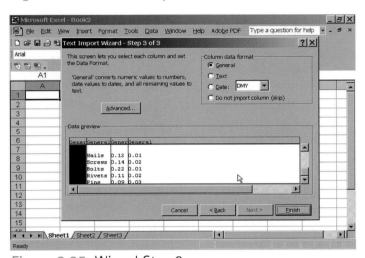

Figure 2.25 Wizard Step 3

Exercise 11

Importing data

1 Insert your floppy disk into the A: drive.

2 Create a data file (figure 2.26) using the Notepad application (Start, All Programs, Accessories and Notepad). Use the tab key to position the information in Notepad (i.e. one tab, enter Item, one tab, enter Cost, etc.). Save the file as Import Data on your floppy disk. It will appear as Import

```
Import Data - Notepad
File Edit Format View Help
This is a test file to demonstrate importing data into Microsoft Excel.

Item     Cost     Profit

Pens     0.17     0.04
Pencils  0.08     0.03
Ink      0.05     0.01
Refills  0.24     0.07
Staples  0.14     0.04
```

Figure 2.26 Notepad

Data.txt to show it is a text file. (In the CLAiT Plus assessment you will be provided with data files to import and you will not need to create them. The file is also available from the Hodder Education website – www.hodderclait.co.uk).

3 Load Microsoft Excel® using either the All Programs menu or the Excel® icon on the desktop.

4 Select the File menu and the Open option. Change the Look in: box to choose floppy disk and you should see your files. If you do not, then it is likely that you need to change the Files of type box to read Text Files or All Files. Double-click on Import Data.txt file and the Wizard Step 1 will appear (figure 2.27). The file is delimited, so click on the Next button. Figure 2.28 shows the appearance of the data in Wizard Step 2.

5 If the data is not laid out correctly you will need to adjust its presentation by using the different delimiters. Experiment with different combinations if you do not know what was used. The best is a combination of tab and space, but you may find it is either space or tab on its own if this was the way the file was created. Figure 2.28 shows you the Wizard view of the data once the correct delimiters were selected. In this example, this should be produced automatically.

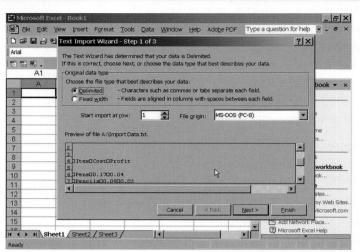

Figure 2.27 Wizard Step 1

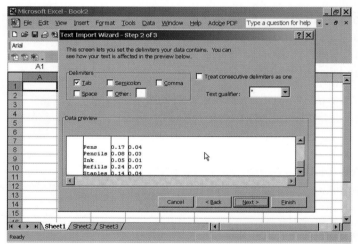

Figure 2.28 Correct delimiters selected

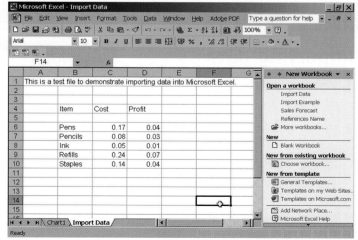

Figure 2.29 Imported data in Microsoft Excel®

continued

6 Click on <u>Next</u> in Wizard Step 3 to import the file into the spreadsheet. Figure 2.29 shows the result of importing the file. The process is complex, so you may need to practise this operation several times. Create new files of test data using different delimiters and experiment with the method until you are confident that you can import a data file.

7 Close Microsoft Excel® by selecting the <u>File</u> menu item and clicking on the E<u>x</u>it option, or by clicking on the Close button in the top right-hand corner of the application window.

House styles

In many organisations, spreadsheets are used by large numbers of staff. In order to ensure the quality of their presentation and use, many organisations have produced standards which are called house styles. Microsoft Excel® provides the means of establishing styles using the <u>Format</u> menu and the <u>Style</u> option.

This allows you to set a style covering factors such as:

- number formats
- fonts
- alignment
- borders
- patterns
- protection.

When you select the <u>Format</u> menu and click on the <u>Style</u> option, you open the Style window. This is shown in figure 2.30. If you click on the <u>Modify</u> button, the Format Cell window is opened, which allows you to choose different formats for your style.

A new style is applied by highlighting the spreadsheet, selecting the style and clicking the OK button. There is obviously an alternative way of applying a house style, which is simply to follow the standard as you create the spreadsheet, or amend each element, one by one. Creating a style helps you automate the process and reduce the potential for errors.

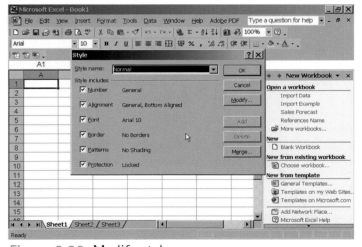

Figure 2.30 Modify style

Linking spreadsheets

In many cases, you will have a number of interrelated spreadsheets dealing with the same area of work. You may need one sheet showing the manufacturing costs, one showing transport costs and one indicating the costs of staff. If you study each of these separately, you will obviously benefit in that you can take more informed decisions. However, each of these areas depends on the others. Ideally, they should be linked directly so that a change in one will have immediate effects on the others. In this way you can see the consequences of any change.

The linked data can be included in formulae so that it can be used to solve problems, identify trends or any of the many other uses of formulae. In Exercise 12 you will link two sheets. The link is between a cell in which a formula has totalled a column of figures to a cell in another sheet. This cell, in turn, is part of a column which is totalled by a formula. This ability to include links into formulae is very useful in developing more complex relationships within spreadsheets.

Exercise 12

Linking spreadsheets

1 Insert a floppy disk into the A: drive.

2 Load Microsoft Excel® using either the All Programs menu or the Excel® icon on the desktop.

3 Set the orientation of the sheet to portrait, margins to 3 cm – right and left, and 2 cm – top and bottom, and header and footer to 1.5 cm (select File menu and Page Setup option).

4 Enter the spreadsheet shown in Figure 2.31. Use the SUM function to total rows and columns. This spreadsheet shows the costs of each factory in January.

5 Select the File menu and click on the option Save to reveal the Save As window. Change the Save in: box to select the floppy disk and add the file name First in the File name box. Click on the Save button. The top line of Microsoft Excel® will change to read 'Microsoft Excel® – First'.

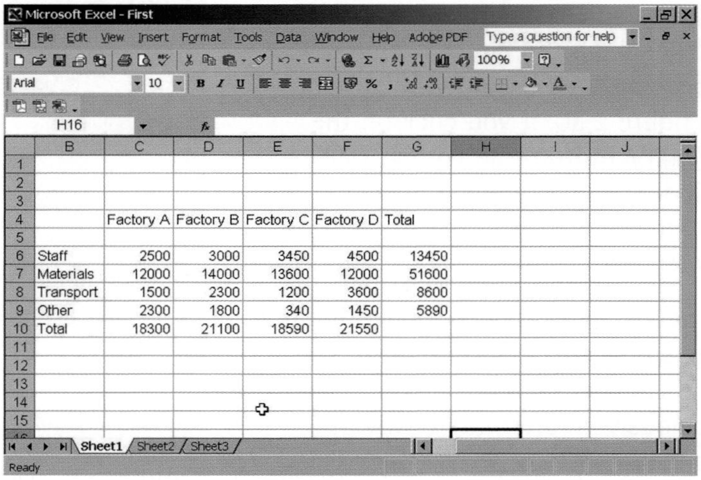

	B	C	D	E	F	G
4		Factory A	Factory B	Factory C	Factory D	Total
6	Staff	2500	3000	3450	4500	13450
7	Materials	12000	14000	13600	12000	51600
8	Transport	1500	2300	1200	3600	8600
9	Other	2300	1800	340	1450	5890
10	Total	18300	21100	18590	21550	

Figure 2.31 First spreadsheet

6 Select the File menu and click on the New option to reveal the New Workbook task pane window on the right of the work area (if this pane is already open then nothing will change). Select the Blank workbook option in the New Workbook pane and click on the OK button. A new blank spreadsheet will appear. Enter the spreadsheet shown in figure 2.32. Use the SUM function to total rows and columns. This spreadsheet represents the staff costs of each factory.

7 Select the File menu and click on the option Save to reveal the Save As window. Change the Save in: box to select the floppy disk and add the file name Second in the File name box. Click on the Save button. The top line of Microsoft Excel® will change to read 'Microsoft Excel® – Second'.

8 Inspection of the two spreadsheets shows that cell C6 of First should equal cell C11 of Second (i.e. staff costs of Factory A in January). You could transfer the information manually, of course, but it is very straightforward to link the two cells.

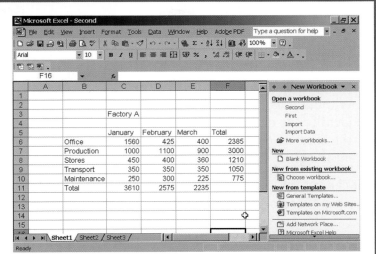

Figure 2.32 Second spreadsheet

9 In cell C6 of First spreadsheet insert = [Second.xls]sheet 1!C11. To make the new formula calculate, click the mouse away from the formula. You will see value change to 2610. Change the values in Second and see how the link operates.

10 To link two cells you simply enter the workbook name, sheet number, an exclamation mark and the cell reference. Practise making more links between the worksheets until you are satisfied that you understand the process.

11 Save the spreadsheets as Link.

12 Close Microsoft Excel® by selecting the File menu item and clicking on the Exit option or by clicking on the Close button in the top right-hand corner of the application window.

Graphs and charts

Often numbers are more easily understood if presented in a visual form. Microsoft Excel® provides the means of converting data into a graph or chart. Figure 2.33 illustrates a chart and shows the different labels that can be applied to it.

The main chart or graph labels are:

- Title – this is optional in a Microsoft Excel® chart or graph and provides a name for the chart. The title should relate to the content of the chart or graph.
- Axis titles – these identify the units that measure the chart or graph.

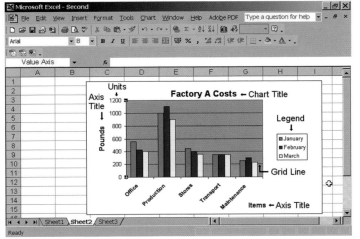

Figure 2.33 Chart

- Labels – these are used to identify the different elements in a chart or graph (eg. label the slices of a pie chart).
- Legend – this provides the key to understanding the data series (e.g. colour coding in a bar chart). Without a legend to correctly identify the displayed data series, the chart or graph is effectively meaningless.

You can set the chart or graph labels by using Microsoft Excel®'s Chart Wizard. The exercises in this chapter will help you to understand how to do this. The main types of charts and graphs are:

- pie charts
- bar/column charts
- line graph charts
- XY scatter graphs.

You can also present information by combining line graphs with column charts.

Figure 2.34 shows the Chart Wizard for Pie charts, which is obtained by selecting the appropriate data in your spreadsheet, then the Insert menu and clicking on the Chart option to reveal the Chart Wizard.

Pie charts are a very effective means of visually presenting a set of values. There is, however, more than one type. For example, the left-hand and middle charts in the second row of choices are exploding and three-dimensional exploding pie charts (figure 2.34).

Figure 2.33 illustrates a column chart; figure 2.35 shows a bar chart; figure 2.36 illustrates a line graph; and figure 2.37 shows a scatter graph. A bar or column chart is useful in comparing a range of results side by side (e.g. rainfall for different months of the year), while a line graph is used to show the relationship between two variables (e.g. how income changes over a period of time).

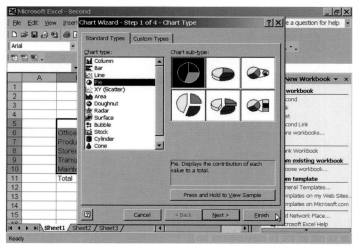

Figure 2.34 Pie charts

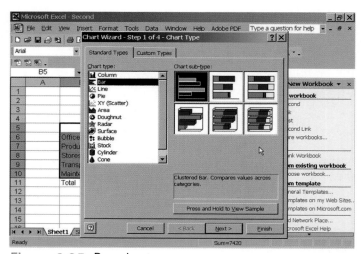

Figure 2.35 Bar chart

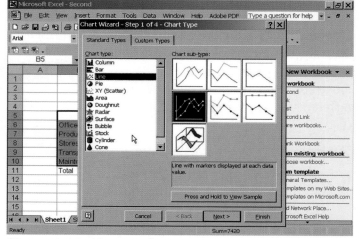

Figure 2.36 Line graph

A scatter graph presents two sets of variable data compared to each other. Often they do not show an obvious relationship, in that, as the name suggests, the data points are scattered over an area. However, it is possible to draw a line through the points to illustrate the trend of the variables against each other.

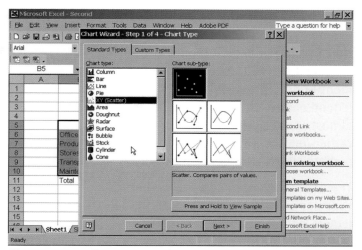

Figure 2.37 Scatter graph

Selecting data sets

The charts and graphs that you create depend on the data you select to base them on. You are free to select a whole spreadsheet, a subset of the data or data from non-adjacent areas. To select data you need to highlight it. If you click in the top left-hand corner of the data you want to select, and hold down the mouse button, you can drag the mouse to the bottom right corner of the data. The subset of data is highlighted when you release the mouse button.

In order to select data from non-adjacent areas you need to highlight the first area using the method described above, and then hold down the Ctrl key while repeating the highlighting operation on the second area. Both areas will be highlighted.

An alternative way of selecting data is to import it from another application. There are several ways of importing or opening information/data from within Microsoft Excel®. The most straightforward is to use the Copy and Paste functions if you are importing data from another Microsoft Office® application. An alternative is to use the Open option within the File menu to reveal the Open window. Microsoft Excel® can import files in a variety of formats. The file format depends on the application that was used to create it. The compatible formats are shown in the Files of type box in the Open window. The file you want to import is located using the Look in: box to identify the floppy disk, drive or folder. The files and folders are shown in the work area and are selected by either highlighting the file with a single click and then clicking on the Open button, or by double-clicking on the file. The chosen file needs to be converted into Microsoft Excel® format. To undertake this task you are helped by a Microsoft Excel® Wizard, which opens automatically when you import a file. The use of the Wizard was explained earlier in this chapter (see page 64).

Earlier (Exercise 8) you created a spreadsheet called Sales Forecast. You are going to use this information to practise choosing different data sets and creating charts.

Setting parameters

What makes a chart or graph meaningful are the titles, data labels,

Figure 2.38 Chart Wizard Step 1

legend and units that you employ. The legend is particularly important in that it is specifically intended to provide a key to the colours used to identify different data series. If a legend is missing or incorrect, it is almost impossible to understand. It is rather like showing in black and white a chart which uses colour coding.

The Chart Wizard allows you to enter the title and position, show the legend and select data labels. The initial step in using the Wizard is to select the data set and then the Insert menu and click on the Chart option. This opens the Chart Wizard. Figure 2.38 shows Step 1 of 4 of the Wizard, in which you select the type of chart or graph you want to create. By clicking on the Next button you move to Step 2, and, subsequently, to Steps 3 and 4. In several of the steps there are tabs which provide access to other functions. In Step 2 (figure 2.39) the Series tab allows you to name, add and remove different data series. The data series can be added or removed and named in the bottom half of the window in the Titles area.

In Step 3 (figure 2.40) of the Wizard you are provided with a series of tabbed windows which provide access to different functions. The Titles tab allows you to give the chart or graph a title, as well as naming the axis.

If you click on the Legend tab, you reveal a window which allows you to show or remove the legend and also to select where to position it (i.e. Bottom, Corner, Top, Right and Left) by clicking on the various checkboxes and radio buttons.

If you click on the Data Labels tab, you reveal a window which enables you to choose not to apply data labels or to choose between different types of label (e.g. names or values). When you have finished then you can move to step 4 (figure 2.41). This offers you the choice of combining your chart or graph with the associated data or presenting it on a separate sheet.

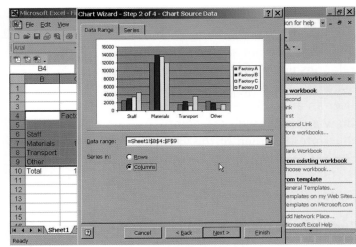

Figure 2.39 Chart Wizard Step 2

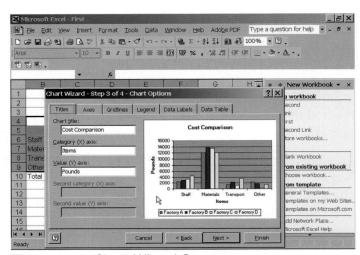

Figure 2.40 Chart Wizard Step 3

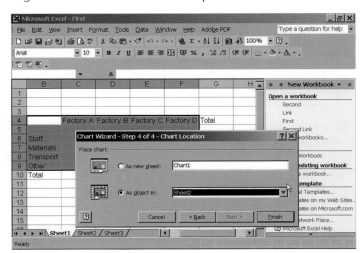

Figure 2.41 Chart Wizard Step 4

Creating an exploding pie chart

1 Insert your floppy disk which contains the Sales Forecast file into the A: drive.

2 Load Microsoft Excel® using either the All Programs menu or the Excel® icon on the desktop. Open the Sales Forecast file by selecting the File menu and clicking on the Open option to reveal the Open window. Change the Look in: box to select the floppy disk and the file name will appear in the work area. Double-click Sales Forecast or single-click it and then click the OK button. The spreadsheet will open in Microsoft Excel®. If you have saved the spreadsheet with the AutoFilter on, you will need to switch it off to avoid obscuring the data (Data menu, highlight Filter and select AutoFilter to remove tick).

3 Highlight the first two columns (i.e. Items and January), excluding the Total row. Select the Insert menu and the Chart option. Click on the Pie chart option and either the two- or three-dimensional exploding items (i.e. the left-hand or middle options of the second row). Check the chart by clicking and holding down the mouse button on the Press and Hold to View Sample button. This allows you to see the chart. Release and click on the next button to move to step 2 of the Chart Wizard (figure 2.42).

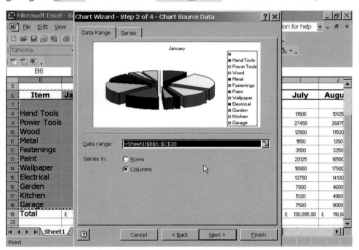

Figure 2.42 Pie Chart Wizard Step 2

4 Consider the data range =sheet1!$B$6:$C$18, which translates to the area in the top left-hand corner, cell B6 to cell C18. The chart shows a blank item in the legend above Hand Tools. This corresponds to the blank row 7, so change the range to B8 to C18 (i.e. =sheet1!$B$8:$C$18), by clicking, deleting and entering new values.

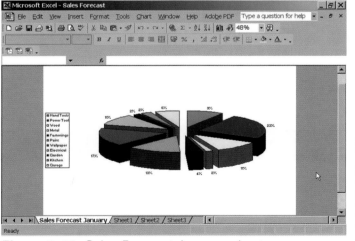

Figure 2.43 Sales Forecast January chart

5 Click on the Next button to reveal Step 3.

6 Click on the FileTitles tab and enter Sales Forecast January. Click on the Legend tab and select left. Click on the Data Labels tab and select the Percentage option. Click on the Next button to reveal step 4.

7 Click on the As new sheet option and enter Sales Forecast January. Click on the Finish button. The exploding pie chart will appear (figure 2.43) on a new sheet linked to your Sales Forecast Data. If you place your mouse pointer on any of the segments of the pie chart you will see an explanation of what the data represents (e.g. Series 1 "Wood" Value 15,000 11%). Take a moment to consider the image and notice how a three-dimensional exploding pie chart is a powerful representation of the data. The size of each segment is shown in relation to the others so that its value is emphasised.

8 Save your chart by selecting the File menu and the Save As option to reveal the Save As window. Save your file as Sales Forecast January on your floppy disk.

9 Close Microsoft Excel® by selecting the File menu item and clicking on the Exit option or by clicking on the Close button in the top right-hand corner of the application window.

Rows and columns presentation

In step 2 of the Chart Wizard (figure 2.39) are two options, Rows and Columns. These options change the presentation of the chart. Figure 2.44 shows the same chart in row presentation. In Column presentation the bars reflect the column values of January, February and March, while the axis shows the row items. In Rows presentation the bars reflect the row values while the axis shows the column items (i.e. the bars are grouped by month).

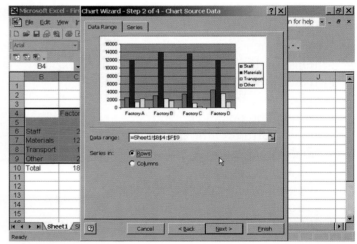

Figure 2.44 Rows presentation

Exercise 14

Selecting data sets

1 Insert your floppy disk into the A: drive.

2 Load Microsoft Excel® using either the All Programs menu or the Excel® icon on the desktop. Open the file Sales Forecast January by selecting the File menu and clicking on the Open option to reveal the Open window. Change the Look in: box to select the floppy disk and the file name will appear in the work area. Double-click on the Sales Forecast January or single-click it and then click the OK button. Select Sheet 1 to reveal the spreadsheet data.

3 You are going to produce a bar chart for three months of data to compare the different results. Highlight the columns Item, January, February and March, excluding the Total row.

4 Select the Insert menu and the Chart option. Click on the Column chart. Notice that in Chart Wizard Step 2 there is an area of the window called Series in: and two choices:

- Rows
- Columns.

Explore what happens when you select rows. When you are finished, select columns.

5 Now work through these steps:

a) Name the chart Quarter Comparison

b) X axis – Items

c) Y axis – Amount

d) Legend – on top

e) No data labels

e) Place chart as a new sheet (i.e. Quarter Comparison Chart).

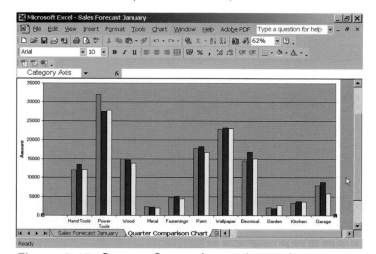

Figure 2.45 Quarter Comparison column chart

6 Save the chart, by selecting the File menu and the Save As option, as the file Quarter Comparison Chart on your floppy disk or a location of your choice.

7 Figure 2.45 illustrates the Quarter Comparison Chart.

8 Repeat this process, but select the columns Item and the months June, July and August. Highlight the Item column and then, holding down the Ctrl key, highlight the other three columns, excluding the

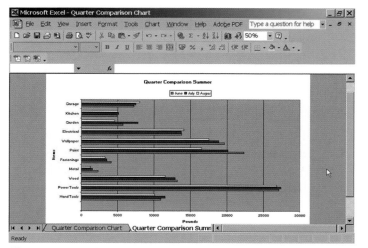

Figure 2.46 Bar chart

Total row. Select the Chart option. Create a bar chart. Use the same axis and legend position, and entitle the column chart Quarter Comparison Summer.

You have created a chart using data from non-adjacent columns.

9 Figure 2.46 shows the bar chart.

10 Save the chart, by selecting the File menu and the Save As option, as the file Quarter Comparison Summer on your floppy disk or a location of your choice.

11 You can present the chart in either portrait or landscape mode by selecting the File menu and clicking on the Page Setup option to reveal the Page Setup window. Click in the appropriate radio button. To check how the chart would appear if printed, click on the Print Preview button. To print the chart, click on the Print button to reveal the Print window.

12 Print your bar chart in both portrait and landscape modes.

13 Close Microsoft Excel® by selecting the File menu and clicking on the Exit option or by clicking on the Close button in the top right-hand corner of the application window.

Line graphs

A line graph shows the relationship between two variables. If you plotted the sales forecast for Hand Tools against months you would obtain a line graph showing how sales of these products fluctuated across the 12 months. It is also possible to combine a line graph with a column chart so that both appear together.

Exercise 15

Line and column graphs

1 Insert your floppy disk into the A: drive.

2 Load Microsoft Excel® using either the All Programs menu or the Excel® icon on the desktop. Open the file Sales Forecast January by selecting the File menu and clicking on the Open option to reveal the Open window. Change the Look in: box to select the floppy disk and the file name will appear in the work area. Double-click Sales Forecast January or single-click it and then click the OK button. Select Sheet 1 to reveal spreadsheet data.

3 Highlight the top three rows of Sales Forecast (Items, Hand Tools and Power Tools), excluding Total and Average columns, and then select the Insert menu and click on the Chart option. Select one of the line graphs (whichever appeals) and create it using the Wizard. However, select:

a) Not to show the legend

b) Title – Tools

c) X axis – Months

d) Y axis – Amount

e) No gridlines

f) No data labels

g) As a new sheet called Tools.

4 Figure 2.47 shows the line graph that you have created.

5 Save the chart, by selecting the File menu and the Save option, as the file Tools on your floppy disk or a location of your choice.

6 Print your line graph in either portrait or landscape.

7 You are now going to produce a graph displaying both a line and columns. Highlight columns Item and October, November and December, excluding the Total row. Remember that to highlight non-adjacent columns you need to hold down the Ctrl key. With the columns highlighted, select the Insert menu and click on the Chart option.

8 Select the Custom Types tab and the Line and Column chart (figure 2.48). Follow the Chart Wizard. Choose the title to be Quarter Comparison Autumn, X axis – Items, Y axis – Amount, Legend – Bottom, and as a new sheet called Quarter Comparison Autumn.

9 Figure 2.49 illustrates a line and column graph. October and November are shown as columns, while December is displayed as a line.

10 Save the chart, by selecting the File menu and the Save As option, as the file Quarter Comparison Autumn on your floppy disk or a location of your choice.

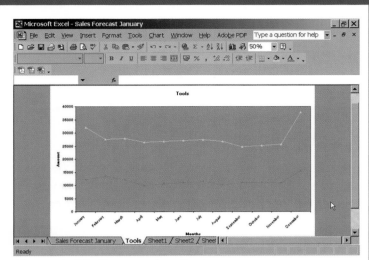

Figure 2.47 **Line graph – Tools**

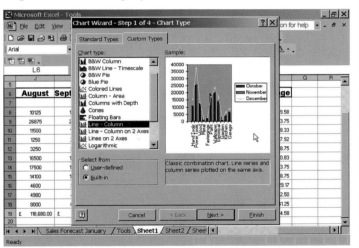

Figure 2.48 **Line and column type – Custom**

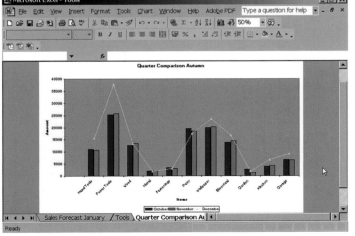

Figure 2.49 **Quarter Comparison Autumn**

11 Print your line and column graph in either portrait or landscape.

12 Close Microsoft Excel® by selecting the File menu item and clicking on the Exit option or by clicking on the Close button in the top right-hand corner of the application window.

XY scatter graph

XY scatter graphs are used to plot the values of two or more variables against each other in order to show the relationship between them. They are often used to present the results of engineering, laboratory or other experimental work.

Exercise 16

XY scatter graphs

1 Normally you will be provided with the data on which your charts and graphs will be based. In this exercise, the table below shows the relationship between actual and predicted rainfall at monthly intervals.

2 Load Microsoft Excel® using either the All Programs menu or the Excel® icon on the desktop. Enter the data below and save the spreadsheet to a floppy disk as a file called Rainfall.

Months	Predicted Rainfall	Actual Rainfall
January	12.50	10.00
February	16.25	15.50
March	23.75	26.55
April	14.15	18.90
May	12.50	11.75
June	9.85	12.55
July	8.65	5.50
August	4.75	3.55
September	15.75	11.85
October	18.75	17.25
November	19.85	25.95
December	15.65	17.45

3 Highlight the whole of the information except the title line. Select the Insert menu and click on the Chart option. Select one of the XY scatter graphs and create it using the Wizard. You will need to use the Series tab in step 2 to change the names of Series 1 to Predicted and Series 2 to Actual. However, select:

continued

a) Title – Rainfall

b) X axis – Months

c) Y axis – Inches

d) Y Major gridlines

e) Legend – Corner

f) No data labels

g) As a new sheet called Rainfall.

4 Figure 2.50 shows the XY scatter graph that we have created. Notice that you appear to have 14 months in a year. We will edit the graph to remove this error later.

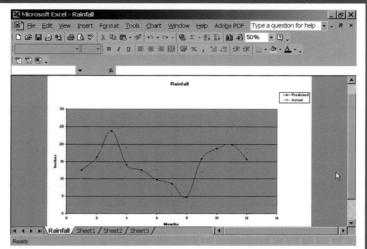

Figure 2.50 Rainfall

5 Save the chart, by selecting the File menu and the Save option, as the file Rainfall on your floppy disk or a location of your choice.

6 Print your XY scatter graph in either portrait or landscape.

7 To help understand the graph, it is possible to add a trendline by selecting the Chart menu to open the Add Trendline window. Select the Linear Trend/Regression type and the

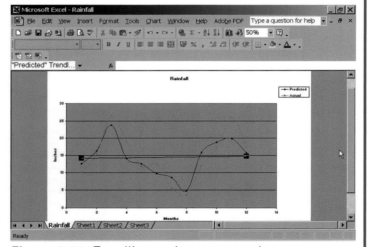

Figure 2.51 Trendline and scatter graph

series the line is based on (i.e. Predicted or Actual Rainfall). Figure 2.51 shows the scatter graph with a trendline. The line helps you to predict the rainfall across the year, or to predict future rainfall by extending the line, while the actual line allows you to consider the variation across the year.

8 It is possible to display the equation by clicking on the trendline so it is highlighted (i.e. each end of the line will have a square handle). Select the Format menu and click on the Selected Trendline option to reveal the Format Trendline window. Select the Options tab and click on the Display equation on chart radio button. The trendline equation is displayed near the graph. In New CLAiT Plus 2006 you will not be assessed on adding a trendline or its equation, but since they are sometimes useful we have included them in the chapter.

9 Save the chart by selecting the File menu and the Save option on your floppy disk or a location of your choice.

10 Print your XY scatter graph with trendline and equation in either portrait or landscape.

11 Close Microsoft Excel® by selecting the File menu item and clicking on the Exit option or by clicking on the Close button in the top right-hand corner of the application window.

Page setup

You can adjust the display of your charts and graphs by selecting the File menu and the Page Setup option to reveal the Page Setup window (assumes chart and graph is being displayed). This allows you to adjust all four margins – top, bottom, left and right. In addition, you can change the size of the header and footer.

By clicking on the Header/Footer tab you can add them to your chart or graph.

Text box

Although an image is often said to be worth a thousand words, it can be enhanced by the addition of some text. Charts and graphs are useful ways of presenting information, but in many cases they need a short statement to help your audience to fully understand their content. Words can be added to charts and graphs using a text box. Click on the Text Box icon on the Draw toolbar to reveal a new mouse pointer. Draw a box by holding down the mouse button and dragging the box open (figure 2.52). Text then can be added to the open box.

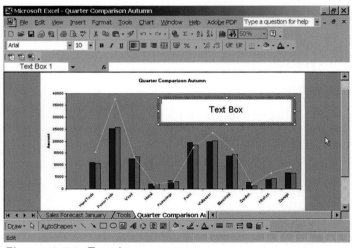

Figure 2.52 Text box

House style

In order to ensure consistency in organisational documents and publications, house styles are often developed. These provide a series of guidelines for staff to follow. An example is given below. House styles are often employed to ensure that a minimum standard of quality is adhered to by employees.

Example house style guidelines:

Pie Charts

Font (typeface)   serif (e.g. Times New Roman)

Character (text) size
                    Title   20, bold
                    Subtitle   20, bold
                    Data Labels   14
                    Legend   14

Bar/column, line and XY scatter charts and graphs

Font (typeface)   serif (e.g. Times New Roman)

Character (text) size

Title   20, bold
Subtitle   20, bold
X axis title   14, bold
Y axis title   14, bold
Other text/numbering on the X axis   12
Other text/numbering on the Y axis   12
Legend   12

Text box labels   12, border invisible

Trendline equation   12

Headers and footers

During your assessment you will be often asked to insert your name and centre number in either the header or footer. Organisations often use the header and footer to record titles, dates and file names.

Formatting graphs and charts

It is possible to edit your charts and graphs employing the techniques that you have learned from using other Microsoft Office® applications. You can change the fonts, character sizes and effects (e.g. bold), apply superscript and subscript effects, change the style and thickness of lines and alter the colours of your charts and graphs.

To edit a chart or graph you must double-click on the element that you are seeking to change. A window will appear (e.g. Format Chart Title, Format Axis, Format Plot Area, Format

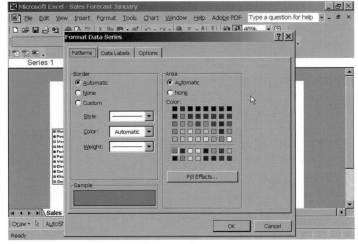

Figure 2.53 Format data series

Legend, Format Data Labels, Format Data Series). Figure 2.53 illustrates the Format Data Series for the Sales Forecast January exploding pie chart that you created earlier. The element that you have double-clicked will be highlighted by being enclosed in a frame with small black squares.

The format window is divided into three tabs – Patterns, Data Labels and Options. Each of these is similarly divided, but in a way appropriate to the element. In the case of Patterns you can alter the colours, fill effects and lines. In the Data Labels tab you can adjust the labels, while in Options you can change the angle of the pie slices. You should notice that the options are customised to the type of chart or graph.

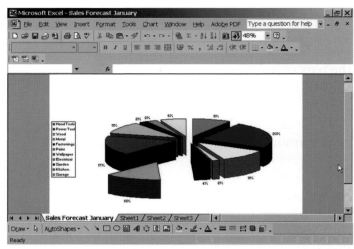

Figure 2.54 Dragging a slice

You can move the various slices of the pie by clicking on a segment and holding down the button to drag it. This is a useful way to emphasise that slice (figure 2.54).

If you click on the axis, the Format Axis window will open. This allows you to change the upper and lower limits, intervals on the axis and numeric formatting. The different functions are grouped together under the various tabs across the top of the window. Figure 2.55 shows the Format Axis for the Quarter Comparison Autumn Chart – notice the tabs of Patterns, Scale, Font, Number and Alignment. The Data Labels Number tab provides you with a wide range of numeric formats for the axes (e.g. fractions, currency, decimal places, date, negative signs and minus signs). The Patterns tab provides you with the means to change the markers on the chart or graph lines, using the options indicated by radio buttons on the right side of the window.

If you select the Font tab, which is available in many of the Format windows, you will reveal the options to change the fonts, including type, style, size and effects. The effects include choosing Strikethrough, Superscript and Subscript, by clicking on the appropriate checkboxes.

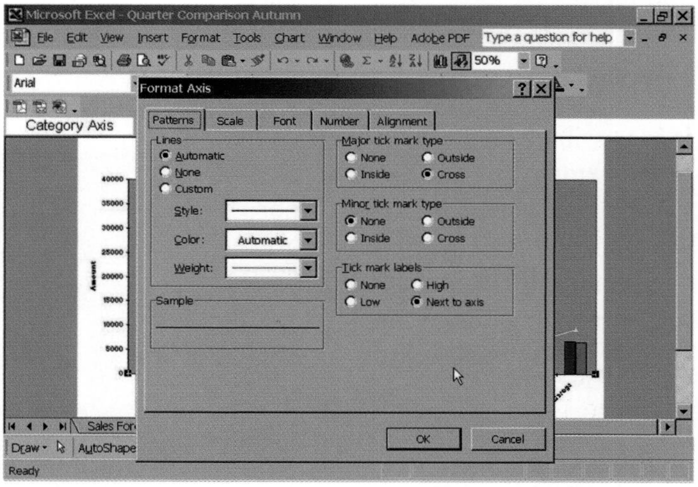

If you double-click in the plot area, you will open the Format Plot Area window. This allows you to change the background colour of the plot or to choose to have no background colour (i.e. select the None option radio

Figure 2.55 Format Axis – Quarter Comparison Autumn

button). You select the colour by clicking on those displayed in the palette and you are shown a sample of the colour. There is also a Fill Effects button, which provides access to a variety of fills. When you wish to apply the changes to the background, click on the OK button.

In a similar way to changing the background colour of the chart or graph, you can change the colour of the bars of a data series by double-clicking on one of the bars. This will open the Format Data Series window (figure 2.56). The new bar colour is chosen from the palette or from the Fill Effects options. To apply the new colour or fill, you need to click on the OK button. Compare figure 2.56 with figure 2.53, since both are called Format Data Series. The difference is that they are customised for different types of chart.

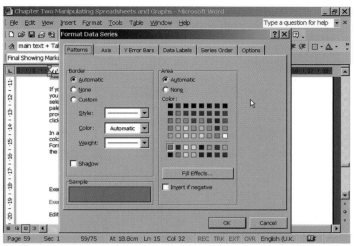

Figure 2.56 Format Data Series window

Exercise 17 provides you with the opportunity to explore many of these options.

Exercise 17

Editing a chart

1 Insert your floppy disk into the A: drive.

2 Load Microsoft Excel® using either the All Programs menu or the Excel® icon on the desktop. Open the file Quarter Comparison Chart by selecting the File menu and clicking on the Open option to reveal the Open window. Change the Look in: box to select the floppy disk and the file name will appear in the work area. Double-click Quarter Comparison Chart or single-click it and then click the OK button.

3 Select the Quarter Comparison Chart by clicking on the tab. You are now going to edit this chart. Double-click on the title to open the Format Chart Title window, and click on the Font tab to show the options. Select the Times New Roman font, character size 20 and embolden the text. You should also explore the other options. When you have completed the changes to conform with the house style, click on the OK button.

4 Double-click on the legend to open the Format Legend window and select Times New Roman and size 14.

5 Double-click on the X and Y axes titles in turn and change them to Times New Roman, emboldened and size 14.

6 Double-click on the text along each axis and change it to Times New Roman and size 12.

7 Once you have made the changes, take the opportunity to explore some other editing possibilities.

8 If you double-click in the plot area you will open the Format Plot Area window, which will allow you to change the background colour or remove it. Experiment with different options until you find one you prefer.

9 If you double-click on the Amount Axis line, you will open the Format Axis window. This provides five tabs – Patterns, Scale, Font, Number and Alignment. Explore the different options. You can select specific numeric formats for your axis. This can be very useful in other charts. In the Patterns tab you will notice three sets of marks (e.g. Major tick mark type). Experiment with the different options.

10 Double-click on one of the data bars and you will open the Format Data Series window. Explore the different options, but choose a new colour for this bar and the other two. Also change the line thickness using the same windows.

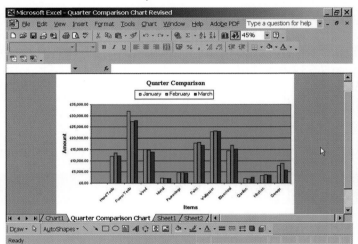

11 Make any other changes that you feel will improve the chart. Figure 2.57 illustrates the changes we have made. Compare your own efforts

Figure 2.57 **Chart edited**

with it. There is no need to be identical, except in respect of the earlier instructions.

12 Save the chart, by selecting the File menu and the Save As option, as Quarter Comparison Chart Revised on your floppy disk or a location of your choice.

13 Print your edited chart in either portrait or landscape.

14 Close Microsoft Excel® by selecting the File menu item and clicking on the Exit option or by clicking on the Close button in the top right-hand corner of the application window.

Editing an XY scatter graph

In Exercise 16, the final chart (Figure 2.51) appears to show that there are 14 months in the year. This can be removed using the editing options.

Exercise 18

Editing XY scatter graph

1 Insert your floppy disk into the A: drive.

2 Load Microsoft Excel® using either the All Programs menu or the Excel® icon on the desktop. Open the file Rainfall by selecting the File menu and clicking on the Open option to reveal the Open window. Change the Look in: box to select the floppy disk and the file name will appear in the work area. Double-click Rainfall or single-click it and then click the OK button.

3 Select the Rainfall chart by clicking on the tab. You are now going to edit this chart.

4 Click on the X axis to open the Format Axis window and select the Scale tab. Change maximum from 14 to 12 and click on the OK button. You will see the scale change to 12.

5 Click on one of the scatter points and the Format Data Series window will open. Select the Patterns tab and change the marker style to one you prefer. Repeat the action, selecting the other series of points. Try to make the scatter graph more legible.

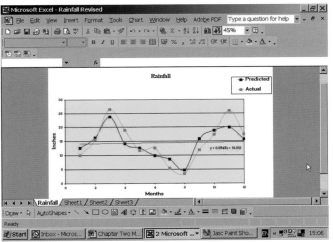

6 Explore the different options and try to improve the clarity of the chart. Our efforts are shown in figure 2.58. However, there is no need to produce an identical copy.

Figure 2.58 Rainfall chart revised

7 Save the chart, by selecting the File menu and the Save As option, as Rainfall Revised on your floppy disk or a location of your choice.

8 Print your edited chart in either portrait or landscape.

9 Close Microsoft Excel® by selecting the File menu item and clicking on the Exit option or by clicking on the Close button in the top right-hand corner of the application window.

Prediction

Graphs and charts are useful ways of presenting numerical information. They can make complex data understandable. Pie, column and bar charts allow you to compare different sets of information so that it is straightforward to understand. However, graphs can also help with prediction, by extending or extrapolating the lines into the future. This requires a graph or chart with one axis being time (e.g. hours, days, months or years).

It is possible to extend the trendline for the actual and predicted rainfall lines and thus estimate rainfall. However, you always need to consider what the data represents. In this case, rainfall is likely to be seasonal, so simply extending the lines may be inaccurate. You need to compare the extended line with the actual values of the months and consider how close the match is.

It is often helpful to extend lines into the future as long as you are careful when considering the context of the information. In this case, there is a distinct cycle to the rainfall throughout the year, which, if you consider it alongside the extrapolations, will provide greater accuracy in your predictions. Weather forecasts are often limited to a few days ahead.

More practice

In the assessment you may be provided with a series of files representing some partly completed spreadsheets and data that you need to import. These additional exercises often require that you enter information to create the spreadsheet. They are also available on the Hodder Education website (www.hodderclait.co.uk) linked to this book, so you can use them rather than having to input the information.

Activity 1

1 Insert a floppy disk into the A: drive.
2 Load Microsoft Excel® using either the All Programs menu or the Excel® icon on the desktop.
3 Set the orientation of the sheet to landscape, margins to 2.5 cm – right and left, and 2.5 cm – top and bottom, and header and footer to 2 cm (select File menu and Page Setup option).
4 Insert a header to read: Sports Results (Arial font and character size 14 bold – in the Centre section).
5 Insert automatic fields in the footer:

   File name – Left section
   Page number – Centre section
   Date – Right section

6 Enter the table of information shown in figure 2.59 to form your first spreadsheet of the average performances of sports club members during the last six months.
7 Check that you have entered the data accurately and correct any mistakes. If you click in the cell that contains the error, you can amend the mistake.
8 Select the File menu and click on the option Save to reveal the Save As window. Change the Save in: box to select the floppy disk and add the file name Sport in the File name: box. Click on the Save button. The top line of Microsoft Excel® will change to read 'Microsoft Excel® – Sport'.

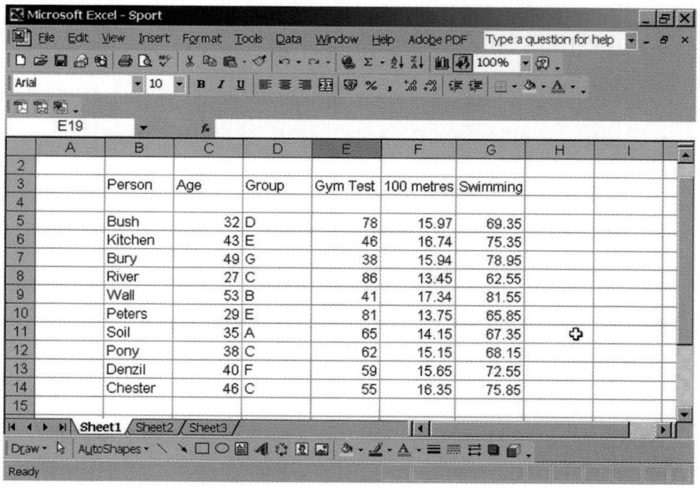

Person	Age	Group	Gym Test	100 metres	Swimming
Bush	32	D	78	15.97	69.35
Kitchen	43	E	46	16.74	75.35
Bury	49	G	38	15.94	78.95
River	27	C	86	13.45	62.55
Wall	53	B	41	17.34	81.55
Peters	29	E	81	13.75	65.85
Soil	35	A	65	14.15	67.35
Pony	38	C	62	15.15	68.15
Denzil	40	F	59	15.65	72.55
Chester	46	C	55	16.35	75.85

Figure 2.59 Sports

9 Change the size of the columns so that you can see the contents clearly. Use the AVERAGE function to average the columns, and add the name Average to the row.

10 Check the appearance of your spreadsheet as a printed document by selecting the **File** menu and the **Print Preview** option.

11 Click on **Sheet 2** to create a new spreadsheet. Enter the table of information in (figure 2.60) to form a second spreadsheet. This shows Bush's last four scores at the three disciplines.

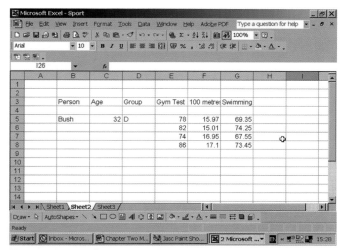

Figure 2.60 Sheet 2 – Bush

12 Change the size of the columns so that you can see the contents clearly. Use the AVERAGE function to average the rows. Name the row Average.

13 Link the three Bush averages to the Sports spreadsheet (i.e. sheet2!E9, sheet2!F9 and sheet2!G9).

14 Save your sheet, by selecting the **File** menu and clicking on the **Save As** option, as file Sport Revised.

15 Return to Sheet 1 and in column H create an IF function to decide if the individual members are fit or unfit, depending on their Gym Test score. Fitness is determined by scoring more than 60 (=IF(E5>60,"Fit","Unfit"). Insert a column heading Fitness.

16 Adjust all the figures in Sheet 1 so they are to two decimal places. Change the font to Arial and character size to 12. Embolden all the headings and centre all the data. You will need to adjust the column widths accordingly.

17 Use the formula for fitness to produce an overall estimate of the fitness of the members. Name this cell Fitness.

17 Figure 2.61 shows the new sheet.

18 Print the sheet without gridlines and row and column headings, and then with them.

19 Print the sheet showing the formulae.

20 Save your sheet by selecting the **File** menu and clicking on the **Save** option.

21 Close Microsoft Excel® by selecting the **File** menu item and clicking on the **Exit** option or by clicking on the **Close** button in the top right-hand corner of the application window.

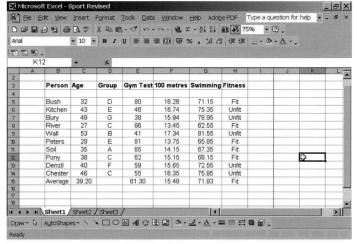

Figure 2.61 Sport Revised

Activity 2

Pie chart

1   Insert a floppy disk into the A: drive.

2   Load Microsoft Excel® using either the All Programs menu or the Excel® icon on the desktop. Open the file Sport Revised by selecting the File menu and clicking on the Open option to reveal the Open window. Change the Look in: box to select the floppy disk and the file name will appear in the work area. Double-click Sport Revised or single-click it and then click the OK button.

3   Using the names of the members and the Gym Test scores, create an exploded pie chart.

   a) Title – Fitness

   b) Label each segment with the member's name.

   c) Do not display the legend.

   d) Create the chart on a separate sheet to the data. Title – Fitness.

   e) Drag Bush's segment out from the others.

4   Add your name to the header.

5   Edit the chart to ensure everything is clear and legible.

6   Print a copy of the pie chart. Figure 2.62 shows the pie chart we created.

7   Save your sheet by selecting the File menu and clicking on the Save option. Call the file Sport Revised Fitness.

8   Close Microsoft Excel® by selecting the File menu item and clicking on the Exit option or by clicking on the Close button in the top right-hand corner of the application window.

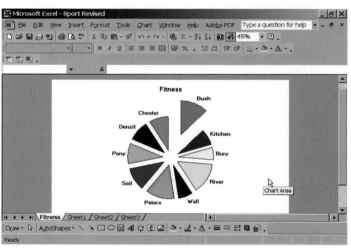

Figure 2.62 Sport pie chart

Activity 3

Scatter graph

1   Insert a floppy disk into the A: drive.

2   Load Microsoft Excel® using either the All Programs menu or the Excel® icon on the desktop. Open the file Sport Revised by selecting the File menu and clicking on the Open option to reveal the Open window. Change the Look in: box to select the floppy disk and the file name will appear in the work area. Double-click Sport Revised Fitness or single-click it and then click the OK button. Sheet 1 contains the spreadsheet data.

3   Using the names of the members and data from 100 metres and swimming, create an XY scatter graph:

a) Title – Relationship

b) Change series names to 100 metres and Swimming.

c) Display the legend at the top.

d) Label X axis – members, and Y axis – seconds.

e) Create the chart on a separate sheet to the data. Title – Relationship.

4 Add your name to the header.

5 Edit the chart to ensure everything is clear and legible.

6 Print a copy of the scatter graph. Figure 2.63 shows the scatter graph we created.

7 Save your sheet by selecting the File menu and clicking on the Save option. Call the file Sport Revised Relationship.

8 Close Microsoft Excel® by selecting the File menu item and clicking on the Exit option or by clicking on the Close button in the top right-hand corner of the application window.

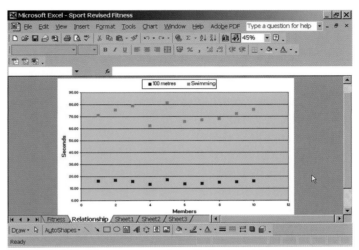

Figure 2.63 Scatter graph – Relationship

Activity 4

Sort and filter

1 Insert a floppy disk into the A: drive.

2 Load Microsoft Excel® using either the All Programs menu or the Excel® icon on the desktop. Open the file Sport Revised by selecting the File menu and clicking on the Open option to reveal the Open window. Change the Look in: box to select the floppy disk and the file name will appear in the work area. Double-click Sport Revised Relationship or single-click it and then click the OK button. Select Sheet 1.

3 Chester has left the sports club, so his records need to be deleted.

4 Filter the data to locate all members who are judged to be fit. Print a copy of the filtered spreadsheet, with row and column headings.

5 Filter the data to locate members with a swimming score less than 71.49 (i.e. use Custom option). Print a copy of the filtered spreadsheet (figure 2.64), with row and column headings.

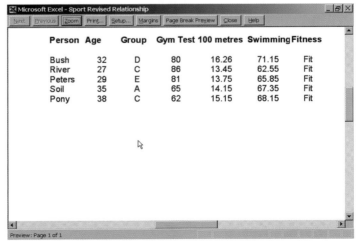

Figure 2.64 Filtered spreadsheet

6 Sort the data into descending order of member names.

7 Create a header. Add your name and file name.

8 Save your sheet by selecting the <u>F</u>ile menu and clicking on the <u>S</u>ave option. Call the file Sport Revised Filter.

9 Close Microsoft Excel® by selecting the <u>F</u>ile menu item and clicking on the E<u>x</u>it option or by clicking on the <u>Close</u> button in the top right-hand corner of the application window.

Activity 5

1 Insert your floppy disk into the A: drive.

2 Create a data file using the Notepad application (<u>Start</u>, <u>All Programs</u>, <u>Accessories</u> and <u>Notepad</u>). Separate the data only with commas:

Staff,January,February,March
Squires,300,700,1200
Johnson,100,300,500
Singh,300,1200,2100
Patel,150,340,800
Gordon,230,560,600
Davies,270,450,560

3 Save the file as Sales Data. (In the CLAiT Plus assessment you will be provided with data files to import and will not need to create them. Sales Data is available on the Hodder Education website – www.hodderclait.co.uk).

4 Load Microsoft Excel® using either the <u>All Programs</u> menu or the Excel® icon on the desktop.

5 Import the file Sales Data. The delimiter is a comma. Figure 2.65 shows the spreadsheet.

6 Enter a formula to total the columns B, C and D and rows 2, 3, 4, 5, 6 and 7. Enter the formula once for a row and once for a column and then replicate it. Insert row and column title – Total.

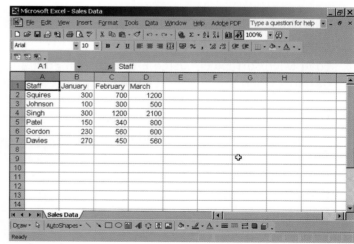

Figure 2.65 Sales

7 Enter a new column heading in F1 called Commission – adjust column widths appropriately. Commission is paid quarterly, at a rate of 9 per cent of sales. Devise a formula to calculate the quarterly commission (i.e. divide quarterly total by 100 and multiply by 9). Enter the formula.

8 Centre and embolden the column headings.

9 Change the format of the commission column to currency.

10 Change the font of the whole spreadsheet, except the column headings, to Times New Roman and character size 12.

11 Insert a new sheet by selecting the <u>I</u>nsert menu and clicking on the <u>W</u>orksheet option. A Sheet 1 tab will appear alongside the Sales Data sheet. Click on the Sheet 1 tab and enter

the data below or import them from the file Sales Data Squires (www.hodderclait.co.uk). This sheet shows the sales performance of Squires, who is also featured in the Sales Data spreadsheet.

Products	Tyres	Brakes	Oil	Filters
January	75	125	50	50
February	125	200	150	225
March	350	250	350	250

12 Total each monthly row using a standard function.

13 The monthly totals for Squires are the same as the content of each entry in the Sales Data sheet (i.e. cells B2, C2 and D2) so link the two sheets. Click away from the fomula to calculate it. Figure 2.66 shows the spreadsheet.

14 Print the sheet without gridlines and row and column headings, and then with them.

15 Print the sheet showing the formulae.

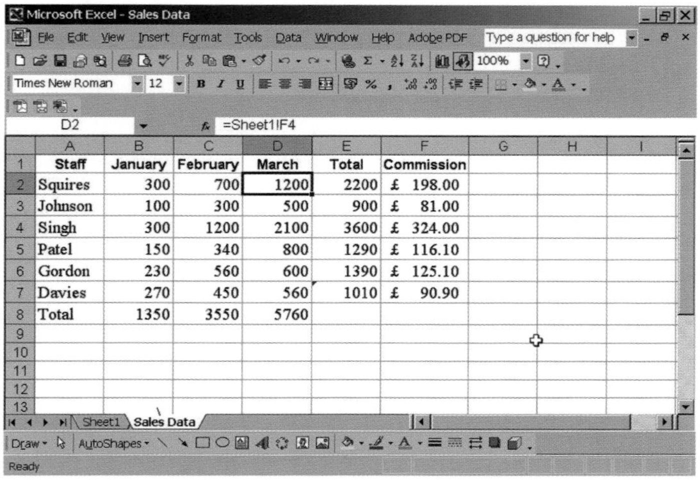

	A	B	C	D	E	F
1	Staff	January	February	March	Total	Commission
2	Squires	300	700	1200	2200	£ 198.00
3	Johnson	100	300	500	900	£ 81.00
4	Singh	300	1200	2100	3600	£ 324.00
5	Patel	150	340	800	1290	£ 116.10
6	Gordon	230	560	600	1390	£ 125.10
7	Davies	270	450	560	1010	£ 90.90
8	Total	1350	3550	5760		

Figure 2.66 Sales Data linked spreadsheet

16 Save your sheet, by selecting the File menu and clicking on the Save option, as a Microsoft Excel® file with the name Sales Data.

17 Close Microsoft Excel® by selecting the File menu item and clicking on the Exit option or by clicking on the Close button in the top right-hand corner of the application window.

Activity 6

Pie chart

1 Insert a floppy disk into the A: drive.

2 Load Microsoft Excel® using either the All Programs menu or the Excel® icon on the desktop. Open the file Sales Data by selecting the File menu and clicking on the Open option to reveal the Open window. Change the Look in: box to select the floppy disk and the file name will appear in the work area. Double-click Sales Data or single-click it and then click the OK button.

3 Using the names of the sales staff and the value of the commission, create an exploded pie chart.

   a) Title – Commission
   b) Label each segment with the commission earned.
   c) Display the legend on the left.
   d) Create the chart on a separate sheet to the data. Title – Commission.
   e) Drag the largest segment out from the others.

4   Add your name to the header.

5   Edit the chart to ensure everything is clear and legible.

6   Print a copy of the pie chart.

7   Save your sheet by selecting the File menu and clicking on the Save As option. Call the file Sales Data Commission.

8   Close Microsoft Excel® by selecting the File menu item and clicking on the Exit option or by clicking on the Close button in the top right-hand corner of the application window.

Activity 7

Column chart

1   Insert a floppy disk into the A: drive.

2   Load Microsoft Excel® using either the All Programs menu or the Excel® icon on the desktop. Open the file Sales Data by selecting the File menu and clicking on the Open option to reveal the Open window. Change the Look in: box to select the floppy disk and the file name will appear in the work area. Double-click Sales Data or single-click it and then click the OK button.

3   Using the names of the sales staff and data from January, February and March, create a column chart:

    a) Title – Sales

    b) X axis – Staff, and Y axis – Amount

    c) Display the legend at the bottom.

    d) Do not display any gridlines.

    e) Create the chart on a separate sheet to the data. Title – Sales.

4   Add your name to the header.

5   Edit the chart to ensure everything is clear and legible.

6   Print a copy of the column chart.

7   Save your sheet by selecting the File menu and clicking on the Save As option. Call the file Sales Data Sales.

8   Close Excel® by selecting the File menu item and clicking on the Exit option or by clicking on the Close button in the top right-hand corner of the application window.

Activity 8

Sort and filter

1   Insert a floppy disk into the A: drive.

2   Load Microsoft Excel® using either the All Programs menu or the Excel® icon on the desktop. Open the file Sales Data by selecting the File menu and clicking on the Open option to reveal the Open window. Change the Look in: box to select the floppy disk and the file name will appear in the work area. Double-click Sales Data or single-click it and then click the OK button.

3   A sales person has joined the team. Insert a new row and the following information.

    Jenkins   125, 450 and 670

4 Calculate a new row total and commission for Jenkins.

5 Filter the data to locate staff who earned more than £115.20p commission (i.e. use Custom option). Print a copy of the filtered spreadsheet (figure 2.67) with row and column headings.

6 Sort the data into ascending order of staff names.

7 Create a header. Add your name and file name.

8 Save your sheet by selecting the File menu and clicking on the Save As option. Call the file Sales Data Filter.

	A	B	C	D	E	F
1	Staff	Januar	Februa	March	Total	Commissi
2	Squires	300	700	1200	2200	£ 198.00
4	Singh	300	1200	2100	3600	£ 324.00
5	Patel	150	340	800	1290	£ 116.10
6	Gordon	230	560	600	1390	£ 125.10

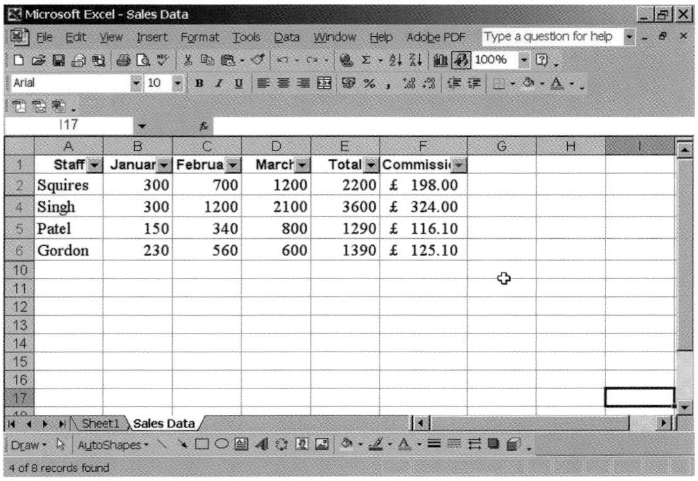

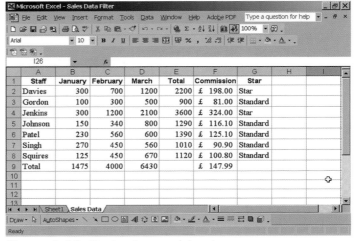

Figure 2.67 Filtered Data

9 Close Microsoft Excel® by selecting the File menu item and clicking on the Exit option or by clicking on the Close button in the top right-hand corner of the application window.

Activity 9

Functions

1 Insert a floppy disk into the A: drive.

2 Load Microsoft Excel® using either the All Programs menu or the Excel® icon on the desktop. Open the file Sales Data by selecting the File menu and clicking on the Open option to reveal the Open window. Change the Look in: box to select the floppy disk and the file name will appear in the work area. Double-click Sales Data Filter or single-click it and then click the OK button. Remove the filter.

3 Add a new heading in column G – Star. In this column, create a formula to identify sales staff who earned more than £150 per quarter, since these are star sales staff. Other staff should be identified as standard.

4 Average the commission earned and name the cell Average. Figure 2.68 shows the revised spreadsheet.

5 Print the sheet without gridlines and row and column headings, and then with them.

6 Print the sheet showing the formulae.

7 Save your sheet by selecting the File menu and clicking on the Save As option. Call the file Sales Data Star.

8 Close Microsoft Excel® by selecting the File menu item and clicking on the Exit option or by clicking on the Close button in the top right-hand corner of the application window.

	A	B	C	D	E	F	G
1	Staff	January	February	March	Total	Commission	Star
2	Davies	300	700	1200	2200	£ 198.00	Star
3	Gordon	100	300	500	900	£ 81.00	Standard
4	Jenkins	300	1200	2100	3600	£ 324.00	Star
5	Johnson	150	340	800	1290	£ 116.10	Standard
6	Patel	230	560	600	1390	£ 125.10	Standard
7	Singh	270	450	560	1010	£ 90.90	Standard
8	Squires	125	450	670	1120	£ 100.80	Standard
9	Total	1475	4000	6430		£ 147.99	

Figure 2.68 Revised spreadsheet

Other resources

1   The table below shows the orders received from five companies in terms of their number and value in 2006.

These resources will allow you to practise creating formulae to total columns, calculate profit and identify the most profitable company. In addition, it is the basis to produce a pie chart and it will also allow you to sort and filter the data.

	Orders	Value	Profit
Company A	156	45000	
Company B	345	230000	
Company C	198	123000	
Company D	112	56000	
Company E	234	97000	
Total			

2   The table below shows the actual hours of sunshine in each month of 2006, compared to the predicted amount.

These resources will allow you to practise creating formulae to identify the average number of hours of sunshine (i.e. actual and predicted) and to identify the month with the most sunshine. It is also the basis to produce a scatter graph, as well as enabling you to sort and filter the data.

Months	Hours of Sunshine Actual	Hours of Sunshine Predicted
January	5.00	4.25
February	4.50	3.25
March	6.50	3.75
April	9.50	4.50
May	10.50	9.50
June	13.50	12.75
July	15.00	16.50
August	14.50	15.75
September	12.25	14.50
October	9.50	7.25
November	7.50	5.65
December	5.75	4.50

3   The table below shows the relationship between sales, costs, fixed assets and annual profit. These resources will allow you to practise creating formula to total columns, calculate profit and identify the most profitable company. It is also the basis to produce a column/bar

chart and to sort and filter the data. It will provide you with the means to link two spreadsheets using the second table of information.

Organisation	Sales	Cost	Assets	Profit
A	230000	178000	198000	
B	340000	212000	430000	
C	390000	234000	357900	
D	410000	395000	230000	
E	440000	340000	178000	
F	560000	456000	76000	
Total				

Organisation A				
A	Sales	Cost	Assets	Profit
Product 1	78000	48000	68000	
Product 2	23000	17000	34000	
Product 3	35000	33000	41000	
Product 4	65000	55000	27000	
Product 5	29000	25000	28000	
Total	230000	178000	198000	

SUMMARY

1 Open Microsoft Excel®
There are several ways of loading an application in Microsoft Windows®. These include:

- clicking on the Start button, highlighting the All Programs item and clicking on Microsoft Excel®
- double-clicking on the Excel® icon on the desktop.

2 Open a file
Select the File menu, click on the Open option to reveal the Open window. Change the Look in: box to select the folder and the file name will appear in the work area.

3 Page layout
Select the File menu and click on the Page Setup option to reveal the Page Setup window. There are four tabs:

- Page – to set the orientation of the sheet (portrait and landscape) and scale your spreadsheet on to a specified number of pages when you are printing it
- Margins – to set the size of all four margins (i.e. left, right, top and bottom) and the header and footer

- Header/Footer – to insert the content of the header and footer, including automatic fields
- Sheet

4 Adjust column width

Change the width of a column by placing the mouse pointer on the line between the two columns. The pointer's appearance will change and you can drag the column wider.

Alternatively, select the Format menu and click on either the Row or Column option, revealing options to change the width of a column or the height of a row.

5 Save

Select the File menu and click on the option Save to reveal the Save As window. Change the Save in: box to select the floppy disk or other drive/folder, and add the file name in the File name: box. Click on the Save button.

6 Close

Select the File menu item and click on the Exit option or click on the close button in the top right-hand corner of the application window.

7 Mathematical operators

The mathematical operators used in Microsoft Excel® are:

+	add
–	subtract
*	multiply
/	divide
<	less than
<=	less than or equal to
>	more than
>=	greater than or equal to

8 Mathematical rules

When a formula consists of several arithmetical operators, they are worked out in a standard way. Everything enclosed in brackets is calculated first, then multiplication and division, and, finally, addition and subtraction. If a formula contains multiplication and division or addition and subtraction, it works out the calculation from left to right.

9 Standard functions

Microsoft Excel® provides a number of standard functions. These include: SUM, AVERAGE, COUNT, MIN, SQRT, MAX and IF. A full list of all the functions can be accessed by clicking on the down arrow next to the Sum function button on the Standard toolbar. This reveals a list of functions and the button More Functions . Click on More Functions to open the Insert Function window.

The Insert Function window allows you to insert the function into the sheet. When you enter a function, a new window will sometimes appear called Function Arguments. Function Arguments asks you to set the parameters for the function.

10 References

The cell reference is given by combining the column letter with the row number (e.g. A4). There are three types of reference:

- relative
- absolute
- named.

The relative reference is the one you normally encounter when you use Microsoft Excel®. If you move the cells (e.g. delete or insert rows or columns), the reference in the formula changes to allow for the new position.

The absolute reference is one which remains unchanged no matter what happens. You create an absolute reference by using the $ symbol (e.g. SUM (A2:A5) uses relative references, while SUM ($A$2:$A$5) uses absolute references).

A mixed reference combines both relative and absolute references within the same formula or function (e.g. H5+$G$3).

Named cell references are created by highlighting a cell or area and entering its name in the left-hand box of the formula bar and pressing Enter.

11 Print

Select the File menu and click on the Print option.

12 Print preview

Select the File menu and click on the Print Preview option to reveal the Print Preview window.

13 Print gridlines, row and column headings

Select the File menu, click on the Print Preview option to reveal the Print Preview window. Click on the Setup button to reveal the Page Setup window. Select the Sheet tab and click in the Gridlines and Row and column headings boxes so ticks appear. Click on the OK button when you are finished and you will see the window disappear and a new print preview appear, showing gridlines and headings.

14 Print options

Select the File menu and click on the Print option to reveal the Print window. In the window is a section called Print What, with three options:

- Selection – print areas that are highlighted
- Active sheet(s) – print all the sheets you have selected
- Entire workbook – print all the sheets within the workbook.

15 Print formulae

Select the Tools menu and click on Options to reveal the Options window. The View tab shows a section called Window options. Clicking on the Formulas box will print the formulas. There are also boxes to select the Gridlines and Row & column headers. When choices have been made, they are enacted by clicking on the OK button.

16 Change format

The Formatting toolbar provides you with a variety of tools to enhance the format of your spreadsheet (e.g. fonts, character sizes, bold, italics, underline and change alignment). They are selected by highlighting the cell or cells and selecting the appropriate tool from the toolbar.

17 Borders
Click on the Borders icon on the Formatting toolbar to reveal a small window of options.

18 Hide Rows and Columns
Select the Format menu and click on either Row or Column options, revealing the options to hide or unhide rows or columns.

19 Orientation of text
Select the Format menu and click on the Cells option to reveal the Format Cells window. The Alignment tab provides options to:

- Align the text both horizontally and vertically
- Wrap text
- Shrink to fit
- Merge Cells
- Change the angle of orientation of the text (i.e. slope the text).

20 Sort data
Select the Data menu and click on the Sort option to reveal the Sort Window, or select either of the two sort icons on the Standard toolbar.

21 Filtering
Select the Data menu, highlight the Filter option and click on AutoFilter.

22 Track changes
Select the Tools menu and highlight the Track Changes option to reveal the Highlight Changes option, which, when clicked, will open the Highlight Changes window.

23 Import files
Use the Copy and Paste functions which are available in all Microsoft Office® applications.

Alternatively, select the File menu and click on the Open option. Select the file you want to import. A Wizard will help you convert your file into the Microsoft Excel® format. It opens automatically when you try to import the file.

24 Logical operators/functions
The three logical operators are:

OR   OR(condition1, condition2) This returns true if one or more of the conditions is true; otherwise it returns false.

NOT   NOT(condition) This reverses the value of the condition.

AND   AND(condition1 and condition2) This returns the value true if both the conditions are true; otherwise it returns the value false.

25 Link spreadsheets

To link two cells, simply enter the sheet number, an exclamation mark and the cell reference. For example:

Sheet1!cell reference (e.g. sheet2!D6)

26 Style

Select the Format menu and click on Style to reveal the Style window. Click on the Modify button to open the Format Cell window to select format options.

27 Select data

Highlight the whole area of data.

28 Chart Wizard

a) Select the Insert menu and the Chart option. Click on the chart/graph type.
b) Check the chart by clicking on and holding down the mouse button on the Press and Hold to View Sample . Click on the Next button to move to Step 2 of the Chart Wizard.
c) Consider the data range (e.g. =sheet1!$B$6:$C$18 translates into the area at the top left-hand corner, cell B6 to cell C18). Click on the Next button to reveal Step 3.
d) Click on the tab of your choice (e.g. Legends). Click on the Next button to reveal Step 4.
e) Click on the radio button of your choice. Click on the Finish button.

29 Trendline

With the Chart visible, select the Chart menu and click on the Add Trendline option to open the Add Trendline window. Select the equation type for the series the line is based on.

30 Header and footer

With the chart or graph visible, select the File menu and the Page Setup option to reveal the Page Setup window. Click on the Header/Footer tab.

31 Text box

Click on the Text Box icon in the Draw toolbar to reveal a new mouse pointer, which allows you to draw a box by holding down the mouse button and dragging the box open.

32 Format graphs and charts

Double-click on the chart or graph element, then the Format window will appear (e.g. Format Chart Title, Format Legend, Format Data Labels and Format Data Series).

33 XY scatter graph – joining points

Double-click on a point to open the Format Data Series window. Select the Custom radio button to choose the Style , Color and Weight (thickness) of the line.

34 Types of charts and graphs

There are several different types of charts and graphs. The main ones are:

■ pie charts – useful way of visually presenting a range of results (e.g. sales results for four quarters of a year)

- bar/column charts – useful way of comparing results side by side (e.g. car sales by garage)
- line graphs – useful way of showing the relationship between two variables
- XY scatter graphs – useful way of comparing two variables which do not have an obvious relationship.

Chapter

3

Unit 3

Creating and Using a Database

This chapter will help you to:

- create a database file, set up fields and enter a range of data
- import data files, update and interrogate database using complex search criteria
- plan and produce database reports in a variety of report formats
- format and present database reports.

This chapter covers unit 3 (Creating and Using a Database). There are no preconditions for studying this unit. However, its content does assume that you have the skills and understanding which are provided by the OCR Level 1 ICT course CLAiT 2006 (e.g. Unit 3: Database Manipulation and Unit 1: File Management and e-Document Production).

Assessment

After studying unit 3, your skills and understanding are assessed during a three-hour practical assignment. This is set by OCR and marked locally. However, the marking will be externally moderated by OCR. This ensures that the standard is being applied correctly across the many different providers of OCR CLAiT Plus 2006. If you are unsuccessful, you can be reassessed using a different assignment.

An alternative approach is for you to be assessed by an assignment set by OCR or designed by your centre. These assignments cover all the assessment objectives included in the unit. You will need to complete an OCR evidence checklist, explaining how each assessment objective has been covered.

Font families

CLAiT Plus uses font families in its assessments rather than font names. In chapter 1 font families are explained, along with how they relate to font names (see page 000). As you undertake each exercise, consider which font family you are using.

Databases

Databases are used extensively, but are often invisible to individuals, who can be unaware when they make contact with them. When you telephone your bank, for example, the staff member dealing with your enquiry is looking at your records stored on a database. This is equally true of almost any financial transaction (e.g. building society, insurance and credit cards). Many organisations keep records on a database of customers details, preferences, order patterns, contacts, and so on. Supermarkets will maintain a database of their stock, while employers are likely to hold information about employees' salary, working hours, rates of pay and holidays on a database.

Databases are extremely useful in organising information. They allow you to manipulate the data to compare different pieces of information and extract any combination of records to aid decision-making. Managers can see the relevant information before they decide what to do. When you tax your car online the system checks several databases (e.g. car insurance) to ensure your vehicle complies with the legal conditions to drive on the road. This happens with amazing speed compared with the alternative of gathering your documents together and visiting a post office to have them checked.

Database applications

This chapter is based on Microsoft Access® XP, which is a modern package that you can employ to create databases. Figure 3.1 shows the Access® application interface. When the application initially loads it shows the New File task pane on the right of the display. This provides a range of options, such as:

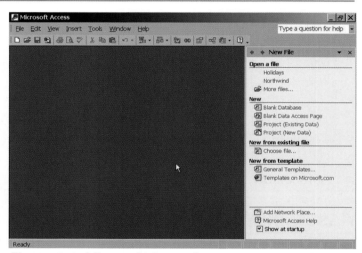

Figure 3.1 Microsoft Access®

- create a new blank database – New section, Blank Database option
- open an existing database – Open a file section, file name of existing database
- create a new database based on a template – New from template section

New database

With any application, it is always tempting to rush ahead and begin to construct something immediately. Modern software applications provide many powerful tools to edit and enhance the outcome and allow you to start straightaway. However, this can produce poorly designed and structured databases. It is not easy to restructure or amend a database once you have constructed it. It is good practice to plan your database before trying to develop it – a few minutes spent planning will save you many problems later.

We are going to develop a database for a sports club, showing the performance of some of the members. We will need to consider what information the database will hold. There are three terms that it is important to remember:

- field – this is an individual piece of information or data (e.g. surname)
- record – a group of fields with a common purpose (e.g. information about a single individual)
- table – a set of records (e.g. information about all the club's sprint runners).

The normal process is to consult the people who are going to use the database in order to identify what information it should contain and how it should be structured. This consultation has taken place and we have been requested to construct a database containing the following information:

- club membership number, date of membership, fees paid, title, first name, surname, street, town and postcode
- sporting events
- career best performance in an event.

When you have identified the information, you need to decide what sort of data it is (i.e. numbers or text). This is vital because the database needs to be able to sort and manipulate the information, so it must be sure what form the data takes. Microsoft Access® needs to know the type of data and how large it is so that it can reserve enough space to hold the information. Microsoft Access® allows you to define nine types of data:

- Text: a text field can hold up to 256 characters, which can be letters, numbers or special characters
- Memo: this allows you to store items such as sales reports, customer details, product information, and so on
- Numbers: a Microsoft Access® database can store numbers and also carry out calculations (e.g. calculate salary based on hours worked and pay rates)
- Date/time: a standard format is provided for dates and times
- Currency: this is a special number type designed for currency
- Autonumber: creates a unique number so that records can be numbered
- Yes/No: a simple type of data that can only be yes or no (e.g. Invoice paid yes/no)
- OLE Object: provides the means of including in the database other Microsoft Windows® objects (e.g. graphic image, spreadsheets and Microsoft® Word® files). When you click on the object, the appropriate application is opened and you can view that object.
- Hyperlink: provides the means to link the database to a website.

For our sports database we need to decide the data type of each field. Table 1 shows the type of each piece of data. There is an important practical issue with regard to dates in that different formats are used across the world. This can cause confusion. For CLAiT Plus 2006 you must use the English format (i.e. day, month and year).

Table 1 Sport data types

Field Name	Data Type
Club membership number	Autonumber – this field will automatically be incremented for each new member
Date of membership	Date
Fees paid	Yes/No
First name	Text – 20 characters
Last name	Text – 50 characters
Event	Text – 50 characters
Career Best performance	Number

In addition to deciding on the data types, you would also consider querying the data (i.e. asking the database questions – how many members ran the 100 metres faster than 12 seconds?), designing standard reports that the people using the database will need (e.g. who has not paid their membership fee?), and also input forms to provide an efficient data entry process. We will consider these issues later.

A key to the usefulness of any database is an obvious one, but is sometimes overlooked. The information contained in a database must be accurate. Potential errors are inserted into a database during data entry. It is essentially that data is entered accurately. It takes far longer to correct an error than any time gained by rushed entry. Inaccurate data can produce misleading reports and queries and lead to poor decisions.

Exercise 19

Creating a database

1 Load Microsoft Access® by selecting Start , highlighting the All Programs menu and clicking on the Microsoft Access® item or click on the Access® icon on the desktop.

2 Microsoft Access® will load (figure 3.1). Select Blank Database option in the task pane. The File New Database window opens to enable you to save your new database. Create the database as a file called Sports on a floppy disk (i.e. change Save in : box to floppy disk, File name : to Sports and click on Create button).

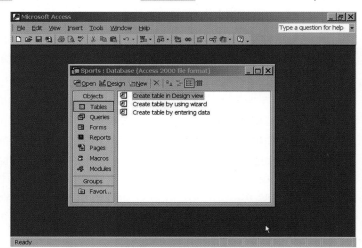

Figure 3.2 **Sports Database window**

The Sports Database window (figure 3.2) shows three options with the Tables object on the left-hand side selected:

■ Create table in Design view

■ Create table by using wizard

■ Create table by entering data

3 Double-click on Create table in Design view and the table window opens.

4 You need to insert your field names and their types. If you enter Club membership in Field Name box and click in the corresponding Data Type box, a small down arrow will appear revealing a list of types. Select autonumber and click in the next Field Name box, then enter Date of Membership. Complete the table, as shown in figure 3.3.

5 When you enter a type, you should observe that in field size a value (e.g. 50) will appear with a text type and long integer with a number type. The value 50 indicates the number

of characters that the field can store, while a long integer is a whole number (i.e. no decimal places). Change First Name to 20 characters, but leave the other text items at 50 characters. If you wanted to show real numbers (i.e. with decimal places) then you would need to click in the Long Integer box to produce a down arrow which, if clicked, gives you other options. In this case, Career Best performance needs to include decimal places, so select the decimal option and insert 2 in the Scale and decimal places fields. This will allow data containing two decimal places to be entered (e.g. minutes and seconds).

You can also add a brief description alongside each field. This can be useful if you need to make changes later. It can be very difficult to understand your own decisions even a few months later.

6 You need to save your table. If you select the File menu and the Save As option, the Save As window appears. Enter Membership and click on the OK button. If you try to close the window without saving, a warning message appears to offer you the option of saving your table.

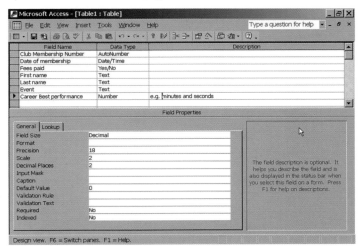

Figure 3.3 Table

7 A warning message will now appear asking you if you need a primary key. In this case you do not need to define one, so click on the No button. A primary key is a unique number which allows different tables to relate to each other. The table window reappears and you should close it by clicking on the close button in the top right-hand corner of the table window. You can now see the Sports Database window, but with an extra item added – membership.

8 Double-clicking on membership allows you to begin entering the data. We will return to this table to enter the data later. Close the window by clicking on the close button in the top right-hand corner of the Sports Database window.

9 Unless you wish to carry on with the next exercise immediately, close Microsoft Access® by clicking on the close button in the top right hand corner of the main application window or select the File menu and the Exit option.

Entering data

This unit stresses the importance of entering data accurately. The value of a database relies on its contents being accurate. Data errors considerably reduce the value of a database and can lead to wrong conclusions being reached and to poor business decisions. Correcting a single error takes considerably longer than entering many items of data, so accuracy is more important than speed of entry.

Table 2 Data input

Date of membership	Fees paid	First name	Last name	Event	Career Best performance
12/01/89	Yes	Michael	Doherty	MA	183.56
15/03/89	Yes	Brian	Dowling	SH	6.4
23/05/89	Yes	Hari	Ghorbani	SP	12.95
30/10/89	Yes	John	Gibbins	TW	120.50
12/12/89	Yes	Clive	Groom	HI	1.80
08/01/90	Yes	Peter	Hanson	SP	12.56
26/02/90	No	Hazel	Hill	TR	13.55
14/05/90	Yes	Jane	Hopwood	MA	200.85
17/09/90	No	Bill	Johnson	MD	14.05
09/12/90	Yes	Latia	Rannie	LO	6.25
03/01/91	Yes	Alice	Luckhurst	MD	16.15
22/02/91	Yes	Cheryl	Ludden	SP	15.75
11/04/91	Yes	Mark	Ludlow	SP	12.15
16/05/91	Yes	Asghar	Malik	HI	1.82
27/07/91	Yes	Christine	Morris	TR	13.10
14/11/91	Yes	Kevin	Steele	TW	118.55
12/01/92	Yes	Gary	Newhouse	MA	175.75
02/02/92	No	James	Night	MA	177.55
07/06/92	Yes	Richard	Palmer	SP	12.68
10/08/92	Yes	Julie	Pandey	MA	203.45
11/10/92	Yes	Pannu	Rasmussen	SP	12.10
04/01/93	Yes	Steven	Salt	TW	110.45
05/03/93	Yes	Rao	Palk	LO	5.95
17/05/93	Yes	Mathew	Peek	SP	12.85
19/07/93	Yes	Paula	Pitman	HI	1.56
23/09/93	No	Paul	Pecan	TW	122.85
30/11/93	Yes	Karl	Polkowski	MA	165.85
05/02/94	No	Oliver	Randall	TW	118.65
09/05/94	Yes	Alan	Rider	TR	15.65
13/07/94	Yes	Linda	Rose	LO	6.05
20/09/94	Yes	Fred	Scrim	SP	13.05
12/02/95	Yes	Kate	Scott	MD	15.35
25/07/95	Yes	Murray	Smith	TW	117.50
29/08/95	Yes	Ben	Sibley	TR	16.05
03/01/96	No	Peter	Swain	MI	3.58
16/05/96	Yes	John	Sutton	JA	55.34
21/09/96	Yes	Susan	Taylor	SH	5.6
22/10/97	Yes	Tom	Turner	HU	18.95
17/03/98	Yes	Dorothy	West	SP	15.65
18/06/98	Yes	Tim	Wilson	LA	52.35

The event column codes are:

- 100 and 200 metres – SP
- 110 and 400 metres hurdles – HU
- 400 metres – LA
- 800 metres – TW
- 1500 metres – MI
- 5000 metres – MD
- Marathon – MA
- Shot – SH
- Javelin – JA
- Discus – DI
- Long Jump – LO
- Triple Jump – TR
- High Jump – HI

Table 2 shows the records of 40 members of the club. The event column shows a two-letter code rather than the full name of the event (e.g. MA – Marathon). This type of encoding is frequently used to save time during data input. Only a few seconds are saved for each entry, but when you are inputting hundreds or even thousands of records, the saving is significant. Errors are also reduced since less needs to be entered. However, this is only half the story in that databases are also concerned with presenting, comparing and contrasting information. A code is of little benefit if it is not understood by the database users. An effective code is one that users recognise and can convert to the full terms. This also helps users enter the data since they are easily able to recognise errors and it is always easier to enter meaningful data than a meaningless set of numbers and letters. A set of random numbers is unlikely to be helpful unless users have a reason to memorise them (e.g. product codes widely used in the company). Database reports that contain encoded information need to be meaningful to the reader or their value will be diminished by the need to translate them into the actual terms. The example in Table 2 shows encoding based on an attempt to use the first two letters of the event name or something relating to the name (e.g. 100 and 200 metres SP or sprint, SH – Shot, 1500 metres – metric mile MI, and 5000 metres – middle distance MD). They are therefore shorter and reasonably meaningful to a sports club user.

Once you have created a database that reflects your needs, it is important that your data is aligned with the types of data you have specified. If the data is different, you will waste time and perhaps produce confusing results. An example of potential confusion is that there are several alternative ways of showing dates (e.g. American – month, day and year). It is important to present dates in the format that your users understand. In the case of Great Britain, this is day, month and year. Often users will wish to search for data relating for a particular date; this will be seriously impaired if dates have been entered in the wrong format. An American format 2/09/02 means 9 February 2002. It is therefore vital that dates are entered correctly. This type of error is difficult to detect and so it is important to ensure accurate and correct input.

Exercise 20

Entering data

1 Load Microsoft Access® by selecting Start, highlighting the All Programs menu and clicking on the Microsoft Access® item or click on the Access® icon on the desktop. Insert your floppy disk into the drive.

2 The New File task pane (figure 3.1) offers you the choice of:

- opening an existing database file
- creating a new blank database.

If you have only recently created the Sports database (see previous exercise), you should see it listed in the Open a file section. If not, select the More files option, which will reveal the Open window to allow you to locate the file Sports and load it.

3 The Sports: Database window should open (figure 3.4). By double-clicking on the membership table item, it will open for data entry.

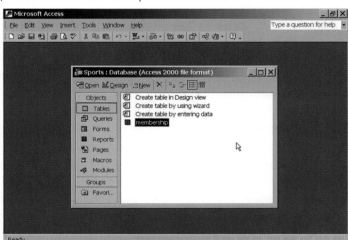

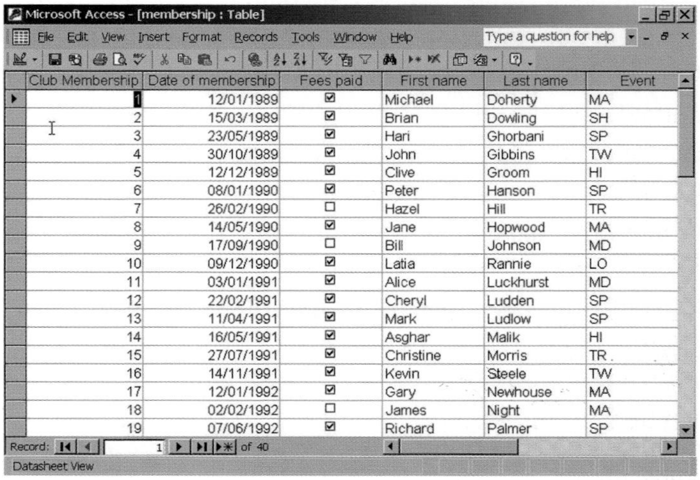

Figure 3.4 Sports database – Membership table

4 Some of the columns are too small to show the whole title. You can adjust the size by placing your mouse pointer over the line separating the columns and it will change shape to form a double arrow. If you hold down the mouse button, you can drag the column line to widen it. Change the column widths so that their titles can be seen.

Club Membership	Date of membership	Fees paid	First name	Last name	Event
1	12/01/1989	☑	Michael	Doherty	MA
2	15/03/1989	☑	Brian	Dowling	SH
3	23/05/1989	☑	Hari	Ghorbani	SP
4	30/10/1989	☑	John	Gibbins	TW
5	12/12/1989	☑	Clive	Groom	HI
6	08/01/1990	☑	Peter	Hanson	SP
7	26/02/1990	☐	Hazel	Hill	TR
8	14/05/1990	☑	Jane	Hopwood	MA
9	17/09/1990	☐	Bill	Johnson	MD
10	09/12/1990	☑	Latia	Rannie	LO
11	03/01/1991	☑	Alice	Luckhurst	MD
12	22/02/1991	☑	Cheryl	Ludden	SP
13	11/04/1991	☑	Mark	Ludlow	SP
14	16/05/1991	☑	Asghar	Malik	HI
15	27/07/1991	☑	Christine	Morris	TR
16	14/11/1991	☑	Kevin	Steele	TW
17	12/01/1992	☑	Gary	Newhouse	MA
18	02/02/1992	☐	James	Night	MA
19	07/06/1992	☑	Richard	Palmer	SP

Figure 3.5 Membership table

5 Enter the data shown in table 2. Remember that the membership number is entered automatically by Microsoft Access®. Click in the field Date of Membership and enter the date. You can enter data into any field providing you click into that field first. The Fees paid field shows a small rectangle that you click in to indicate that the fees have been paid. It is left blank if the fees have not been paid.

continued

6 Figure 3.5 shows the completed table in full screen view. It is very important to check that each record has been entered accurately. If you find a mistake, click on the appropriate field and enter your correction.

7 Save your data by selecting the File menu and the Save option.

8 Close the membership: Table window by clicking on the close button in the top right-hand corner of the window.

9 Close Microsoft Access® by clicking on the close button in top right-hand corner of the main application window or select the File menu and the Exit option.

Reports

The information stored in a database is only part of the story. The real value of databases lies in accessing the information in a form that is useful to you. This involves designing reports, which are the means of presenting selected data. Microsoft Access® provides two ways of helping you extract information in the form of a report. They are:

- using the Access® Wizard to assist your design (i.e. Create report by using wizard)
- developing the report manually (i.e. Create report in Design view).

If you look at the Sports Database window you will see that down the left-hand side is a series of buttons. If you select Reports, figure 3.6 will appear, showing you the two approaches to creating reports.

Figure 3.7 is an example of a simple report listing all the members of the Sports Club in order of their membership number.

Reports are intended to present information to users. It is therefore

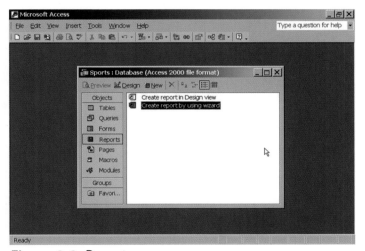

Figure 3.6 Reports

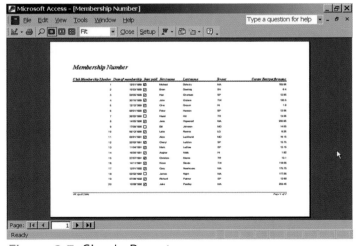

Figure 3.7 Simple Report

important that the information is displayed effectively so that it is easy to understand. This means that you need to control the alignment of the data and how it is presented. The presentation and alignment of a report can be changed by highlighting the report you wish to amend and clicking on the Design icon on the toolbar. This will open the report showing the structure (figure 3.8). If you click on the text boxes and headers you will see they are enclosed in a frame with small rectangles; these allow you to resize and move them. You can also use the Format menu Align option to align the text (i.e. left, right, top, bottom and to grid).

When you print or review a report on the screen you will sometimes notice that the fields are not printed or shown in full. This is sometimes the result of different text boxes overlapping, so you need to move and resize them. This is important because:

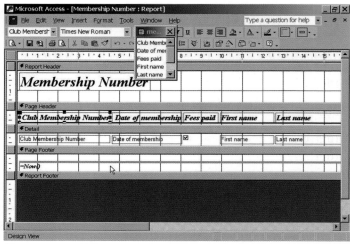

Figure 3.8 Edit reports

■ It avoids confusing readers of the report, who may be misled by shortened title or data. This is important if decisions are being taken on the basis of the information.

■ Presentation of a report will help convince managers that they need to act on the information it contains. A poorly presented

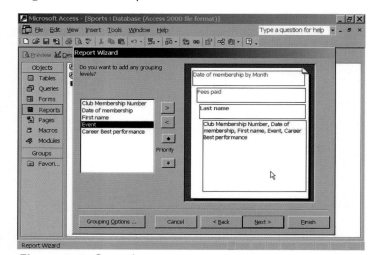

Figure 3.9 Grouping

report will not help to persuade managers to treat the information with the importance it deserves.

An important approach to presenting a report is to group records together with some common characteristic. This could be the year when the members joined the sports club or any other characteristic (i.e. a specific field). Using the Report Wizard you are offered the opportunity to group your information by a specific field. Figure 3.9 shows this aspect of the Wizard.

For example, comparing the presentation of grouped information with a list of the same information:

List of Orders

1999 Order ABC
2001 Order BHK
2000 Order DGH
2000 Order HJY
1999 Order JCF
2001 Order JKY

Orders Grouped by Year

1999

Order ABC
Order JCF

2000

Order DGH
Order HJY

2001

Order JKY
Order BHK

The Report Wizard provides a systematic process to the design of reports. The first step is to identify the fields that will be included in the report. Figure 3.10 shows the Wizard's first step. This window allows you to select the table or query on which to base the report. We will consider queries later in the chapter. Once a table or query has been selected, you can choose the individual fields from it to include in the report.

The second step is to choose how to group the fields. This is shown in figure 3.9. The third step is to order your fields and this is shown in figure 3.11.

The fourth step in creating a report is to select its layout. There are three options Columnar, Tabular and Justified. The layout associated with each presentation type is shown in the window. This window also provides you with the option to select the orientation of the report (i.e. Portrait or Landscape) and adjust the field widths so they all appear on the page. Figure 3.12 shows the fourth step.

Step 5 (figure 3.13) offers you a variety of styles in which to present your report. The sixth and final step (figure 3.14) allows you to name your report and modify the report.

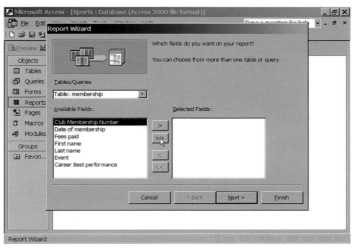

Figure 3.10 First step

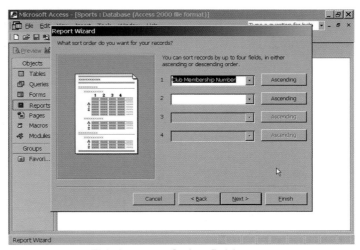

Figure 3.11 Third step – Order fields

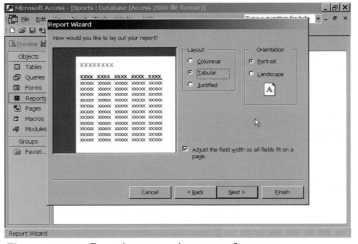

Figure 3.12 Fourth step – Layout of report

When you open a report by clicking on it in the database report window, a small (dialog) window will open sometimes called Enter Parameter Value. Simply click on the OK button to proceed.

Printing

You will often need to print a report or a table of information in order to provide the information to a wider audience than those who have direct access to the database. Presentation of the information is important, so you should preview the document before you print it to check it. The Print Preview option is available from the File menu and operates in the same way that it does in other Microsoft Office® applications. You are presented with an image of the report or table as it will appear when printed. Sometimes, because of the density of the information, you will need to use the zoom function (i.e. a magnifying glass) on the toolbar to see the detail.

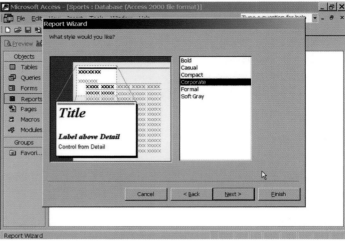
Figure 3.13 Fifth step – Styles

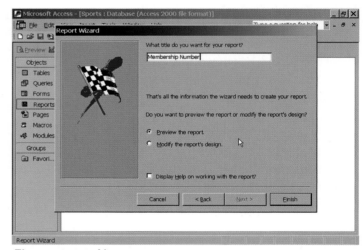
Figure 3.14 Name report

If the preview is acceptable, you can either print it directly from the preview window by selecting the Print icon on the toolbar, or close the window and select the File menu and then the Print option to reveal the Print window. By clicking on the OK button the report or table will be printed. If the preview is not satisfactory you may need to select the File menu and Page Setup to change the margins, orientation and column settings. If you are printing a report you may have to use the Design option to move and resize the boxes.

Exercise 21

Reports

1 Load Microsoft Access® by selecting the Start button, highlighting the All Programs option and clicking on the Microsoft Access® item or click on the Access® icon on the desktop. Insert your floppy disk into the drive.

2 The New File task pane (figure 3.1) offers you the choice of:

- opening an existing database file
- creating a new blank database.

If you have only recently created the Sports database (see previous exercise), you should see it listed in the Open a file section. If not, select the More files option, which will reveal the Open window to allow you to locate the file Sports and load it.

3   If the Reports button is not pressed, click on it to show the two options for creating a report.

4   Select Create report by using a wizard and the Report Wizard window (figure 3.10) will appear. This shows the table that the report will be based on in the box below the Tables/Queries title. It allows you to change the table or to select a query on which to base your report. The process is the same in both cases. This window allows you to select which fields you wish to include in your report. You select a field by highlighting it and clicking on the single arrow button pointing towards the right-hand box. If you click on the double arrow button you will select all the fields. If you accidentally select a field by mistake you can correct it by highlighting it and using the left-pointing arrow button.

5   Select Club Membership, First name and Last name to produce a report which is essentially a list of the members.

6   When you have successfully selected your fields, click on the Next button to reveal the next window that allows you to group your information by again highlighting the item and using the arrow button. Experiment with different groupings. However, return to the original state when you have finished and click on the Next button. You should note that there is a Back button that lets you to return to the previous window if you have made an error.

7   The next window enables you to sort your records into ascending or descending order. In this example we do not wish to sort the records, so simply click on the Next button. This allows you to change the orientation of the report from portrait to landscape, as well as selecting the layout of the report – Columnar, Tabular or Justified. You can explore these options since this window provides you with a preview facility. Select Portrait and Tabular and click on the Next button.

8   The next window offers you a choice of styles and you can explore the options by watching the preview area. Select Formal and click on the Next button.

9   You are now approaching the end of the Wizard process and by using the window you can choose the title of your report – enter Membership List. You can preview your report or modify its design. Click on the Finish button. The report will now appear (figure 3.15).

Figure 3.15 Membership report

continued

10 Select the File menu and the Print Preview option to check the report. Print the report by selecting the File menu, clicking on the Print option and then clicking on the OK button to print with the default settings or select the printer icon in the Print Preview window. Before you print, check that the printer is switched on and has paper.

11 Close the Report window using the control buttons in the top right-hand corner of the window. You will now see the Sports database window with the new report, Membership List, included.

12 If you wish to stop now, close the Sports: Database window using the Close button in the top right-hand corner of the window; to move to the next exercise ignore this step.

13 Close Microsoft Access® by clicking on the close button in the top right-hand corner of the main application window or selecting the File menu and the Exit option.

Amending a report

Although you have created a report using the Wizard it is possible to make changes to the layout and presentation. You can alter the report's:

- margins (i.e. left, right, top and bottom)
- orientation (i.e. portrait or landscape)
- headers and footers
- automatic fields (i.e. date, page and file name).

Exercise 22

Amending the report

1 Load Microsoft Access® by selecting the Start button, highlighting the All Programs option and clicking on the Microsoft Access® item or by clicking on the Access® icon on the desktop. Insert your floppy disk into the drive.

2 The New File task pane (figure 3.1) offers you the choice of:

- opening an existing database file
- creating a new blank database.

If you have only recently created the Sports database, you should see it listed in the Open a file section. If not, select the More files option, which will reveal Open window to allow you to locate the file Sports and load it.

3 If the Reports button is not pressed, click on it to show the Membership List report. Click on Membership List to reveal the report. Investigate the report – move to page 2. Notice that at the bottom of page 2 the date is shown, as well as page 1 of 2. These are produced by automatic fields, inserted into the report by the Wizard, that calculate the date and page length.

continued

4 It is straightforward to change the report's margins and orientation by selecting the File menu and the Page Setup option, or if the report is open, select the Setup button. Both methods will open the Page Setup window (figure 3.16), allowing you to change the margins; if you select the Page tab, you can alter the orientation. You can also select the size of paper that the report will be printed on.

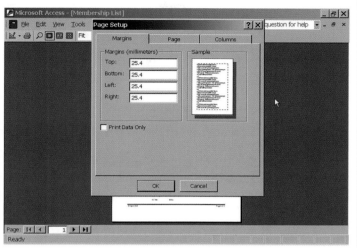

Figure 3.16 **Page Setup window**

5 Change all four margins to 34.99 mm and the orientation to landscape. Inspect the result of these changes. Close the Report window using the control buttons in the top right-hand corner of the window.

6 Microsoft Access® also provides tools to alter the details of the report. If you highlight Membership List and click on the Design icon on the toolbar, the structure of the report is revealed (figure 3.8). You can now manipulate the various elements of the report. Investigate changing the structure by resizing and moving the boxes, and use the Align option in the Format menu to change alignment. For example, resize the Membership List text box so it fills the whole width, and explore different alignments. Continue until you are confident.

7 If you click on the element Membership List you will see that the title is enclosed in a frame (figure 3.17). This is the equivalent of highlighting it. You can drag the frame and its contents – the mouse pointer changes to a small hand and you can move the frame by holding down the mouse button and dragging it. Move the title Membership List to the centre of the report.

8 With the Membership List enclosed in a frame you can also change the font and character size. Change the font to Arial and character size to 28, using the toolbar. You will need to adjust the size of the frame to this by placing the pointer on the frame edge – it will change to a double-headed arrow. If you hold down the left mouse button you can drag the frame edge to make it larger.

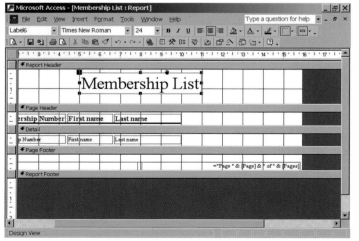

Figure 3.17 **Adjust framer**

9 Now change the character size of the subheading (Page Header) to 12. You will need to rearrange the three headings. In order to align the information you will also need to align the detail to the Page Header subtitles.

10 If you consider the Page Footer you will see:

=Now() – this is the date automatic field

="Page " & [Page] & "of" & [Pages] – this is the page automatic field

These are inserted using the Insert menu and either the Page Numbers or Date and Time option. If you left or right double-click on the Report Footer, a window will appear providing a range of options. Explore the options and you will notice that you can alter the presentation of the date and pages. In a similar way, Report Header can be changed. Try to add your name to the footer (Right-click to open a pop-up box, select Toolbox and use the Label tool).

11 When you have finished you can close the design view of the report using the control buttons in the right-hand corner of the window. You will be presented with a message window asking you if you would like to save the changes you have made. Click on the Yes button.

12 Close the Sports: Database window using the close button in the top right-hand corner of the window.

13 Close Microsoft Access® by clicking on the close button in the top right-hand corner of the main application window, or select the File menu and the Exit option.

AutoReport

There is another quick way to produce reports other than using the Wizard. This is the AutoReport. This can be accessed by selecting the New button in the Report window. This opens the New Report window, which contains a range of options (figure 3.18), including AutoReport: Tabular and AutoReport: Columnar. In this window you need to select the table or query that the report is based on by using the down arrow.

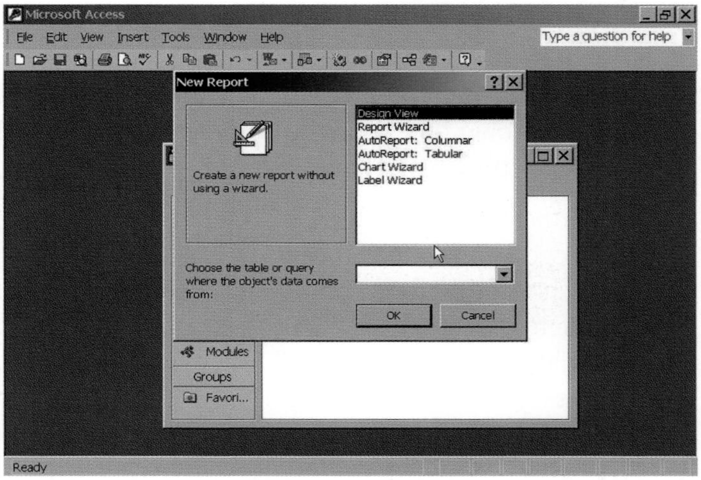

Figure 3.18 AutoReport

If you select one of the AutoReport options, a report showing the contents of the selected table or query will appear in the chosen layout. Figure 3.19 shows the columnar option.

You can give the report a name and save it. The AutoReport can be amended using the Design option in the same way that a report produced using the Wizard can be.

Data entry forms

When entering information into a database, it is important that the source of the data is designed to make data entry as easy as possible. This will improve productivity and reduce errors. The source is normally some type of form. In the example we have been using of a Sports Club, the source document could be the membership application form. A common problem is that the membership form's layout does not correspond to the database table. This is often made worse by the use of abbreviations in the database, so that mistakes can easily be made.

Microsoft Access® allows you to design a data entry form that resembles the source document, to avoid errors and make the process efficient. Figure 3.20 shows Sports: Database in forms view (i.e. the Forms button has been clicked) and the two ways that Microsoft Access® provides of creating forms:

- Create form in Design view
- Create form by using wizard.

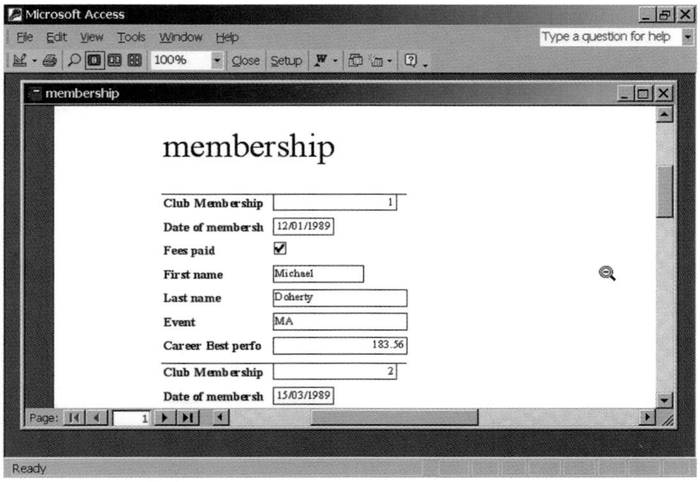

By printing out the data entry form you have created a form which serves both as an input document and as a membership application form. This will minimise errors and reduce the need to transfer data between documents. CLAiT Plus 2006 does not require you to be skilled in the development and use of forms. However, it is included to provide you with the opportunity to understand the use of forms if you wish.

Figure 3.19 Membership Columnar AutoReport

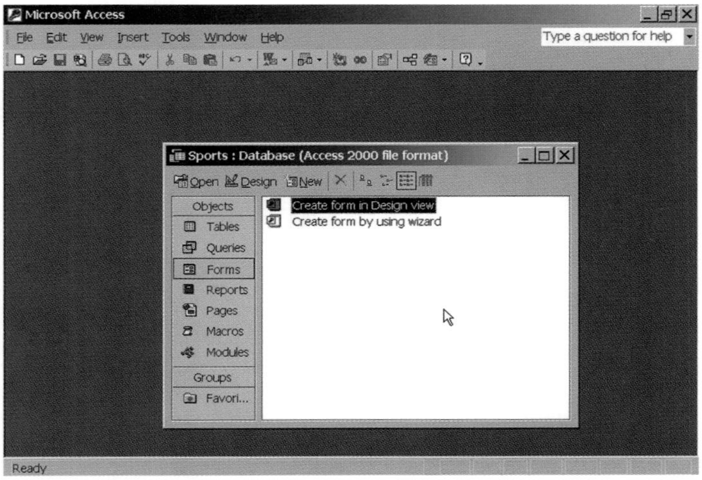

Figure 3.20 Sports: Database forms view

Exercise 23

Data entry form

1 Load Microsoft Access® by selecting the Start button, highlighting the All Programs option and clicking on the Microsoft Access® item or by clicking on the Access® icon on the desktop. Insert your floppy disk into the drive.

2 The New File task pane (figure 3.1) offers you the choice of:

- opening an existing database file
- creating a new blank database.

If you have only recently finished the last exercise, the Sports database will still be listed in the Open a file section. If not, select the More files option, which will reveal Open window to allow you to locate the file Sports and load it.

3   Click on the Forms button on the left-hand side of the window and you will reveal two options to create a form. This is shown in figure 3.20. Click on the Create form by using wizard option to open the Form Wizard window. The fields to include in the form are chosen by highlighting the field and clicking on the single arrow keys. If the double arrow is selected, all the fields are included. In this case, select all the fields (figure 3.21).

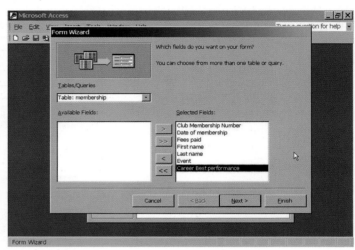

Figure 3.21 **Form Wizard**

4   Click on the Next button to move to the next stage of the Wizard. This gives you a choice of six layouts. In this case, select Justified and click on the Next button to reveal figure 3.22, which provides you with a variety of style choices.

5   Select the Standard style, but you should also explore the different options. Click on the Next button to reveal figure 3.23. This allows you to select a

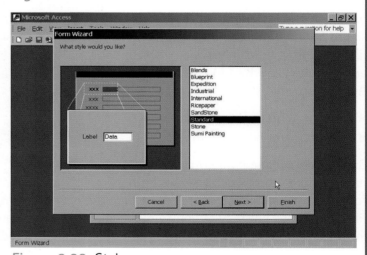

Figure 3.22 **Styles**

name for your form. Enter Membership Form and complete the process by clicking on Finish button.

6   The Membership Form is shown in the Sports Database window when the Forms button is pressed. By double-clicking on Membership Form you can see the completed form, showing the first record of the membership table (figure 3.24).

7   The forms for all members can be printed out by selecting the File menu, the Print option and the OK button. All the records will be printed in the form layout. Print the data forms. The printout can help administer the Sports Club by allowing you to work manually on the membership list (e.g. copies can be provided for all members of the management team).

continued

8 A blank form can be produced by selecting the Arrow Star button on the bottom line of the form. New members can also be added directly through the form into the database. In this case, you would need to find record 41. The membership number is automatically generated.

9 Close the Sports: Database window using the close button in the top right-hand corner of the window.

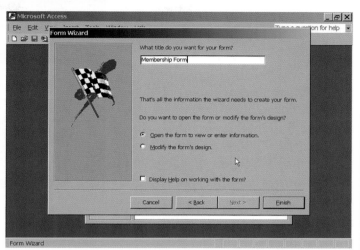

Figure 3.23 Form name

10 Close Microsoft Access® by clicking on the close button in the top right-hand corner of the main application window or select the File menu and the Exit option.

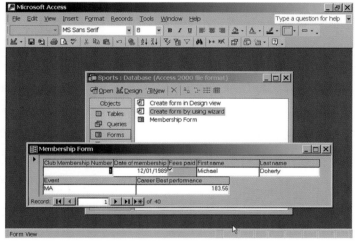

Figure 3.24 Completed Membership Form

Presentation of data – Labels

You have already investigated some of the possibilities of presenting the information contained in a database so that it is more useful to you. Reports and forms allow you to extract data in a way that meets your needs. You can group information, present it as a table, in a column or in justified form. One way that is often required is extracting information in order to produce address labels.

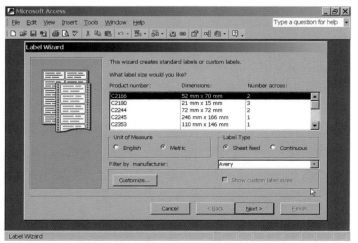

Figure 3.25 Size of labels

If you click on the New button in the Report window, a new window will appear called New Report (figure 3.18). This provides access to the Label Wizard, which will assist you to design a label.

In order to use the Label Wizard you need to select a table from which to supply the information. The table can be inserted in the New Report window or selected from the list available if the down arrow button at the end of the box is clicked.

Figures 3.25 to 3.31 show the sequence of steps to produce the labels. Step 1 (figure 3.25) allows you to select the size of lables to match the ones you use.

Step 2 (figure 3.26) allows you to select the font, character size and colour of your text.

Step 3 (figure 3.27) provides you with the means to design your label (i.e. selecting the fields, layout and adding extra text).

Step 4 (figure 3.28) enables you to sort your labels by a chosen field (e.g. membership number or name).

Step 5 (figure 3.29) is the final stage, where you can name your label report, choose to preview it and modify the design.

Figure 3.30 illustrates an example label, based on the membership database table.

When you close the labels window (figure 3.30), the report is saved and added to the window (figure 3.31).

Reports can be designed to present data in many forms, such as a particular field order, table/list/group format and summaries. During the Report Wizard process, you select the order of presentation of the fields, the options to present your data in table form or columns and to group the data.

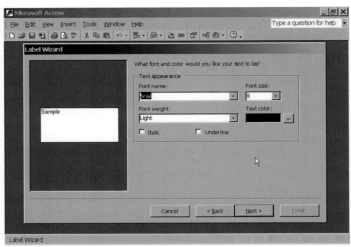

Figure 3.26 Font and character size

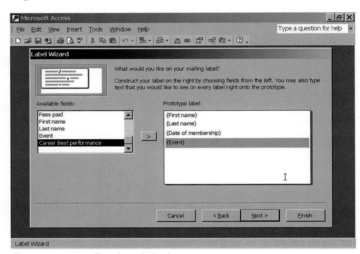

Figure 3.27 Design label

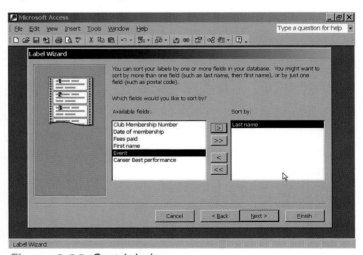

Figure 3.28 Sort labels

Queries can also be designed to present the data in your chosen order by using the Query Wizards (i.e. Simple and Crosstab Query Wizard) in a similar way to producing a report. If you produce a query in design view, the order of presentation is determined by the order in which you select the fields. We will consider queries later in this chapter.

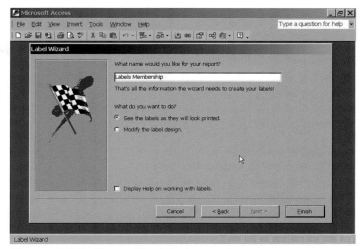

Figure 3.29 Name the label report

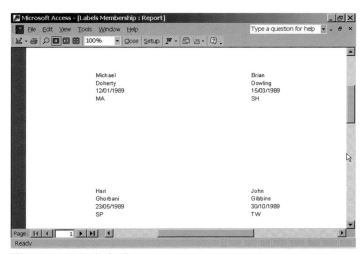

Figure 3.30 Labels

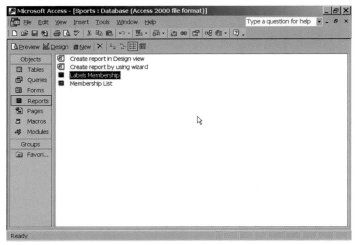

Figure 3.31 Report Window

Importing a Data file

Unit 3 requires that you are able to import or open a data file in Microsoft Access®. Access® provides a standard approach to importing data using the File menu, highlighting the Get External Data and clicking the Import option to reveal the Import Window (figure 3.32). The option is only available when a database window is open, so you will need to create a new database or open an existing one.

The Import Window allows you can select files that can be imported into a Microsoft Access® database. Figure 3.33 shows the spreadsheet files created in chapter 2 that can now be imported into Microsoft Access®. The file is selected by double-clicking on it or by single-clicking on the file and then on the Import button. Microsoft Access® will then guide you through the process of converting the data into a database format. Figure 3.33 shows the Import Spreadsheet Wizard.

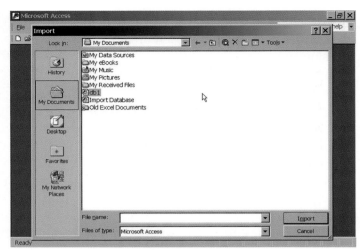

Figure 3.32 Import Window

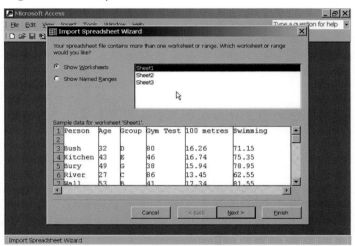

Figure 3.33 Import Spreadsheet Wizard

Exercise 24

Importing a data file

1 Load Microsoft Access® by selecting the Start button, highlighting the All Programs option and clicking on the Microsoft Access® item or clicking on the Access® icon on the desktop. Insert your floppy disk into the drive.

2 The New File task pane (figure 3.1) offers you the choice of:

- opening an existing database file
- creating a new blank database.

Select Create a blank database. The File New Database window opens. Save the database as a file called Import on a floppy disk. An alternative is to open an existing database, in which case, the imported data is saved either in a new table or combined with an existing table.

3 Click on the File menu and highlight Get External Data to reveal the Import option. Click on Import to show the Import Window (figure 3.32). You are going to import one of the spreadsheets you created in chapter 2 – Sales Forecast – so you need to adjust the

continued

Look in: box to the location you saved the spreadsheet (e.g. floppy disk). When Sales Forecast is in the window, double-click on the file to load it into Microsoft Access®.

4 The Import Spreadsheet Wizard will appear with the contents of Sales Forecast within the window. The display shows each spreadsheet sheet. In this case you want to select Sheet 1. Click the Next button to open the next window, which will ask you to select the database fields. Click on the radio button – First Row Contains Column Headings and then on the Next button to see if the row headings are suitable to become the field titles. In this case you will see a warning message that informs you that the first row contains data that cannot be used in valid Microsoft Access® field names. Click on OK. This means that you cannot import the column titles as your field names, but we can correct this later, so go on.

5 The next window to appear asks you to choose between storing the imported information In a New Table or In an Existing Table. In this case, select In a New Table and click on the Next button.

6 The new window that is shown offers you the opportunity to modify the fields in the database table. You select the column of the field by clicking in it. You can now change the fields selected by Microsoft Access® back to those from the imported spreadsheet. Change Field 1 to Item, Field 2 to January, Field 3 to February, and so on, until you have replaced all the fields. Click on the Next button.

7 The next step is revealed. Now you can add a primary key, which is essentially a unique record identifier. However, in this case you do not need a primary key. Select No primary key by clicking in the radio button and then click on the Next button.

8 The final step allows you to complete the process of importing data by clicking on the Finish button. However, you need to name your new table, so enter Sales Office® in the Import to Table: box in the centre of the window and then click Finish. An information window will appear to tell you when you have finished importing the file. Click the OK button on the information window after you have read it.

9 You will now see that your new table has been listed in the database window you created originally. In this case, it was the Import Database.

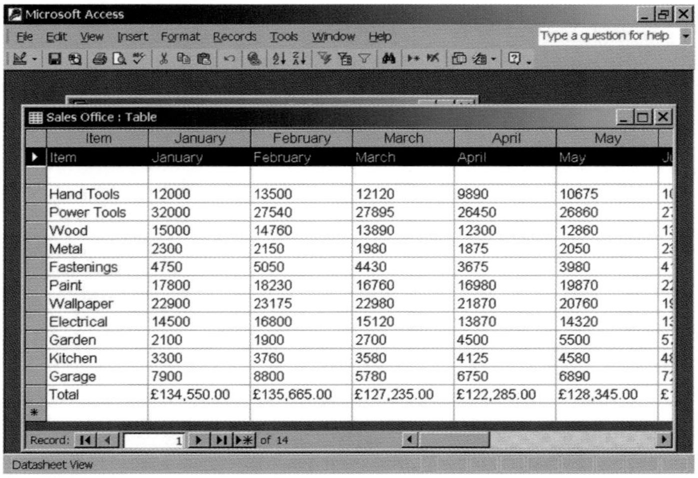

Item	January	February	March	April	May
Item	January	February	March	April	May
Hand Tools	12000	13500	12120	9890	10675
Power Tools	32000	27540	27895	26450	26860
Wood	15000	14760	13890	12300	12860
Metal	2300	2150	1980	1875	2050
Fastenings	4750	5050	4430	3675	3980
Paint	17800	18230	16760	16980	19870
Wallpaper	22900	23175	22980	21870	20760
Electrical	14500	16800	15120	13870	14320
Garden	2100	1900	2700	4500	5500
Kitchen	3300	3760	3580	4125	4580
Garage	7900	8800	5780	6750	6890
Total	£134,550.00	£135,665.00	£127,235.00	£122,285.00	£128,345.00

Figure 3.34 Sales Office® table

10 The table you have created by importing the spreadsheet data has been added to the database window as the file Sales Office®.

11 If you double-click on the file Sales Office®, the table will open and you can see the new data (figure 3.34). There is one final step to take and that is to remove the spreadsheets column headings and blank line. Delete rows 1 and 2 by highlighting them and selecting the Edit menu and the Delete option.

continued

12 Close the window by clicking on the close button in the top right-hand corner of the Sales Office® window.

13 Close Microsoft Access® by clicking on the close button in the top right-hand corner of the main application window or select the File menu and the Exit option.

Maintenance

The maintenance of any database requires that occasionally you need to add, amend and delete records and fields. To amend a field is a straightforward task in that you need to click in it, delete the contents and enter the new data. It is also possible to delete an entire column (i.e. remove a field from all records) or an individual row (i.e. an individual record). By placing your pointer over the column or row heading you will see it change shape to become a thick black arrow. If you click now, the whole column or row is highlighted. To delete the row or column, select the Edit menu and click on the Delete, Delete Record or Delete Column option (figure 3.35). Before the row or column is removed, a message window will ask you to confirm that you want the record or field deleted permanently.

This type of approach is effective if you want to change an individual data item or delete a record or entire field, but if you want to change a

Figure 3.35 Delete a record

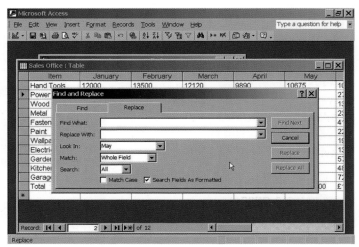

Figure 3.36 Find and Replace window

recurring piece of the information, then Microsoft Access® provides a more productive method called Find and Replace. If you select the Edit menu and click on Replace, then the Find and Replace window will appear (figure 3.36). This window provides two different functions. It can simply search your data to locate a particular piece of information or it can locate an item and then replace it. The latter is very useful when you have to change an item which occurs in several places in your database. The functions allow you select a particular table to search and specify the degree of match you are seeking (i.e. any part of the field, the whole field or the start of a field).

The Find and Replace function ensures that you find every item that you are seeking to find or to replace. A manual search is likely to miss items, so the function is a method of guaranteeing a perfect result. It is also considerably quicker.

Sorting

Microsoft Access® provides a number of ways of presenting information. One of the most straightforward is sorting. Information can be ordered alphabetically or numerically so that it is ascending (i.e. lowest to highest) or descending (i.e. highest to lowest). The sort functions are available on the toolbar.

Figure 3.37 shows the results of sorting the Sales Office® table by descending alphabetical value. Compare the effects on the data of the different types of sorting.

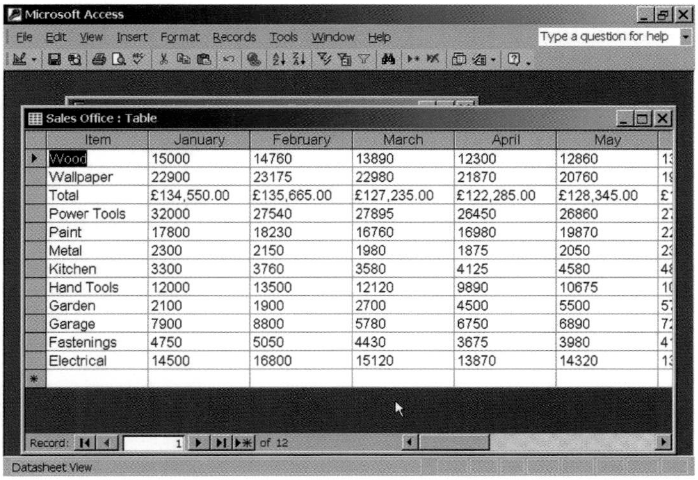

Queries

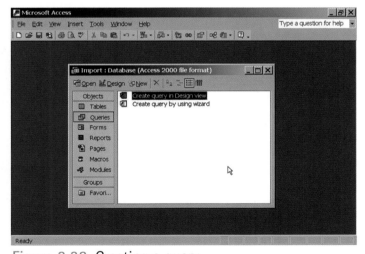

Figure 3.37 Sorted Data

A major requirement of any database is the ability to extract the information that it contains. Microsoft Access® enables you to find out what information is held within the database in any form or combination you require. Extracting data is called querying the database. The starting point for producing a query is the database window. Figure 3.38 shows the two ways of producing a query which are available once you have selected the Queries button on the left-hand side of window. They are:

- Create a query in Design view
- Create a query using wizard.

Figure 3.38 Creating a query

Exercise 25

Querying data

1 Load Microsoft Access® by selecting the Start button, highlighting the All Programs option and clicking on the Microsoft Access® item or clicking on the Access® icon on the desktop. Insert your floppy disk into the drive.

2 The New File task pane (figure 3.1) offers you the choice of:

- opening an existing database file

- creating a new blank database.

 If you have only recently finished the previous exercises, the Sports database will still be listed in the Open a file section. If not, select the More files option, which will reveal Open window to allow you to locate the file Sports and load it. The Sports database window will open. Click on the Queries button to reveal figure 3.38.

3 Select Create query in Design view and you will see an overlaid window Show Table appear. Click on the Add button and you will notice a small window called Membership. Now click on the Close button in Show Table to reveal figure 3.39.

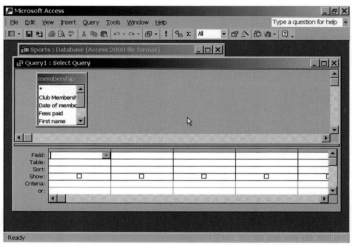

Figure 3.39 Select Query

4 The cursor will be flashing in the Field: box, and if you click on the down arrow all the Membership table fields are available for you to select from. Select the Club Membership item by clicking on it and you will see it appear in the Field: box. Now click in the Sort: box and you will see another

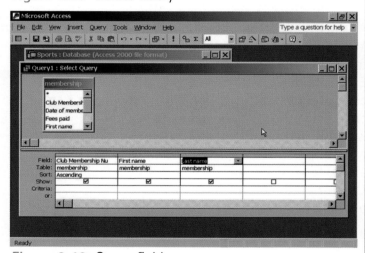

Figure 3.40 Query fields

down-arrow button that provides access to sorting functions. Select the Ascending option.

5 Now click in the next column and select First name in the Field box. Repeat this action in the third column, selecting Last name. Figure 3.40 shows the result you should have obtained.

6 Now close the window using the button in the top right-hand corner. A message window will appear asking you if you want to save the query as Query1. Click on the Yes button and another window (dialog) box will appear, to offer you the opportunity to name your query. Change the name to List and click on the OK button. You will see your query appear in the Sports: database window (assuming the Queries button has been selected).

7 You have created a straightforward query to produce a list of members' names and their membership numbers (i.e. only the fields you have selected will appear in your query). If

you double-click on the query (List), you will see the results of the query appear (figure 3.41).

8 If you need to change your query because, for example, it is producing incorrect results, you need to select the Design icon on the toolbar with List highlighted.

9 Highlight List and click on the Design icon. You are now going to change the list to select only those members who have not paid their membership fees.

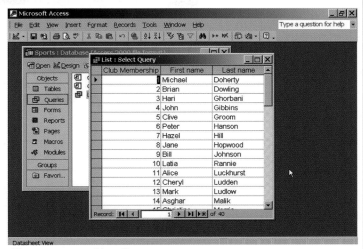
Figure 3.41 List Query

10 Select the fourth column and in the Field box insert the fees paid field. Now click in the Criteria row and enter =No. You are telling Microsoft Access® only to present records of members who have a value equal to No (i.e. not paid) in this field (figure 3.42). Fees Paid can only have two values Yes or No. Close the window and you will be asked if you want to save your

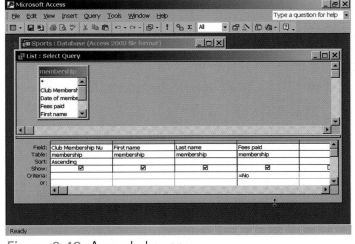
Figure 3.42 Amended query

changes. Click on the Yes button to return to the Sports: Database window with List showing. Double-click on List to see your new query.

11 Close Microsoft Access® by clicking on the close button in the top right-hand corner of the main application window, or select the File menu and the Exit option.

Criteria

In the previous exercise you had your first experience of using a criterion to select information (e.g. =No). This was relatively simple, but you can use a variety of symbols to be more precise. These are:

>   greater than

<   less than

>= greater than or equal to

<= less than or equal to

<> not equal to

These symbols are available on the keyboard:

> greater than – hold the shift key down and then the full stop key

< less than – hold the shift key down and then the comma key

>= greater than or equal to – hold the shift key down and then the full stop key, release the keys and press the equal key

<= less than or equal to – hold the shift key down and then the comma key, release the keys and press the equal key

<> not equal to – hold the shift key down, press the comma key and then the full stop key

In addition to these symbols are the logical operators:

- AND
- OR.

AND combines two different criteria, both of which must be true before the action can be undertaken. For example:

Club Membership >=10 AND <=20

This selects records of members who have a membership number greater than or equal to 10 and also less than or equal to 20 (i.e. records for Club Members 10 to 20 inclusive).

OR allows two criteria to be selected so that if either is true, the action can take place. For example:

Fees Paid = No OR Date of Membership <01/01/90

This selects the records of members who have not paid their fees or who were members before 01/01/1990. In this example, notice that we are linking two fields. Both AND and OR can be used within a single field and also combining fields.

Exercise 26

Queries and criteria

1 Load Microsoft Access® by selecting the Start button, highlighting the All Programs option and clicking on the Microsoft Access® item or clicking on the Access® icon on the desktop. Insert your floppy disk into the drive.

2 The New File task pane (figure 3.1) offers you the choice of:

- opening an existing database file
- creating a new blank database.

If you have only recently finished the previous exercise, the Sports database will still be listed in the Open a file section. If not, select the More files option, which will reveal Open window to allow you to locate the file Sports and load it. The Sports database window will open. Click on the Queries button to reveal figure 3.38.

3 Select Create query in Design view and you will see an overlaid window Show Table appear. Click on the Add button and you will notice a small window called Membership appear on the query window. Now click on the Close button in Show Table to reveal figure 3.39.

4 The cursor will be flashing in the Field: box, and if you click on the down arrow all the Membership table fields are available for you to select from. Select the Date of Membership. Click in the Sort: box and you will see another down-arrow button appear that provides access to sorting functions. Select the Descending option.

5 Now click in the criteria row and enter >=01/01/94. You are selecting all members who joined the club on or after 1 January 1994.

6 Now click in the OR row and enter <= 01/01/99. You are adding an extra condition to select members who joined on or before 1 January 1999. If the criteria are too long, press the Shift and F2 keys together, with the cursor in the criteria box. This opens a Zoom window to let you see the whole criterion. Try it.

7 Now click in the next column and select First Name in the Field: box. Repeat this action, selecting Last name in the third column, Fees Paid in the fourth and Event in the fifth. Figure 3.43 shows the result you should have obtained.

8 Now close the window using the button in the top right-hand corner. A message window will appear asking you if you want to save the query as Query1. Click on the Yes button

and another window (dialog) box will appear offering you the opportunity to name your query. Change the name to Fees then click on the OK button. You will see your query appear in the Sports: database window (assuming the Queries button has been selected).

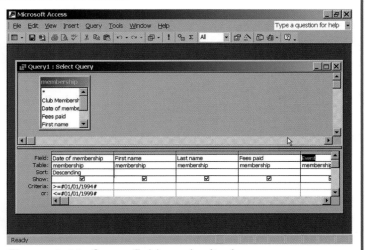

Figure 3.43 Query fields and criteria

9 You have created a straightforward query, producing a list of members with a particular range of membership dates. If you double-click on the query (Fees), you will see the results of the query appear (figure 3.44). Print the query you have created.

10 You are now going to change this query by highlighting Fees and clicking on the

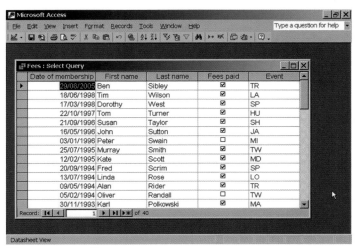

Figure 3.44 Fees query

Design icon on the toolbar. You want to select those members who have paid their membership fees, so in the criteria row of the Fees Paid column enter =Yes.

11 Close the window and save the query. Double-click on Fees to see the result of your change. Notice the change in the number of records now selected (i.e. changes from 40 to 34). Print out the new query.

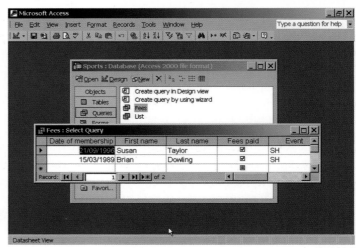

Figure 3.45 Event amendment

12 We will now change the query by adding an extra criterion to the Event column. Enter =SH (i.e. Shot putting). The results of the new query are shown in figure 3.45.

13 Amend Date of membership column criteria to read >=01/01/94 AND <=01/01/99 and remove the criteria from Event column. Compare the result with the OR criteria. Figure 3.46 shows

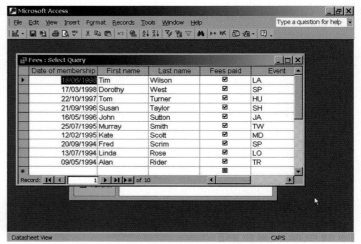

Figure 3.46 Amend Date of membership

the results of the new query. This shows the different effects of AND and OR. Experiment with the logical operators until you are a confident user of them.

14 Close Microsoft Access® by clicking on the close button in top right-hand corner of the main application window, or select the File menu and the Exit option.

Wild Cards

When designing criteria for searching, it is possible to use a device called a wild card. This is useful when you only know part of a name or title. Say you wanted to list all the members in our database beginning with the letter S. This would be shown as S*, the * indicating that any combination of letters is acceptable. * is the wild card.

Calculations

It is sometimes necessary to perform a calculation on information contained in a table. In the Import Database (Sales Office Table) we created earlier we have information about the sales of various items. However, there is no field to calculate VAT(Valued Added Tax). This may be occasionally needed. Microsoft® Access allows you to add an additional field which is known as a calculated field.

In order to add a calculated field you need to enter a calculated field name, a colon and then the calculation when you are creating a query into an empty row. If you include a table field in the calculation it must be enclosed in a square bracket.

Example

VAT:[January]*0.175

The example shows that the sales in January for an item multiplied by 0.175 will produce the VAT for that item. In this example the calculated field name is VAT and since January is a table field it is enclosed in square brackets. The value of sales in January for an item is multiplied by 0.175, the equivalent of 17.5% (i.e. a current VAT rate).

In this example we have used multiplication (*) but you can also use addition (+), subtraction (-) or division (/). It is important to notice that the symbols for the different ma matical operators are different from the conventional ones in some cases.

Exercise 27

Calculated Fields

1 Load Microsoft Access® by selecting the Start button, highlighting the All Programs option and clicking on the Microsoft Access® item or clicking on the Access® icon on the desktop. Insert your floppy disk into the drive.

2 The New File Task Pane (Figure 3.1) offers you the choice of:

   ■ Opening an existing database file

   ■ Creating a new blank database

Select the More files option which will reveal the Open window to allow you to locate the file, import and load it. The Import database window will open. Click on the Queries button.

3 Select Create query in Design view and you will see an overlaid window, Show Table, appear. Click on the Add button and you will notice a small window called Sales Office appear on the query window. Now click on the Close button in Show Table.

4 The cursor will be flashing in the Field: box and if you click on the down arrow all the Sales Office table fields are available for you to select from. Select the item. Click in the Sort box and you will see another down arrow button appear that provides access to sorting functions. Select the Descending option.

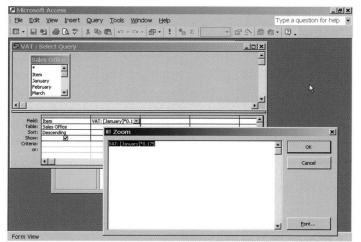

Figure 3.47 Calculated Field (Zoom View)

5   In the next column enter VAT:[January]*0.175 (figure 3.47). The space to enter the expression is limited and if you need more right click and select the Zoom option which will provide you with sufficient space to enter even large complex calculations.

6   Now close the window using the button in the top right hand corner. A message window will appear asking you if you want to save the query as Query1. Click on the Yes button and another window (dialogue) box will appear offering you the opportunity to name your query. Change the name to VAT, then click on the OK button. You will see your query appear in the Import: database window (assuming the Queries button has been selected).

7   You have created a calculated field in a query to

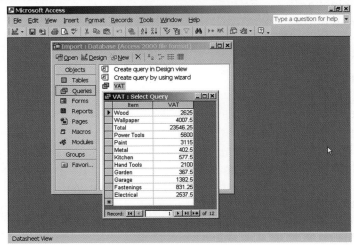

Figure 3.48 **VAT**

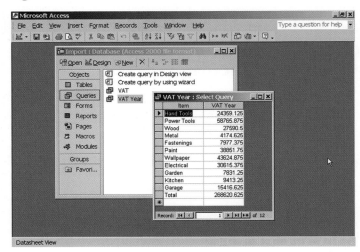

Figure 3.49 **VAT Year Query**

show VAT on the January sales. If you double click on the query (Fees) you will see the results of the query appear (Figure 3.48). Print the query you have created.

8   You are now going to create a new query to add a calculated field in order to calculate the VAT for each item for the whole year. The calculation you need to insert is VAT Year:[Total]*0.175.

9   Explore creating other calculated fields until you are confident.

10 Print out each new query. Figure 3.49 shows the VAT Year.

11 Close Access by clicking on the Close button in the top right hand corner of the main application window or select the File menu and the Exit option.

Summaries

There are many occasions when you want to summarise the information that is held in a database table and Microsoft Access® provides you with a straightforward way of summarising data using a Query. If you select Create a query using Wizard or the Simple Query Wizard (New button), you will reveal the Simple Query Wizard (figure 3.50).

The Wizard allows you to select the fields you want to include in the query by highlighting a field and clicking the arrow button; the field will be moved to the Selected Fields area. When you have completed your selection, you can move forward by clicking on the Next button. As you move through the Wizard, you will be offered the choice of displaying the details of the fields or a summary. If you select Summary and Summary Options, then figure 3.51 will appear, offering you the options to display the Sum, Average, Minimum and Maximum values of the fields.

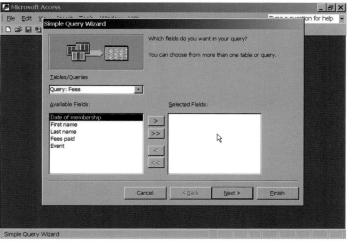

Figure 3.50 Simple Query Wizard

More practice

Activity 1

Database

1 Create a new database called Equipment Orders based on table 3.

Table 3 Equipment Orders

Field Name	Data Type
Customer Reference	Autonumber – this field will automatically be incremented for each new customer
First Order	Date
Name	Text
Address	Text
Equipment Ordered	Text
Cost	Decimal number
Credit Customer	Yes/No

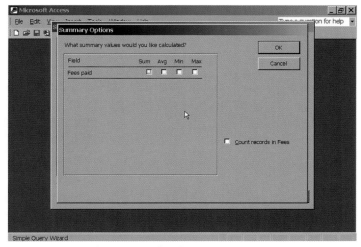

Figure 3.51 Summary Options

2 Enter the data in table 4 into the Equipment Orders database. The equipment ordered is coded to improve speed of input. Call the table Orders.

Table 4 Data Input

First Order	Name	Address	Equipment Ordered	Cost	Credit Customer
01/02/86	Brown	Liverpool	A12	1110	Yes
03/02/87	Clare	Manchester	B67	650	No
06/08/83	Davies	London	K17	230	Yes
11/09/95	Edwards	Brighton	P11	345	Yes
15/05/92	Frame	Leicester	N45	890	Yes
10/04/93	Gornski	Newcastle	A12	1110	No
02/05/89	Davies	Stoke	B34	120	No
21/07/93	Smith	Bristol	A09	560	No
31/01/95	Rao	Poole	B67	650	Yes
18/03/90	Weatherall	Exeter	P11	345	Yes
12/04/99	Weston	London	N45	890	No
16/02/92	Hunter	Manchester	A09	560	Yes

3 Amend your table in the following ways:

Add these new records:

13/02/99	Giles	Bury	A12	1110	Yes
25/08/98	Singh	Halifax	B34	120	Yes
03/11/01	Harris	Manchester	N45	890	No

Delete this record:

31/01/95	Rao	Poole	B67	650	Yes

Change Credit Customer to No:

11/09/95	Edwards	Brighton	P11	345	Yes

Change Date of First Order to 12/05/00:

12/04/99	Weston	London	N45	890	No

4 Systematically check that your data has been entered accurately and then save the database.

Activity 2

Report

1 Open the database Equipment Orders and produce a tabular report using formal style in portrait orientation, showing all the fields, but in the following sequence:

Equipment Ordered

Name

Address

Cost

Credit Customer

First Order

2 Give the report the title Orders List.

3 Sort the information in descending order of First Order.

4 In the header and footer, show the date and add your name to the footer.

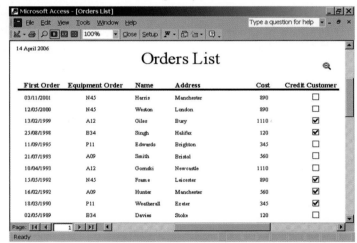

Figure 3.52 Report – Orders List

5 Preview the printout to check that the report is clear and shows all the information. Figure 3.52 shows our efforts. Some text boxes needed to be moved to ensure that columns were aligned. You may have made other choices, so the figure may not be identical to your report.

6 Print the report.

7 Save the report.

8 Create a label for each customer – call the report Customer Labels.

Equipment

Address

First Order

9 Sort the data in order of address.

10 In the footer show:

Your name

Page number.

11 Check that all the labels are correct and print them.

12 Close the database.

Activity 3

Query

1 Open the database Equipment Orders and produce a query to identify customers who placed their first order on or after 01/02/93; include all the fields except Customer Reference.

2 Save the query as Date of First Order (figure 3.53).

3 Use the Date query to produce a tabular report in portrait orientation in corporate style, with the title Date of First Order. The report could be sorted on First Order ascending.

4 Show the following fields in this sequence:

First Order

Cost

Equipment Ordered

Name

Address

Credit Customer

5 In the footer show:

Your name

Page numbers

Date.

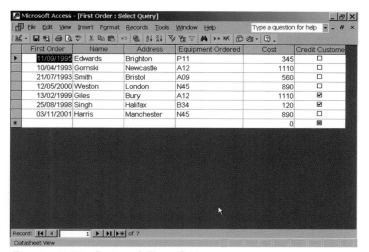

Figure 3.53 Date of First Order query

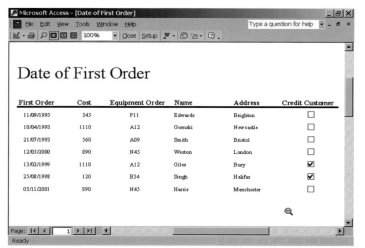

Figure 3.54 Date of First Order report

6 Check the report for clarity and make any necessary changes.

7 Save the report and print. Figure 3.54 shows our effort.

Activity 4

New database

1 Create a new database called Paint, based on table 5.

Table 5 Paint

Field Name	Data Type
Product Name	Text
Volume	Integer
Type	Text (10 characters)
Unit Cost	Currency
Supplier	Text

2   Enter the data in table 6 into the Paint database. The type of paint is coded to improve speed of input (i.e. E – Emulsion and G – Gloss).

Table 6 Data Input

Product Name	Volume	Type	Unit Cost	Supplier
Light Green	950	E	1.5	Justin
Dark Green	560	G	2.1	King
Red	350	G	2.2	Lord
Light Blue	1200	E	1.7	Lord
Dark Blue	125	E	1.8	Justin
White	550	G	2.0	King
Cream	230	G	1.4	Justin
Yellow	175	E	2.3	King
Black	900	E	1.1	Lord
Brown	750	G	1.6	King

3   Systematically check that your data has been entered accurately and then save the database.

Activity 5

Reports

Using the Import Database (Sales Office® table), create reports which show:

- a list of items and sales in April, May and June (figure 3.55)
- a list of items and total sales.

In both cases, explore columnar, tabular and justified layouts.

Activity 6

Queries

Using the Sales Office® database, create queries that present a list of the items and sales in June (figure 3.56)

Explore creating a variety of queries and reports.

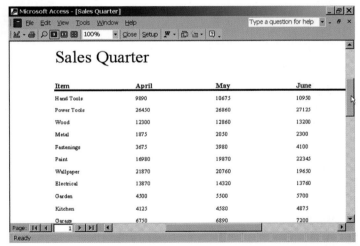

Figure 3.55 Sales Quarter

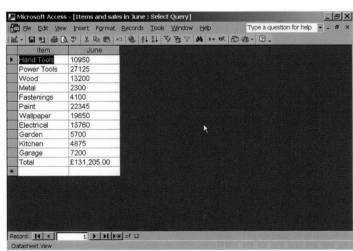

Figure 3.56 Query – Sales in June

SUMMARY

1 Open Microsoft Access®

There are several ways of loading an application in Microsoft Windows®. These include:

- clicking on the Start button, highlighting the All Programs item and clicking on Microsoft Access®
- double-clicking on the Access® icon on the desktop.

2 Create a blank database

Microsoft Access® will load and reveal the New File task pane, which offers you the choice of:

- opening an existing database file
- creating a new blank database.

Select Blank Database. The File New Database will open to enable you to save your new database.

3 Open an existing database

Microsoft Access® will load and reveal the New File task pane, which offers you the choice of:

- opening an existing database file
- creating a new blank database.

If you have only recently created the database, it will be listed in the section. If not, select the More files option, which will reveal the Open window to allow you to locate the file and load it.

4 Create a new table

Once you have saved your new database, the Database window will open to show three options, with the Table object on the left-hand side selected:

- Create table in Design view
- Create table by using wizard
- Create table by entering data.

Double-click on Create a table in Design view and the Table window opens. Insert your field names and their types. If you enter a name in the Field Name box and click in the corresponding Data Type box, a small down arrow will appear, revealing a list of types. Select the appropriate type, and so on, to complete the table.

Save your table by selecting the File menu and the Save As option. The Save As window appears. Enter the table name and click on the OK button.

5 Types of Microsoft Access® data

Microsoft Access® allows you to define nine types of data. They are text, memo, numbers, date/time, currency, autonumber, yes/no, OLE Object and hyperlink.

6 Enter data in a table

Double-click on the table in the Database window and it will open. If it is a new table, the columns may be too small to show the whole field name. Adjust the size by placing your mouse pointer over the line separating the columns and it will change shape to form a double arrow. If you hold down the mouse button, you can drag the column line to widen it.

Click in the fields and enter the data. It is very important to check that each record has been entered accurately. If you find a mistake, click on the appropriate field and enter your correction.

7 Reports
In the Database window, click on the Reports button (left hand side of window) and the two ways of producing a report will be revealed. These are:

- Create report in Design view
- Create report by using wizard.

Reports can be based on tables or queries.

8 AutoReport
In the Reports window, select the New button. This opens the New Report window, which contains a range of options, including AutoReport: Tabular and AutoReport: Columnar).

9 Page setup
Select the File menu and Page Setup. This will open the Page Setup window. Margins can be adjusted and orientation changed by additionally selecting the Page tab.

10 Amend report layout
Highlight the report and click on the Design icon on the toolbar. The structure of the report will be revealed. Clicking on an element will enclose it in a frame. The frame and its contents can be manipulated using the mouse pointer (i.e. pointer changes to a small hand). Items enclosed in a frame can also have their font and character size changed.

11 Header and footer (report)
With the report in Design view, automatic functions – Page Numbers or Date and Time – can be added using the Insert menu. To add your name, right-click on the page footer to reveal a pop-up menu, select Toolbox and use the Label tool.

12 Forms
From the Database window, select the Forms button on the left-hand side of the window and the two options to create a form will be revealed. Click on
Create a form using the Wizard. This will help you through the process of producing a form.

13 Labels
From the Database window, with the Reports button selected, click on New on the toolbar and a new window will appear called New Report. This allows you to choose the Label Wizard, which will assist you in designing a label.

14 Import a data file
Select the File menu, highlight the Get External Data item and click the Import option. The option is only available when a database window is open, so you need to create a new database or open an existing one.

15 Query

Select the Queries button in the Database window and click on the Create query in Design view option.

Alternatively, you can select the Create query by using wizard option. This allows you to create a summary query.

16 Delete records and fields

Highlight your chosen row or column. Select the Edit menu and click on the Delete option. Before the row or column is removed, a message window will appear to ask you to confirm whether you want the record or field deleted permanently.

17 Find and Replace

Select the Edit menu and click on Replace. The Find and Replace window will appear.

18 Update

With the design view grid open, select the Query menu and click on the Update Query option.

19 Customised calculations

Insert a calculation into an empty field with the design view grid, enter the calculated field name, a colon and the calculation. If a table field is included in the calculation it needs to be enclosed in square brackets (e.g. Month: [March] $\times$ 7).

20 Sort

The Sort function is available on the toolbar and allows you to sort data into ascending or descending order. It sorts on numerical, alphabetical and chronological information.

21 Add calculated field in query

With the design view grid open, add the Total row by clicking on the Totals icon on the toolbar. The down-arrow button in the Total row gives access to a range of standard mathematical functions.

Customised calculations can be inserted into an empty field within the design view grid.

Chapter 5

Unit 5

Designing an e-Presentation

This chapter will help you to:

- create a presentation
- set up a master slide
- insert and manipulate data
- control a presentation
- save, print and produce support documents for a presentation.

This chapter covers unit 5 (Design an e-Presentation). There are no preconditions for studying this unit. However, their content does assume that you have the skills and understanding which are provided by the OCR Level 1 ICT course CLAiT 2006 (e.g. Unit 5: Create an e-Presentation and Unit 1: File Management and e-Document Production).

Assessment

After studying unit 5, your skills and understanding are assessed during a three-hour practical assignment. This is set by OCR and marked locally. However, the marking will be externally moderated by OCR. This ensures that the standard is being applied correctly across the many different providers of OCR CLAiT Plus. If you are unsuccessful, you can be reassessed using a different assignment.

An alternative approach is for you to be assessed by an assignment set by OCR or designed by your centre. These assignments cover all the assessment objectives included in the unit. You will need to complete an OCR evidence checklist, explaining how each assessment objective has been covered.

Presentation graphics

Over recent years there has been a large increase in the use of presentation graphics to support business meetings, conferences and teaching. They allow individuals to create a set of slides and handouts quickly to illustrate and support their presentations. These can be projected from the computer through a video (data) projector or printed on transparencies for use with an overhead projector. In either case, high quality visual aids can be produced straightforwardly.

Microsoft PowerPoint® XP is the presentation graphics application on which this chapter is based (figure 5.1). It is a modern tool for creating presentations and offers users a wide range of facilities to combine text and graphics. However, it is good practice to develop a consistent format for your slides that does not overuse colour, images or text effects. Many organisations provide their staff with a house style to follow, which incorporates standard features such as the organisation's logo. Microsoft PowerPoint® provides you with the means of creating a standard template or master for your presentations.

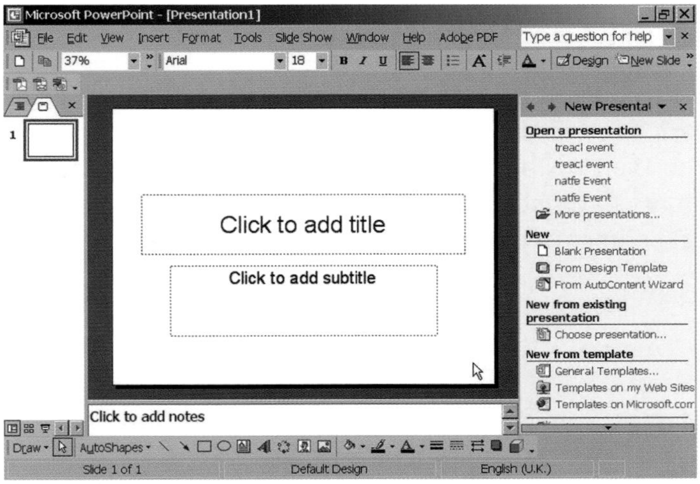

A master/template will include:

- background colour
- standard graphics (e.g. logo)
- slide number
- presenter's name and date (this will help you manage your presentations when you have several)
- heading style (i.e. font, size, colour and style)
- bullet style (i.e. font, size, colour and style)
- sub-bullet style (i.e. font, size, colour and style).

Figure 5.1 Microsoft PowerPoint® XP

It will also specify the location of different elements (e.g. pictures, slide numbering and dates) and the use of Microsoft PowerPoint® effects. Microsoft PowerPoint® and other presentation graphics packages allow you to employ animation techniques to add interest to presentations. However, it is good practice not to overuse these effects.

In exercise 34 you are going to create a master style. The house style that you are going to follow is:

Master slide

Feature	Colour	Position	Comments
Background	none		
Graphic		Left corner of text area	
Number slides		Bottom right-hand corner of the slide	
Text (footer)		Bottom centre of the slide	Enter your name and centre
Date		Bottom right-hand corner of the slide	
Timings			Each slide 60 seconds
Transitions			1 effect on every slide
Builds			1 effect on every slide

Text

Style name	Typeface	Point size	Feature	Alignment
Heading	Sans serif	40	Bold/blue	Centre
Bullet (level 1)	Serif	28	Include bullet character	Left
Sub-bullet (level 2)	Serif	24	Include bullet character	Left
Sub-bullet (level 3)	Serif	20	Include bullet character	Left

Table

Style name	Typeface	Point size	Feature	Colour	Alignment
Text	Serif	24	No bullet characters	Black	Left
Currency					Use decimal tabulation

Typeface (font)

The house style sheets use the term typeface, which is an alternative to the term font. There are two types of font (or typefaces), sans serif and serif. A serif type font has small projections on the ends of the characters, while a sans serif type font does not. You might say that serif fonts have more fancy characters or that sans serif fonts have plain characters. You need to experiment with your choice of fonts to find the ones that you like. For example:

Serif

Courier New
Serifa BT
Times New Roman

Sans serif

Arial
Helvetica

Microsoft PowerPoint®

Figure 5.1 shows the initial view of Microsoft PowerPoint® when it loads. It shows a display divided into four main areas. Across the top are a series of menus and toolbars, which are similar to those provided by other Microsoft Office® applications. A further toolbar (i.e. Drawing) is shown across the bottom. On the right-hand side is the New Presentation task pane. On the left-hand side is an Overview pane, showing the slides that you have created in the presentation – at the moment, one blank slide. In the middle is the work area, showing a blank slide and an area to add notes for your presentation.

Exercise 34

Starting a new presentation master slide

1 Insert a floppy disk into the computer's drive.

2 Load Microsoft Publisher® by selecting Start , highlighting the All Programs menu and clicking on the Microsoft PowerPoint item or by clicking on the PowerPoint icon on the desktop.

3 Select the Blank Presentation option from the New Presentation task pane on the right of the display. This will display the Slide Layout task

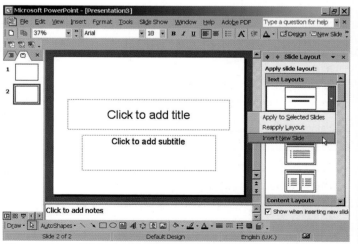

Figure 5.2 Slide Layout task pane

pane (figure 5.2), which offers you a variety of outline slides in a scrolling box to choose from. If you place the pointer on an outline, a button with a down arrow will appear on the right of slide (figure 5.2), along with a description of the slide type. The first outline is a title slide, which is identical to the opening display. Scroll down the outlines and explore the options, then return to the first one and click on the button to reveal a short menu. Select Insert New Slide (figure 5.2).

4 The title slide will appear in the work area of Microsoft PowerPoint®. However, since it is identical to the original display, you will only notice a flicker as the display is refreshed.

5 You are now going to create a master slide for this presentation. Select the View menu, then highlight the Master option to reveal a sub-menu (Figure 5.3). Click on the Slide Master option. The master slide template will show in the Microsoft PowerPoint® work area (figure 5.4). A small Slide Master View toolbar will also appear. If you drag the toolbar down to the Drawing toolbar, it will merge with it.

6 To edit the master (i.e. to change the characteristics) you need to click on the different slide features (e.g. Title). However, before you start to change the master, you should decide on the

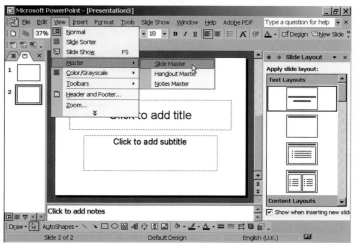

Figure 5.3 Master option

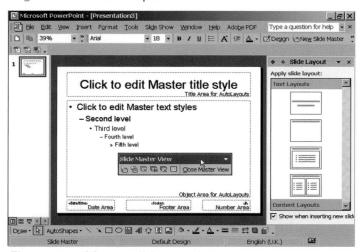

Figure 5.4 Master slide template

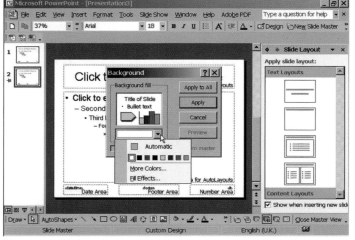

Figure 5.5 Background

Designing an e-Presentation

325

background colour for the slide. Select the Format menu and click on the Background option to reveal the background window (figure 5.5). This allows you to choose a background colour for your slides. If you click on the down-arrow button you are given access to more choices. In this case, we will select no colour and click on Apply to All.

7 Click on the Master title style and from the toolbar choose Tahoma (font), size 40, bold and centred (figure 5.6). Click on Master text style (i.e. first-level bullet point) and choose Times New Roman, size 28 and left-justified. Click on Second level and choose Times New Roman, size 24 and left-justified. Click on Third level and choose Times New Roman, size 20 and left-justified. Delete the fourth and fifth levels.

8 The bottom left-hand side box contains the date (i.e. date/time) and is left-justified. Click on the box and highlight the date and time. Select the Insert menu and click on the Date and Time option to reveal the Date and Time window (figure 5.7). Select the layout dd/mm/yyyy and click the automatic update radio button.

9 Click on the footer to highlight it and enter your

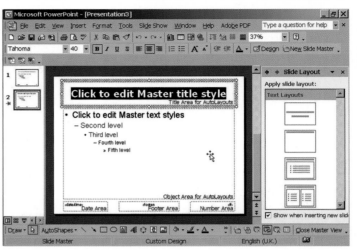

Figure 5.6 Master title

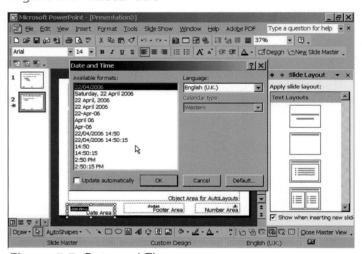

Figure 5.7 Date and Time

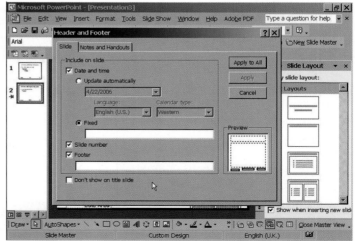

Figure 5.8 Header and Footer window

CLAiT Plus 2006 for Office® XP

name, which should be centred.

10 Click on the right-hand box Number Area. Select I̱nsert menu and click on Slide Nu̱mber. This will reveal the Header and Footer window (figure 5.8). Click in the Footer radio button to show the footer you have created on the slides. Click on the radio button Slide number and then the Apply to All button. The Preview area will show positions of date/time, footer and number boxes.

11 The next step is to select a font colour. The default colour is black, which is acceptable, except for the title, so click in the title box and then select the Font Color icon on the Drawing toolbar (figure 5.9). Choose blue.

12 The last step is to place a graphic image in the bottom right-hand corner of the text area. Select the I̱nsert menu,

Figure 5.9 Drawing toolbar

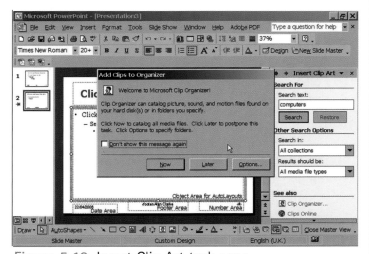

Figure 5.10 Insert Clip Art task pane

highlight Pi̱ctures to reveal the sub-menu and click on Clip Art. This will open the Insert Clip Art task pane (figure 5.10). A message will overlay the display (Add Clips to Organizer). Click on Later to remove the message.

13 The Insert Clip Art task pane lets you search for an image to fit your presentation theme. The results of a search are displayed in the task pane in a scrolling box. Explore the pictures. When you place the pointer over the image, a description of it will appear, as well as a button with a down arrow along the right edge of the picture. When you click the button, a menu of options appears. Select the I̱nsert option to add an image to the master slide.

14 The Clip Art image will appear on the slide, enclosed in a frame, with small rectangles at the corners and centres of the lines. These allow you to change the shape and size of the image. You can move the image by positioning the mouse over the image, holding down the mouse button and dragging the image around. The mouse pointer is shaped

like crossed arrows. To resize or change the shape of the image, position your mouse over one of the rectangles and it will change to a double-headed arrow. By holding down the mouse button and dragging, you can change the shape and size of the picture. Experiment, but remember that changing its shape and size may distort the image, so you need to ensure the image's proportions are acceptable when you have finished.

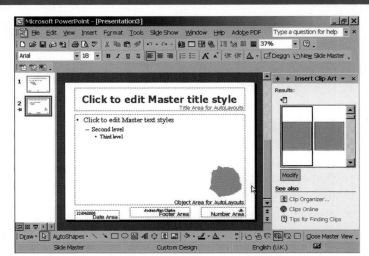

Figure 5.11 Master slide

15 You have now established your master and need to save it. Select the File menu and the Save option. The Save As window will appear. Save the master as a file called Presentation1 on your floppy disk. You will need to change the Save in: box to floppy disk and enter the file name in the File name: box.

16 The master is shown in figure 5.11. Notice that in overview pane it shows that we have two slides. This is simply the result of the process we have followed and the first slide is the original default master before the changes we have made. We therefore need to remove it, otherwise presentations developed using our master will default to the original design. Click on the first slide in the overview and press the delete key. The slide will be removed, leaving your revised master. Save this again.

17 Close the application either by selecting the File menu and clicking on the Exit option or by clicking on the Close button in the top right-hand corner of the application window.

Transition and other effects

A slide show is a presentation of a set of individual slides. Microsoft PowerPoint® allows you to control the change from one slide to the next by using transition effects. For example, you can slowly dissolve the closing slide and gradually reveal the next one. These effects can add considerable interest to a standard presentation. Among the transition effects is the control of time, so you can display each slide for a set period and then change it. This is very useful for providing a continuous presentation for an exhibition stand or similar function.

The transitions are accessed by selecting the Slide Show menu and clicking on the Slide Transition option to reveal the Slide Transition task pane (figure 5.12). This lets you select the type of transition and either have a standard change for the whole presentation or a different transition between each slide.

In figure 5.12 you will notice that there is a down-arrow button which you need to click to reveal the rest of the task pane. At the top of the pane, in the Apply to selected slides: area, is a scroll box that gives you a choice of different transition effects. Below this area is Modify transition, which allows you to vary the speed of change and also to add sound effects. Below this section is one called Advance slide, which gives the choice of manually controlling the move from one slide to the next by clicking your mouse button, or allowing the slides to change automatically after a set time.

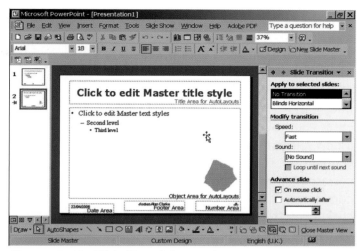

Figure 5.12 Slide Transition task pane

If you click on the down-arrow button at the bottom of the pane you reveal a series of choices of which slides to apply the transition effect to:

- Apply to Master (only appears when you are working on the master slide)
- Apply to All Slides
- Play (so you can see effect)
- Slide Show.

At the top of the pane, an up arrow will appear to allow you to return to the original display.

In addition to adding transitions to each slide, you can also add animation to the individual slide elements (e.g. title). The main effects are available by selecting the Slide Show menu and clicking on the Custom Animation option. This reveals the Custom Animation task pane.

Although Microsoft PowerPoint® provides a wide variety of effects, it is good practice to limit their use since they can distract from your overall message. One or two carefully chosen effects can enhance your presentation, whereas too many can leave your audience confused.

Charts

When starting a new presentation or inserting a new slide, you are offered the choice of a variety of different layouts (figure 5.2). Among the choices is to have slides which are:

- text only
- graphics (picture) only
- text and graphics
- charts only
- text and charts
- organisational charts
- organisational charts and text.

When you scroll down the outline they are divided into sections, and the charts are displayed in the Other layout section. If you select either the chart only or text and chart slides, you will see a chart placeholder, which, if you double-click it, will reveal a chart with its corresponding data in the form of a datasheet (figure 5.13). The datasheet contains sample information indicating where you can enter your own information to create a new chart. If you enter information, you will see the chart change in a corresponding way. When you have completed entering your data, just click away from the chart or datasheet and you will see the datasheet disappear and the new chart will be inserted into the slide.

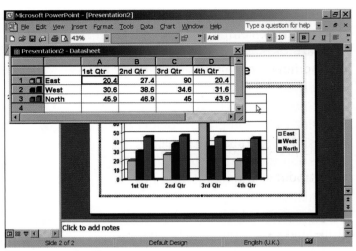

Figure 5.13 Chart

You can also insert a Microsoft Excel® chart into a slide by selecting the Insert menu and clicking on the Object option to reveal the Insert Object window. This provides you with two choices: to create a new object or select an existing one. An object is a file produced by a variety of applications. The Insert Object window displays a list of suitable applications.

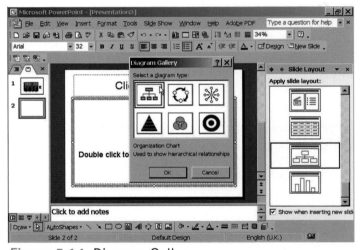

Figure 5.14 Diagram Gallery

Microsoft PowerPoint® also provides a special type of chart called an organisational chart. If you select the organisational chart slide, you will see an organisational chart placeholder. If you double-click on it, the Diagram Gallery window will be revealed (figure 5.14). Select the top left-hand corner option (i.e. Organization chart) to reveal the Organization toolbar and slide (figure 5.15). You can enter your own labels into the chart and then extend it by using the toolbar options.

Create a presentation

You have created a master slide or a template for your slides. You now need to employ it to guide you

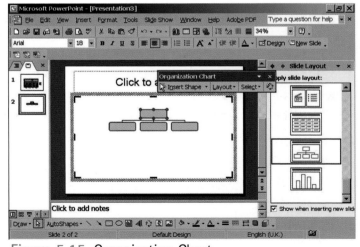

Figure 5.15 Organisation Chart

through producing a slide show. Your master can still be amended or adapted. When you have used Microsoft PowerPoint® for a period you will begin to develop a library of presentations and different master slides to suit different purposes.

You are going to create a presentation for a senior manager who is demonstrating a new product to the company directors. It is always useful to plan your presentations before you rush to create the slides. Outline what you would like to say, what the objectives of the presentation are and how long you plan to speak. People often produce more material than they can fit into the time available. Consider carefully what are the key things you need to say and how best to present them. It is often appropriate to finish early to allow time for questions. Few audiences appreciate speakers who finish late or have to rush their final slides in order to keep to time.

For this presentation, the manager wants to:

- introduce himself (1 slide)
- explain the new product (2 slides)
- discuss prices (1 slide)
- discuss sales approach (1 slide)
- discuss customers (1 slide)
- forecast chart (1 slide)
- conclude the presentation (1 slide).

Your final presentation will consist of eight slides. These will be based on the master you have already developed.

Exercise 35

Creating a presentation

1 Insert a floppy disk into the computer's drive.

2 Load Microsoft Publisher® by selecting Start, highlighting the All Programs menu and clicking on the Microsoft PowerPoint® item or by clicking on the PowerPoint® icon on the desktop.

3 If you have only recently completed exercise 34, then you may see Presentation1 in the Open a presentation section of the New Presentation task pane. If it is not visible, click on the More presentations option to reveal the Open window. Change the Look in: box to floppy disk to locate Presentation1. Double-click on Presentation1 to load it.

4 The master slide Presentation1 will load into the Microsoft PowerPoint® work area. It is useful now to save the presentation under a new name to avoid overwriting the master slide, which you may want to use later for a different presentation. Select the File menu and the Save As option. This will open the Save As window. Change the Save in: box to floppy disk and enter New Product into the File name: box, then click on the Save button.

5 You now need to create your presentation. Select the View menu and click on the Normal option. The master slide will be replaced by the Title slide in the master slides style. Enter AMEX STATIONERY in the Click to add title area. In this case, you do not have a subtitle, so select the Insert menu and click on the New Slide option.

6 The Slide Layout task pane will appear. Select a text-only layout with a single column, and use

the Apply to Selected Slides option to change the new slide to this layout. Click on Click to add title and enter Leather Bound Notebook. Click on Click to add text and insert Pocket Size, then press the enter key. The cursor will move to the next line and a new bullet will appear. Enter Desk Size and then press the enter key to move to a new line. Enter Different Formats. Figure 5.16 shows the result.

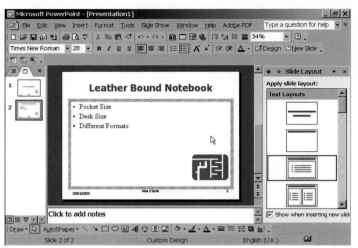

Figure 5.16 Initial Slide 2

7 Figure 5.16 shows that your bullet point text is presented on the left side of the slide. The text area is enclosed in a box, with small squares at the corners and in the centre of each side. These squares allow you to change the shape of the text area and adjust the position of the text. If you place your mouse point on the enclosure lines, but not on the squares, the pointer changes shape to a star. If you hold down the mouse button while the pointer is in this shape,

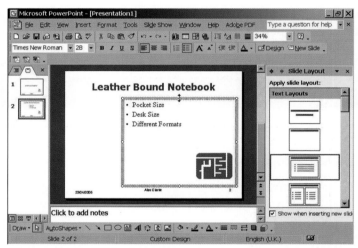

Figure 5.17 Slide 2

you can move the whole text area. Try to move the text area, but return it to its original place when you have finished.

8 If you place your mouse over a square, the mouse pointer changes to a double-headed arrow. If you hold down the button you can drag the text area to change its size and shape. Experiment changing the shape until you are content with the new appearance. Figure 5.17 shows the method.

9 Select Insert menu and click on the New Slide option. The Slide Layout task pane will appear. Select the Text in Two columns layout and use the Apply to Selected Slides option to change the new slide to this layout. Insert the title Options. Insert in the left-hand column: Lined Paper, Squared Paper and Plain Paper; and in the right-hand column: Address Book, Diary and Folder. You will notice that each column is enclosed so that it can be moved, resized or its shape adjusted. Change the columns to improve the presentation of the slide.

10 Now create a further four slides:

Slide 4 – Text slide: the title of the slide is Price; add a WordArt image of the pound symbol to represent money, and in the text column add Wholesale, Retail, Independent and Chains.

Alternatively, select a slide with a text column and a Clip Art column and then insert a clip to represent money. When inserting Clip Art you may be asked to insert the Microsoft Office® CD-ROM containing the Clip Art if this has not been installed on the hard disk.

Slide 5 – Text only slide: the title of the slide is Sales Staff; add to text National Sales Manager, Regional Sales Manager and Sales Representatives; again, position the text box to conform with your earlier decisions.

Slide 6 – Text only slide: the title of the slide is Customers; add the text Independent Stationers, Chains, Bookshops, General Retail, Wholesale and Postal; again, position the text box to conform with your earlier decisions.

Slide 7 – Chart only slide: the title of the slide is Forecast; the data sheet for the slide is:

	1st Quarter	2nd Quarter	3rd Quarter	4th Quarter
Address	15	16	21	23
Diary	27	22	31	26
Folder	8	11	9	12
Notebook	35	34	30	32

Slide 8 – Text only slide: the title of the slide is Conclusions; add to the text Product Launch, Advertising and Sales Effort.

11 Adjust the layout to improve the appearance of all slides. When you are adjusting the shape and size of a graphic, there is a danger that you will alter its proportions so that a poor image results. Figure 5.18 shows the whole presentation. As you created your presentation, you will have noticed an overview of

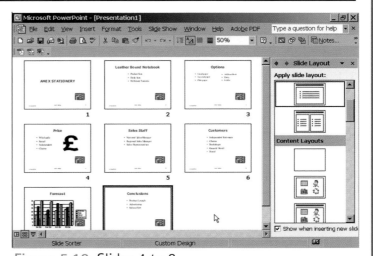

Figure 5.18 Slides 4 to 8

the presentation appear in the left-hand column of the work area. If you select the first tab (Outline), an overview of the text appears (figure 5.19).

12 Save your presentation by selecting the File menu and clicking on Save. No window will appear since the system assumes you are saving in the current location, using the same file name.

continued

13 Close the application by either selecting the File menu and clicking on the Exit option or by clicking on the Close button in the top right-hand corner of the application window.

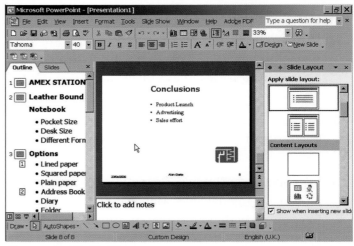

Figure 5.19 Outline

Exercise 35A

Create Timings

1 Insert a floppy disk into the computer's drive.

2 Load Microsoft PowerPoint® by selecting Start, highlighting the All Programs menu and clicking on the Microsoft PowerPoint® item or by clicking on the PowerPoint® icon on the desktop.

3 If you have only recently completed Exercise 35 then you may see New Product in the Open a presentation section of the New Presentation Task Pane. If it is not visible then click on the More Presentations option to reveal the Open window. Change the Look in: box to Floppy Disk to locate New Product. Double click on New Product to load it.

4 The presentation will load into the PowerPoint® work area. You are now going to set times between slides so that they will change automatically. This is useful if you are running a presentation as part of an exhibition.

5 Select the Slide Show menu and the Slide Transition option to open the Slide Transition task pane. In the section Advance Slide is a radio button Automatically which you need to click in order to insert a tick. Immediately below the button is a box in which you can enter times either from the keyboard or by clicking on the up or down arrows. Enter 15 seconds.

6 Click on the Apply to All Slides button which you may need to scroll down to.

7 Now run the presentation by selecting the Slide Show menu and View Show option. Watch as the slides change automatically every 15 seconds.

continued

12 Save your presentation as New Product Automatic by selecting the File menu and clicking on Save. No window will appear since the system assumes you are saving in the current location using the same file name.

13 Close the application by either selecting the File menu and clicking on the Exit option or by clicking on the Close button in the top right hand corner of the application window.

Editing a presentation

Microsoft PowerPoint® provides functions so you can edit the presentation. You are able to:

- change the order of the presentation
- delete slides
- insert new slides
- edit individual slides (e.g. text, graphics)
- hide slides.

You can gain an overview of the whole presentation by selecting the View menu and clicking on the Slide Sorter option. This reveals a display showing a small (thumbnail) picture of each slide. Slides can be dragged around the presentation by clicking on them to highlight them. A highlighted slide is enclosed in a rectangle. Highlighted slides (figure 5.20) can be dragged to new positions in the presentation, or deleted by pressing the delete key. New slides can be added by clicking the position (figure 5.21) you would like to add a new slide to, and then selecting the Insert menu and clicking on the New Slide option.

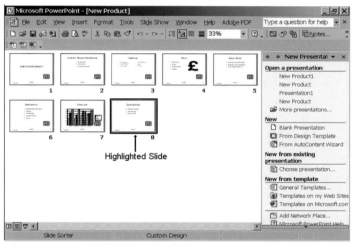

Figure 5.20 Highlighted slide

An alternative approach is to scroll through the slides from the work area. You can return from the Slide Sorter display by selecting the View menu and clicking on the Normal option. Slides can be inserted using the Insert menu and clicking on New Slide or deleted by selecting the Edit menu and clicking on the Delete Slide option.

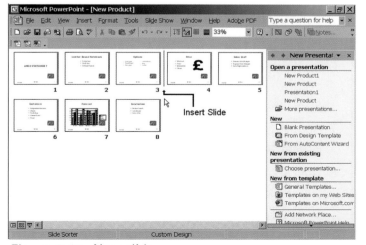

Figure 5.21 New slide

It may seem a little odd that you would want to hide a slide, but there are occasions when you want to show different information to different groups. For example, you may have created a presentation for internal staff that you later need to show some customers. Hiding slides allows you to change the presentation quickly.

To hide a slide, select the V̲iew menu and click the Sli̲de Sorter option. Click on the slide you want to hide to highlight it, and select the Slid̲e Show menu, click the H̲ide Slide option. The slide is now hidden. This is indicated by the slide number being crossed. To reverse the process, click on the H̲ide Slide option.

You can create a link from another slide to the hidden one so that by clicking on a word, image or button, you can present the hidden slide. The Hyperlinks section explains how to create links to hidden slides.

Exercise 36

Editing

1 Insert a floppy disk into the computer's drive.

2 Load Microsoft Power Point® by selecting Start, highlighting the All Programs menu and clicking on the Microsoft PowerPoint® item or by clicking on the PowerPoint® icon on the desktop.

3 If you have only recently completed exercise 35, you may see New Product in the Open a presentation section of the New Presentation task pane. If it is not visible, click on the More presentations option to reveal the Open window. Change the Look i̲n: box to floppy disk to locate New Product. Double-click on New Product to load it.

4 You are going to insert an additional slide between slides 5 and 6, showing the organisation of the sales staff. Select the V̲iew menu and click on the Sli̲de Sorter option. You will see all eight slides appear as small images. Click between slides 5 and 6 and you will see a line appear between them.

5 Select the I̲nsert menu and click on the N̲ew Slide option. A new slide will appear in the position you have selected and the Slide Layout task pane will be displayed. Select the organisational chart layout from the task pane and click on the Apply to S̲elected Slides option.

6 Double-click on the new slide and you will return to the work area, with the new slide occupying the display. The slides are automatically renumbered so that the new one is now number 6.

7 Double-click on the slide to reveal the Diagram Gallery window (figure 5.14). Select the Organization Chart image in the left-hand corner to insert the organisational chart.

8 The Organization Chart toolbar is opened with the blank organisation chart (figure 5.15). This allows you to create a chart. Click on the top box of the chart and enter National Sales Manager. Now move to the next row down. Enter into each box Regional Sales Manager (three times).

9 Click on the centre Regional Sales Manager box and then on the down arrow on the Insert Shape option on the toolbar. Select the Subordinate option and a new box will be added, linked to the central Regional Sales Manager box. Click in the new box and enter Sales Representative. Your chart should now look like figure 5.22.

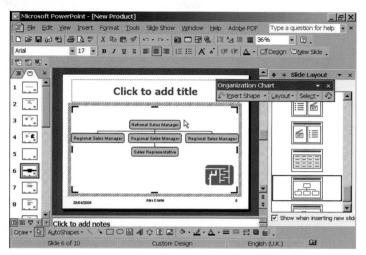

Figure 5.22 Sales organisational chart

10 Close the Organization Chart toolbar.

11 Click on the Title and enter Sales Organisation.

12 Save your new presentation by selecting the File menu and clicking on the Save option.

13 Select the View menu and click on Slide Sorter. You are going to change the order of the slides by moving slide 4, Price, to appear after slide 7, Customers. Click on the Price slide to highlight it (enclose it) and, holding down the mouse button, drag the slide to the new position. A line will appear in this new position. You can then release the button.

14 Save your new presentation by selecting the File menu and clicking on the Save option.

15 Close the application by selecting either the File menu and clicking on the Exit option or by clicking on the Close button in the top right-hand corner of the application window.

Hyperlinks

Hyperlinks are the means by which you can add extra slides to your presentation which only appear if you click on a sensitive area or the button on an existing slide. This allows you to customise a presentation to meet the needs of different audiences or to provide more control over the presentation. Figure 5.23 shows the connection between the main presentation slides and the hyperlink ones. Hyperlinks can also link your presentation to a document, a website, an intranet location or an e-mail address.

To add a hyperlink, select the text on the slide, click on the Insert menu and select the Hyperlink option. The Insert Hyperlink window will appear, which allows you to link the

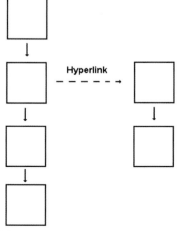

Figure 5.23 Hyperlink

slide to a chosen location where the other slides or documents are stored. If you are linking to other slides and want to return to the original presentation, you must create a second hyperlink back to your original slide. The link text will change colour and be underlined to show the hyperlink.

You can add standard hyperlink buttons to a slide by clicking on the Slide Show menu and highlighting the Action buttons option to reveal a small menu of buttons. Click on the button of your choice and the pointer changes to a cross to let you position it on the slide. Once it is located, the Action Settings window opens to allow you to select the action which will take place when the button is pressed. You can establish buttons to link you to the previous, next, first or last slides, giving you considerable control over the presentation.

Earlier we discussed hiding slides to protect confidential information. It is possible to create links to hidden slides so that you have the option of showing the slide. You need to highlight the text or image, then select the Insert menu and click on the Hyperlink option. This will reveal the Insert Hyperlink window (figure 5.24). Select the Place in This Document button to reveal a list of the slide titles. To complete the link, choose the hidden slide by clicking on it. The hidden slide will appear in the Preview area. Click the OK button to finish the task. This

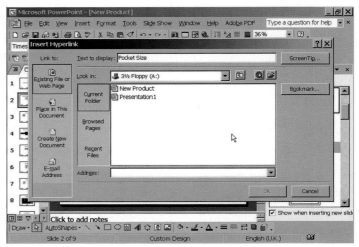

Figure 5.24 Insert Hyperlink window

method can be used to establish links within a presentation, not simply to hidden slides.

Using blank slides

One of the major difficulties in designing a presentation is to time the slide show. You do not know how many questions you will be asked or if a previous presenter will not arrive and you will have more time than you planned for. One way of maintaining control is to insert blank slides into the presentation.

This gives you the opportunity to pause or to stop if time runs out. Blanks should be inserted at logical places to allow you to pause, perhaps to provide an opportunity for questions or comments.

Tables

One of the layout options is a table, which you can select from the Slide Layout task pane and a table slide is placed within the presentation (figure 5.25). Click on the Insert Table icon to

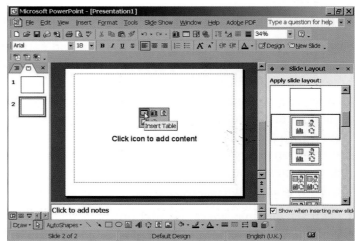

Figure 5.25 Table slide

open the Insert Table window in which you can choose the number of rows and columns. When you have selected the size of the table and clicked on the OK button, you will see the table on the slide, and the Tables and Borders toolbar (figure 5.26) appears (alternatively, View menu, highlight Toolbar and Tables and Borders option). This lets you change the appearance of the table. When you have made your selections you are presented with an empty table in which to enter your information. The mouse pointer looks like a pen.

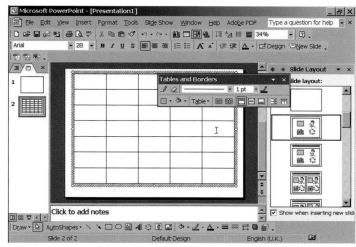

Figure 5.26 Tables and Borders

You can also insert a table into an existing slide by selecting the Insert menu and the Table option to reveal the Insert Table window, which allows you to set the number of rows and columns. This will produce a table for you to enter text into. The table can be resized and moved using the mouse pointer to position it on the slide.

Tables are one means of aligning information on a slide, but you can also use the tab key. The justification icons on the toolbar also let you align the text left, right and centre, in the same way that text is aligned in Microsoft Word®.

Exercise 37

Transitions and effects

1 Insert a floppy disk into the computer's drive.

2 Load Microsoft PowerPoint® by selecting Start, highlighting the All Programs menu and clicking on the Microsoft PowerPoint® item or by clicking on the PowerPoint® icon on the desktop.

3 If you have only recently completed Exercise 36, you may see New Product in the Open a presentation section of the New Presentation task pane. If it is not visible, click on the More presentations option to reveal the Open window. Change the Look in: box to floppy disk to locate New Product. Double-click on New Product to load it.

4 You are now going to apply a transition effect to each slide of the presentation. Select the Slide Show menu and click on the Slide Transition option to reveal the Slide Transition task pane (figure 5.12). Click on the down-arrow button below Apply to selected slides to display a list of transition options. Select an option and you will see it demonstrated on the slide in the work area. Explore the options and choose one you feel is effective. You are also provided with three speeds as transitions (i.e. slow, medium and fast). To select a new speed, click on your choice. You will again see it demonstrated in the work area.

5 In the Advance Slide area you are going to set the presentation to change slides automatically. The house style sets 60 seconds as the time for each slide, so click in the automatic box and adjust the time to read 60 seconds or 1 minute. Both the On Mouse Click and Automatically after options now have a tick in them, so you can manually change slides or they will change themselves after a minute. Now click on the Apply to All button (you may need to click on the down arrow to reveal the options).

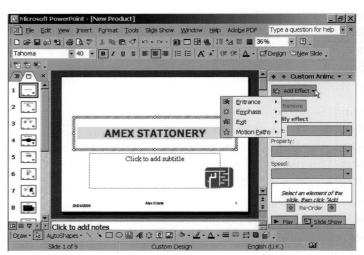

Figure 5.27 Custom Animation task pane

6 You are now going to add animation effects to each slide. The house style is for one effect for each slide. Scroll through the slides until you reach the title one. Click on the title to highlight it (i.e. enclosed in a frame). Select the Slide Show menu and the Custom Animation option to reveal the Custom Animation task pane. Click on the down arrow of the Add Effect box to reveal a series of options (figure 5.27). Choose Entrance and the Fly In option. The option will be demonstrated on the working slide as soon you select it. You can modify the effect using the other parts of the task pane.

7 Repeat the process for each slide.

8 Save your new presentation by selecting the File menu and clicking on the Save option.

9 Two other ways of enhancing your presentation are by using hyperlinks and hiding slides. You may want to use this presentation for external audiences and some slides will not be appropriate (e.g. forecasts of income). Let us hide the Forecast slide. Select the View menu and click on the Slide Sorter option. Thumbnail images of each slide will appear. Click on the Forecast slide to highlight it (i.e. it will be enclosed in a rectangle). Now select Slide Show menu and click on the Hide Slide option. The number of the slide will be crossed.

10 In some cases you may want to show the hidden slide. This can be achieved by using hyperlinks. Move to the slide prior to the Forecast slide and highlight the text you want to make the link (e.g. Slide Title). Select the Insert menu and click on the Hyperlink option to reveal the Insert Hyperlink window (figure 5.24). Click on the Place in This Document button, since you are linking to a slide in this presentation. A list of slide titles will appear. Double-click on the Forecast slide and you will return to the slide working area. You have linked the slides.

11 Save your revised presentation by selecting the File menu and clicking on the Save option.

12 Close the application either by selecting the File menu and clicking on the Exit option or by clicking on the Close button in the top right-hand corner of the application window.

Importing text and graphics

Microsoft Office® applications enable you to cut, copy and paste text and graphics between applications. It is possible to cut or copy text from Microsoft Word® and paste it into PowerPoint®. You can also send text from Microsoft Word® to Microsoft PowerPoint® directly, using the option Send To, which is available from the File menu. This reveals a sub-menu with the option Microsoft PowerPoint. This will change the file into a Microsoft PowerPoint® presentation.

Graphics can be inserted into Microsoft PowerPoint® by selecting the Insert menu and highlighting the Picture option to reveal a sub-menu of options (figure 5.28). This provides you with a series of choices, including inserting Clip Art or selecting a graphic image from a file, a scanner or a digital camera.

Figure 5.28 Picture option

Find and replace

When you need to make changes to a presentation, you can do it manually by locating the slide, deleting the text and then inserting the replacement text. Alternatively, you could employ the Replace function, available by selecting the Edit menu and clicking on the Replace option (figure 5.29). This lets you search for a word or phrase and replace it throughout the whole presentation.

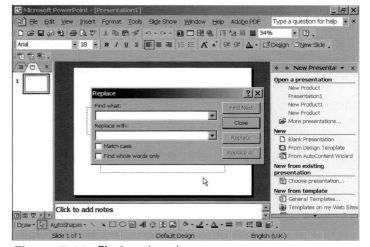

Figure 5.29 Find and replace

Spellchecker

One of the most frequent problems with presentations is showing a misspelt word to an audience. They will see the error immediately, and often you are only aware of it when someone tells you after the presentation. Microsoft PowerPoint® provides a spellchecker and it is good practice to check your completed presentation. The spellchecker is available by selecting the Tools menu and clicking on the Spelling option. However, you should not simply rely on the checker, but also proofread your slides.

Showing a Presentation

There are several ways of running a presentation. These are:

1 Select the View menu and click on Slide Show option.

2 Select the Slide Show menu and click on the View Show option (figure 5.30).

3 Click on the Slide Show button in the bottom left-hand corner of the display (figure 5.30). This shows the presentation from the slide in the work area.

Microsoft PowerPoint® allows you to save your slides in the Presentation format, which lets the slide show be shown immediately. With Save As or Save, you need to select the Save as type: to select Presentation. When you double-click on the Presentation, the slides open immediately.

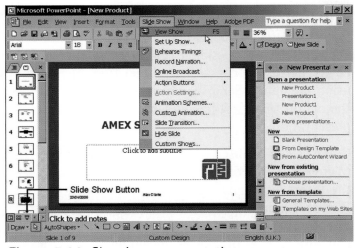

Figure 5.30 Showing a presentation

Moving a presentation to a new computer

The computer on which the presentation is created is frequently not the one used for actually showing it. Therefore you need to move the presentation. You can simply transfer the file using a memory stick or other portable method. However, this does assume the new computer will have all the resources that you need to run the show (e.g. images, sounds and fonts). You do not want to discover that it does not during a presentation.

Microsoft PowerPoint® provides a Pack and Go facility to ensure your presentation is complete. Select the File menu and the Pack and Go option. This opens a Wizard, which will take you through the process step by step (figure 5.31).

To install the pack presentation on the new computer, you need to double-click on Pngsetup (i.e. Pack and Go setup file) and select the folder in which you want to save the presentation, then click on OK. The system will tell you when the unpacking is successful. You can then run the presentation in the normal way.

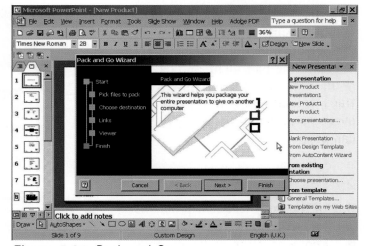

Figure 5.31 Pack and Go

Exercise 38

Showing a presentation

1 Insert a floppy disk into the computer's drive.

2 Load Microsoft PowerPoint® by selecting Start, highlighting the All Programs menu and clicking on the Microsoft PowerPoint® item or by clicking on the PowerPoint® icon on the desktop.

3 If you have only recently completed exercise 37, you may see New Product in the Open a presentation section of the New Presentation task pane. If it is not visible, click on the More presentations option to reveal the Open window. Change the Look in: box to floppy disk to locate New Product. Double-click on New Product to load it.

4 Run the presentation using one of the options. You will see the slide occupy the whole screen. You may need to click your mouse to see the transition effects. Observe what happens when you move between slides. Try waiting for 60 seconds to see the slides change automatically. The precise change will depend on your previous choice of effects.

5 Run the presentation several times, including linking to the hidden slide.

6 Close the application either by selecting the File menu and clicking on the Exit option or by clicking on the Close button in the top right-hand corner of the application window.

Printing supporting documents

As well as producing slides using Microsoft PowerPoint®, you can also create a variety of printed documents to support the presentation. The slides themselves can be printed on to transparencies for use with an overhead projector. In addition, you can print:

- copies of individual slides
- a set of notes for the presenter
- handouts which allow audience to add notes
- a copy of the presentation in outline view.

These are all available by selecting the File menu and clicking on the Print option to reveal the Print window (figure 5.32). This gives you a variety of options. In the Print what: area you can select from a list. The Handouts options lets you print copies of slides as small thumbnail images in a number of different formats (e.g. six images to a page). You can also print

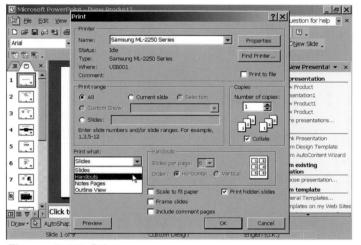

Figure 5.32 Print

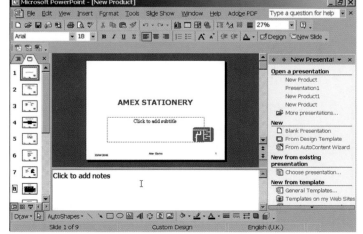

Figure 5.33 Speaking notes

Designing an e-Presentation

343

full-size copies of individual slides, groups or the whole presentation, using the Print range options.

When you are creating your slides you can also produce a set of speaking notes to accompany them, using the Slide notes area below the working area (figure 5.33).

Screen prints

Microsoft Windows® provides you with the means of capturing the display on the computer screen. To do this, press the PrtSc (Print screen) button. The display is captured and stored in a special area of the computer's memory called the clipboard. If you open Microsoft Word® or another suitable application, you can paste the captured display into the document. This is useful in that you can capture the slides as they appear on the screen, so you can document the build-up of the slide and other special effects. CLAiT Plus 2006 requires that you use screen prints as evidence of transitions, builds and hyperlinks.

Exercise 39

Printing

1 Insert a floppy disk into the computer's drive.

2 Load Microsoft PowerPoint® by selecting Start, highlighting the All Programs menu and clicking on the Microsoft PowerPoint® item or by clicking on the PowerPoint® icon on the desktop.

3 If you have only recently completed exercise 38, you may see New Product in the Open a presentation section of the New Presentation task pane. If it is not visible, click on the More presentations option to reveal the Open window. Change the Look in: box to floppy disk to locate New Product. Double-click on New Product to load it.

4 Notice that under the slide is an area labelled Click to add notes. Click in this area, since you are going to produce a set of speaker's notes. In slide 1 enter:

Good morning. I am pleased that you were able to find the time in a busy day to attend my presentation. I am sure that you will find its contents beneficial.

In the final slide, Conclusions, enter:

This is an exciting new product that will potentially generate substantial profits for the company. However, it requires an effort from everyone in this room in order to be successful.

Now enter appropriate text for the other slides to produce a full set of notes.

5 Select the File menu and click on the Print option to reveal the Print window. Print:

- copies of all slides – full size

- handouts with six, four and two copies of the slides on each page

- notes pages

- outline view.

Explore all the options until you are confident that you can produce the desired documents.

6 Now run the presentation and practise capturing the screen displays using the PrtSc key. Paste your captures into Microsoft Word® or Microsoft Windows® Paint. Print the resulting document. Continue until you are confident.

7 Close the application either by selecting the File menu and clicking on the Exit option or by clicking on the Close button in the top right-hand corner of the application window.

Importing data

You can import information from other Microsoft Office® applications into PowerPoint®. There are many occasions when you need to show an audience information from your company. The obvious way is to copy and paste information between the applications. The copied object is transferred to Microsoft PowerPoint®. However, you can also transfer an object and maintain a link with its original application. It is therefore able to change as it is updated. This is useful when you are presenting a spreadsheet that will change. Your presentation is automatically kept up to date.

In order to establish the link, you need to copy the object (e.g. spreadsheet) and select Paste Special to reveal the Paste Special window (figure 5.34). If you use Paste Special without establishing a link, it is still useful, since the table is transferred to the slide. When you simply use paste, the data but not the table is transferred.

Once you have imported an object you can edit it by double-clicking on it. You will return to the original application if the object is linked to it and can therefore edit it. If the object is not linked, it is enclosed in a spreadsheet frame, allowing you to edit it. To return to Microsoft PowerPoint®, select the File menu and the Exit option in the linked case, and simply click away from the table when not linked.

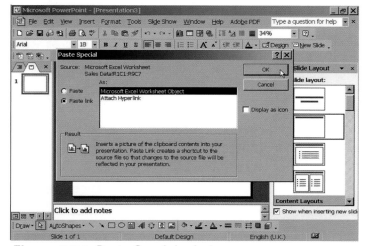

Figure 5.34 Paste Special window

More practice

Activity 1

Master slide

1 Create a master slide based on the specification below:
Orientation is landscape

Master slide

Feature	Colour	Position	Comments
Background	none		
Graphic		Bottom right corner of text area	
Number slides		Bottom right hand corner of the slide	
Text (footer)		Bottom centre of slide	Enter your name
Date		Bottom left hand corner of the slide	
Timings			Each slide 30 seconds
Transititions			1 effect on every slide
Builds			1 effect on every slide

Text

Style name	Typeface	Point size	Feature	Alignment
Heading	Sans serif	44	Bold/red	Centre
Bullet (level 1)	Serif 36	Include bullet character	Left	
Sub-bullet (level 2)	Serif 32	Include bullet character	Left	

2   Save the master presentation as News. Figure 5.35 shows the master slide.

3   Close Microsoft PowerPoint® or proceed to activity 2.

Activity 2

1   Create a presentation for a manager who wants to explain some changes to the employees of a company. The structure and text is shown below:

- introduction (1 slide)
- explain the changes (3 slides)
- current organisation (1 slide)
- new organisation (1 slide)
- invite questions (1 slide)
- conclude the presentation (1 slide).

Text for the slides

Slide 1	Kingston Computing Ltd
Slide 2	Changes Global Competition More Efficient Structures Reduce Costs
Slide 3	Changes Flexibility Team Working Learning Organisation Insert a Clip Art image alongside the text relevant to change
Slide 4	Changes Streamline Organisation Reduce Management More Delegation

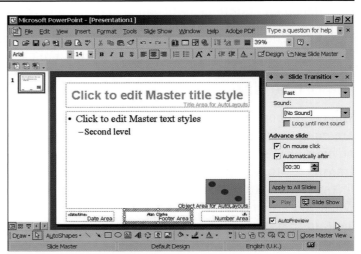

Figure 5.35 Master slide

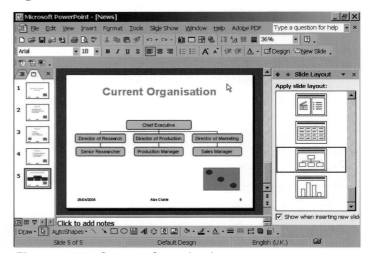

Figure 5.36 Current Organisation

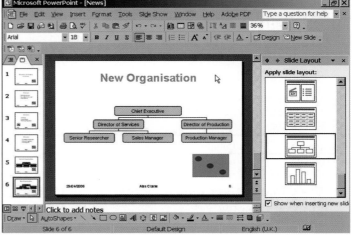

Figure 5.37 New Organisation

Slide 5	Current Organisation Insert organisation chart (figure 5.36)
Slide 6	New Organisation Insert organisation chart (figure 5.37)
Slide 7	Questions Please ask any questions
Slide 8	Conclusion Change Cooperation Thank you

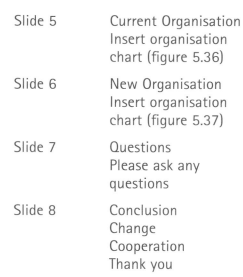
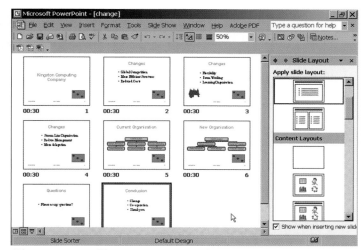

Figure 5.38 Change presentation

2 Figure 5.38 shows the presentation slides.

3 Save the presentations as Change.

4 Close Microsoft PowerPoint® or proceed to activity 3.

Activity 3

1 Create an additional slide between the existing slides 1 and 2, showing the current financial position of the company.

2 The new slide is based on the spreadsheet shown below and saved as Finance.

	Income	Expenditure	Profit
2003	22.30	21.80	0.50
2004	21.90	21.65	0.25
2005	21.20	21.35	−0.15

Import data from spreadsheet and display on new slide 2.

3 Insert slide title – Financial Position.

4 Format the table:
column headings – sans serif, character size 16, bold
row headings – sans serif, character size 14, bold
data – sans serif, character size 12.
(Tip: double-click on the table)

5 Figure 5.39 shows the imported table.

6 Save the revised presentation.

7 Close Microsoft PowerPoint® or proceed to activity 4.

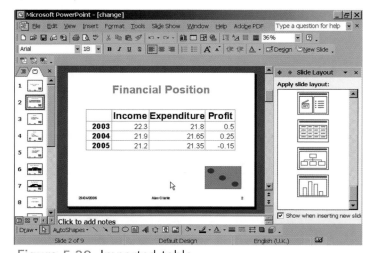

Figure 5.39 Imported table

Activity 4

1 Slide 2 of the Change presentation contains sensitive information, so hide the slide with a hyperlink from slide 1 so that the presenter can choose when to show it.

2 Hide slide 2.

3 Create a hyperlink from slide 1 to hidden slide.

4 Test the link (figure 5.40).

5 Add the speaker's notes below to the slide 1:

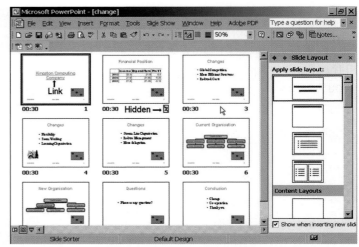

Figure 5.40 Hyperlink and hidden slide

Thank you for coming along at short notice. I would like to explain the nature of my presentation and what it will include. The company has been struggling for several years to maintain its profit margins and is now making a loss. It is therefore important to take action to bring us into profit. In the next few minutes I plan to give an overview of the financial position and explain the nature of the changes we want to introduce to save costs and make us more efficient.

6 Save your revised presentation as Change.

7 Close Microsoft PowerPoint® unless you are going on to activity 5.

Activity 5

Transitions and animation

1 Revise the Change presentation to add a single transition between each slide and a single animation in each slide.

2 Test the presentation transitions and animations.

3 Now print:
- all the slides as handouts – four slides per page
- outline view
- speaker's notes on slide 1.

4 Save the presentation as Change.

5 Close Microsoft PowerPoint®.

SUMMARY

1 Loading Microsoft PowerPoint®
Select Start, highlight the All Programs option and click on the Microsoft PowerPoint® item or click on the PowerPoint® icon on the desktop.

2 Save
Select the File menu and the Save option. The Save As window will appear.

3 Blank presentation

Select the Blank presentation option from the New Presentation task pane on the right of the display. This will display the Slide Layout task pane, which offers you a variety of outline slides in a scrolling box to choose from.

4 Master slide

Select the View menu, highlight the Master option to reveal a sub-menu. Click on the Slide Master option. The Master Slide template will appear in the Microsoft PowerPoint® work area.

5 Edit master

To edit the master (i.e. to change the characteristics) you need to click on the different slide features (e.g. Title) and select the new characteristics (e.g. font, text colour and character size).

6 Background colour

Select the Format menu and click on the Background option to reveal the Background window. This allows you to choose a background colour for your slides.

7 Date and time

Select the Insert menu and click on the Date and Time option to reveal the Date and Time window.

8 Page numbers

Select the Insert menu and click on the Slide Number option to reveal the Header and Footer window.

9 Font colour

Select the Font color icon on the Drawing toolbar and choose your colour.

10 Hyperlinks

Select slide text, click on the Insert menu and select the Hyperlink option.

To add hyperlink buttons, click on the Slide Show menu and highlight the Action buttons option. Select a button, position it on the slide and select an action from the Action Setting window.

11 Transitions

Select the Slide Show menu and click on the Slide Transition option. This will reveal the Slide Transition task pane.

12 Animation

Select the Slide Show menu and click on the Custom Animation option. This will reveal the Custom Animation task pane.

Alternatively, Select the Slide Show menu and highlight the Animation Scheme option to reveal the Slide Design task pane options.

13 Open an existing presentation

Presentation may be visible in the Open a presentation section of the New Presentation task pane. If it is not, click on the More presentations option to reveal the Open window.

14 New slide
Select the Insert menu and click on the New Slide option.

15 Manipulate text and graphics
The text and graphic areas are enclosed in a box, with small squares at the corners and in the centre of each side. These squares allow you to change the shape of the text area and adjust the position of the text or graphics.

Placing your mouse pointer on the enclosure lines, but not on the squares, changes its shape to a star. If you hold down the mouse button while the pointer is in this shape, you can move the whole text area.

If you place your mouse pointer on the squares, it will change shape to a double-headed arrow. If you hold down the mouse button, you can drag the enclosure to change the shape and size of the area.

16 Overview
Select the View menu and click on the Slide Sorter option.

17 Manipulate slides in slide sorter
Highlight a slide, then drag it to a new position in the presentation or delete it by pressing the delete key. New slides can be added by clicking at the position in which you would like to add a new slide and then selecting the Insert menu and clicking on the New Slide option.

18 Organisation chart
Select the Organization Chart layout from the Slide Layout task pane.

19 Import text
Cut or copy text directly between Microsoft Word® and PowerPoint®.

Send text from Microsoft Word® to PowerPoint® directly by using the option Send To, which is available from the File menu in Microsoft Word®. This reveals a sub-menu with the option Microsoft PowerPoint. This will change the file into a Microsoft PowerPoint® presentation.

20 Import graphics
Select the Insert menu and highlight the Picture option to reveal a sub-menu of options.

21 Find and replace
Select the Edit menu and click on the Replace option to reveal the Replace window.

22 Spellchecker
Select the Tools menu and click on the Spelling option.

23 Show a presentation
Select the View menu and click on the Slide Show option.

Alternatively, select the Slide Show menu and click on the View Show option.

OR, click on the Slide Show button in the bottom left-hand corner of the display.

24 Printing
Select the File menu and click on the Print option to reveal the Print window.

25 Close application
Select the File menu and click on the Exit option or click on the close button in the top right-hand corner of the application window.

26 Chart/graph
Select a chart slide from the Slide Layout task pane and click on the chart/graph placeholder to reveal a chart and its corresponding datasheet. Enter your data to produce a new chart.

To insert a Microsoft Excel® chart, select the Insert menu and click on the Object option to reveal the Insert Object window.

27 Speaker's notes
Click on the area below the slide working area, labelled Click to add notes. Enter your notes.

You can print your notes by using the Print option in the File menu. Print what: allows you to select Notes Pages.

28 House styles
Many organisations have developed standards for their presentations. This ensures consistency and quality in the use of them. To ensure standards, it is often useful to develop a master slide. Many organisations provide this to ensure their standards are adhered to. Standards are often called house styles.

29 Microsoft PowerPoint® show
Select Save As or Save and choose Save as type to select PowerPoint Show.

30 Pack and Go
Select the File menu and the Pack and Go option. This opens a Wizard which will take you through the process step by step.

31 Unpack
Double-click on Pngsetup (i.e. Pack and Go setup file) and select the folder in which you want to save the presentation, then click on OK. The system will tell you when the unpacking is successful.

32 Import spreadsheet file
Copy the highlighted object in the application and select the Edit menu in Microsoft PowerPoint® to reveal the options. Choose the Paste Special option to reveal the Paste Special window. This lets you simply paste in the object or link the object to the original file.

33 Edit object (spreadsheet table)
Double-click on the object. If linked, the object will transfer the display to original application (i.e. spreadsheet), in which you can edit it before returning by selecting File menu and Exit option. If the object is not linked, then it is enclosed in a frame and you can edit it within Microsoft PowerPoint®.

8

Electronic Communication

This chapter will help you to:

- use advanced e-mail features to coordinate information

- set up distribution lists and use an address book

- manage mailbox and folders,

This chapter covers unit 8 (Electronic Communication). There are no preconditions for studying this unit. However, its content does assume that you have the skills and understanding that are provided by the OCR Level 1 ICT course CLAiT 2006 (e.g. Unit 8: Online Communication and Unit 1: File Management and e-Document Production).

Assessment

After studying unit 8, your skills and understanding are assessed during a three-hour practical assignment. This is set by OCR and marked locally. However, the marking will be externally moderated by OCR. This ensures that the standard is being applied correctly across the many different providers of OCR CLAiT Plus. If you are unsuccessful, you can be reassessed using a different assignment.

An alternative approach is for you to be assessed by an assignment set by OCR or designed for your centre. These assignments cover all the assessment objectives included in the unit. You will need to complete an OCR evidence checklist, explaining how each assessment objective has been covered.

Microsoft Outlook® XP

Microsoft Outlook® XP (2002) is an application designed to help you organise yourself. It is widely used by employers and other organisations to help their staff. It provides you with a variety of systems, including:

- a comprehensive e-mail system
- a personal and group work scheduler
- a contact and address book
- a desk diary

- a project manager
- a work monitor.

The application is illustrated in figure 8.1. This shows the view of the Microsoft Outlook® XP e-mail inbox. The application is divided into a series of areas. These are, from left to right:

- Shortcuts – there are three sets (i.e. Outlook, My Shortcuts and Other Shortcuts)
- Folder List
- List of e-mails in the inbox – top area
- Preview of the current e-mail – bottom area.

Across the top of the application are the normal menu and toolbars, which are part of many Microsoft Windows® applications.

The Shortcuts area provides a list of icons that link you to the various functions of Microsoft Outlook®. The three sets of shortcuts are accessed by buttons at the bottom of the area. The Outlook® Shortcuts are displayed by default and provide you with connections to:

- Outlook® Today
- Calendar
- Contacts
- Tasks
- Notes
- Deleted items.

The My Shortcuts group provides links to:

- Inbox
- Drafts
- Journal
- Outlook® Update.

The Other Shortcuts group provides links to:

- My Computer
- My Documents
- Favorites.

These allow you to access the files and folders of the other applications on the computer.

The Folders List shows you the folders associated with Microsoft Outlook® (e.g. Inbox, Sent items and Outbox).

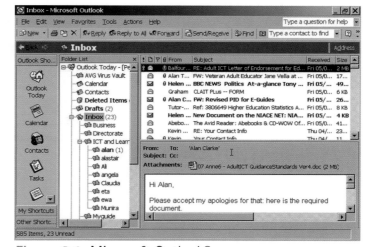

Figure 8.1 Microsoft Outlook®

You can add folders to your list to store e-mails (e.g. Ali, Alastair and Angela). The Inbox holds e-mails sent to you, Sent Items stores messages you have sent and Outbox holds those messages before they are sent. You can create additional folders so that you can store your messages in any way that you choose.

Creating an e-mail message

E-mail is an effective communication medium for almost everyone. In business, e-mail has had an enormous effect on communications. It combines a rapid transmission method with useful record-keeping features. The e-mail system automatically records the date and time the message is sent, while the sender's details are attached so that the recipient can easily identify who has sent the communication. The initial message is retained in the reply, making it simple to understand the context of the message without having to look at files or other records. E-mail can be stored in an appropriate folder, enabling complete records of transactions to be maintained.

This is very useful if misunderstandings happen or people disagree about decisions that have been made. Paper communications suffer from often only providing a partial record in that dates, names and details are sometimes missing. It is often not clear what they are responding to or who has been sent copies.

E-mail automatically provides this information and filing is a simple matter. Paper records are more easily lost or misfiled.

E-mails are created by selecting the New button on the standard toolbar to reveal the Message window. This is divided into two main areas:

- the address area in which you place the e-mail address of the person(s) you are e-mailing (i.e. To... box), the address of any other people you want to copy the message to (i.e. Cc) and, finally, the subject of the message. When you address an e-mail it is critical to ensure that you are accurate. A single mistake (eg. reversing letters, misspelling) will ensure that the message is not received. There is also the danger that the message will be sent to the wrong person. Perfection is required with all addresses. If you send a message with an incorrect address you will later receive an e-mail containing an error message, such as Mail delivery failed: Returning message to sender. The sender is the Mail Delivery System.
- the message area where you enter your communication.

There is an extra box called Bcc, which you can add to the message. This enables blind copying in which you copy the message to another person or persons, but their names will be hidden in the recipient's copy of the message. Blind copying is used to maintain confidentiality. The option is added to the message by selecting the down-arrow button next to the Option button on the toolbar, to reveal a list of options, and clicking on the Bcc option. The new message window is shown in figure 8.2.

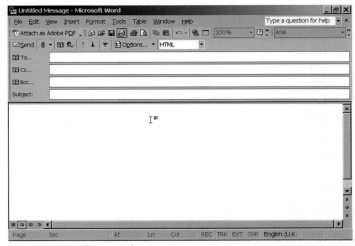

Figure 8.2 Bcc option

Format options

Microsoft Outlook® offers three format options. The ability of e-mail recipients to read the different formats varies. The three choices are:

- Plain text
- Rich text (RTF)
- HTML.

Plain text

These messages do not have any formatting or other features. You cannot use images within plain text messages. Attachments can be included in plain text messages, but there is a risk that they cannot be read by the recipient of the message.

Rich text (RTF)

This is a format designed to be read by most word-processing applications. It allows you a range of formatting opportunities, such as font sizes, alignments and lists. Some recipients may receive attachments that they cannot read.

HTML

Almost everyone can read an HTML e-mail message. It also provides some formatting possibilities for your messages.

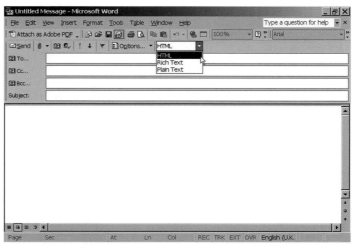

Figure 8.3 Format

The e-mail toolbar provides access to the three choices (figure 8.3). You need to consider who you are sending the message to in order to select the most appropriate format.

Priorities

When you send an e-mail it is possible to indicate whether the message is important by adding a particular symbol. This is achieved by clicking on the icon indicated by an exclamation mark (figure 8.3). Other related options are low importance and the follow-up flag. This provides a means of creating a reminder to follow up a message.

Most e-mail users get a large number of messages. Within a company you

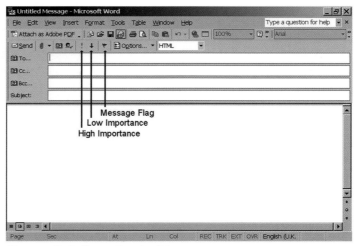

Figure 8.4 E-mail priorities

will get messages about your work, social matters, car parking, people selling items and many other issues. It is therefore useful to indicate when one is important so that recipients can identify that it needs immediate attention. Figure 8.4 shows the purpose of some of the icons on the standard toolbar.

Creating an e-mail

1 Microsoft Outlook® is opened either by selecting the Start button, highlighting the All Programs option and clicking on the Outlook® option, or by double-clicking on the Outlook® icon on the Microsoft Windows® desktop.

2 Create a new e-mail by clicking on the New icon to reveal the message window. Add a blind copy option to the message window by selecting the down-arrow button next to the Option button on the toolbar, to reveal a menu of options, and clicking on the Bcc option. You will notice an extra line is added to the message window (figure 8.2).

3 Create the message below:

To: Janet123@yahoo.co.uk
Cc: John456@yahoo.co.uk
Bcc: Sheila789@yahoo.co.uk

Practice

This is a practice e-mail

If you are working with a group of other learners, substitute the three e-mail addresses with those of your peers. Send the e-mail and see how it appears to the recipient (figure 8.5). You can also send e-mails to television or radio programmes if you would like to practise. Many programmes give their e-mail addresses so you can respond to their content.

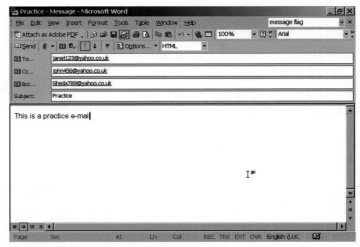

Figure 8.5 **Practice message**

4 Give the message a high priority by selecting the High Importance icon on the toolbar.

5 If you are interrupted before you can finish your e-mail, you can save it to complete later. Select the File menu and click on the Exit option. A message will appear asking you if you want to save your message. Click on the Yes button. Your message will be saved as a draft in the folder list (i.e. Drafts) and you will see the number of drafts increased by one. To retrieve it, simply click on Drafts and a list of them will appear in the main work area. Click on the Practice message and send the e-mail.

6 To send the message, click on the Send button on the toolbar. If your system is connected to the Internet the message will be sent. If not, it will be stored in the Outbox until the next time you make a connection (figure 8.6). Observe in the folder list that the Outbox item has a number in brackets indicating the number of messages waiting to be sent.

7 Close Microsoft Outlook® by selecting the <u>F</u>ile menu and clicking on the E<u>x</u>it option or by clicking on the close button in the top right-hand corner of the application. You may be presented with a message informing you that there are unsent messages in your Outbox and asking if you would still like to close the application. Say yes.

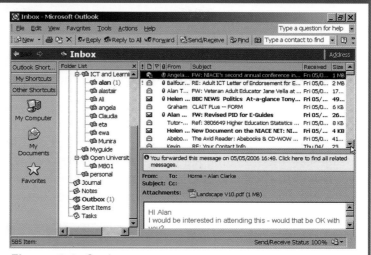

Figure 8.6 Outbox

Receiving e-mails

E-mails may be received every time you connect to the Internet. They will be held in your Inbox until you are ready to open them. Figure 8.1 shows the Inbox, with a series of messages listed in the top box, while the contents of the highlighted e-mail are shown in the preview box. There are several choices of displaying your inbox available to you through the View menu, highlighting Current View and selecting from one of the options that is revealed.

Mail folders

Most people find that the number of messages they receive grows rapidly when they begin to use e-mail. This indicates the value of e-mail, but to benefit from e-mail once the numbers start to grow, you need to be organised. You will often want to refer back to messages in order to take advantage of them, so you need to store them in a way that makes retrieving them a straightforward process. The normal way of storing e-mails is to establish a series of mail folders for the main people who send you messages. By creating a series of folders in which to store mail, you

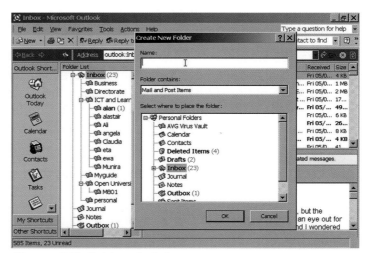

Figure 8.7 Folders in Inbox

make it quicker to locate the ones you need. If they are all stored in a single folder, you will quickly find hundreds if not thousands of messages stored in it, so that finding a particular one is very difficult. A single folder is the equivalent of keeping all your papers in a pile on your desk. You will find it difficult to find the papers you need.

To create a new mail folder in the Inbox, highlight the Inbox folder and select the File menu, highlight the New option and click on the Folder option. This will open the Create New Folder window (figure 8.7).

The folder is created by entering the folder name and then highlighting where to locate the folder in the Select where to place the folder area. In Figure 8.7 the folder will be placed within the Inbox folder. When you are ready, click on the OK button to create the mail folder.

Once you have created a series of mail folders, you may want to move messages between them. This can be achieved by dragging and dropping – open the mail folder in which the messages are stored, click on the selected message and hold down the mouse button. The message can then be dragged over the new folder and the button released. The message will have moved to the new location (folder). Dragging and dropping needs to be practised, but is an efficient and effective way of moving messages between folders.

Move messages

In the last section we created folders in which to store e-mail messages. E-mails were moved between folders manually. The emphasis was on creating archives of old e-mails, but there is another aspect of mail folders, which is to create ones so that incoming messages can be sorted into them. Outlook® provides functions to establish rules that will sort e-mails automatically into different folders. This is the equivalent of manually sorting your mail into different groups, depending on who sent them.

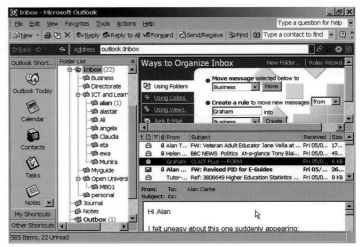

Figure 8.8 Organize

The Organize button in the Inbox area of Microsoft Outlook® provides the function to create rules to automatically move e-mail into different folders. Alternatively, select the Tools menu and Organize option. Either method will open the Ways to Organize Inbox window. Figure 8.8 shows the Ways to Organize Inbox window with a rule displayed. If you highlight an incoming message and then select Organize, you can choose to move future e-mails sent from that address to a specific folder. This requires you use the option Using Folders.

To access the moved e-mails you need to select the folder. The e-mails that the folder contains are then displayed in the working area.

Within Organize are other options, such as:

- Using Colors
- Using Views
- Junk E-mail.

Using Colors allows you to colour-code e-mails sent from particular addresses so that they are easy to identify in a crowded inbox. Using Views changes the way that e-mails in the Inbox or selected folder are displayed. Some of the options include:

- By sender
- Unread messages
- Messages with autopreview.

This again offers you the opportunity to organise your e-mails to meet your needs.

The final option, Junk E-mail, allows you to colour-code junk mail and that with adult content, based on filters within Microsoft Outlook®. You can also automatically move or delete unwanted e-mail using junk mail options.

Signatures

You can add a signature to your e-mail by selecting the Tools menu on the toolbar of the message window, then Options. Next choose the General tab and click on E-mail Options, and finally the E-mail Signature tab. The E-mail Options window will be revealed (figure 8.9).

You can now create a signature for your e-mail. An alternative approach is to select the Tools menu on the

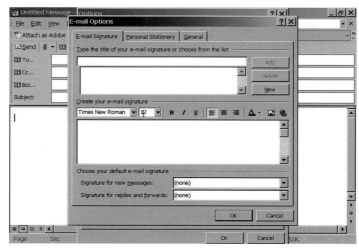

Figure 8.9 E-mail Options window

main application (e.g. Inbox) and click on the Options item, then on the Mail Format tab. This will reveal a Signatures button, which will open a Create Signature window.

Attachments

One of the major advantages of using e-mail is that you can attach files of information to your messages. These can be of any type, but you must always remember that in order to open the attached file, your recipient must have access to the application that created it, or a compatible one, otherwise the file cannot be opened; unfortunately, this is a regular problem with e-mail attachments. You can reduce this problem by considering what applications your recipient is likely to have, or by asking them. If you do not know if a recipient has the particular application, it is sometimes useful to convert files into generic formats. For example:

Microsoft Word® file – convert into a text file or a rich text file, which are opened by most word processors.

You can attach many files to a single e-mail and they can be a mix of different formats. However, it is useful to consider the size of each file and the overall size of the attachments. Some e-mail systems limit the size of e-mails that they will accept, so you may have your messages refused unless you limit their size. Also, if you are sending a message with attachments to a home computer, it is likely to have a low speed connection to the Internet, so large attachments will be downloaded very slowly. Few home recipients will be pleased if your e-mail takes 20, 30 or 60 minutes to download. They are paying the telephone costs.

It is good practice to consider file sizes and, if they are too large, send several e-mails with a single attachment or compress the files so that their size is reduced.

Compress

In order to reduce the size of an attachment you can compress the file using a compression application or utility. There are several available. WinZip® is one of the best known and can significantly reduce the size of a file. You can compress one file or many. The result is called an archive. In order to access the individual files in an archive you need to decompress the files. This requires either the full application or the WinZip Self-Extractor, which will only decompress an archive. The self-extractor is free.

Compressing files is very useful in that you can send large amounts of information as an attachment efficiently, without causing recipients problems of slow downloads or exceeding system limits.

You can download WinZip from its website for a trial period.

E-mail problems

E-mail attachments are often associated with virus infections. It is therefore important to have up-to-date virus protection. Most modern virus protection software can be configured to check all incoming and outgoing messages. Both are critical to prevent the spread of viruses. Whatever virus protection product you choose, it is important to pick one that regular updates the software, since viruses are continuously changing and new versions are being released.

In addition to virus infection, there is also the potential of being infected with spyware, which seeks to monitor your system and could be recording your passwords and other sensitive data. Spyware is also often passed between systems through e-mail, so it is important to have good protection on your system. There is a range of spyware protection applications available. It is important to have a system that is regularly updated.

A final threat is simply to receive advertising e-mails. These are called spam and often advertise offensive products. In some cases, they are associated with attempts to get money from you fraudulently. Microsoft Office® allows you to block spam, using the Organize function to stop junk mail.

Exercise 55

Signatures and attachments

1 Microsoft Outlook® is opened either by selecting the Start button, highlighting the All Programs option and clicking on the Outlook® option, or by double-clicking on the Outlook® icon on the Microsoft Windows® desktop.

2 You are going to create a new signature, so select the Tools menu and click on the Options item to open the Options window. Click on the Mail Format tab and the Signatures button to reveal the Create Signature window. Click on the New button and Create New Signature will open (figure 8.10). Enter your name and click on the Next, then Finish buttons. Close the open windows. You will now be able to select your name as a signature for your messages.

3 Click on New to create a new e-mail message. Click in the message area and select the

---

Insert menu and highlight the AutoText option and then the Signature option to reveal a signature list you can choose from. Select your own name and it will be inserted at the cursor in the message area.

4 Now enter the following message

To: Janet123@yahoo.co.uk
Cc: John 456@yahoo.co.uk
Bcc: Sheila789@yahoo.co.uk

More Practice

This is a practice e-mail to demonstrate adding a signature and an attachment

Signature

If you are working in a group, address your e-mail (To: Cc: and Bcc:) to other members of the group. This will allow everyone else to practise receiving e-mail and let you see what your message looks like when it is received. Figure 8.11 shows the finished e-mail.

5 E-mails are not limited to the message you enter at the keyboard. You can attach files of any type. To add an attachment, select the Insert menu and the File option to reveal the Insert File window. Change the folder in the Look in: box to locate the file of your choice. Select it to add to your message (figure 8.12) by double-clicking on the file. You can add many files to the same e-mail by repeating the process. An alternative

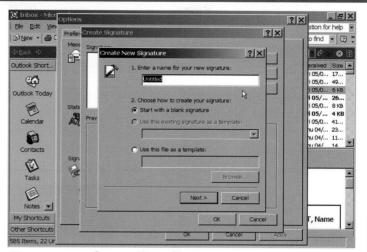

Figure 8.10 Create New Signature

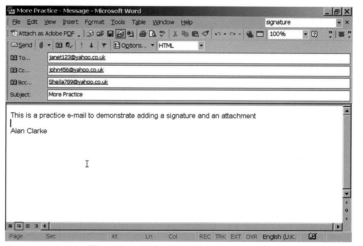

Figure 8.11 E-mail with signature

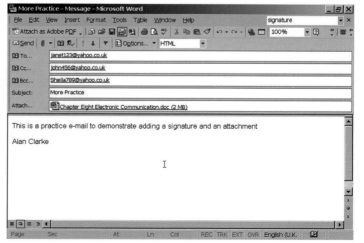

Figure 8.12 E-mail with attachment

Electronic Communication

approach is to select the paperclip icon on the toolbar, which will open the Insert File window.

6 Send the message by clicking on the Send button on the toolbar.

7 Close Microsoft Outlook® by selecting the File menu and clicking on the Exit option or by clicking on the Close button in the top right-hand corner of the application. You may be presented with a message informing you that there are unsent messages in your Outbox and asking if you would still like to close the application. Say yes.

Address book

In addition to sending and receiving messages, Microsoft Outlook® also provides facilities to store the e-mail addresses and details of your contacts. Without these components you would need to maintain a paper address book. An electronic system not only duplicates the features of a paper address book, but in addition allows you to establish mailing lists or groups, so that you can send a message to a group of users as easily as sending one to an individual. This is very useful in any organisation (e.g. members of a team).

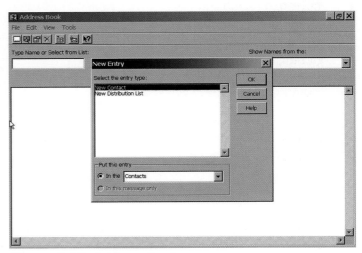

Figure 8.13 Address Book

Microsoft Outlook® provides you with an address book (figure 8.13). You can enter new contacts or create distribution lists. By selecting the New Entry icon on the address book toolbar, you reveal the New Entry window, with two choices – New Contact and New Distribution List. This allows you to add individual contact details or establish a mailing group.

There is a legal aspect to keeping contact details of individuals. The Data Protection Act ensures that you register information kept on individuals. If you intend to create records of individuals as part of your business, then you need to seek advice.

Alternative approach to creating a group/distribution list

There is an alternative method of creating a distribution list. Select the

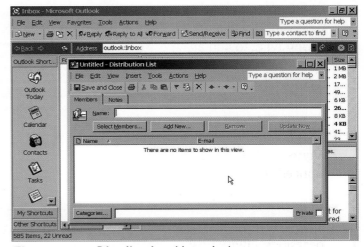

Figure 8.14 Distribution List window

File menu, then highlight the New option to reveal a menu of choices. Click on the Distribution List option to open the Distribution List window (figure 8.14). To select from the existing address book contacts, you need to click on the Select Members button. New contacts are added to the list by clicking on the Add New button.

Exercise 56

Address book

1 Microsoft Outlook® is opened either by selecting the Start button, highlighting the All Programs option and clicking on the Outlook® option, or by double-clicking on the Outlook® icon on the Microsoft Windows® desktop.

2 Select the Tools menu and click on the Address Book option. This will reveal the address book (figure 8.13). To add a new contact or new group (i.e.

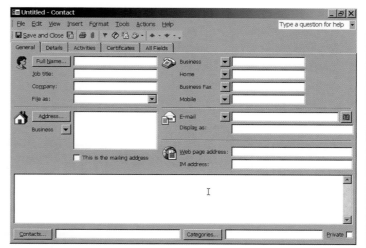

Figure 8.15 Contact window

distribution list), click on the New Entry icon to reveal the New Entry window, with two options. Click on the New Contact option to reveal the Contact window (figure 8.15). You will notice a series of tabs across the top of the window that allow you to categorise your information. Explore the different tabs until you are familiar with them.

3 Return to the General tab and enter the following contact in the Full Name and E-mail boxes:

Ms Jane Ann King, JAKing@example.co.uk

Accuracy is important since you will later rely on this entry for your e-mails. Check each entry carefully.

Click on the Save and Close button. The new contact will appear in the work area.

4 Add the following contacts:

Dr William MacDonald, William.Mac@example.co.uk

Miss Belinda Lomas, Belinda@example.co.uk

Mr Albert Woods, awoods@example.co.uk

Figure 8.16 shows the address book after the contacts have been added. You will have noticed that you have not entered any information beyond name and e-mail address. You can extend your entries by double-clicking on the item (e.g. Albert Woods), which will open the Contact window and allow you to add extra information. Obviously you could have entered all the information when you first added the new contact, but there are occasions when you initially have only partial data.

continued

5 The other option available from the New Entry icon is to create a new distribution list. If you click on the New Distribution List option you will reveal the Distribution List window. Enter a group name – Example – and click on the Select Members button to reveal the Select Members window (figure 8.17).

6 You can create a group based on existing contacts, new contacts or a mixture. To add existing contacts to your group, highlight the contacts and click on the Members button. Add the four contacts you created earlier to your group. To add a new contact, click on New Contacts button to reveal the New Entry window and enter a contact (e.g. E Example) in the normal way. As soon as you click on the Save and Close button the entry appears in the list of existing contacts for you to select for your group. When you have completed your selections, click on the OK button to return to the Example Distribution List window. Click on the Save and Close button again and your group will be added to your list of contacts.

7 Close the Address Book by clicking on the close button in the top right-hand corner of the window. To access the address book contacts, open a new e-mail by clicking on the New icon on the toolbar to reveal the message window.

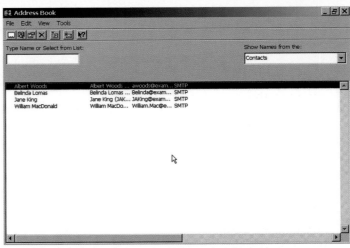
Figure 8.16 Completed address book

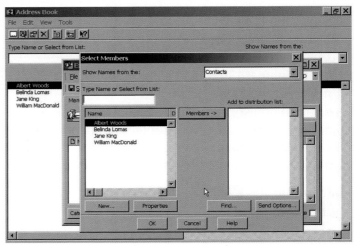
Figure 8.17 Example Distribution List

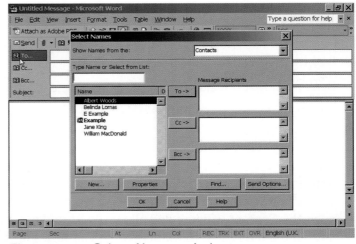
Figure 8.18 Select Names window

CLAiT Plus 2006 for Office XP

364

Select the To... button to show the Select Names window (figure 8.18). You can place any contact or group into the To, Cc or Bcc fields by highlighting the entry and clicking on the appropriate field button.

8 Practise using the window to select different contacts until you are confident that you can use the address book.

9 Microsoft Outlook® also provides you with the means to print your contacts and groups. Select the Print icon on the Contact or Distribution List window toolbar to print the information.

10 Close all the open windows by clicking on the close button in the top right-hand corner of each window.

11 Close Microsoft Outlook® by selecting the File menu and clicking on the Exit option, or click on the Close button in the top right-hand corner of the application. You may be presented with a message informing you that there are unsent messages in your Outbox and asking if you would still like to close the application. Say yes.

Personal information manager

Microsoft Outlook® provides a number of functions to help you to organise your life. The three main ones are (figure 8.19):

■ a calendar
■ a to do list
■ notes.

The calendar allows you to schedule your work on a daily, weekly or monthly basis, over many months, while the to do list lets you create a list of tasks you need to complete. The notes are essentially the electronic equivalent of post-it notes – brief pieces of information, reminders and useful items of data.

The to do list of tasks can be presented in a variety of ways. Select the View menu, then highlight the Current View item to reveal a list of options (figure 8.20). Figure 8.19 shows the Day/Week/Month View with AutoPreview.

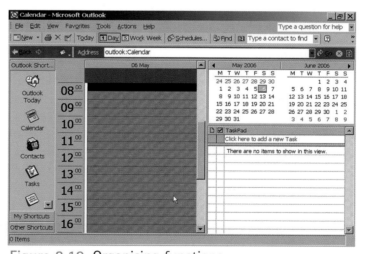

Figure 8.19 Organising functions

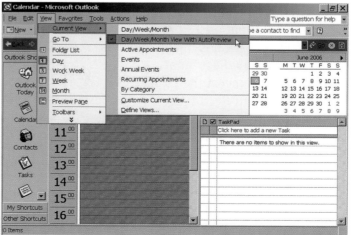

Figure 8.20 Current views

Exercise 57

Planning your work

1 Microsoft Outlook® is opened either by selecting the Start button, highlighting the All Programs option and clicking on the Outlook® option, or by double-clicking on the Outlook® icon on the Microsoft Windows® desktop.

2 You are going to create a calendar for a typical business person, complete with a to do list of tasks and notes.

3 Click on the Calendar icon in the Outlook® Shortcuts list on the left-hand side of the display. Close the Folder List pane if it is open. Select the View menu and highlight the Current View option to reveal a list of options. Click on the Day/Week/Month View with AutoPreview. It will change the display to show the calendar and to do list (figure 8.19). The calendar will show the date you are working on and offers you the choice of a complete 24-hour period to book appointments in. If you want to change the date, simply click on the desired one in the monthly calendar in the top right-hand corner. Change the date to your birthday – you can change the month by clicking on the arrow buttons to move backwards and forwards through the year.

4 You can change the view of your calendar to show a single day, a working week (i.e. five days), a seven-day week or a month, by selecting the View menu and clicking on the options (figure 8.19). Explore the different options and return to a single-day view once you are confident.

5 In the calendar you are going to enter the appointments for the first Monday in June (in my case, 5 June 2006), so change the date. The appointments for this day are influenced by the organisation always having a staff meeting on the first Monday of every month. Enter Staff Meeting at 10.00. As you enter Staff Meeting, you will notice it is enclosed in a box. If you place your mouse pointer over the box outline, it will change shape and you can drag the box to cover more time. Your staff meeting will last three hours (e.g. 10 am to 1 pm).

6 The staff meeting is a recurring appointment every month and the calendar allows you to set this up without having to enter the same information 12 times. Select the Actions menu and click on New Recurring Meeting to reveal the Appointment Recurrence window (figure 8.21). Click on the Monthly radio button in the Recurrence pattern area and you will see that the first Monday of each month is offered as an option. Click on

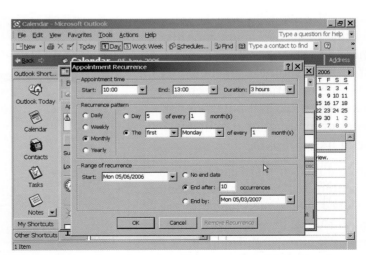

Figure 8.21 Appointment Recurrence window

the radio button alongside the option to set the pattern. You can also set the end date for the recurrence – No end date, End after: a set number of events or End by: a given date. Set it to End after: 10 occurences. Click the OK button to close the window and set the meeting.

7 You will notice that the window under the Appointment Recurrence window is still open. It is called Untitled – Meeting. This lets you name your meeting and also invite other people to participate in the meeting using e-mail. If you are working in an organisation with an electronic network, Microsoft Outlook® can be used to schedule meetings by sending e-mails to everyone who needs to attend. This adds an extra dimension to managing your individual information. Close the window.

8 If you double-click on the appointment in the calendar, the window will reappear. In the middle of the window is a picture of a bell and Reminder item. This enables you to ask Microsoft Outlook® to remind you about your appointments. The down arrow next to the reminder provides you with a range of choices of how long before the meeting or appointment you want to be reminded. Explore the options and choose two hours. Click on Save and Close to exit the window and return to Calendar.

9 Now enter a lunch appointment at 1.00 for one hour with Jim Brown, and a meeting with the Sales Manager at 3.00 for 30 minutes.

10 It is good time management to write lists of the key tasks that need to be done. In this case, we are going to create a new list:
   ■ Reply to the enquiry from Acme Tools
   ■ Begin work on the quarterly business report
   ■ Telephone the production manager
   ■ Write a letter to James Little plc
   ■ Send samples to King Ltd

11 Click in the area Click here to add a new task (TaskPad) and, when you have completed an entry, click elsewhere to see it added to the list. Enter all five tasks. Figure 8.22 shows a completed list and calendar. When you have completed a task, click in the radio button alongside it to insert a tick and see a line placed through it to show the task has been completed.

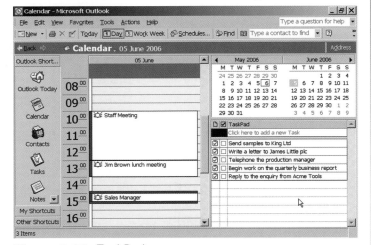

12 Explore the different ways of presenting the to do list by selecting the View menu, then highlighting the Current View and Task Pad View to show the list of options. Consider each option in turn. If you double-

Figure 8.22 TaskPad

click on any of the to do tasks or on the Click here to add a new task area, the Task window will open (figure 8.23), letting you add more detail to your tasks.

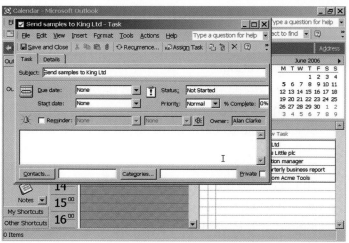

Figure 8.23 **Task window**

13 Revise each of your to do list entries to show start and finish dates:

Start Date: Monday
Due Date: Wednesday
Reply to enquiry from Acme Tools

Start Date: Monday
Due Date: Tuesday
Begin work on quarterly business report

Start Date: Tuesday
Due Date: Thursday
Telephone production manager

Start Date: Wednesday
Due Date: Thursday
Write letter to James Little plc

Start Date: Thursday
Due Date: Friday
Send samples to King Ltd

14 Most days you will need to make a note of events, pieces of information or simply things to remind you to take action. Microsoft Outlook® allows you to do this by selecting the File menu, highlighting the New option and clicking on Note to reveal a blank note. Enter "Remember to ask Mary about the statistic report". Close the note by clicking on

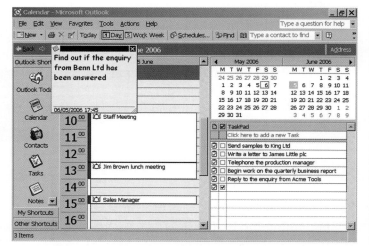

Figure 8.24 **Creating a note**

the X button. Enter another note – "Find out if the enquiry from Benn Ltd has been answered" (figure 8.24). Close the note when you have finished.

15 Notes are of little use if you cannot recall them. Click on the Notes icon on the

CLAiT Plus 2006 for Office XP

Outlook® Shortcuts area to the left of the display. Figure 8.25 shows you your notes. If you double-click on the one you want to see, it will expand. To remove the message, highlight the note with a single click and press the delete key.

Figure 8.25 Displaying notes

16 You can copy and paste into your notes using the menu available when you right-click in the note. This enables you to insert large amounts of information into a note, including the contents of a file.

17 To print the calendar, select the File menu and click on Print Preview. If the preview is satisfactory, click on the Print button.

18 To print a note with it visible on the screen (click on the Note icon), select the File menu, click on the Print option and the OK button.

19 To print a to do list, click on the Tasks icon so the list is visible, then select the File menu, click on the Print option and the OK button.

20 Print your calendar, to do list and notes. Hard copy is useful since there are many occasions when you need to know your schedule, to do lists or notes while away from the computer.

21 Close Microsoft Outlook® by selecting the File menu and clicking on the Exit option, or click on the Close button in the top right-hand corner of the application. You may be presented with a message informing you that there are unsent messages in your Outbox and asking if you would still like to Close the application. Say yes.

Updating your calendar

Establishing a calendar is only a part of the overall task, since it is just as important to be able to change entries or even delete them.

To remove an item you need to single-click on the item to highlight it, then select the Edit menu and click on the Delete option. This will remove the entry, unless it is a recurring item, when it will open the Confirm Delete window where you can delete the single item or all occurring items.

To alter a calendar item, all you have to do is to highlight it. You can then change the text, add extra items or a new entry.

If you double-click on the item, the appointment window will open, allowing you to change start and end times, set the alarm reminder and invite attendees.

It is important to keep your calendar up to date, including removing any conflicting appointments. A calendar's effectiveness is seriously reduced by inaccurate information. If it is not maintained, it will lead to mistakes. You will not gain anyone's confidence if you miss an appointment or prepare for one which has actually been cancelled.

Exercise 58

Creating an e-mail with an attachment

1 Microsoft Outlook® is opened either by selecting the Start button, highlighting the All Programs option and clicking on the Outlook® option, or by double-clicking on the Outlook® icon on the Microsoft Windows® desktop.

2 Create a new e-mail by clicking on the New icon to reveal the message window.

3 Create the message below:

To: Frank.Williams@practiceattachment.co.uk

Attachment

This is an e-mail to show you how to add an attachment.

If you are working with a group of other learners, substitute the e-mail address with one of your fellow learners. You can send the e-mail and see how it appears to the recipient.

4 Add an attachment by clicking on the Insert file icon (it looks like a paperclip). This opens the Insert File window. Select the folder in which your attached file is stored in the Look in: box, then highlight the file and click on the Insert button. Your attached file will appear in the Attach... line of your e-mail. You can attach several files by repeating the process. Each attachment can be a different type of file (e.g. word-processing, images).

5 To send the message, click on the Send button on the toolbar. If your system is connected to the Internet, the message will be sent. If not, it will be stored in the Outbox until the next time you make a connection. Observe in the folder list that the Outbox item has a number in brackets, indicating the number of messages waiting to be sent.

6 Practise sending messages with attachments, either to imaginary addresses or, preferably, to other learners on your course. Continue to practise until you are confident that you understand the process.

7 Encourage your colleagues to send you e-mails with attachments, but if you are on your own, you can send yourself a message.

8 When you receive an e-mail with an attachment, you can read the file by double-clicking on it. This will open the file, providing you have the associated application software on your system (e.g. Word files require Microsoft Word®). You can save the file using the application software in the normal way anywhere on the system, and read the attachment later using the application software. Practise with the attachments.

9 If you do not have a suitable application, you will be presented with a warning message.

10 An alternative to opening a file is to select the File menu and the Save Attachments option to reveal the Save Attachments window, which allows you to save your file in any folder. Practise saving your attachment in this way.

11 A third way to save your attachment is to select the File menu and the Move to Folder option. You can save the e-mail and attachment to a folder within the mail system. This is useful should you want to save messages to particular folders.

12 A fourth way of saving an attachment is to simply drag it to your new folder. Highlight the attachment and hold down the mouse button, then drag it to the new folder and release. It will have been copied to the new location. Copy the attachment to the Notes icon and your attached file will now be available from within a note. This is useful when you are dealing with several e-mails and want to refer to the attachment as soon as you have completed dealing with the messages.

13 It is important to spend as much time as you can practising the different approaches to dealing with attachments.

14 Close Microsoft Outlook® by selecting the File menu and clicking on the Exit option, or click on the Close button in the top right-hand corner of the application. You may be presented with a message informing you that there are unsent messages in your Outbox and asking if you would still like to close the application. Say yes.

Page setup

You may want to display or print your calendar in a variety of formats. With the Calendar selected and displayed, you can change its appearance by selecting the File menu, then highlighting the Page Setup option to reveal a menu of choices.

The choices include:

- Daily Style
- Weekly Style
- Monthly Style
- Tri-fold Style
- Calendar Details Style
- Memo Style
- Define Print Styles

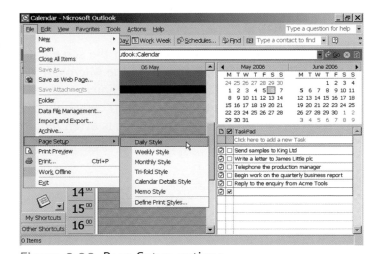

Figure 8.26 **Page Setup options**

When you click on the option, the Page Setup style window opens, providing additional choices. In particular, you can add a header and footer to the printout to identify the calendar (figure 8.27). Simply enter the text into the template provided.

With the calendar, the to do list, notes or contacts displayed, you can choose from a variety of page setups to show and print.

Printing

E-mail, calendars, to do lists and electronic notes are all extremely useful, but they do not eliminate the need for paper. If you are away from your office, unless you have everything stored on a laptop computer, you will need a copy of the key documents and messages. In many locations it is difficult to use a laptop, while paper can normally be studied in almost any location. When travelling, a printout of your calendar is very useful. If you add copies of

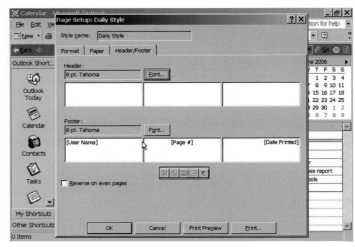

Figure 8.27 Header and Footer

contact details for the people you are meeting and any relevant e-mail messages, then you are well prepared.

Microsoft Outlook® provides extensive facilities for printing messages, calendars and contact details. Printing e-mails, calendars or contact details requires that you select the File menu and click on either the Print or Print Preview options. It is good practice to preview before you print. If you are then satisfied with the appearance of the printout, you can simply click on the Print option within the preview window. If it is not correct, then close the window and select the Page Setup option to change its appearance.

Screen print

If you need to capture what appears on the screen, press the Print Screen key. A copy of your screen display is made and stored on the Microsoft Windows® clipboard. You can then paste the image into an application of your choice, such as Microsoft Windows® Paint, from where you can print the display. If you want to copy only the contents of the active window, press the Alt and Print Screen keys together. This is often required during the assessment to provide evidence that you have undertaken the required tasks.

More practice

Take screen prints to practice providing evidence that you have completed the tasks.

Activity 1

1   Add these new contacts to your address book (figure 8.28):

Name: Mrs Wendy James
Title: Personnel Manager
Address: Queens Ltd
                   23 Long Lane
                   Leicester
                   LE12 9LL
Telephone: 0116 567 4599
E-mail: wendy.james@queensleicester.co.uk

Name:	Ms Lori Davis
Title:	Personal Assistant
Address:	Square Paints Ltd
	Alliance Drive
	Manchester
	M34 9RL
Telephone:	0161 777 9999
E-mail:	ld_Square@squarepaints.co.uk

Name:	Dr Paul Brookes
Title:	Director
Address:	Unicorn Ltd
	West Way
	Nottingham
	NG38 9KK
Telephone:	0115 678 9888
E-mail:	Paul_Brookes@unicorntoday.co.uk

Name:	Ms Jane Raymonds
Title:	Human Resource Manager
Address:	Highways Ltd
	567 South County Road
	Mansfield
	NG45 7JK
Telephone:	0999 567 3400
E-mail:	Jane.Raymonds@highways.co.uk

Name:	Mr Tom Jenkins
Title:	Personnel Officer
Address:	Sunshine Ltd
	Kingsway
	Liverpool
	L89 3DD
Telephone:	0151 768 1111
E-mail:	Tomj@sunshine.co.uk

2 Establish an e-mail distribution list based on the five contacts.

3 Call your distribution list Humanresources.

4 Save your distribution list.

5 Print a copy of the five contacts, showing their full name, telephone and e-mail address. Figure 8.29 shows a copy of the distribution list.

6 Print a copy of the distribution group.

Figure 8.28 New contact

Activity 2

1 Create a sub-folder within the Inbox to store e-mails about human resource matters from the five contacts and any internal messages. Name the folder Human.

2 Save an incoming e-mail message within this folder and also in a folder outside of Outlook® Today.

3 Create three more sub-folders within the Inbox, called First, Second and Third.

4 Move the e-mail message stored in Human to the folder called Second.

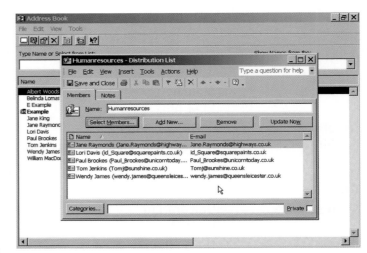

Figure 8.29 Distribution List

Activity 3

1 Decompress a zipped (compressed) archive.

2 Save the files to a folder outside the Outlook® Today folder.

3 Compress the files again, using a suitable application to form a new archive called New.

Activity 4

1 Enter the following appointments and meetings into your calendar:

Day	Start Time	Finish Time	Appointment/Meeting	Notes
Monday	10.00	11.00	Staff Meeting	Recurring every week
Tuesday	9.00	9.30	Conference Update	
	11.00	15.00	Interviews for Receptionist	
	16.00	17.00	Annual Review – David Jones	
Wednesday	10.30	11.45	Telephone Conference	
	14.30	16.00	Meeting with Training Manager	
Thursday	9.00	9.45	Progress Report	
	15.00	16.30	Review of Annual Report	
Friday	10.45	11.45	Meeting with Dr Lord	
	12.30	14.00	Lunch meeting with Production Director	

2 Print a copy of your diary for the week, making sure that all the information is shown in the printout. Add a header to the printout, showing your name.

3 For the same week, prepare a list of tasks to do. Enter the list below:

Subject	Due Date
Prepare for interviews for Receptionist	Tuesday
Make notes for the telephone conference	Wednesday
Read Annual Report	Thursday
Confirm lunch with Production Director	Friday

Figure 8.30 illustrates the calendar and to do list.

4 You need to make some notes. Create the two notes below:
Note 1 (figure 8.31):

Key points for the telephone conference on Thursday

- costs must be covered by the project
- project completion date is likely to be missed
- we need an extra month to finish our tasks

Note 2:

Annual Report

Check that in the report:

- the department has been accurately described
- details of all the personnel mentioned are correct – job titles, spelling of names, etc.
- costs and sales figures are right

5 Print copies of your to do list and notes:

To Do list – print in Table Style

Notes – print both notes in Memo Style

For all the printouts, add a header containing your name, centre number and date.

Activity 5

1 After you have read the Annual Report, you need to contact the editor of the report to comment on the contents. If you are working within a group, ask a colleague to act the part of the editor and reply to your comments.

2 Create a signature for yourself:

Your Name

With a sentence describing yourself (e.g. I am 54 years old and have grey hair)

3 Create the e-mail below:

To: Janet@madeup.co.uk (substitute the correct address)

Subject: Annual Report

Dear Janet,

I have now had an opportunity to study the Annual Report. I liked the new layout which I thought presented the information better. However, there are one or two small errors in the spelling of people's names which need to be corrected. I have attached a file of staff names.

Best wishes

Alan

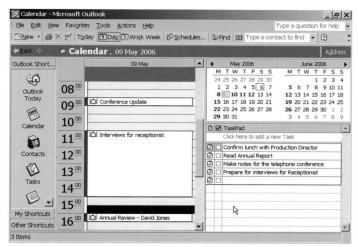

Figure 8.30 Calendar

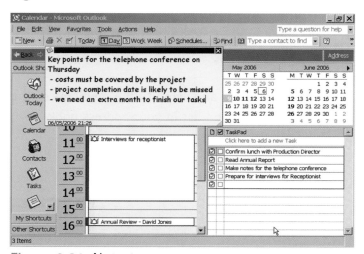

Figure 8.31 Note 1

4 Add the signature you have created to this e-mail.

5 Attach one or more files to this e-mail to practise sending an attachment. Figure 8.32 shows the e-mail.

6 If you are working in a group, ask one of your colleagues to send you a similar e-mail with an attachment.

7 Drag and drop the attachment into the Notes to copy the file.

8 Copy the e-mail that has been sent to you to another member of the group.

9 Save the original e-mail into the Human folder you created in activity 2.

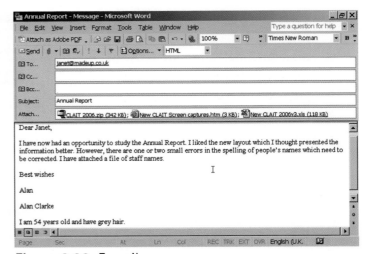

Figure 8.32 E-mail

Activity 6

1 You need to send an e-mail to the members of the Humanresources distribution group.

2 Use the distribution list in your address book.

3 Create the e-mail below:

Subject: Meeting

Next Thursday at 3pm I would like to hold a meeting to discuss the changes to Human Policy that the board have agreed at their last meeting. Could you please let me know if you are able to attend.

4 Add the signature you created in activity 5.

5 Attach three files of your choice to the e-mail.

6 Indicate that the message is being sent with High Importance.

7 Blind copy the message to another person. Figure 8.33 shows the e-mail.

8 Print a copy of the e-mail.

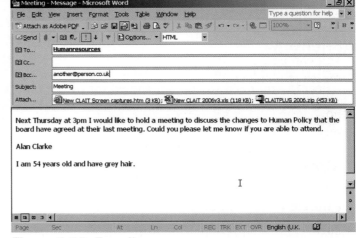

Figure 8.33 E-mail

Activity 7

In order to become a competent user of Microsoft Outlook®, you need to practise a range of tasks. The main ones are:

■ sending and receiving e-mails

■ saving the messages to folders within Outlook® Today

■ creating new folders within the Inbox and Outlook® Today

- decompressing archives and saving the files to appropriate folders outside the Outlook® Today area
- copying and moving files between folders
- creating and applying signatures
- adding new contacts to your address book
- creating distribution lists
- sending e-mails to distribution lists
- adding meetings and appointments to your calendar
- creating to do lists and notes.

SUMMARY

1 Open
Select the Start button, highlight the All Programs option and click on the Outlook® option or double-click on the Outlook® icon on the Microsoft Windows® desktop.

2 Create an e-mail
Select the New button on the standard toolbar to reveal the Message window.

3 Blind copies (Bcc)
Select the down-arrow button next to the Option button on the toolbar to reveal a short list of options and click on the Bcc option.

4 Priorities – High Importance
Click on the icon indicated by an exclamation mark (i.e. High Importance) in the message window.

5 Create a signature
You can add a signature to your e-mail by selecting the Tools menu on the toolbar of the message window, then Options . Next choose the General tab and click on E-mail options and finally the E-mail Signature tab. The E-mail Options window will be revealed. You can now create a signature for your e-mail. An alternative approach is to select the Tools menu on the main application (e.g. Inbox) and click on the Options item, then on the Mail Format tab. This will reveal a Signatures button, which will open a Create Signature window.

6 Address book
Select the Tools menu and click on the Address Book option. This will reveal the address book.

7 Add new contact
Click on the New Entry icon. Click on the New Contact option to reveal the Contact window.

8 New distribution list
Click on the New Entry icon and then on the New Distribution List option, to reveal the Distribution List window; or select the File menu, highlight the New option and click on the Distribution List option to open the Distribution List window.

9 Calendar
Click on the Calendar icon in the Outlook® Shortcuts list on the left-hand side of the display.

10 Change date
Click on the desired date of the monthly calendar.

11 Change calendar view
Select the View menu and click on the option of your choice.

12 Recurring appointments
Select the Actions menu, click on New Recurring Appointment to reveal the Appointment Recurrence window.

13 Notes
Select the File menu, highlight the New option and click on the Note option.

14 Print
Select the File menu. Click on Print Preview and then on the Print button.

15 Page setup
Select the File menu, highlight the Page Setup option, to reveal a menu of choices, and select your option.

16 New folder
Select the File menu, highlight the New item and click on the Folder option to reveal the Create New Folder window; or click on the down arrow next to the New button on the toolbar.

17 Attachment
Click on the Insert file icon (i.e. a paperclip) to open the Insert File window.

18 Save an attachment
Double-click on the attachment to open the file in the associated application software (e.g. spreadsheet files require Microsoft Excel®). Save the file using the application software.

Alternatively, single-click on the file to highlight it and then select the File menu and the Save Attachments option to reveal the Save Attachment window. Or, drag the attachment to a folder, highlight the attachment and hold down the mouse button to drag the attachment to the new folder, then release.

19 Save messages and attachments to folders
Select the File menu and the Move to Folder option to reveal the Move Item window, which lists mail system folders.

20 Enter tasks
Click in the area Click here to add a new task (TaskPad) and enter the item.

21 Change task views
Select the View menu and highlight the Current View and TaskPad items to reveal a list of options.

22 Task details
Double-click on the entry to reveal the Task window.

23 Message formats
Option on the e-mail toolbar provides access to the three choices (i.e. Plain text , RTF and HTML). You need to consider who you are sending the message to in order to select the most appropriate format.

24 Block spam
The Organize button in the Inbox area of Outlook® provides the function to create rules to automatically move e-mail into different folders. Alternatively, select the Tools menu and Organize option. Either method will open the Ways to Organize Inbox window.

Glossary

Application – a software program designed to perform a task such as desktop publishing, designing a database or designing a web page.

Bar Chart – a chart which represents numerical information as bars of different lengths.

Bitmap – an image composed of many dots called pixels. The more pixels in a given amount of space (e.g. a square inch) the clearer the image or the higher the resolution of the picture.

Boot – the process that occurs when you switch on the computer. It involves the loading of the operating system (e.g. Microsoft Windows® 98) and checking of the equipment to ensure that everything is ready for you to use.

Browser – an application which allows you to access a World Wide Web page. Each page has a unique address which is called a URL (uniform or universal resource locator) which, when entered into the browser, allows it to find the site and view its contents.

Byte – the basic measure of memory. A byte is sufficient memory to store one character (e.g. a letter or a number).

Column Chart – a chart which represents numbers and columns of different lengths.

CPU – central processing unit: a silicon chip which controls the operation of the computer.

Database – a way of storing information so that its contents can be extracted in many different combinations and ways.

Desktop – the main display of the operating system and normally the first display you see after the computer has loaded the operating system (e.g. Microsoft Windows®).

Desktop Publishing – an application which allows text and images to be combined in many different ways so that many different forms of printed document can be designed (e.g. newsletters and posters).

Directory – a list of World Wide Web addresses related to a particular topic or subject.

DTP – see Desktop Publishing

E-mail – a message which is sent electronically through the Internet or over a local network.

Field – an individual piece of information stored on a database, usually as part of a record.

File – a collection of digital (computer) information. There are many types of file, such as word-processing, graphic and spreadsheet files.

Floppy Disk – a small magnetic disk on which you can store a small amount of information in the form of files.

Folder – a location on the computer in which you can store files.

Font – characters can be printed and displayed in many different styles. These styles are known as fonts.

Format – a way of structuring the computer information stored in a file on a disk or drive. There are many different types of file format.

Formula – a method of calculating parts of a spreadsheet automatically.

Greyscale – a way of describing an image which is shown in a range of shades of grey rather than in different colours.

GUI – graphical user interface: a Microsoft Windows® 95 type display in which icons, windows and a mouse pointer interact to produce an easy-to-use environment.

Hard Disk – a large magnetic disk, which is located inside the computer, on which a large amount of information can be stored.

Hardware – the physical components which make up the computer.

HTML – Hypertext Markup Language: a specialist language which is used to design World Wide Web pages so that they can be read using a browser.

HTTP – Hypertext Transfer Protocol: specifies how to access documents on the World Wide Web (e.g. http://www.bbc.co.uk)

Hypertext – Pages of a website are linked together through a number of hypertext connections. These are shown by underlined words, coloured words, icons and graphic pictures. The links allow the user to jump between different parts of the site or even between sites.

Icon – a small picture which represents a computer function or operation.

Internet – a super network of networks which links millions of computers throughout the world.

ISP – Internet service provider: a commercial company that provides connections to the Internet for individuals and companies.

Justification – a way of laying out text (e.g. left justification means that text is aligned so that its left edge is parallel with the paper's edge when it is printed).

KB – kilobyte: a measure of memory (i.e. 1024 bytes).

Laptop – a portable computer with a screen built into its cover.

Line Graph – a graphical way of comparing two or more sets of numerical information.

MB – megabyte: a measure of computer memory (approximately a million bytes).

Memory – a measure of the computer's capacity to perform tasks and store information.

Menu – a method of displaying options.

Operating System – software that provides the instructions to make the hardware work.

Password – a series of alphanumeric characters that limits access to a computer system.

Personal Computer – an individual computer which is normally used by one person at a time.

Pie Chart – a graphical representation of information by showing it as slices of a circle so that the size of each slice is proportional to the data.

Pixel – graphic images are made up of many small rectangular areas which are called pixels.

Port – a way of connecting peripheral devices (e.g. printers) to a computer.

Query – a way of asking a database of information a particular question. Normally, this takes the form of identifying particular combinations of information (e.g. all customers whose orders total more than £100,000 during the last three months).

QWERTY – the order of the top line of alphabetical keys on the keyboard.

RAM – random access memory: the computer's working memory in which the computer carries out its functions once it is switched on. It only exists while the machine is on. If the power is switched off, so is the memory.

Record – a group of related fields of information which you find in a database.

Resolution – this is a way of describing the quality of an image, monitor or printer. The quality is described in terms of the dots which make up the image. That is, the more dots the higher the quality of the image, monitor display or printer output.

ROM – read-only memory: the computer's permanent memory, built into the structure of the silicon chips. It is not lost if the power is switched off.

Search Engine – an application that allows you to search the World Wide Web for a web page containing information on a specific topic or to search within a website for a particular item of information.

Software – computer programs written to allow you or the computer to carry out certain tasks, such as constructing databases.

Sort – a way of presenting information in a spreadsheet or database (e.g. alphabetically).

Surfing – the process of wandering around the World Wide Web in search of interesting information.

Table – the part of a database in which information is stored as a series of records and fields.

URL – uniform resource locator: the unique address of a World Wide Web site that allows a browser to locate the site.

Vector – an image that is defined by mathematical formulae rather than pixels. This defines the start and finish of the line and allows it to be changed easily . A vector image can be resized and it will stay in perfect proportion.

Virus – a computer program designed to cause harm to a computer.

Web Page – a document which forms part of a website.

Website – a collection of pages on the Internet.

Word Processor – an application which allows you to create and manipulate documents.

WWW – World Wide Web: a collection of millions of websites and documents spread across the world as part of the Internet.

Window – rectangular area of the screen in which computer applications and information are displayed.

Wizard – Many Microsoft Windows® applications include Wizards that are used to perform complex tasks more easily by allowing the user to choose between options.

Index